Projecting Resilience Across the Mediterranean

Eugenio Cusumano · Stefan Hofmaier
Editors

Projecting Resilience Across the Mediterranean

palgrave
macmillan

Editors
Eugenio Cusumano
Leiden, The Netherlands

Stefan Hofmaier
The Hague, The Netherlands

ISBN 978-3-030-23640-3   ISBN 978-3-030-23641-0 (eBook)
https://doi.org/10.1007/978-3-030-23641-0

© The Editor(s) (if applicable) and The Author(s), under exclusive license to Springer Nature Switzerland AG, part of Springer Nature 2020

This work is subject to copyright. All rights are solely and exclusively licensed by the Publisher, whether the whole or part of the material is concerned, specifically the rights of translation, reprinting, reuse of illustrations, recitation, broadcasting, reproduction on microfilms or in any other physical way, and transmission or information storage and retrieval, electronic adaptation, computer software, or by similar or dissimilar methodology now known or hereafter developed.

The use of general descriptive names, registered names, trademarks, service marks, etc. in this publication does not imply, even in the absence of a specific statement, that such names are exempt from the relevant protective laws and regulations and therefore free for general use.

The publisher, the authors and the editors are safe to assume that the advice and information in this book are believed to be true and accurate at the date of publication. Neither the publisher nor the authors or the editors give a warranty, expressed or implied, with respect to the material contained herein or for any errors or omissions that may have been made. The publisher remains neutral with regard to jurisdictional claims in published maps and institutional affiliations.

Cover image: © imaginima/Getty Images

This Palgrave Macmillan imprint is published by the registered company Springer Nature Switzerland AG

The registered company address is: Gewerbestrasse 11, 6330 Cham, Switzerland

Contents

1. **Introduction** — 1
   Eugenio Cusumano and Stefan Hofmaier

2. **Resilience in the European Union External Action** — 17
   Rosanne Anholt and Wolfgang Wagner

3. **Projecting Stability to the South: NATO's "New" Mission?** — 37
   Jeffrey A. Larsen and Kevin Koehler

4. **The EU, Resilience and the Southern Neighbourhood After the Arab Uprisings** — 63
   Emile Badarin and Tobias Schumacher

5. **EU Counter-Terrorism Cooperation with the Middle East and North Africa** — 87
   Christian Kaunert, Sarah Léonard and Ori Wertman

6. **Sanctions as a Regional Security Instrument: EU Restrictive Measures Examined** — 103
   Francesco Giumelli

7	European Energy Security and the Resilience of Southern Mediterranean Countries Luca Franza, Coby van der Linde and Pier Stapersma	125
8	Libya: From Regime Change to State-Building Matteo Villa and Arturo Varvelli	147
9	Resilience to What? EU Capacity-Building Missions in the Sahel Luca Raineri and Edoardo Baldaro	169
10	Resilience and Conflict Resolution: UN Peacekeeping in Mali Chiara Ruffa, Sebastiaan Rietjens and Emma Nygren	189
11	Resilience in the Eye of the Storm: Capacity-Building in Lebanon Nick Pounds and Rudolf Keijzer	205
12	The Horn of Africa: NATO and the EU as Partners Against Pirates Stefano Ruzza	227
13	Paths to Resilience: Examining EU and NATO Responses to the Tunisian and Egyptian Political Transitions Maria Giulia Amadio Viceré and Andrea Frontini	247
14	Civil-Military Cooperation in the Mediterranean Sea: Lessons Not Learnt Hernan del Valle	269
15	Conclusions Eugenio Cusumano and Nathan Cooper	295
Index		315

Notes on Contributors

Maria Giulia Amadio Viceré is a Postdoctoral Fellow and an Adjunct Professor in Political Science at LUISS University (IT). Before that, she has been an Assistant Professor at Leiden University (NL). She has held visiting positions at the European University Institute (IT); at the University of Washington (USA); and at King's College (UK). She is the author of *The High Representative and EU Foreign Policy Integration: A Comparative Study of Kosovo and Ukraine* (Palgrave Macmillan, 2018).

Rosanne Anholt is lecturer and Ph.D. candidate at the faculty of social sciences of the Vrije Universiteit Amsterdam. Her research interests include humanitarian action and development assistance in fragile and conflict-affected states.

Emile Badarin is a Postdoctoral fellow at the European Neighbourhood Policy Chair, College of Europe, Natolin Campus. He holds a Ph.D. in Middle East Politics from the University of Exeter. His research cuts across fields of international politics, foreign policy, with the EU and the Middle East as areas of study, critical theory, and Israel–Palestine conflict. He is the author of *Palestinian Political Discourse: Between Exile and Occupation* (2016).

Edoardo Baldaro is a Postdoctoral Fellow in International Relations at the University of Naples "L'Orientale" (Naples, Italy) and holds a Ph.D. from the Institute of Human and Social Sciences of the Scuola Normale Superiore (Florence, Italy). His main areas of interest include security studies, North–South relations, African politics and security, and the redefinition of statehood in Africa.

Nathan Cooper holds an M.A. degree in international relations from Leiden University and is currently a Policy Advisor at the British Department of Business, Energy and Industrial Strategy. He has an interest in migration governance, stabilisation, and democratic institutions, particularly in the European neighbourhood.

Eugenio Cusumano is an Assistant Professor of international relations at the University of Leiden, and Jean Monnet Fellow at the European University Institute. His research on military organisations, private security companies, and NGOs' involvement in international crisis management has been published in leading security studies journals. He also contributed to and edited volumes for Oxford and Stanford University Press, Palgrave, and Routledge.

Hernan del Valle is a lawyer specialised in international law and human rights. For the past 20 years, he led humanitarian aid operations assisting people affected by armed conflict and forced displacement in Africa, Asia, Latin America, and the Middle East. As *Médecins Sans Frontières* (MSF) Head of Advocacy and Communications he was in charge of rescue operations in the Mediterranean Sea. He is currently Rita E. Hauser Fellow at the Radcliffe Institute for Advanced Studies at Harvard University.

Luca Franza is a researcher at the Clingendael International Energy Programme (CIEP) since 2012. He is also a lecturer at SciencesPo, Paris and a Ph.D. candidate at the University of Groningen. His main areas of research are natural gas and LNG supply and demand, European gas markets, pricing, and the societal, macroeconomic, and geopolitical dimensions of energy.

Andrea Frontini is a Policy Assistant in the European Commission, working on EU defence and security markets and industry. Prior to that, he was a Policy Analyst at the European Policy Centre (EPC), a leading European think tank in Brussels, Belgium, and held earlier job positions in the private, public, and not-for-profit sectors, both in Italy and Belgium. He graduated *cum laude* from the University of Trieste, Italy. He writes here in a personal capacity.

Francesco Giumelli is an Assistant Professor in international relations and deputy head of the international department at the University of

Groningen. He has published extensively on sanctions and restrictive measure, and dedicated two books to European Union sanctions specifically.

Stefan Hofmaier is a Lieutenant Colonel in the German Army and the chief of the Concept, Interoperability and Capabilities Branch of the Civil-Military Cooperation Center of Excellence (CCOE). He holds an M.A. degree in Business and previously served as department head of the German Army Centre for Lessons Learnt and Deputy Commander of the Afghan National Army 2nd Brigade NATO operation ISAF mentoring team in Kunduz, Afghanistan.

Professor Christian Kaunert is Chair of Policing and Security, as well as Director of the International Centre for Policing and Security at the University of South Wales. He published extensively on Policing and International Security, especially in the area of EU counterterrorism. He is the author of several articles on EU counterterrorism, EU asylum and migration, EU Justice and Home Affairs, and wider global security matters.

Rudolf Keijzer retired as Lieutenant Colonel from the Royal Netherlands Marine Corps in 2017 and he is the former Branch Chief Training and Education at the NATO CCOE.

He has master's degrees in economics, marketing, and information management, and he is now an independent stability adviser on Security Force Assistance, Civil-Military Cooperation, and Hybrid Threats. He developed extensive experience on these subjects through deployment to Afghanistan, Bosnia, Iraq, Lebanon, and other countries.

Kevin Koehler is an Assistant Professor of Comparative Politics at Leiden University. He previously served as a Research Advisor at the Middle East Faculty of the NATO Defense College and an Assistant Professor of Comparative Methods at the American University in Cairo. He received his Ph.D. from the European University Institute in Florence in 2013.

Jeffrey A. Larsen is a Research Professor in the Department of National Security Affairs, US Naval Postgraduate School, Monterey, CA, and president of Larsen Consulting Group. From 2013 to 2018, he served as Director of the Research Division at the NATO Defense College. He previously completed a 21-year career in the US Air Force, retiring as a

Lt Colonel, followed by 16 years as a senior policy analyst with a major US defense contractor. He is the author or editor of more than 150 books, journal articles, chapters, and monographs.

Sarah Léonard is a professor of Social Sciences at the University of the West of England. She was previously Associate Professor in International Affairs at Vesalius College, Vrije Universiteit Brussel (Belgium). Her research lies at the intersection between Security Studies and European Studies. She is particularly interested in the study of securitization processes and the development of the European Union's internal security policies.

Emma Nygren holds a Bachelor's degree from the Department of Peace and Conflict Research at Uppsala University.

Nick Pounds retired from the Royal Marines in 2005, as a Brigadier. He has a master's degree in Post War Recovery Studies from the University of York and he is now an independent consultant on conflict stabilisation and security sector reform—with experience from Afghanistan, Iraq, Lebanon, Libya, and Ukraine. He is also a member of the UK Government Stabilisation Unit's panel of senior advisers and both writes and lectures widely on the subject.

Luca Raineri is a Research Fellow in International Relations and Security Studies at the Sant'Anna School of Advanced Studies in Pisa, Italy. He is also a member of the Research School on Peace and Conflict in Oslo. His areas of expertise include critical security studies, African politics, geopolitics, and peace and conflict studies.

Sebastiaan Rietjens is full professor of Intelligence & Security at the Netherlands Defence Academy. He has done extensive fieldwork in military exercises and operations (Afghanistan, Mali, Greece) and has published in international books and journals including *Disasters, Armed Forces & Society, International Journal of Public Administration* and *Journal of Intelligence and Counter Intelligence*.

Chiara Ruffa is Academy Fellow at the Department of Peace and Conflict Research at Uppsala University and Associate Professor in War Studies at the Swedish Defense University. Chiara's research, published in several international journal, lies at the cross-road between political science, sociology and focuses on the study of peacekeeping operations. Her book, Military Cultures in Peace and Stability Operations, has been published with the University of Pennsylvania Press (in May 2018).

Stefano Ruzza is an Assistant Professor of "Conflict, Security and Statebuilding" at the University of Turin. He lectures regularly in advanced educational programmes of the Italian Army, and is a co-founder of the Torino World Affairs Institute (T.wai), where he leads the "Violence and Security" research programme. His research interests are conflict transformation, non-state armed actors in international relations and private military and security companies.

Professor Tobias Schumacher is Chairholder of the ENP Chair at the College of Europe in Natolin. He is a Senior Associate Researcher at the Center for International Studies at the Lisbon University Institute and was a Kennedy Memorial Fellow at the Minda de Gunzburg Center for European Studies at Harvard University. He is the lead editor of *The Routledge Handbook on the European Neighbourhood Policy* (2018) and co-editor of *The Revised European Neighbourhood Policy: Continuity and Change in EU Foreign Policy* (Palgrave, 2017).

Pier Stapersma is a senior researcher at the Clingendael International Energy Programme (CIEP) since 2012. He was previously business analyst at Delta NV. His main areas of research are power markets, solar and wind value chains and issues related to decarbonization and the energy transition, particularly in North-Western Europe.

Coby van der Linde is the director of the Clingendael International Energy Programme (CIEP). She is a professor at the University of Gronigen and a lecturer at Sciences Po, Paris. She is also non-executive director of two energy companies. Her main areas of research are international oil and gas markets and energy transition issues.

Arturo Varvelli, Ph.D. is Head of the MENA Centre at the Italian Institute for International Political Studies (ISPI). He specialises in Libya and writes extensively on the subject. He is author or editor of many books on the country, such as *L'Italia e l'ascesa di Gheddafi*, *Dopo Gheddafi. Democrazia e petrolio nella nuova Libia*, *Libia: Fine o rinascita di una nazione?*, and *Foreign Actors in Libya's Crisis*.

Matteo Villa, Ph.D. is a Research Fellow at the Italian Institute for International Political Studies (ISPI). He specialises in European policies and politics, especially on migration, focusing on quantitative, evidence-based analysis. Over the past years he provided scholarly expertise to the G20, the European Parliament, the Italian Parliament, the Lombardy Region, and the Municipality of Milan.

Wolfgang Wagner is professor of international security at the faculty of social sciences of the Vrije Universiteit Amsterdam. His research interests include the foreign policies of the European Union and its member states.

Ori Wertman is a Ph.D. candidate at the University of South Wales. He previously was a foreign affairs and political adviser to former Israeli Labour Party chairman Isaac Herzog, former deputy chairman of the Israeli Labour Party Youth, and a candidate on the Israeli Labour Parliament (Knesset) list.

Acronyms

3RP	Regional Refugee and Resilience Plan
ACT	Allied Command Transformation
ALNAP	Active Learning Network for Accountability and Performance in Humanitarian Action
AMISOM	African Union Mission in Somalia
AU	African Union
AWACS	Airborne Warning and Control System
CA	Comprehensive Approach
CAR	Conflict Armament Research
CCOE	Civil-Military Cooperation Centre of Excellence
CENTCOM	United States Central Command
CFSP	Common Foreign and Security Policy
CGPCS	Contact Group on Piracy Off the Coast of Somalia
CIEP	*Clingendael International Energy Programme*
CIMIC	Civil-Military Cooperation
CMF	Combined Maritime Forces
CMI	Civil-Military Interaction
COE	Centre of Excellence
CSDP	Common Security and Defence Policy
CSP	Concentrated Solar Power
CTF-151	Combined Task Force 151
DCB	Defence and Related Security Capacity Building
DCFTA	Deep and Comprehensive Free Trade Agreement
DDR	Disarmament, Demobilisation and Reintegration
DG ECHO	Directorate-General for European Civil Protection and Humanitarian Aid Operations

DPRK	Democratic People's Republic of North Korea
DRR	Disaster Risk Reduction
EBRD	European Bank for Reconstruction and Development
EC	European Commission
ECJ	European Court of Justice
EEAS	European External Action Service
EEC	European Economic Community
EMP	Euro-Mediterranean Partnership
ENP	European Neighbourhood Policy
EOR	Enhanced Oil Recovery
ESS	European Security Strategy
EU	European Union
EUBAM	European Union Border Assistance Mission
EUCAP	European Union Capacity Building Mission
EUGS	European Union Global Strategy
EUMS	European Union Military Staff
EUNAVFOR Med	European Union Naval Force Mediterranean
EUTM	European Union Training Mission
FAC	Foreign Affairs Council
FEXWEB	Fleet Exercise Web
FJP	Freedom and Justice Party
Frontex	European Border and Coast Guard Agency
FSRU	Floating Storage Regasification Unit
FYROM	Former Yugoslav Republic of Macedonia
G5 Sahel/G5S/FC-G5S	Group of Five for the Sahel/*Force Conjointe du G5 Sahel*
GALSI	*Gasdotto Algeria Sardegna Italia (Algeria-Sardinia gas pipeline)*
GAR-SI SAHEL	*Groupe d'Action Rapide—Surveillance et Intervention au Sahel*
GCC	Gulf Coordination Council
GNA	Government of National Accord
GNC	General National Congress
GSP	General System of Preference
HoR	House of Representatives
HP	High Representative of the European Union for Foreign Affairs and Security Policy
HQ	Headquarters
HR	High Representative of the Union for Foreign Affairs and Security Policy
HRA	High Risk Area

ICC	International Chamber of Commerce
ICC	International Criminal Court
ICI	Istanbul Cooperation Initiative
ICP	Individual Cooperation Programme
ICRC	International Committee of the Red Cross
ICTY	International Criminal Tribunal for the former Yugoslavia
IED	Improvised Explosive Device
IFOR	Implementation Force
IHL	International Humanitarian Law
IHRL	International Human Rights Law
IMB	International Maritime Bureau
IMO	International Maritime Organization
IO	International Organisation
IPCP	Individual Partnership and Cooperation Programme
IRTC	Internationally Recommended Transit Corridor
IS/ISIL/ISIS	Islamic State/Islamic State of Iraq and the Levant/Islamic State of Iraq and al-Sham
KFOR	Kosovo Force
LAS	League of Arab States
LCG	Libyan Coast Guard
LNA	Libyan National Army
LNG	Liquefied Natural Gas
LOPM	Military Orientation and Programming Law (*Loi d'Orientation et de Programmation Militaire*)
LOPSI	Orientation and Programming of Internal Security Law (*Projet de Loi d'Orientation et de Programmation sur la Sécurité Intérieure*)
LPA	Libyan Political Agreement
LT	Lisbon Treaty
MARLO	United States Maritime Liaison Office
MD	Mediterranean Dialogue
MEDA	Mesures D'Accompagnement (Measures to Accompany ENP Reforms)
MEE	Middle East Eye
MINUSMA	United Nations Multidimensional Integrated Stabilization Mission in Mali
MOAS	Migrant Offshore Aid Station
MOU	Memorandum of Understanding
MRCC	Maritime Rescue Coordination Center
MS	Member State
MSCHOA	Maritime Security Centre—Horn of Africa

MSF	*Médecins sans Frontières*
MSPA	Maritime Security Patrol Area
NAC	North Atlantic Council
NATO	North Atlantic Treaty Organization
NAVCO	Naval Coordination Cell
NDCs	National Determined Contributions
NFZ	No-fly Zone
NGL	Natural Gas Liquids
NGO	Non-Governmental Organisation
NTC	National Transitional Council
NTM-A	NATO Training Mission in Afghanistan
NTM-I	NATO Training Mission in Iraq
OSCE	Organization for Security and Co-operation in Europe
OUP	Operation Unified Protector
PAP-DIB	Partnership Action Plan on Defence Institution Building
PCM	Partnership Cooperation Menu
PFG	Petroleum Facility Guard
PfP	Partnership for Peace
PMA	Panama Maritime Authority
PP	Partnership Priorities
PSC	Political and Security Committee
R/P	Reserve-to-Production
RELEX	Working Party of Foreign Relations Counsellors
SACT	Headquarters Supreme Allied Command Transformation
SAR	Search and Rescue
SEMED	Southern and Eastern Mediterranean
SFOR	Stabilisation *Force* in Bosnia and Herzegovina
SGC	Southern Gas Corridor
SHADE	Shared Awareness and Deconfliction
SHAPE	Supreme Headquarters Allied Powers Europe
SHQ	Sector Headquarter
SNAF	Somali National Armed Forces
Solar PV	Solar Photovoltaics
SoS Med	*SoS Méditerranée*
SPRING	Support for Partnership, Reform and Inclusive Growth
SRSG	Special Representative of the Secretary General
SSF	Single Support Frameworks
SSR	Security Sector Reform

TACIS	Technical Assistance to the Commonwealth of Independent States
TEU	Treaty of the European Union
TFEU	Treaty on the Functioning of the European Union
TPES/Pop	Total Primary Energy Supply Per Capita
UAE	United Arab Emirates
UfM	Union for the Mediterranean
UKMTO	United Kingdom Marine Trade Operations
UN	United Nations
UNCLOS	United Nations Convention of the Law of the Sea
UNCTAD	United Nations Conference on Trade and Development
UNDG	United Nations Development Group
UNDP UN	United Nations Development Programme
UNFCCC	United Nations Framework Convention on Climate Change
UNGA	United Nations General Assembly
UNHCR	United Nations High Commissioner for Refugees
UNMIK	United Nations Mission in Kosovo
UNOCHA	United Nations Office for the Coordination of Humanitarian Affairs
UNODC	United Nations Office on Drugs and Crime
UNSC	United Nations Security Council
UNSMIL	United Nations Support Mission in Libya
USSR	*Union of Soviet Socialist Republics*
WFP	World Food Programme
WHS	World Humanitarian Summit
WMD	Weapons of Mass Destruction

List of Figures

Graph 7.1	Volumes and value of crude oil exports between Algeria and the EU	132
Graph 7.2	Worldwide annual CSP installations and total CSP capacity (left); CSP and PV totals worldwide (right)	140
Graph 12.1	Number of pirate attacks per year, 2008–2016 (*Source* Adaptation from IMB)	229

List of Tables

Table 4.1	EU resilience-building initiatives in the Middle East and North Africa	79
Table 6.1	EU restrictive measures per type of crisis since 1993	109
Table 7.1	Key figures on Southern Mediterranean countries	128
Table 7.2	Energy disruptions in SEMED countries	130
Table 8.1	Timeline of the Libyan crisis	162
Table 9.1	CSDP missions in the Sahel	181
Table 12.1	The 'Big Three' counter-piracy naval missions	236

CHAPTER 1

Introduction

Eugenio Cusumano and Stefan Hofmaier

In the introduction to the previous volume edited under the auspices of the Centre of Excellence for Civil-Military Cooperation (CCOE), we noted how pervasive the adjective 'hybrid' had become in the Euro-Atlantic security jargon (Cusumano and Corbe 2018). Anybody playing a 'European security conference drinking game' (Gramer 2017) where participants have to drink a shot each time 'hybrid threats' and 'hybrid war' were mentioned would soon end up drunk. Repeating the same game with the noun 'resilience' and the adjective 'resilient' would guarantee an equally painful hangover.

Initially used in scientific disciplines like psychiatry, ecology, and engineering, the notion of resilience eventually spilled over into the social sciences. Security scholars and practitioners discovered the concept relatively recently. Over the last few years, however, the concept of resilience has rapidly gained traction, becoming a *leitmotiv* of both North Atlantic

E. Cusumano (✉)
University of Leiden, Leiden, The Netherlands
e-mail: e.cusumano@hum.leidenuniv.nl

S. Hofmaier
Civil-Military Cooperation Center of Excellence (CCOE),
The Hague, The Netherlands
e-mail: Hofmaier.S@cimic-coe.org

© The Author(s) 2020
E. Cusumano and S. Hofmaier (eds.),
Projecting Resilience Across the Mediterranean,
https://doi.org/10.1007/978-3-030-23641-0_1

Treaty Organisation (NATO) and European Union (EU) declarations and policy documents. In the 2016 Warsaw Summit Communiqué, NATO heads of state and government referred to member states' resilience as 'the basis for credible deterrence and the effective fulfilment of the Alliance's core tasks'. The European Union Global Strategy (EUGS), published in the same period, elected resilience as the guidance principle of EU external action. Both documents forcefully acknowledge that efforts to enhance resilience cannot be limited to strengthening EU and NATO member states. As illustrated by the Arab uprisings and their aftermath, conflict and unrest in the Southern and Eastern Mediterranean have severe implications for the security of the Euro-Atlantic region. Consequently, creating resilient state institutions and societies in Maghreb, Sahel, and Middle East countries is imperative for the EU, NATO, and their member states alike.

Nine years after the uprisings, upheaval at the Southern end of the Mediterranean basin continues. In the spring of 2019, street protests in Algeria and Sudan forced presidents Bouteflika and Al-Bashir to resign after over twenty years in power, showing that the region keeps demanding democracy (*The Economist* 2019). As epitomised by the case of Libya, however, not all this turmoil is bloodless. Renewed clashes between Tripoli's Government of National Accord (GNA) and general Haftar's Libyan National Army (LNA) caused over 250 casualties and the displacement of 30,000 people in the first two weeks of April 2019, raising concerns about growing migratory flows and terrorist infiltrations at Europe's maritime Southern border (Chorin 2019).

This book examines the activities conducted by NATO and the EU to foster resilience across the Mediterranean, ranging from deterrence, force projection, and crisis management operations to capacity building, diplomacy, development cooperation, and humanitarian assistance. By doing so, the volume simultaneously pursues several goals. First, examining the scope and varying effectiveness of the humanitarian, diplomatic, and military initiatives carried out at Europe's Southern borders contributes to several topical academic and policy debates, including migration management across the Mediterranean, conflict resolution in Syria and Libya, counterterrorism, state-building, the trade-off between democratisation and stability, and the security-development nexus.

Various studies and collections have explored the influence of EU external policies on these countries, such as, inter alia, Schumacher et al. (2017) and Bruns et al. (2016). Existing research, however, has mainly concentrated on EU policy instruments such as the European Neighbourhood Policy (ENP). Consequently, these studies have simultaneously examined both the Eastern and Southern Neighbourhood and dedicated limited attention to security policies, largely disregarding the role of other regional organisations like NATO. Although many scholars have examined NATO's contribution to European security as well as Transatlantic relations in a broader sense, this literature has focused nearly exclusively on NATO's traditional role of providing deterrence and reassurance at its Eastern flank and conducting operations 'out of area' in Afghanistan and the Balkans (Johnson 2017; Sloan 2016; Auerswald and Saideman 2014; Michta and Paal Sigurd 2014). In light of the Alliance's renewed activism in the Mediterranean, epitomised by the air campaign against Libya in 2011 and the recent establishment of a Southern Hub in Naples, NATO's initiatives in the Maghreb and the broader Middle East warrant deeper attention. Our simultaneous examination of Euro-Atlantic diplomatic and military initiatives south of the Mediterranean will contribute to the study of EU–NATO relations, helping to map synergies, redundancies, inconsistencies, and potential tensions between these two organisations. At a time when Transatlantic relations are increasingly strained, this collection will thus provide fresh insights into the cohesion of the North Atlantic Alliance and the future trajectory of NATO–EU relations. In addition, the study of peace-keeping operations in Mali and Lebanon allows us to examine the role of the United Nations (UN) in the Sahel and the Middle East. Besides analysing the policies of international organisations and their member states, the book also explores the involvement of non-state actors in resilience-building initiatives, examining both commercial entities such as the shipping and oil industries and non-governmental organisations (NGOs) like *Médecins Sans Frontieres*.

Reappraising the role of states, international organisations and non-state actors in enhancing the resilience of countries and communities will not only provide novel empirical insights with timely policy implications. The study of resilience-based approaches to foreign policy also sheds new light on consensus-building strategies in international institutions, highlighting the ability of broad, open-ended notions like resilience to serve as 'bridging concepts' (Baggio et al. 2015) and catalysts for agreement within divided alliances and regional organisations. The term resilience has recently attracted considerable attention among international relations scholars. Most notably, Philippe Bourbeau (2015, 2018a, b), David Chandler (2014; Chandler and Coffee 2016), Jon Coaffee (Chandler and Coaffee 2016; Coaffee 2006), and Jonathan Joseph (2018) have conducted insightful examinations of the genealogy, analytical potential, and normative implications of the concept of resilience. International relations scholarship on resilience, however, has primarily been developed by academics and for academics only. The existing literature has mainly investigated resilience from a theoretical standpoint, without analysing in detail how the concept has guided the activities of international organisations like NATO, the EU, and their member states' military forces. Moreover, these studies do not adopt a specific geographical focus, collecting empirical evidence from a host of different areas without systematically examining any region in detail.

Our volume departs from these studies in two different ways. First, as already mentioned, we primarily focus on the initiatives carried out by NATO and the EU in order to provide an in-depth examination of the potentials and pitfalls of resilience-building in the broader Middle East, Maghreb, and Sahel regions specifically. Second, we have attempted to use the study of resilience as a bridge between academic and practitioner communities. Efforts to enhance resilience far exceed the capabilities of military organisations, thus presupposing unity of effort across a host of government institutions, international, non-governmental, and commercial actors. Consequently, building resilience requires dialogue and cooperation between academics and practitioners, and between military and civilian communities. As such, the study of resilience-based approaches to foreign and security policy sheds new light on the importance of civil-military interaction and cooperation in today's foreign and security policies. In the very spirit of civil-military cooperation, this collection includes contributors with different perspectives and professional backgrounds, ranging from renowned scholars of EU external relations to practitioners from international organisations, armed forces, think tanks, and humanitarian NGOs. By drawing on such a diverse body of expertise, we hope to strengthen the dialogue between academia and various segments of the policy community, thereby bridging the gap between academics and practitioners, and between civilian and military professionals.

The two sections below will introduce the key concepts used in this volume and briefly outline its content.

Key Concepts:
From Hybrid Threats to Resilience

The physical and psychological property known as resilience—usually referred to as the ability of a material or an individual to absorb shocks without getting permanently damaged—already started to be borrowed by social scientists in the late 1960s. Drawing on an article by Walker and Cooper (2011), several scholars have argued that resilience has entered the study of international relations through biology, and specifically ecology. Accordingly, many have seen the concept as imbued with a Darwinian logic implying that the recovery from and adaptation to environmental changes ultimately entails the survival of the fittest. For these scholars, the concept of resilience has spawned into international relations due to its resonance with the social Darwinism that implicitly underlies today's neoliberal consensus, betraying the willingness of countries in the Global North to relinquish any responsibility for conflict, unrest, and extreme poverty at their periphery.

As shown by Bourbeau (2018b), however, this is not necessarily the case. Resilience has simultaneously entered the field of international relations through different disciplinary avenues. Scholars with an interest in the robustness of state institutions, for instance, have drawn on engineers' understanding of resilience as the property of materials capable of bending but not breaking (Hasenclever et al. 1997), while experts of violent extremism have primarily built on psychiatrists' conceptualisation of resilience as individuals' ability to cope with traumatic experiences (Wimelius et al. 2018). Consequently, resilience should not be dismissed as a morally problematic concept imbued with a darwinistic understanding of international politics and an uncritical belief in neoliberal modes of governance (Schmidt 2015). Resilience-based approaches to foreign policy are not inherently incompatible with inclusive agendas attempting to mitigate local communities' vulnerability to economic, environmental, and security challenges.

By 2012, the notion of resilience had spawned into the language of foreign and policy practitioners too. Most notably, the US Department of Homeland Security (2010), the US and UK agencies for International Development (USAID 2012; DFID 2011), as well as Dutch, Swiss, Swedish, French and Australian government agencies have all made extensive reference to the concept of resilience.

International organisations with a focus on development also adopted the concept, referring to resilience as the antidote to state fragility in Africa and the Middle East. Most notably, the UN Development Programme (2011) referred to human resilience as an objective of the UN Millennium Development Goals. A comprehensive genealogy of the concept of resilience has already been provided elsewhere (Bourbeau 2018b; Chandler 2014; Anholt and Wagner in this volume) and is beyond the scope of this introduction. As noted by Joseph (2018: 18), resilience often means somewhat different things to different actors. In order to maximise contributors' academic freedom and obtain insights into how different practitioner and academic communities use such an elusive notion, we decided not to straitjacket our contributors with an overarching definition of resilience, leaving authors free to develop their own definitions and resort to the terminology used by the discipline and organisations examined by each chapters. Accordingly, we also left our contributors free to develop their own conclusions regarding the heuristic utility and normative implications of resilience-based approaches to foreign and security policies. In the conclusions to this volume, we will then reappraise the concept of resilience in light of the evidence provided by the case studies, taking stock of the insight provided by the contributors to reassess the potential and shortcomings of resilience-based approaches to foreign and security policymaking.

The next section will only examine how NATO and the EU have conceptualised resilience and its projection abroad, mapping similarities and differences in the terminology employed by both organisations.

Resilience in NATO and EU Documents

Resilience entered NATO's official parlance in the Final Communiqué of the 2014 Wales Summit (NATO 2014). It was only at the 2016 Warsaw summit, however, that resilience—mentioned 11 times—became a core programmatic objective of the Alliance. In Warsaw, NATO member states made a 'commitment to continue to enhance our resilience against the full spectrum of threats' (NATO 2016). The awareness that hybrid threats are too multifaceted to be anticipated and deterred in full informed the commitment to enhancing NATO members institutions' and societies' ability to 'resist and recover from a major shock' (NATO 2018).

Around the same period, the EU outlined its own strategic objectives in its Global Strategy, published in June 2016. The concept of resilience—already outlined in a 2012 Communication and developed in the 2013 Council Conclusions on the EU Approach to Resilience—features especially prominently in the EUGS, where it is iterated 41 times and used as a *leitmotiv* of external action (Wagner and Anholt 2016). Indeed, the EUGS mentions the commitment to 'state and societal Resilience to our East and South' as the main objective of EU external action.

Although both NATO and the EU adopted the concept of resilience, the way the concept has been employed by the two organisations differs. NATO defines resilience as 'society's ability to resist and recover easily and quickly from shocks' such as 'a natural disaster, failure of critical infrastructure or an armed attack'. Such an ability 'combines both civil preparedness and military capacity' and is seen as 'essential to NATO's collective security and defense' (NATO 2018). In the 2013 EU Council Conclusions, resilience is 'understood to mean the ability of an individual, a household, a community, a country, or a region to prepare for, to withstand, to adapt, and to quickly recover from stresses and shocks without compromising long-term development prospects'. The EUGS more vaguely defines resilience as 'the ability of states and societies to reform, thus withstanding and recovering from internal and external crises' (European Union 2016: 26). The document's commitment to 'targeting the most acute cases of governmental, economic, societal and climate/energy fragility' (European Union 2016: 60) confirms that the EU has developed a broader approach to resilience-building that embraces a much wider array of policy instruments, ranging from trade and development to security and defence.

Given its nature as a regional security organisation, NATO's narrower conceptualisation of resilience is unsurprising. Where EU and NATO's understanding of the concept differs most starkly, however, is not the scope of the concept, but in its empirical referents. As explained in detail in Chapter 2 by Anholt and Wagner, the EU is committed to building resilience both 'at home and abroad'. Consequently, the notion of resilience is employed with reference to both EU member states and 'states and societies to the east stretching into Central Asia, and to the south down to Central Africa' (European Union 2016: 9). By contrast, NATO unclassified documents tend to narrow the usage of resilience to member states' societies only. Although occasionally used in regards to allies like Ukraine, resilience is primarily employed with reference to NATO members' ability to withstand external shocks. Accordingly, the Baseline

Requirements for National Resilience (*NATO Review* 2016) are formulated with a view to ensuring continuity of government and essential services, security of critical civilian infrastructure, and support to military forces with civilian means within NATO countries. Strategic documents like the Warsaw Summit Final Communiqué (2016) forcefully acknowledge that NATO is surrounded by an arc of instability, and stress that the security of its member states cannot be disentangled from that of the regions surrounding them. NATO's commitment to preventing and mitigating turmoil outside the Euro-Atlantic region, however, goes under the different rubric of 'projecting stability' (NATO 2016). As explained by Larsen and Koehler in this volume, resilience is nevertheless present in NATO's definition of stability, seen as a situation where 'well-functioning institutions and a resilient state/society create the conditions in which the risk for outbreak, escalation, recurrence of conflict is reduced to acceptable levels'. Consequently, resilience seems to be implicitly understood as a precondition for NATO stability-projection efforts consisting of 'a range of military and non-military activities', such as 'regional partnerships and capacity building efforts' (*NATO Review* 2018).

In sum, both the EU and NATO have formulated a forceful commitment to address crises at their Southern flank and strengthen their neighbours' ability to cope with both internal fragilities and external shocks. The terminology used by both organisations, however, is not identical. The EU seems to have replaced the concept of stability (mentioned only 4 times in the entire EUGS) with the notion of resilience, applied to both within and outside of the EU. NATO, by contrast, has persisted in using both concepts, but with different geographical referents. NATO members are the targets of a number of specific initiatives aimed at strengthening their resilience, primarily seen as their preparedness against those threats usually referred to as hybrid, including cyber-attacks, energy disruptions, and disinformation campaigns (Corbe and Cusumano 2018). States and regions outside NATO's borders, by contrast, are the beneficiaries of less specific efforts intended to project stability.

Structure of the Book

The remainder of this volume will examine a host of different initiatives that are tightly connected to enhancing state and societal resilience at Europe's Southern periphery. To that end, the book is divided as follows.

Chapter 2, by Rosanne Anholt and Wolfgang Wagner, examines the genesis and development of the notion of resilience within the framework of EU external action. To this end, it examines the broader academic debate on resilience, arguing that despite its shortcomings, the concept of resilience offers a useful contribution to policymakers by stressing the importance of local contexts and providing practitioners from the military, diplomatic, and development communities with a common language to engage with each other. Drawing on these insights, the chapter then analyses EU policy documents such as the EUGS, where resilience features much more prominently than the commitment to promote democracy and human rights that dominated previous strategies and statements. After identifying resilience as a new *leitmotiv* of EU external action, Anholt and Wagner assess the prospects and pitfalls of resilience-based approaches, focusing on the impact of this paradigm shift on EU external action.

Chapter 3, by Jeffrey A. Larsen and Kevin Koehler, shows that projecting stability is not a novel mission for NATO. Indeed, two waves of stability projection can be identified: one directed eastwards and launched after the end of the Cold War, and another targeting the Alliance's south, ongoing since the 2016 Warsaw Summit. The chapter argues that although NATO stability-projection eastwards was successful, the Alliance may currently be unfit for the purpose of projecting stability across the Mediterranean. Wider cultural differences, a deeply ingrained wariness of organisations perceived as aligned to US national interests, and the impossibility of rewarding recipient countries' reforms with NATO membership inevitably make projecting stability to Europe's South more problematic. Keeping these caveats in mind, the chapter concludes by offering some policy recommendations on how to increase the effectiveness of current NATO initiatives in the Middle East and Maghreb.

Chapter 4, by Emile Badarin and Tobias Schumacher, focuses on the influence of resilience-based foreign policy on the EU Neighbourhood Policy (ENP) framework. It argues that the notion of resilience in EU foreign policy towards its southern 'near abroad' is unsettled and continues to undergo a seemingly endless process of reconceptualisation. Accordingly, the chapter treats resilience not only as a work in progress, but also as a discursive means through which the EU attempts to conceal its struggle to come to terms with instability in the Southern Neighbourhood and downplay its recent shift from transformative to *status quo*-oriented foreign policy aspirations. Drawing on concrete examples of EU resilience-building in Egypt, Jordan, Lebanon and Palestine, Badarin and Schumacher show that the elusiveness of resilience and the frequent inconsistencies in its applications have rendered the EU unable to both democratise and stabilise its Southern Neighbourhood.

Chapter 5, by Christian Kaunert, Sarah Léonard, and Ori Wertman, focuses on EU attempts to develop counterterrorism cooperation with countries in the Middle East and North Africa (MENA). It examined four main dimensions and types of initiatives: border control, countering the financing of terrorism, fostering regional cooperation, as well as strengthening the rule of law and the protection of human rights. Despite attempts to promote judicial reforms intended to protect individual rights from security forces' abuse, EU counterterrorism assistance has primarily focused on strengthening the ability of partner country institutions to effectively disrupt terrorist groups. In line with EU traditional approaches towards the MENA region, counterterrorism cooperation has therefore given priority to state resilience over societal resilience.

Chapter 6, by Francesco Giumelli, discusses whether the EU's use of sanctions and restrictive measures is consistent with its efforts to strengthen the resilience of states and societies in the MENA region. To this end, it provides an in-depth examination of EU restrictive measures enacted towards Tunisia, Libya, Egypt, and Syria between 2010 and 2018, arguing that EU targeted sanctions in the Southern Neighbourhood had mixed results. Although not effective to a full extent, the sanctions designed to support regime consolidation in Tunisia and Egypt were appropriately tailored around the needs of local actors, and can ultimately be seen as successful in increasing state resilience. Sanctions aimed at fostering regime change by impairing the ability of authoritarian governments to tackle the uprisings, on the other hand, had nearly no noticeable effects on societal resilience, ultimately departing from the principled pragmatism enshrined in the EUGS.

Chapter 7, by Luca Franza, Coby van der Linde, and Pier Stapersma, notes that although energy security plays an increasingly prominent role in Euro-Atlantic agendas, NATO and the EU's renewed emphasis on the safety of fossil fuel supplies is primarily motivated by concerns over European countries' dependence on Russian gas. These fears have overshadowed energy security challenges in the Southern and Eastern Mediterranean regions, where fossil fuel supply disruptions have actually occurred more frequently than along the Russian-Ukrainian transit corridor. Reliable flows of hydrocarbons across the Mediterranean are not only important for Europe's energy security, but also vital for the economy of large fuel exporters like Algeria and Libya. In order to mitigate the risks of unrest in the Southern Mediterranean, EU, and NATO member states should also consider the unintended repercussions of their energy policies on the resilience of states and societies in the Maghreb and the Middle East.

Chapter 8, by Arturo Varvelli and Matteo Villa, examines the relations between Libya and countries in the Euro-Atlantic communities from the ousting of Muhammar Gaddafi's regime in 2011 to the present day. As this chapter shows, NATO operation Unified Protector was successful on military grounds. However, ensuing attempts to stabilise the country failed to produce significant results, glossing over the most delicate phases of nation-building. The lack of meaningful EU support and the interference of external actors complicated an already fragile political transition. Taking stock of these lessons, Varvelli and Villa offer timely policy recommendations on how to overcome such obstacles, stressing the importance of involving militias in the peace process, redistributing oil revenues more equitably within Libyan society, and ensuring a more effective cooperation between NATO and the EU and among each organisation's member states.

Sahelian states like Niger and Mali are often seen as specimens of state fragility. Chapter 9, by Luca Raineri and Edoardo Baldaro, offers an in-depth analysis of the three Common Security and Defence Policy (CSDP) missions currently deployed in the Sahel: European Union Capacity Building Mission (EUCAP) Sahel Niger, EUCAP Sahel Mali, and European Union Training Mission (EUTM) Mali. According to Raineri and Baldaro, these missions have mainly conceptualised resilience in terms of sector-specific, quick-impact capacity-building measures seeking to enable local states' security forces to better tackle terrorism, radicalisation, and irregular migrations. By reducing resilience as states' preparedness against external shocks, the EU has ultimately overemphasised the magnitude of foreign threats, underestimating the risks arising from Sahelian states' internal political and socioeconomic fragilities. Such miscalculations may undermine the impact of EU efforts to enhance the resilience of Mali, Niger, and Sub-Saharan Africa's countries at large.

In 2013, the UN Department of Political Affairs launched an Integrated Strategy for the Sahel, aimed at 'building the resilience of people and communities' through both capacity building and political inclusion. Due to its protracted instability, Mali has been the target of the UN Multidimensional Integrated Stabilisation Mission (MINUSMA), one of the largest UN peacekeeping missions ever launched. Chapter 10, by Chiara Ruffa, Sebastiaan Rietjens, and Emma Nygren, uses this mission as a source of insights into the role of UN peacekeeping operations in enhancing resilience. By focusing on the protection of civilians, MINUSMA has successfully enhanced human security among Malian communities. The effectiveness of the mission, however, has been hindered by widespread incoherence and insufficient cooperation between its different components. Moreover, the structure and mandate of the mission have been primarily geared towards security and military objectives, disregarding the promotion of inclusive, bottom-up development.

Chapter 11, by Nick Pounds, and Rudolf Keijzer, zooms into the resilience of Lebanese state institutions and society. Despite ethnic and religious divisions, the legacy of a long civil war, Syrian and Iranian interference, Israeli invasions, and the highest inflow of refugees worldwide per capita, Lebanon has largely remained unaffected by the widespread unrest that followed the Arab uprisings. Hence, the Lebanese case can shed light on the underpinnings of resilience, providing crucial insights into how to address the fragility of states in the Middle East. Specifically, this chapter argues that the seven baseline requirements identified by NATO as the foundations of state and societal resilience cannot serve as a blueprint for the stabilisation of Lebanon, which entails addressing other priorities such as reducing economic inequalities and curbing other countries' interference in Beirut's internal politics.

While Lebanon has remained unaffected by the Arab uprisings, other countries in the MENA region have experienced a political transition. Chapter 12, by Maria Giulia Amadio Viceré and Andrea Frontini, focuses on the EU and NATO's responses to the unfolding of the Arab uprisings, arguing that Euro-Atlantic diplomacy vis-à-vis Egypt and Tunisia has prioritised state resilience at the expense of broader societal resilience. The political transitions in Egypt and Tunisia alike arose from pressures to democratise and address socioeconomic problems. Despite the different priorities and instruments available to both organisations, EU and NATO responses to the Arab uprisings eventually converged. As the EU and NATO alike grew increasingly wary of the risk of state failure at their Southern periphery, they both focused on strengthening government institutions at the expense of civil society, ultimately leaving the root causes of instability unaddressed.

Chapter 13, by Stefano Ruzza, examines piracy off the Horn of Africa. Maritime crime off the Somali coast seriously threatened both global maritime trade and regional stability in the Red Sea basin. NATO, the EU, and other regional powers worked in close synergy with the shipping industry, complementing the best management practices developed by the International Maritime Bureau with policing operations at sea such as NATO mission Ocean Shield and the EU operation EUNAVFOR Atalanta and capacity-building missions on land such as EUCAP Nestor. The international response to Somali-based piracy succeeded in boosting the resilience of maritime trade thanks to effective cooperation between all relevant stakeholders. Consequently, the policies developed to tackle Somali piracy are not only relevant for studying the efforts of projecting stability at Europe's Southern borders. Such initiatives also serve as a valuable case study into the importance of EU-NATO and civil-military cooperation alike.

As shown by Hernan Del Valle in Chapter 14, however, civil-military cooperation at sea is not always effective or frictionless. Between 2014 and 2018, the mobilisation of European civil society resulted in the launching of several non-governmental Search and Rescue (SAR) missions off the coast of Libya. NGO ships cooperated effectively with European naval assets, saving more than 110,000 asylum seekers. Since 2017, however, European and Italian authorities grew increasingly wary of non-governmental SAR operations. Del Valle, then head of advocacy and communication for the Amsterdam branch of MSF, shows that the political imperative of stemming irregular entries into the EU-led European governments to criminalise not only human smuggling, but also humanitarian activities such as NGOs' rescue operations. European border agencies' insufficient awareness of humanitarian principles prevented effective dialogue between NGOs and law enforcement authorities, triggering a confrontational approach that undermined a novel and otherwise effective form of maritime civil-military cooperation.

The conclusions reassess the concept of resilience in light of the insights offered by the contributors. We stress that the recent emphasis on the projection of resilience has several advantages, serving as a reminder of the need for local ownership, a bridge across academic and policy communities, and an enabler of civil-military cooperation. Moreover, the constructive ambiguity of resilience has eased consensus-building within

NATO and the EU, serving as a catalyst for agreement at a time of growing disagreement within the Euro-Atlantic community. On the other hand, however, the notion of resilience is in danger of becoming overly stretched. The unclear relationship between state and societal resilience is a case in point. Although the EU and NATO see states and societal resilience as two sides of the same coin, strengthening the resilience of illiberal state institutions may yield short-term stability at the price of long-term societal resilience. After raising some theoretical and policy questions that help prevent the concept of resilience from becoming too ambiguous to be truly constructive, the conclusion briefly outlines some policy directions on how to enhance the effectiveness of future resilience-building initiatives. Most notably, we stress the importance of a comprehensive approach bringing together the military, diplomatic, development and humanitarian communities and combining NATO force-projection capabilities with the EU's development assistance and post-conflict stabilisation instruments.

References

Auerswald, D., & Saideman, S. (2014). *NATO in Afghanistan*. Princeton: Princeton University Press.

Baggio, J. A., Brown, K., & Hellebrandt, D. (2015). Boundary Object or Bridging Concept? A Citation Network Analysis of Resilience. *Ecology and Society, 20*(2).

Bourbeau, P. (2015). Resilience and International Politics: Premises, Debates, Agenda. *International Studies Review*: n/a–n/a.

Bourbeau, P. (2018a). *On Resilience*. Cambridge: Cambridge University Press.

Bourbeau, P. (2018b). A Genealogy of Resilience. *International Political Sociology, 12*, 19–35.

Bruns, B., Happ, D., & Zichner, H. (Eds.). (2016). *The European Neighbourhood Policy*. Basingstoke: Palgrave.

Chandler, D., & Coaffee, J. (Eds.). (2016). *The Routledge Handbook of International Resilience*. London: Routledge.

Chandler, D. (2014). *Resilience: The Governance of Complexity*. London: Routledge.

Chorin, E. (2019, April 19). Libya's Perpetual Chaos. *Foreign Affairs*.

Coaffee, J. (2006). From Counterterrorism to Resilience. *The European Legacy, 11*(4), 389–403.

Corbe, M., & Cusumano, E. (2018). Conclusions. In E. Cusumano & M. Corbe (Eds.), *A Civil-Military Response to Hybrid Threats*. Palgrave: Basingstoke.

Cusumano, E., & Corbe, M. (2018). Introduction. In E. Cusumano & M. Corbe (Eds.), *A Civil-Military Response to Hybrid Threats*. Basingstoke: Palgrave.

European Union. (2016). *Shared Vision, Common Action: A Stronger Europe. A Global Strategy for the European Union's Foreign and Security Policy.*

European Union Council Conclusions on the EU Approach to Resilience. (2013). https://www.consilium.europa.eu/uedocs/cms_Data/docs/pressdata/EN/foraff/137319.pdf. Accessed 26 April 2019.

Gramer, R. (2017, February 17). The Definitive European Security Conference Drinking Game. *Foreign Policy*.

Hasenclever, A., Meyer, T., & Rittberger, V. (1997). *Theories of International Regimes*. Cambridge: Cambridge University Press.

Joseph, J. (2018). *Varieties of Resilience: Studies in Governmentality*. Cambridge: Cambridge University Press.

Johnson, S. (2017). *How NATO Adapts: Strategy and Organization in the Atlantic Alliance Since 1950*. Baltimore: Johns Hopkins University Press.

Michta, A., & Paal, S. H. (Eds.). (2014). *The Future of NATO: Regional Defense and Global Security*. Ann Arbor: University of Michigan Press.

NATO. (2014, September 5). *Wales Summit Declaration*. https://www.nato.int/cps/ic/natohq/official_texts_112964.htm. Accessed 26 April 2019.

NATO. (2016, July 9). *Warsaw Summit Communiqué*. https://www.nato.int/cps/en/natohq/official_texts_133169.htm. Accessed 26 April 2019.

NATO Review. (2016). Resilience: A Core Element of Collective Defence. https://www.nato.int/docu/review/2016/Also-in-2016/nato-defence-cyber-resilience/EN/index.htm. Accessed 26 April 2019.

NATO Review. (2018). Projecting Stability: An Agenda for Action. https://www.nato.int/docu/review/2018/Also-in-2018/projecting-stability-an-agenda-for-action-nato-partners/EN/index.htm. Accessed 26 April 2019.

Schmitd, J. (2015). Intuitively Neoliberal? Towards a Critical Understanding of Resilience Governance. *European Journal of International Relations, 21*(2), 402–426.

Schumacher, T. Marchetti, & Demmelhuber, A. (Eds.). (2017). *The Routledge Handbook on the European Neighbourhood Policy*. Oxon: Routledge.

Sloan, S. (2016). *Defense of the West: NATO, the European Union and the Transatlantic Bargain*. Manchester: Manchester University Press.

The Economist. (2019, April 17). Sudan and Algeria Overthrow Despots but Not Their Political Systems. https://www.economist.com/international/2019/04/20/sudan-and-algeria-overthrow-despots-but-not-their-political-systems. Accessed 26 April 2019.

United Kingdom Department of International Development. (2011). *Defining Disaster Resilience: A DFID Approach Paper*. London: UK Department of International Development.

United Nations Development Programme. (2011). *Towards Human Resilience: Sustaining MDG Progress in an Age of Economic Uncertainty*. New York: United Nations Development Programme (UNDP).
United States Agency for International Development (USAID). (2012). *Building Resilience to Recurrent Crisis*. USAID Policy and Programme Guidance.
United States Department of Homeland Security. (2010). *Quadrennial Homeland Security Review Report: A Strategic Framework for a Secure Homeland*. Washington, DC: Department of Homeland Security.
Wagner, W., & Anholt, R. (2016). Resilience as the EU Global Strategy's New Leitmotif: Pragmatic, Problematic or Promising? *Contemporary Security Policy, 37*(3), 414–430.
Walker, J., & Cooper, M. (2011). Genealogies of Resilience: From Systems Ecology to the Political Economy of Crisis Adaptation. *Security Dialogue, 42*(2), 143–160.
Wimelius, M., Eriksson, M., Kinsman, J., Strandh, V., & Ghazinour, M. (2018). What Is Local Resilience Against Radicalization and How Can It Be Promoted? A Multidisciplinary Literature Review. *Studies in Conflict & Terrorism*. https://doi.org/10.1080/1057610x.2018.1531532.

CHAPTER 2

Resilience in the European Union External Action

Rosanne Anholt and Wolfgang Wagner

On a rhetorical level, the European Union's policy towards its Southern neighbourhood has undergone a change in paradigm (see chapter by Badarin and Schumacher in this volume). From the 'Barcelona Process' of the 1990s to the European Security Strategy of 2003 (European Council 2003, hereafter: ESS), EU policy documents often read like contemporary applications of Immanuel Kant's treatise *'Perpetual Peace'*. Just as the enlightenment philosopher, the EU championed democracy, multilateral institutions, and trade as the pillars of a blueprint that had proven its usefulness for the EU itself and was next to be exported to its Southern periphery. The EU portrayed itself as a 'normative power' (Manners 2002) whose influence was based on being an exemplary source of peace, wealth, and democracy. An emulation of the EU by its Southern neighbours was assumed to be a common interest, whose realization appeared as challenging but feasible as the accession of the former Warsaw Pact countries in the East.

R. Anholt (✉) · W. Wagner
Faculty of Social Sciences, Vrije Universiteit Amsterdam, Amsterdam, The Netherlands
e-mail: r.m.anholt@vu.nl

© The Author(s) 2020
E. Cusumano and S. Hofmaier (eds.),
Projecting Resilience Across the Mediterranean,
https://doi.org/10.1007/978-3-030-23641-0_2

In the wake of the 'Arab Winter', the optimism and self-assuredness of the 'Barcelona Process' and the 2003 European Security Strategy seemed out of sync with the political and social realities in the MENA region. Soon after Federica Mogherini was appointed as the High Representative of the European Union for Foreign Affairs and Security Policy in 2014, she began a comprehensive review of the EU's external policies (Tocci 2016). The resulting Global Strategy (High Representative of the EU 2016, hereafter GS) was presented in June 2016 and introduced resilience as a new *leitmotif* (Wagner and Anholt 2016), mentioned far more frequently than the notions of 'human rights', 'democracy/democratization', and 'human security' which had dominated previous strategic documents.

In this chapter, we discuss the implications of the advent of resilience as a new guiding principle for the EU's approach to its Southern neighbourhood. We first examine how the EU conceptualizes 'resilience' (section "The EU's Understanding of Resilience"). We argue that new rhetoric notwithstanding, key elements of the EU's previous approach, such as democracy and human rights promotion, have survived the paradigm shift and continue to guide EU policy. At the same time, the introduction of resilience indicates a turn towards local ownership and bottom-up peacebuilding. We then examine the broader debate about resilience, and review its main merits and shortcomings identified in this literature (section "Resilience—Problems and Promises"). We identify three main themes from criticism, namely the perceived inevitability of protracted crises, the resemblance of resilience-based governance practices with neoliberal styles of governance reasoning, and the construction of a 'resilient subject' onto whom responsibility is shifted (section "Key Criticisms"). At the same time, increased attention to local actors and existing capacities has been highlighted as a key prospect of resilience-based approaches. In addition, resilience provides practitioners, including diplomats, UN and NGO staff, with a common language to engage with each other (section "Key Prospects"). In summary, resilience appears to aptly capture the two major changes in EU policy towards the Southern neighbourhood: the acceptance of protracted crises as the new normal, and a key role for local actors and practices (section "Conclusion").

The EU's Understanding of Resilience

The 2012 Commission Communication on the EU approach to resilience offered a general definition of resilience as 'the ability of an individual, a household, a community, a country or a region to withstand, adapt and quickly recover from stresses and shocks' (European Commission 2012: 5). This understanding echoes widespread usage of the concept in ecology, engineering, and psychology and is in line with definitions by EU member state governments, international organizations, and non-governmental organizations. Resilience contrasts with previous paradigms in security and peacebuilding by acknowledging the inevitability of shocks and stresses. As a practical consequence, efforts are no longer focused exclusively on the prevention of shocks, but on the capacity of a community to sustain its core functions in the event of a shock, and to recover from shocks in a timely manner.

The Commission's definition is by and large silent on the strategies, means, and instruments for achieving resilience. To some extent, this silence is deliberate and signals an openness towards local practices and priorities. Proponents of the resilience paradigm are generally cautious with one-size-fits-all blueprints and instead emphasize the importance of the context as well as of local knowledge and ownership. Notwithstanding its recent appreciation of the local, the EU has of course been developing its own approach to promote resilience. The Global Strategy of June 2016 was one of the first key document in this regard, and the Joint Communication of the Commission and the High Representative 'A Strategic Approach to Resilience in the EU's external action' (European Commission and High Representative 2017; hereafter: Strategic Approach) published a year later, translates the Global Strategy's new leitmotif into tangible priorities and actions. As we will argue in the remainder of this section, both documents conceptualize resilience as a continuation of previous policies aimed at promoting democracy and human rights. However, the Global Strategy in particular also introduces 'principled pragmatism' as a guidepost, i.e. the combination of a commitment to universal values and a pragmatic approach towards implementing them (Juncos 2017).

The Global Strategy reveals that key ideas of the 2003 European Security Strategy (henceforth: ESS) are still very much alive: The ESS held that 'the best protection of our security is a world of well-governed democratic states'. In a similar vein, the 2016 strategy states that 'at the heart of a resilient state' (GS: 24) lies a resilient society, which is further described as 'featuring democracy, trust in institutions, and sustainable development' (GS: 24). The 2017 Joint Communication reaffirmed that EU action 'will be grounded in the EU's commitment to democracy and human and fundamental rights' and further elaborates that shortcomings in governance, democracy, human rights and the rule of law, gender equality, corruption or the shrinking space for public participation and civil society, pose a fundamental challenge to the effectiveness of any society's development efforts. (Strategic Approach: 4)

Continuities vis-à-vis the role of states are also discernable across policy documents. While the state is by no means the exclusive addressee of EU actions, the 2003 strategy considered 'state failure' to be a key threat. In a similar vein, the Global Strategy juxtaposes resilience to 'fragility', which 'threatens all our vital interests' (23). Fragility is again linked to democracy and human rights, as 'repressive states are inherently fragile' (25). The 2017 Communication also mentions strengthening of states' capacity as a key strategy but hastens to qualify this strategy, so that capacity building should be pursued 'in a manner that ensures respect for democracy, rule of law, human and fundamental rights and fosters inclusive long-term security and progress' (Strategic Approach: 3).

Regarding the EU's policy towards its Southern neighbourhood, the relationship between resilience and migration is particularly interesting. Whereas the Global Strategy made rather vague references to 'shared global responsibilities' (GS: 28), addressing the root causes of displacement, and the need to 'stem irregular migration flows' (GS: 27), the Joint Communication mentions migration 'as a legitimate adaptation strategy to severe external stresses' (Strategic Approach: 10) at an individual level. While echoing concerns about the root causes of irregular migration, the Joint Communication shows more sensitivity to the needs of refugees and calls for 'a new people-centred development-oriented approach for the forcibly displaced and their host communities that supports access to education, housing, decent work, livelihoods and services, and aims to end dependence on humanitarian assistance' (Strategic Approach: 11) (on the inconsistencies of EU approaches to migration, see chapter by Del Valle in this volume).

Although the 2016 strategy echoes several key themes of the ESS, at least two differences are worth noting. (from 129ff) "The ESS states that 'security is a precondition of development', whereas the 2016 strategy conceives of development as a requirement for resilience: 'states are resilient when societies feel they are becoming better off and have hope in the future' (GS: 26). Moreover, in the latter strategy, resilience is said to echo the United Nations Sustainable Development Goals (GS: 24)." The

2016 strategy also calls for development policy to be 'better aligned with our strategic priorities' (GS: 11). Thus, development is simultaneously upgraded to a more crucial instrument in and of itself, but also continues to retain its instrumental value in achieving resilience.

The second difference concerns the assertion that 'there are many ways to build inclusive, prosperous and secure societies' (GS: 25). According to the GS, the EU will pursue a 'multifaceted approach to resilience in its surrounding regions' (GS: 25). Compared to the ESS, such an emphasis on 'tailor-made policies' (GS: 25) is new. This resonates with the doctrine of 'principled pragmatism', which would be set to 'guide our external action in the years ahead' (GS: 8). The 2017 Joint Communication maintains its emphasis that the

> EU should … continue to support domestic efforts, tailored to the needs and context of each society … The involvement of local governments, communities and civil society stakeholders will be given particular attention. (Strategic Approach: 5)

This again emphasizes not only the recognition of context-specificity, but also local ownership. These differences between the ESS and the GS echo other changes in the EU's strategic discourse more broadly. One is the emergence of hybrid threats, i.e. 'those threats posed by adversaries with the ability to simultaneously employ conventional and non-conventional means' (Cusumano and Corbe 2018: 2), as a new concern to the EU strategic community. Just as the concept of resilience, the notion of hybrid threats resonates with a 'comprehensive approach' or a 'joint up approach' (GS: 26) that emphasizes collaboration across traditionally separated communities.

Resilience—Problems and Promises

Despite its ubiquity on the global policy level, the concept of resilience is rarely unpacked (Bourbeau 2013). Moreover, there may be, as is suggested by some, a 'worrying consensus across government, business, and some quarters of academia that resilience is an unquestionably "good" value to be striven for, invested in, and cultivated throughout society at whatever cost' (Brasset and Vaughan-Williams 2015: 46). In the previous sections, we introduced the EU's understanding of resilience, and indicated how the new paradigm retains key elements of previous strategies, not least in terms of the principles of democracy and human rights-promotion. Although the new *leitmotif* of resilience is thus compatible with previous priorities in EU foreign policy, the question remains of what the choice for this new term implies. In this section, we review the broader debate on resilience in the social sciences to better understand the prospects and challenges associated with the EU's reorientation of its foreign and security policy around this concept.

Key Criticisms

Key criticisms of resilience revolve around a number of themes, including (i) the implications of assumptions about contemporary risks and crises that underlie resilience-based approaches to addressing (in)security; (ii) the governance practices that define resilience-based approaches and their resemblance to neoliberal or even post-liberal styles of governance; and (iii) the impact of resilience-based approaches on the normative construction of the 'resilient subject'.

First, the rise and spread of the concept of resilience in international discourses on crisis management and complex emergencies indicates both a profound shift in our understanding of the world and a faltering belief in our ability to control it. Contemporary challenges, including terrorism, complex and chronic political crises, climate change-induced natural disasters, and global financial volatility have engendered the idea that our world is increasingly insecure. This understanding is in striking contrast with previous EU documents' rhetoric (Tocci 2017). Whereas the ESS opened with the assertion that 'Europe has never been so prosperous, so secure, nor so free' (European Council 2003: 1), the GS opens with the acknowledgment that 'we need a stronger Europe. This is what our citizens deserve, this is what the wider world expects. We live in times of existential crisis, within and beyond the European Union' (GS, p. 13). Moreover, crisis and instability are increasingly framed as normal, and peace and stability as the exception. A 2015 policy memo of the European Council on Foreign Relations called on Europeans to 'accept that crisis and conflict in their "near abroad" is [sic] the new normal – and that there is much less they can do about it than they once hoped' (Witney and Dennison 2015: 1).

Underlying this sense of fundamental insecurity is not just the amount of crises and threats within Europe and beyond, but also the understanding that they are inherently complex: Today's crises are characterized by multiple interdependencies, transcending not just geographical borders, but also technical, political, and disciplinary boundaries, and lacking straightforward solutions—so-called 'wicked problems' (Rittel and Webbel 1973). This is particularly true for crises of a more protracted or chronic nature, characterized 'by long-term political instability, (episodes of) violent conflict, and vulnerability of the lives and livelihoods of the population' (Macrae and Harmer 2004: 15). Protracted crises such as those across the Middle East and much of North and Central Africa, may generate unpredictable but significant spill-over effects. Syria is a case in point: violence between an intricate web of international and local, state and non-state armed groups caused 5.6 million people to seek refuge abroad (UNHCR 2018). Many of Syria's neighbouring countries were ill-prepared to accommodate such large influxes of people—in the case of Lebanon, for example, amounting to approximately one-sixth of its total population—exacerbating the pre-existing vulnerabilities of host societies. It could be argued that exactly these pre-existing vulnerabilities by and large determine the impact of shocks (Raineri and Baldaro, this volume).

Current approaches to crises and crisis governance systems seem ill-equipped to deal with the complexity and unpredictability of contemporary risks and crises. Peacebuilding, emergency relief, and development assistance have not fulfilled their promises of a safer, better world, but instead have been criticized not only for being ineffective, but also for being inappropriate, illegitimate, and having harmful unintended consequences (Paris 2010). Despite the significant growth of financial and human resources, the international humanitarian system is 'falling short … in meeting the … needs of populations in chronic crises, which are by far the bulk of its caseload' (ALNAP 2015: 11). Perhaps unsurprisingly, the World Humanitarian Summit (WHS) in 2016 saw various commentators question whether the international system was 'broken' (Barder and Talbot 2016; Dickinson 2016). Indeed, in a profoundly complex world where life exists naturally 'on the edge of extinction' (Duffield 2011: 762), predicting, identifying, and responding to risks and crises becomes problematic (Aradau and van Munster 2011). Moreover, it makes modernist approaches of accumulating ever more scientific knowledge to continue to improve policy outcomes rather redundant (Chandler 2017).

Resilience is not so much about preventing all possible risks, but rather about accepting that crises are inevitable precisely because it is impossible to prevent them all (Bulley 2013). Resilience moves beyond a utopia of security, and 'preaches the impossibility and folly of thinking we might resist danger, and instead accept living a life of permanent exposure to endemic dangers' (Evans and Reid 2013: 95). It is this fatalistic worldview—wherein shocks can only be prepared for, not stopped—that underlies much of resilience thinking (Joseph 2017).

Second, limited knowledge of catastrophes to come necessitates new ways of thinking about security (Aradau and van Munster 2011). New modes of security and crisis governance must be 'attuned to the unexpected and unknowable, rather than purporting to prevent, anticipate or protect against the unexpected and the uncertain' (Aradau 2014: 7). Or as Schmidt (2015) puts it: 'in an ontologically complex world, decisions must naturally acquire a different character; that is, they can no longer be conceived in terms of goal-oriented decisions that make a change in the world and are then to be accounted for and evaluated on this basis' (p. 407). Resilience thinking provides this new basis on which to engage with complexity and uncertainty (Cavelty et al. 2015: 5).

A key characteristic of resilience-based modes of governance is that responsibility for security is shifted away from the state, and onto members of society, who become 'active and responsible contributors to security' (Reid 2012). In more traditional conceptions of security the state has the ultimate duty to keep citizens safe, yet resilience decentralizes power and shifts responsibility to the local, thereby 'inverting traditional security logics based on state level control' (Coaffee and Fussey 2015: 87), and replacing traditional top-down structures with (seemingly) bottom-up ones (Howell 2015a). In other words, inasmuch as governments are unable to provide security since they cannot control nor direct the external world, citizens are tasked with organizing themselves locally to provide for their own communities' security. Consequently, security practices are integrated into the everyday (Coaffee and Rogers 2008), while government instead is reduced to the mere 'administration of life' (Chandler 2013b: 221). In times of austerity and depletion of funds, resilience may be used as a justification for further budget cuts. For example, the EU Approach to Resilience explicitly states that resilience is a cost-effective strategy, not only better for the people involved, but also *cheaper* (EC 2012: 3), underscoring the neoliberal nature of resilience-based governance approaches (Joseph 2017).

Resilience also conforms to other neoliberal governance practices, such as regulation from a distance (Duffield 2012). Here, citizens are not completely left to their own devices, but rather, states 'nudge' (Chandler 2013b; Coaffee 2013) citizens towards self-organization and control through protocols, as a kind of regulated self-organization (Kaufmann 2013). The state steps back and encourages certain behaviours from a distance, such as competitive conduct and entrepreneurial skill through public–private partnerships, networked governance, and active citizenship (Joseph 2017). For example, in its Supporting Horn of African Resilience (SHARE) and l'Alliance Globale pour l'Initiative Résilience Sahel (AGIR) projects, the EU promotes local ownership (Joseph 2014)—an ideal also widely embraced at the WHS. The risk here however, is that 'rather than genuinely devolving powers and letting local actors decide for themselves, [resilience] represents a devolution of responsibilities, instructing us on how we ought to behave backed up with a strict interpretation of what constitutes "best practice"' (Joseph 2017: 164). Resilience thus runs the risk of being no more than (external) interventions reconceptualised as empowerment (Chandler 2012).

On the other hand, Schmidt (2015) argues that 'resilience … originates from but no longer operates within the neoliberal problematic of epistemological complexity' (p. 419). Whereas neoliberal governance employs self-governing techniques to achieve desired policy outcomes because of the known limits to our knowledge—'known unknowns', resilience instead operates on the basis of *ontological* complexity (Chandler 2017) and '*unknown* unknowns'. Resilience-based approaches are therefore 'a radically distinctive approach to governing complexity (bringing complexity into governmental reason), through reposing complexity as an ontological rather than an epistemological problem' (Chandler 2017: 142). Although neoliberalism first brought complexity into the sphere of governmental reasoning (Chandler 2017), resilience should perhaps be understood as a response to neoliberalism's inherent frustrations, rather than a continuation of it (Schmidt 2015).

Third, another line of critique is concerned with how resilience creates vigilant, entrepreneurial, and de-politicized subjectivities responsible for non-resilient outcomes: how it normatively constructs the 'resilient subject'. In a dangerous world, where states cannot provide final security, we are asked to 'accept that one is fundamentally vulnerable' (Evans and Reid 2013: 84), and subsequently to prepare for, adapt to, and live with a spectrum of possible—but unknowable—risks (Brasset et al. 2013). This fear of vulnerability within societies may however, be instrumentalized by governments (Duffield 2012; Lentzos and Rose 2009), for example to increase the credibility of state leaders' claims that they are keeping citizens safe (Coaffee et al. 2009), or to secure public support of increasingly pervasive security technologies. A rhetoric of imminent danger may also encourage citizens to report anything they find suspicious (Coaffee and Fussey 2015), turning citizens into micro-vigilantes tasked with policing their locales (Evans and Reid 2014).

Resilience is not only vigilance, but is also about using danger, or crises, as 'an opportunity for transformation' (EC 2013: 3). As learning is understood to result from exposure (Rogers 2013), it is through exposure that can one develop the 'desirable attributes of foresight, enterprise, and self-reliance' by which 'the ability to change and adapt becomes a virtue in itself' (Duffield 2011: 757). This raises the question of whether resilience presupposes the *necessity* and *positivity* of human exposure to danger (Evans and Reid 2013): do we have to expose ourselves to danger, to embrace risk, and 'thrive on chaos' (O'Malley 2010: 489)? Here, resilience may risk becoming a neo-Darwinist measure of the fitness to survive (Duffield 2012; Walker and Cooper 2011).

Resilience itself is portrayed as a *learnable* skill rather than a natural capacity, a human attribute that can be reconfigured into coping strategies and skills that can be learned by anyone, making resilience 'a technology of the self that can be both learnt and taught' (Duffield 2012: 487). If resilience can be learned however, it can also be failed to learn. For example, in the US military, resilience training is used to prevent military personnel from developing (symptoms of) post-traumatic stress disorder (PTSD) following deployment—effectively making them responsible for their own mental well-being (O'Malley 2010; Walklate et al. 2014). Doing so erases the moral basis upon which veterans can claim healthcare entitlements (Howell 2015b), because subjects are made responsible for their own vulnerabilities (Bulley 2013)—regardless of whether these stem from their inherent weaknesses, or from socio-economic and political inequalities. With a view to conflict-affected societies, resilience seems to assign responsibility for threats and insecurities to affected societies themselves, and disregards the role of outside actors— including western governments—in their instability (Chandler 2013a).

Despite these concerns, resilience conceives of subjects as active agents rather than passive or lacking agency (Chandler 2012). Indeed, resilience is about the 'agential capacities to turn inner lives and inner workings into the site of effective, intentional and transformative agency based on the stimuli received from environments one is embedded into' (Schmidt 2015: 420). However, in a world that is fundamentally complex and uncertain, and over which little control can be exerted, agency is limited to choosing whether or not to adapt to the conditions of our suffering (Reid 2012). Or as Chandler and Reid (2016) put it, 'the resilient subject is a subject that must permanently struggle to accommodate itself to the world: not a subject that can conceive of changing the world' (p. 53).

As such, resilience has a profoundly depoliticizing effect (Cavelty et al. 2015). By disavowing 'the transformative capacity of collective political action' (Aradau 2014: 15), politics become a mere 'technical practice' (Evans and Reid 2014: 91). Within the resilience paradigm, addressing (in)security is about enhancing the ways in which affected systems respond to risks and crises, rather than interrogating the structural factors that drive them.

Key Prospects

Aside from the critiques discussed in the previous section, there are also a number of important prospects related to the concept of resilience. This section will address these by first highlighting the functionality of the conceptual ambiguity that still surrounds resilience, and then by examining how it has allowed for new practices and forms of cooperation to emerge, particularly within the field of humanitarian action and development assistance.

There is no uniform understanding (Walklate et al. 2014), and perhaps not only multiple, but also competing logics of resilience (Coaffee and Fussey 2015). The ambiguity of resilience is not necessarily due to conceptual obscurity, nor a product of diverse genealogies (Zebrowski 2012). Rather, in abstraction, resilience might mean as little as an ontological fact (Schmidt 2015: 419) or 'a capacity of life itself' (Evans and Reid 2014: 33). Ambiguous concepts do not necessarily make for useful analytical tools, but conceptual ambiguity is useful insofar it facilitates collective action (Paris 2001). Ultimately, the search for a conceptual agreement should not come at the expense of doing things differently to address vulnerabilities of crisis-affected populations (Levine 2014). Because it is a highly context and issue specific concept, resilience first requires specifying the answers to questions like 'resilience to what?', 'resilience of whom?', and 'resilience by what means?' As the concept can be interpreted differently according to the answers to these three questions, resilience is fluid enough to be applied to various contexts, adapted to different institutional visions, and translated into diverse strategies.

Indeed, resilience may fulfil the role of a 'lingua franca'—a common language able to effectively cross disciplinary boundaries (Duffield 2012). For example, resilience provided a common ground for traditional donors to engage with 'non-traditional donors' (e.g. the BRICS, Turkey, Indonesia, and the Gulf States), who rejected the term 'failed state' (Pospisil and Kühn 2016). Resilience instead helped to 'emphasise … commonalities, while downplaying policy differences' (Pospisil and Kühn 2016: 7–8). As a convening concept, resilience has a brokering capacity 'to bring people (practitioners, policy makers), organizations with different initial agendas, and communities of practice from different sectors, together around the same table with the shared objective of "strengthening resilience"' (Béné et al. 2012: 45). Besides providing a unifying rationale for greater international cooperation (Flynn 2011), resilience also creates opportunities to think more creatively about hybrid solutions and to build on what already exists (de Weijer 2013). Exactly because of this conceptual ambiguity, resilience has been abstract and malleable enough to incorporate different research and policy domains (Walker and Cooper 2011), allowing it to enable new practices and forms of cooperation—for example, within the field of humanitarian aid and development assistance. This notably includes, first, a focus on local ownership, foregrounding and building upon the response capacity of national and local actors within crisis-affected societies, and second, the cooperation between a diverse set of actors as crucial to building resilience.

First, the so-called 'resilience paradigm' enables renewed attention to be focussed on national and local actors as first responders and providers of aid (Hilhorst 2018). Strong national and local ownership is described in the New Way of Working, one of the WHS outcome documents, as a 'shift to "reinforce and do not replace" the roles of national and local actors in the prevention and delivery of assistance … [that] is central to the change in mindset and behaviour required to sustainably reduce need, risk and vulnerability' (UNOCHA 2017: 7). In a study of the UN Development Programme (UNDP) Infrastructures for Peace programme, resilience enabled a focus on developing the capacities of poor or fragile states to deal with, and overcome, the circumstances that block their development—thereby recognizing and respecting local agency, institutions, and systems (Ryan 2012).

Similarly, the Regional Refugee and Resilience Plan (3RP) places national plans and decision-making central to emergency response.

In this consortium co-led by the UN Refugee Agency (UNHCR) and UNDP, the governments of Jordan, Lebanon, Turkey, Iraq, and Egypt, with the help of some 270 partners, including UN agencies and international and local NGOs, lead the response to both the assistance and protection needs of Syrian refugees, and the stabilization and resilience of host societies (3RP 2018). While this represents a move away from more paternalistic approaches that frame aid recipients as passive victims, the 'renewed appreciation of state control of humanitarian responses' within the resilience paradigm (Hilhorst 2018: 6) also carries with it certain dangers, such as the politicization and manipulation of aid. Moreover, national control of crisis response may not necessarily mean that affected communities themselves (i.e. refugees and vulnerable host communities) are in the lead of the response. Whereas former UN Secretary-General Ban Ki-Moon wrote in his WHS report that 'any effort to reduce the vulnerability of people and strengthen their resilience must begin at the local level, with national and international efforts building on local expertise, leadership and capacities' (UNGA 2016: 30), it remains to be seen whether this holds true in the context of responses to insecurity caused by political violence and armed conflict.

Second, the cooperation between a diverse set of actors is understood to be crucial to resilience-building. For example, in the Action Plan for Resilience in Crisis Prone Countries, the EU asserts that achieving resilience 'requires all EU actors (humanitarian, development, political) to work differently and more effectively together' (EC 2013: 4), echoing the GS' emphasis on a comprehensive or joint-up approach. Similarly, the new European Consensus on Development asserts that 'the EU and its Member States must be united in diversity, using a variety of experiences and approaches, bearing in mind their respective comparative advantages' (EC 2017: 6). Indeed, the resilience paradigm ushers in a more systematic attention to a plurality of actors—not only local or national, but also humanitarian, peacebuilding, and development actors, as well as the private sector (Hilhorst 2018). Underlying this perceived need to include a diverse set of actors in response to insecurity and protracted crises, is the sense that achieving different (better) outcomes, requires doing things differently:

> We operate in silos created by mandates and financial structures rather than towards collective outcomes by leveraging comparative advantage. We measure success by projects achieved, people deployed, structures set up

and funds released, rather than the results they produce. Achieving ambitious outcomes for people, particularly in fragile and crisis-affected environments, requires a different kind of collaboration among Governments, international humanitarian and development actors and other actors: one that is based on complementarity, greater levels of interoperability and achieving sustainable, collective outcomes rather than the coordination of individual projects and activities. (UNGA 2016: 29)

Some of these actors—notably, humanitarian and development actors—are, and have been throughout history, significantly distinct from each other: Humanitarian action, as a rapid response mechanism to crisis, and the more medium and long-term development action, are two fields of action that differ not just in term of time horizons, but also in terms of instruments and measures, and principles and values (Stamnes 2016). So much so that, when the former UN Secretary-General called for the international aid system to 'transcend the humanitarian-development divide by working towards collective outcomes' (p. 29) at the WHS, *Médecins Sans Frontières*, a decidedly humanitarian organization, walked out of the summit (MSF 2016). Whereas strengthening the humanitarian-development nexus may be understood as a clearer delineation of the roles of actors involved in responding to crisis as well as an understanding and appreciation of how they may be complementary, the above shows that this will not be without challenges. Notably, humanitarian organizations may be concerned that such partnerships will put the humanitarian principles of neutrality, impartiality, and independence in jeopardy.

As a final note on the key prospects for resilience, some authors observe that resilience thinking is taking a turn towards more transformative notions of the concept (Weichselgartner and Kelman 2014). As one of the few definitions to acknowledge this transformative potential, a position paper by the United Nations Development Group (UNDG) describes resilience as 'the ability of households, communities and societies to cope with shocks and stresses, to recover from those stresses, and to work with households, communities and national and local government institutions to achieve *sustained, positive and transformative change* [emphasis added]' (UNDG 2014: 13). Such understandings may provide an opening, both theoretically as well as practically, for resilience to start engaging with notions of equity, power, and justice. These are issues that the concept of resilience tends to avoid when regarding risks and crises as inevitable and crises-affected individuals and communities as having to adapt to existing structures rather than challenge and change them. This is an important point in particular because the potential of resilience is to decrease disparities between those who have/have not, and those who survive/survive not by increasing protective factors and decreasing risk factors (Jennison 2008).

Conclusion

Over the last 25 years or so, the EU's policy towards its Southern neighbourhood has changed considerably. The concept of resilience can capture two of the most significant of such changes. First, the concept cautions expectations. Rather than suggesting the EU will help overcome protracted crises *tout court*, the new resilience-inspired approach suggests that crises will persist, but the EU may help affected states and societies to cope with them. Consequently, policies may increasingly focus on resilience at the expense of understanding and addressing the root causes of (protracted) crises. Second, the new *leitmotif* of resilience signals a shift in responsibilities. Rather than promoting a one-size-fits-all, made-in-Brussels blueprint, resilience suggests an appreciation for local actors and the development of existing capacities. This is not without challenges. For example, in 2016 the EU eased trade regulations with Jordan in order to encourage trade and investment, as well as create jobs for both Jordanians and Syrian refugees (EC 2016). In return, the Jordanian government pledged to issue 200,000 work permits for Syrian refugees. Whereas these and other measures are presumed to help Jordan cope with hosting some 1.3 million Syrians—including 655,000 refugees registered with UNHCR (Hashemite Kingdom of Jordan, Ministry of Planning & International Cooperation 2018), in terms of job creation, resilience may prove difficult to realize in a country with an unemployment rate of over 18%—even over 37% for people aged between 20 and 24 (Hashemite Kingdom of Jordan, Ministry of Labour 2018). Another challenge with regard to localization concerns who or what is meant by 'local actor': The 'local' is not one, uniform entity, but consists of diverse actors at different levels with divergent and possibly conflicting interests. Equating 'local' with national (host) governments, may risk sidestepping those directly affected, i.e. refugees and vulnerable host communities. Finally, only a thin line separates a genuine appreciation for local capacities from attempts to relieve the EU of expensive commitments. The overall message that is conveyed to the EU's Southern neighbourhood therefore seems ambivalent. While the local receives more appreciation than before, the Southern neighbours are also expected to accept prime responsibility for 'wicked problems' that are expected to persist.

References

ALNAP. (2015). *State of the Humanitarian System: ALNAP Study*. London: ALNAP/ODI.

Aradau, C. (2014). The Promise of Security: Resilience, Surprise and Epistemic Politics. *Resilience International Policies, Practices and Discourses, 2*(2), 73–87.

Aradau, C., & van Munster, R. (2011). *Politics of Catastrophe: Genealogies of the Unknown*. Abingdon: Routledge.

Barder, O., & Talbot, T. (2016). *The World Humanitarian Summit: The System's Broken, Not Broke*. Center for Global Development.

Béné, C., Godfrey Wood, R., Newsham, A., & Davies, M. (2012). *Resilience: New Utopia or New Tyranny? Reflection About the Potentials and Limits of the Concept of Resilience in Relation to Vulnerability Reduction Programmes* (Working Paper 405). Institute of Development Studies.

Bourbeau, P. (2013). Resiliencism: Premises and Promises in Securitisation Research. *Resilience, 1*(1), 3–17.

Bourbeau, P. (2015). Resilience and International Politics: Premises, Debates, Agenda. *International Studies Review, 17*(3), 374–395.

Brasset, J., & Vaughan-Williams, N. (2015). Security and the Performative Politics of Resilience: Critical Infrastructure Protection and Humanitarian Emergency Preparedness. *Security Dialogue, 46*(1), 32–50.

Brasset, J., Croft, S., & Vaughan-Williams, N. (2013). Introduction: An Agenda for Resilience Research in Politics and International Relations. *Politics, 33*(4), 221–228.

Bulley, D. (2013). Producing and Governing Community (Through) Resilience. *Politics, 33*(4), 265–275.

Cavelty, M. D., Kaufmann, M., & Søby Kristensen, K. (2015). Resilience and (In)Security: Practices, Subjects, Temporalities. *Security Dialogue, 46*(1), 3–14.

Chandler, D. (2012). Resilience and Human Security: The Post-interventionist Paradigm. *Security Dialogue, 43*(3), 213–229.

Chandler, D. (2017). Resilience and Neoliberalism. In D. Chandler & J. Coaffee (Eds.), *The Routledge Handbook of International Resilience* (pp. 135–146). Abingdon: Routledge.

Chandler, D. (2013a). International Statebuilding and the Ideology of Resilience. *Politics, 33*(4), 276–286.

Chandler, D. (2013b). Resilience and the Autotelic Subject: Toward a Critique of the Societalization of Security. *International Political Sociology, 7,* 210–226.

Chandler, D., & Reid, J. (2016). *The Neoliberal Subject: Resilience, Adaptation and Vulnerability.* London: Rowman & Littlefield International.

Coaffee, J. (2013). Rescaling and Responsibilising the Politics of Urban Resilience: From National Security to Local Place-Making. *Politics, 33*(4), 240–252.

Coaffee, J., & Fussey, P. (2015). Constructing Resilience Through Security and Surveillance: The Politics, Practices and Tensions of Security-Driven Resilience. *Security Dialogue, 46*(1), 86–105.

Coaffee, J., & Rogers, P. (2008). Rebordering the City for New Security Challenges: From Counter-Terrorism to Community Resilience. *Space and Polity, 12*(1), 101–118.

Coaffee, J., Wood, D. M., & Rogers, P. (2009). *The Everyday Resilience of the City: How Cities Respond to Terrorism and Disaster.* Basingstoke: Palgrave Macmillan.

Cusumano, E., & Corbe, M. (2018). Introduction. In E. Cusumano & M. Corbe (Eds.), *A Civil-Military Response to Hybrid Threats* (pp. 1–14). Basingstoke: Palgrave Macmillan.

de Weijer, F. (2013). *Resilience: A Trojan Horse for a New Way of Thinking?* (Discussion Paper No. 139). European Centre for Development Policy Management.

Dickinson, E. (2016, May 24). *Humanitarian System: Just Broke, or Also Broken?* Devex.

Duffield, M. (2011). Total War as Environmental Terror: Linking Liberalism, Resilience, and the Bunker. *South Atlantic Quarterly, 110*(3), 757–769.

Duffield, M. (2012). Challenging Environments: Danger, Resilience and the Aid Industry. *Security Dialogue, 43*(5), 475–492.

European Commission. (2012, March 10). *Communication from the Commission to the European Parliament and the Council. The EU Approach to Resilience. Learning from Food Security Crises.* COM (2012) 586 final. Brussels.

European Commission. (2013). *Action Plan for Resilience in Crisis Prone Countries 2013–2020.* Commission Staff Working Document. SWD (2013) 227 final.

European Commission. (2016, July 20). *EU-Jordan: Towards a stronger partnership.* European Commission - Press release. IP/16/2570. See http://europa.eu/rapid/press-release_IP-16-2570_en.htm.

European Commission. (2017). The New European Consensus on Development 'Our World, Our Dignity, Our Future' (2017/C 210/01). *Official Journal of the European Union.*

European Commission/High Representative of the Union for Foreign Affairs and Security Policy. (2017, June 7). *Joint Communication to the European Parliament and the Council. A Strategic Approach to Resilience in the EU's External Action.* JOIN (2017) 21 final. Brussels.

European Council. (2003). *European Security Strategy—A Secure Europe in a Better World.* Brussels.

Evans, B., & Reid, J. (2013). Dangerously Exposed: The Life and Death of the Resilient Subject. *Resilience: International Policies, Practices and Discourses, 1*(2), 83–98.

Evans, B., & Reid, J. (2014). *Resilient Life: The Art of Living Dangerously.* Cambridge: Polity Press.

Flynn, S. (2011). A National Security Perspective on Resilience. *Resilience: Interdisciplinary Perspectives on Science and Humanitarianism, 2,* i–ii.

Hashemite Kingdom of Jordan, Ministry of Labour. (2018). *The National Labour Market Indicators (2013–2017).*

Hashemite Kingdom of Jordan, Ministry of Planning & International Cooperation. (2018). *Jordan Response Plan for the Syria Crisis (2018–2020).*

High Representative of the EU. (2016). *Shared Vision, Common Action: A Stronger Europe. A Global Strategy for the European Union's Foreign and Security Policy.*

Hilhorst, D. (2018). Classical Humanitarianism and Resilience Humanitarianism: Making Sense of Two Brands of Humanitarian Action. *Journal of International Humanitarian Action, 3,* 15.

Howell, A. (2015a). Resilience as Enhancement: Governmentality and Political Economy Beyond 'Responsibilisation'. *Politics, 35*(1), 67–71.

Howell, A. (2015b). Resilience, War, and Austerity: The Ethics of Military Human Enhancement and the Politics of Data. *Security Dialogue, 46*(1), 15–31.

Jennison, V. (2008). Networking to Improve Community Resiliency in Disaster Planning and Response. *International Journal of Public Policy, 3*(5/6), 338–353.

Joseph, J. (2014). The EU in the Horn of Africa: Building Resilience as a Distant Form of Governance. *Journal of Common Market Studies, 52*(2), 285–301.

Joseph, J. (2017). Resilience, Governmentality and Neoliberalism. In J. Coaffee & D. Chandler (Eds.), *The Routledge Handbook of International Resilience* (pp. 159–168). Abingdon: Routledge.

Juncos, A. (2017). Resilience as the New EU Foreign Policy Paradigm: A Pragmatist Turn? *European Security, 26*(1), 1–18.

Kaufmann, M. (2013). Emergent Self-Organisation in Emergencies: Resilience Rationales in Interconnected Societies. *Resilience, 1*(1), 53–68.

Lentzos, F., & Rose, N. (2009). Governing Insecurity: Contingency Planning, Protection, Resilience. *Economy and Society, 38*(2), 230–254.

Levine, S. (2014, July). *Political Flag or Conceptual Umbrella? Why Progress on Resilience Must Be Freed from the Constraints of Technical Arguments.* Humanitarian Policy Group, Policy Brief 60.

Macrae, A., & Harmer, J. (2004). *Beyond the Continuum: The Changing Role of Aid Policy in Protracted Crises.* Humanitarian Policy Group Report 18.

Manners, I. (2002). Normative Power Europe: A Contradiction in Terms? *Journal of Common Market Studies, 40*(2), 235–258.

Médecins Sans Frontières. (2016). *MSF to Pull Out of World Humanitarian Summit.*

O'Malley, P. (2010). Resilient Subjects: Uncertainty, Warfare and Liberalism. *Economy and Society, 39*(4), 488–509.

Paris, R. (2001). Human Security: Paradigm Shift or Hot Air? *International Security, 26*(2), 87–102.

Paris, R. (2010). Saving Liberal Peacebuilding. *Review of International Studies, 36*(2), 337–365.

Pospisil, J., & Kühn, F. (2016). The Resilient State: New Regulatory Modes in International Approaches to State Building? *Third World Quarterly, 37*(1), 1–16.

Reid, J. (2012). The Disastrous and Politically Debased Subject of Resilience. *Development Dialogue, 58,* 67–80.

Rittel, H. W. J., & Webber, M. M. (1973). Dilemmas in a General Theory of Planning. *Policy Sciences, 4,* 155–169.

Rogers, P. (2013). The Rigidity Trap in Global Resilience: Neoliberalisation Through Principles, Standards, and Benchmarks. *Globalizations, 10*(3), 383–395.

Ryan, J. (2012). Infrastructures for Peace as a Path to Resilient Societies: An Institutional Perspective. *Journal of Peacebuilding & Development, 7*(3), 14–24.

Schmidt, J. (2015). Intuitively Neoliberal? Towards a Critical Understanding of Resilience Governance. *European Journal of International Relations, 21*(2), 402–426.

Stamnes, E. (2016). *Rethinking the Humanitarian-Development Nexus* (Policy Brief 24). Norwegian Institute of International Affairs (NUPI).

Tocci, N. (2016). The Making of the EU Global Strategy. *Contemporary Security Policy, 37*(3), 461–472.

Tocci, N. (2017). *Framing the EU Global Strategy: A Stronger Europe in a Fragile World.* Cham: Palgrave Macmillan.

UNHCR. (2018). *Situation Syria Regional Refugee Response.* Operations Portal Refugee Situation.

United Nations Development Group. (2014). *A Resilience-Based Development Response to the Syria Crisis.*
United Nations General Assembly. (2016). *One Humanity: Shared Responsibility—Report of the Secretary-General for the World Humanitarian Summit (A/70/709).*
United Nations Office for the Coordination of Humanitarian Affairs. (2017). *New Way of Working Regional Refugee & Resilience Plan (3RP) 2018–2019 in Response to the Syria Crisis: Regional Strategic Overview (2018).*
Wagner, W., & Anholt, R. (2016). Resilience as the EU Global Strategy's New Leitmotif: Pragmatic, Problematic or Promising? *Contemporary Security Policy, 37*(3), 414–430.
Walker, J., & Cooper, M. (2011). Genealogies of Resilience: From Systems Ecology to the Political Economy of Crisis Adaptation. *Security Dialogue, 42*(2), 143–160.
Walklate, S., McGarry, R., & Mythen, G. (2014). Searching for Resilience: A Conceptual Excavation. *Armed Forces and Society, 40*(3), 408–427.
Weichselgartner, J., & Kelman, I. (2014). Geographies of Resilience: Challenges and Opportunities of a Descriptive Concept. *Progress in Human Geography*, 1–9.
Witney, N., & Dennison, S. (2015). *Europe's Neighbourhood: Crisis as the New Normal.* European Council on Foreign Relations. Policy Memo.
Zebrowski, C. (2012). *The Biopolitics of Resilience.* PhD thesis, Keele University.

CHAPTER 3

Projecting Stability to the South: NATO's "New" Mission?

Jeffrey A. Larsen and Kevin Koehler

In 2014, the North Atlantic Treaty Organization was surprised by the sudden emergence of a renewed danger from Russia on its Eastern flank that threatened the sovereignty and security of its member states and their home territories. The Alliance found itself forced to return its attention back to Europe and its previous core missions of collective defence and deterrence, reversing a 20-year trend that was driven by one general assumption: since Europe was free from traditional military threats, the member states were also free to pursue larger ambitions on a global scale. The end of the Cold War contributed to the emergence of crises in the eastern periphery of the Alliance, including in the Balkans, which led to the first wave of NATO out-of-area operations. Nevertheless, the perspective that Europe no longer faced an existential threat was formalised in the 2010 Strategic Concept, which

J. A. Larsen
Department of National Security Affairs, US Naval Postgraduate School, Monterey, CA, USA

K. Koehler (✉)
Leiden University, Leiden, The Netherlands
e-mail: k.koehler@fsw.leidenuniv.nl

© The Author(s) 2020
E. Cusumano and S. Hofmaier (eds.),
Projecting Resilience Across the Mediterranean,
https://doi.org/10.1007/978-3-030-23641-0_3

emphasised the three pillars of NATO strategy: collective defence, crisis management, and cooperative security. While each was nominally equal in importance, in reality the Alliance and its member states had pursued the latter two pillars at the expense of the former for nearly a generation. The concept of "projecting stability" was highlighted in the 2016 Warsaw Summit Declaration as a way of accommodating both of those two pillars. This document emphasised projecting stability as one of the most important missions for the Alliance, almost on a par with the core missions of collective defence and deterrence.

This chapter argues that projecting stability is not a novel concept for the Alliance—it has in fact been applied to Eastern Europe for nearly 30 years since the end of the Cold War. While we question whether NATO is the international organisation best suited for this mission, we also propose some suggestions which focus on states in the Middle East and North Africa, and the particular challenges they face, for ensuring the success of this mission.

We approach these issues in the following way: the next two sections examine the origins and development of the projecting stability agenda with an emphasis on the particular conception of projecting stability from the military perspective, which has recently been adopted by NATO's Military Committee. The following two sections then examine two waves of projecting stability, one directed eastward after the end of the Cold War, the other aimed at the Alliance's southern neighbourhood and ongoing since the Warsaw Summit in 2016. Based on these considerations, we offer some thoughts on the extent to which the Alliance is fit for the purpose of projecting stability and how current activities could be improved, before closing with recommendations to increase the likelihood of NATO successfully achieving its mission of projecting stability to the South.

Background

One would have expected general agreement on the need to reaffirm collective security in Europe as a result of the events of 2014, given that since the end of the Cold War nearly all of NATO's national military forces had become much smaller, and less prepared for collective defence. This trend resulted from two factors: the perceived peace dividend that accompanied the disappearance of the Soviet threat, and the concomitant need to provide more agile and lightweight forces to deal with out-of-area challenges, especially after 9/11. The latter required a different set of equipment than what the armour-heavy Cold War militaries could provide. The necessary retooling and restructuring for military operations beyond Europe were expensive, took years to complete, and resulted in a new mindset among Western militaries regarding their perceived purpose and role in the post-Cold War world. There was, accordingly, little desire to once again reverse course after 2014. The result was considerable push-back within the Alliance against any return to collective defence. "We don't want a return to the Cold War" was a refrain heard regularly in the halls of NATO for more than two years, until the Warsaw Summit declaration of July 2016 set collective defence once again as the primary responsibility of the Alliance. Instead, there was a push for continued emphasis on out-of-area issues, especially threats emanating from the South of course, there is no reason that the Alliance could not accomplish both missions. Members of the Alliance simply have to make a determined effort to do so, and to pay the necessary price. After all, each member state can, in principle, determine where and in what manner they will contribute to the various security missions.

In fact, NATO has been projecting stability outside its borders for a long time—since the first days of the post-Cold War era—and thus the concept is hardly novel. NATO's expansion to the East in the second half of the 1990s was explicitly referred to as an exercise in "projecting stability" by some analysts at the time, and the notion has reappeared regularly since in statements by NATO officials (Hunter 1995). Indeed, in a 2006 speech, Secretary General Jaap de Hoop Scheffer referred to projecting stability as "NATO's new approach to security." "[T]o defend our values," de Hoop Scheffer affirmed, "NATO, as a political-military Alliance, requires a range of tools: stronger partnerships and partnerships with key Nations; not a global NATO but a NATO with global partners that share our values" (de Hoop Scheffer 2006). The same idea was reflected more recently by current NATO Secretary General Jens Stoltenberg, who suggested in a speech at the Graduate Institute in Geneva in March 2017 that "when our neighbors are more stable, we are more secure" (Stoltenberg 2017). In this sense, the agenda of projecting stability can be seen as the Alliance's answer to the increasingly interconnected nature of the security environment at its periphery.

Yet, despite this historic precedence, and notwithstanding the fact that projecting stability experienced a renaissance of sorts following the 2016 Warsaw Summit, important questions remain. To begin with, the Alliance has yet to provide a coherent political definition of stability and how it can be projected. Currently, the Alliance's military bodies are ahead of their political masters in delineating the concept, a situation which creates tensions and inconsistencies. This gap between political ambition, and strategic thinking and planning severely hampers Alliance efforts. In fact, NATO Assistant Secretary General for Operations, John Manza, recently suggested that NATO deserved an "F" for projecting stability (Rousselet 2017). On a more general level, there are those who question whether such a broad mission as is implied by the projecting stability agenda is really the best fit for a political-military alliance like NATO. Would this agenda be better served if led by a different organisation, such as the European Union (EU), the Organization for Security Cooperation in Europe (OSCE), or the United Nations?

Origins and Development of the Concept

Shortly after the end of the Cold War, the Alliance decided to go out of area in an attempt to stabilise its neighbourhood. It hoped that by doing so it would reduce conflict, improve the living standards of the recipients of such stability, and thereby increase Europe and NATO's own security by damping down dangerous tendencies along its periphery (Moore 2007).

NATO's strategic concepts after the end of the Cold War never made explicit reference to projecting stability. In the document published in 2010, the substantive idea of securing Alliance territory by stabilising the security environment in the periphery is visible in the fact that the classical core task of collective defence was complemented by an emphasis on crisis management and cooperative security. However, projecting stability had not reached the level of a strategic concept (NATO 2010). In brief, even though the concept is two-decades old, its function still does not extend far beyond the fundamental hypothesis that "when our neighbors are more stable, we are more secure." In short, the Alliance lacks a focused political reflection on the actual meaning of projecting stability.

In lieu of such reflection, NATO has developed a military concept for projecting stability that has been approved by the Military Committee and, at the time of writing, awaits approval by the North Atlantic Council (NAC). While the latest draft of this document, MC 0655/4, remains classified, previous versions suggest a "means-focused" approach to projecting stability with a little effective reflection on the desired political end-state. The latest, unclassified draft document, MC 0655/3, contains working definition of both stability and projecting stability.[1] According to this document, stability refers to:

> A situation where capable, credible, legitimate and well-functioning institutions and a resilient state/society create the conditions in which the risk for outbreak, escalation, recurrence of conflict is reduced to acceptable levels, leading to a more secure and less threatening environment.[2]

Building on this definition, as well as on prior guidance contained in MC 0400/3, projecting stability is therefore defined as:

> a range of military and non-military activities that influence and shape the strategic environment in order to make neighbouring regions more stable and secure in support of both NATO's strategic interests and those of its neighbours.[3]

Two observations regarding these definitional efforts should be made. First, in terms of the military function of the document, the definitions appropriately refrain from specifying a concrete political end-state. In fact, MC 0655/3 clearly states that projecting stability "includes both political and military efforts, recognizing that all efforts should serve a clear political aim."[4] Reflecting NATO's character as a political-military alliance, this political guidance should come from the political level.

Second, the definition of stability is rather ambitious. Its formulation not only implies activities far beyond NATO's traditional area of functioning, but also suggests that the Alliance take an active interest in the domestic political configurations of non-allied countries. While this does not necessarily suggest that the Alliance is in the business of democratisation, it does imply that, as a recently commissioned report from Allied Command Transformation describes, "local political institutions… need to be sufficiently resilient and representative of local societies as to avoid and resist further crises in the near future" (Costalli 2017: 25; on

---

[1] MC 0655/3 is an unclassified draft document. The fourth version, MC 0655/4, which has been adopted by the MC remains classified. The definitions quoted here might have changed in the final document.

[2] MC 0655/3, para. 5a.

[3] MC 0655/3, para. 5b.

[4] MC 0655/3, para. 4.

NATO's role in the political transition of Tunisia and Egypt, see Amadio Viceré and Frontini in this volume).

In the larger scheme of things, the Alliance has thus put the cart before the horse in its approach towards its periphery, explicating means without having first discussed the ends. Indeed, in the absence of a coherent policy and appropriate direction and guidance at the political level, NATO's military authorities are left with the task of translating an overly vague concept into a concrete set of activities.

While such attempts to develop definitions of central concepts *in abstracto* are welcome, the political implications of Alliance efforts to project stability are best understood in reference to concrete historical settings. In the following section, we trace two waves of projecting stability, which have taken place in two major compass directions and some 20 years apart: to the East in the 1990s and to the South in the 2010s.

The First Wave of Projecting Stability: Partnership with and Enlargement to the East

In the early post-Cold War years of the 1990s, a belief arose that even though Europe was now peaceful, facing no imminent threats, it could not achieve genuine security if instability reigned along its periphery. With the disappearance of the Warsaw Pact, the dissolution of the Soviet Union, and the end of the dangerous long peace, many analysts thought that NATO had accomplished its mission and outlived its usefulness.

Others, however, felt that instead of fading away, the Alliance should now take on a new role: helping erase the divisions of the Cold War, and creating a Europe that was whole, free, and at peace. This was an opportunity for the United States to push its longstanding desire to expand NATO's focus beyond Europe. This new world order would be based on NATO's core values and shared beliefs: democracy, personal freedom, the rule of law, and a just international order. As an American publication opined, it was "time to transform NATO from an alliance based on collective defence against a specific threat into an alliance committed to projecting democracy, stability, and crisis management in a broader strategic sense" (Asmus et al. 1993).

The idea of projecting stability was born from this context immediately after the end of the Cold War and was based on the idea that, as US Senator Richard Lugar expressed in 1993, NATO had to go "out of area or out of business" (quoted in Rosenfeld 1993). At NATO's London Summit in July 1990, Alliance members thus made a pledge to construct a new security environment in Europe. They declared that the Soviet Union was no longer an enemy. Such revisions were a way to maintain Alliance cohesion in an uncertain time by providing a new mission for NATO. Years after, it would also provide a new home for the nations of the former Warsaw Pact by telling them that they were all part of greater Europe, and would not be left out in the cold. For all of this to work, however, the Alliance would have to project stability and democracy to its former enemies in the East. As Vaclav Havel put it, "If the West does not stabilize the East, the East will destabilize the West" (Havel 1997).

At the Rome Summit in 1991, the Alliance took the next step and declared that it would pursue dialogue and cooperation as well as security. One tangible result of this decision was the creation of the North Atlantic Cooperation Council (later renamed the Euro-Atlantic Partnership Council). In 1994, the Alliance created the Partnership for Peace (PfP), which grew to include 21 member states, including all the independent republics that came out of the former USSR, and all the neutral states of Europe. In 1997, the Alliance signed the NATO-Russia Founding Act, which put relations between the two on a more equal footing.

These initiatives towards NATO's eastern neighbourhood constituted concrete efforts to project stability (Hunter 1995; also see Yost 1998). An article by US permanent representative Robert Hunter, published in *NATO Review* in 1995, for example, declared NATO's enlargement as "part of a strategy for Projecting Stability into Central Europe" (Hunter 1995). The idea was to fundamentally transform the security environment in Central Europe: to "move Eastward one of the most thrilling human achievements of the past half century: the abolition of war itself among the states of Western Europe" (Hunter 1995: 3). NATO would offer its erstwhile adversaries to the East various levels of cooperation ranging from potential membership, to close consultation through the framework of the PfP, or through specialised procedures such as the NATO-Russia Founding Act (Hunter 1995: 3). Hunter outlined the Alliance's three-pronged approach: engaging countries from the former Warsaw Pact through consultations in the framework of the PfP initiative; offering a long-term prospective to these countries either through membership, or through sustained partnership; and putting the NATO–Russia relationship on a new footing by winning "Russia's confidence in

NATO's intentions by developing a rich and productive relationship with Moscow" (Hunter 1995: 7).

In addition to the effects of NATO's eastward expansion, members of the Alliance also conducted a series of out-of-area kinetic and non-kinetic operations to the East. At the time, these operations generated considerable debate on both sides of the Atlantic, as experts and politicians considered the future role of the Alliance, whether it should be conducting operations outside its traditional area, whether it should be conducting offensive military operations at all or remain a defensive alliance, and whether an alliance decision obligated all members to comply. But these existential considerations did not prevent the Alliance from acting when it saw a pressing need for some organisation—any organisation—to take prompt action in a crisis. NATO discovered that it was the only organisation available and capable of taking action in most cases of crisis during this period. Some of its actions included:

- Allied Goodwill I and II, humanitarian aid and medical expertise provided to Russia and former Soviet states, 1992
- US arms embargo in the Adriatic, supported by NATO, 1992–1993
- Operations Deadeye and Deliberate Force, countering Bosnian Serb actions, 1995
- International Force (IFOR), Bosnia, 1995–1996
- Security Force (SFOR), Bosnia, 1996–2004
- Operation Allied Freedom, air campaign over Serbia to protect Kosovo, 1999
- Kosovo Force (KFOR), 1999–present
- Operations Essential Harvest, Amber Fox, and Allied Harmony, Former Yugoslav Republic of Macedonia (FYROM), 2001–2003
- NATO Headquarters in Skopje, FYROM, 2002–present.

Each of these missions included air, sea, and land military forces of multiple NATO member states, which greatly inflated the Alliance's view of itself, its purpose in the new world order, and its ability to conduct relatively small-scale military operations in the pursuit of stability for Europe and its immediate neighbourhood.

The ultimate step in projecting stability, for many Partner nations, was an invitation to join NATO as a full member. For some nations, this was also the best indicator of success of the entire projecting stability effort. This logic guided much of the enlargement debate of the 1990s.

The original thinking was based on valid liberal principles: the belief that NATO's enlargement would be a beneficial contribution to the democratisation, and hence pacification, of Eastern Europe. Increased membership was required for more nations to abide by the norms espoused by NATO and the OSCE. This assertion had a political purpose as much as one of military expediency. The lure of membership would create a positive link between the development of a state's foreign and defence policies and its prospects for membership. The Membership Action Plan became the bible for states wishing to become members and served as a tool for outreach and a way of projecting the values of the Alliance. The importance of this assertion for the Alliance is present in today's continued support of NATO's "Open Door" policy for all European states, in accordance with Article 10 of the Washington Treaty.

The success of projecting stability to the East can be explained in part by the fact that European Partner states were motivated by the possibility of eventual NATO membership. In addition, parallel and simultaneous efforts by the European Union to enlarge its zone of peace through shared economic, social, and cultural relationships also supported NATO's efforts in the region. As we shall see, the Mediterranean Dialogue (MD) and Istanbul Cooperation Initiative (ICI) partnership programmes were hamstrung to some extent since they did not carry the same incentivising aspects of future membership to either organisation. This made cooperation with NATO in the MENA region more pragmatic, and seen primarily through the prism of military-to-military programmes.

The Second Wave of Projecting Stability: NATO Looks South

Having shaped NATO's approach to its Eastern neigbourhood in the immediate post-Cold War era, the notion of projecting stability has undergone a renaissance of sorts since the 2016 Warsaw Summit—this time with an emphasis on the South (Díaz-Plaja 2018). The development of the military concept for projecting stability, moreover, constitutes an attempt to give concrete meaning to this abstract notion. This renewed emphasis on projecting stability, somewhat paradoxically, must be seen against the backdrop of increased Alliance efforts in collective defence and deterrence since 2014. Given the Alliance's renewed focus on its classical core task after Russia's 2014 annexation of Crimea (Kroenig 2015), including the return of the nuclear issue (Kamp 2018), the simultaneous resurgence of projecting stability reflects NATO's attempt to balance different risk perceptions by its Eastern and Southern members (Vito 2015).

The second wave of projecting stability is directed towards the South, more specifically towards North Africa and, to a lesser extent, the Eastern Mediterranean. To the extent that the projecting stability agenda as applied to the South is perceived as paralleling earlier efforts in the East, it is important to identify a number of core differences in the regional and global context which might impact the effectiveness of such an agenda.

First, even though the Alliance maintains its "open door policy," there is no prospect for membership when it comes to Partners in the South. While fiercely criticised at the time (Perlmutter and Carpenter 1998) and controversial due to its effects on NATO–Russia relations (Dannreuther 1999), NATO's eastward enlargement must be considered successful from a technical point of view. With four waves of enlargement between 1999 and 2017, NATO has integrated a total of 13 new member states in Central and Eastern Europe since the end of the Cold War. This certainly transformed the security environment in the region and had significant effects on domestic security sectors as well. In the absence of a membership prospective—and the corollary prospect of being allowed under the security umbrella of Article 5—comparable transformations are unlikely in the MENA. In other words, incentives for Southern Partners to adapt their policies and open up their security sectors are limited when compared to former and present candidate countries in Central and Eastern Europe.

Second, NATO does not have the best of reputations in the Southern neighbourhood. Despite lacking systematic public opinion data, public attitudes towards NATO in most MENA countries range from ignorance to opposition. Even at the level of security professionals and military officers, NATO is considered with some scepticism, and Alliance intentions in the south are generally perceived as unclear.[5] The Libya intervention—or rather its aftermath—certainly did not help to present

---

[5] Based on the authors' regular interaction with officers and officials from MENA countries at the NATO Defense College in Rome, 2013–2018.

NATO in a better light in the MENA region. NATO thus starts from a difficult position in the south, underlining the importance of outreach and confidence building activities.

Third, NATO's enlargement to the East occurred in parallel to the EU's eastern enlargement, and it is therefore difficult to disentangle the causal effects of these two processes. It must be understood, however, that similar incentives for, and pressures towards, larger political reforms do not exist in the MENA region. Quite to the contrary, given strategic interests, major Western powers have traditionally supported authoritarian regimes with dubious security practices in the region (Brownlee 2012). For example, Egypt is probably one of the countries furthest removed from the standards of security sector governance encouraged by NATO, even though the country is one of the largest recipient of Western military aid, and has long cooperated with Western powers on a bilateral level and with NATO as part of the MD.

Finally, Western attempts to project stability (or influence) to the MENA do not occur in a vacuum. Russia's September 2015 intervention in the Syrian crisis has proven beyond doubt that Russia is, and will remain, a crucial player in the Middle East (Trenin 2013, 2018). This not only has the potential to transpose some of the re-emerging East–West confrontation into the MENA region, but also means that the West and NATO are not the only game in town. Research has shown that ties with non-democratic patrons can help stabilise authoritarian regimes (Tansey et al. 2017). From the perspective of regional countries, cooperating with Russia might thus appear more attractive, given the fact that Russian support does not come with strings attached regarding domestic political processes. While the first wave of projecting stability to the East occurred during a period of reduced geopolitical competition, NATO's attempts to project stability to the South occurs in the context of resurgent NATO–Russia tensions—not least in the MENA region itself given Russia's role in Syria, but also its increased engagement in Egypt and Libya (Cook 2018).

Given this less-than-optimistic starting point, what can NATO hope to achieve with regard to regional security? We argue that NATO should focus its efforts around the vision of a cooperative (and in the long term, integrated) regional security order. Such a regional security order is currently a long way off, but it is not an entirely unrealistic prospect for the long terms. Indeed, NATO's existing partnership frameworks, the MD and the ICI, can both be seen as efforts in the right direction.

Regional Security Integration

In terms of regional security integration, the Middle East and North Africa lag behind other regions (Aarts 1999). This is because, to begin with, the League of Arab States (LAS) does not have a security component and is largely ineffective as a political organisation (Pinfari 2009). Similarly, while the Gulf Coordination Council (GCC) had shown some signs of increasing cooperation in military and security matters, the current crisis between Qatar on the one hand, and Saudi Arabia and the United Arab Emirates (UAE) on the other has largely blocked what progress had been achieved up to that point (Samaan 2017). In brief, the MENA region remains one of the least integrated regions of the world—economically, politically, and in terms of security. Instead of forming a regional security order, the regional security complex (Buzan and Wæver 2003) in the Middle East is shaped by a high degree of international penetration on the one hand (Hinnebusch 2003), and by a Saudi-Emirati hegemonic projection based on strategic competition with Iran on the other (Lynch 2016).

These systemic processes are punctuated by sub-regional security cooperation, largely based on necessity. Examples include the G5 Sahel (G5S) formed by Burkina Faso, Chad, Mali, Mauritania and Niger and supported by the EU. Founded in 2014, the G5S has set up a joint military force (FC-G5S) in an effort to contribute more efficiently to security provision in the region (International Crisis Group 2017). Further examples include the Peninsula Shield Force of the Gulf Cooperation Council, and steps towards establishing a framework for joint command and missile defence coordination—largely driven by increased demands on Gulf militaries resulting from their countries' more militarily assertive posture since 2011 (Samaan 2017; also see Young 2013). However, as the current GCC crisis illustrates, GCC integration was not strong enough to prevent political differences between the UAE and Saudi Arabia on the one hand, and Qatar on the other to escalate into a full-blown diplomatic crisis since June 2017 (Lenderking et al. 2017).

NATO's partnership formats, the MD and the ICI, have played no significant role in these developments. Cooperation between NATO and the G5S, for example, has been limited to the participation of G5S representatives—along with officials from the European Union delegation in Mauritania and representatives from the African Union (AU)—in the fifth Mediterranean Dialogue Policy Advisory Group Meeting in Nouakchott, Mauritania, in October 2017 (NATO 2017a). Moreover, while both the UAE and Qatar (but not Saudi Arabia) are members of NATO's ICI, and while all parties to the dispute—including Saudi Arabia, the UAE, and Egypt—have continued to participate in NATO partnership activities alongside Qatari participants, the fact that most parties to the GCC crisis share membership in NATO partnership initiatives did not play a role. In other words, despite their relatively long history, NATO partnership initiatives in the MENA region have not developed into effective drivers of cooperative (much less collective) security, nor did they live up to their potential as fora for Track 2 or Track 1.5 political dialogue on security issues.

Part of the reason for this somewhat sobering state of affairs can be seen in the context in which these initiatives emerged. In the case of the MD, initiated in 1994, this background crucially included the Oslo Peace Process between Israel and the Palestinians, and the associated prospects of a resolution to this longstanding conflict (Kaim 2017). Given this backdrop, it made political sense to include countries as diverse as Algeria, Egypt, Israel, and Jordan in the same dialogue initiative. After the failure of the Oslo process, however, and given the current political setting—including the blockage of the Middle East peace process, but also significant shifts in the regional distribution of power in the wake of 2011, as well as the crises in Syria and Libya—it is unclear whether the format of the MD still makes political sense. Similar assessments apply to the ICI.

Set up in the wake of the 2001 terrorist attacks against the United States, and in the context of the global war on terror, the ICI was initially envisaged mainly as a tool to help NATO increase its cooperation with Gulf countries, not least in terms of counterterrorism (Kaim 2017). The fact that two important players, Oman and Saudi Arabia, never joined the ICI, however, signalled the limitations of this approach from the beginning. Moreover, Iraq remained outside NATO's regional partnership programme as a NATO Partner across the Globe together with countries such as Afghanistan, Australia, Colombia, Japan, and Pakistan, among others (NATO 2017b). A structured form of interaction with Iran was never envisaged, even though Iran is arguably one of the main powers in the region. In brief, the ICI did not and does not incentivise regional cooperation, and political developments since its inception in 2004 again suggest that its current format should be revised.

Moreover, in contrast to the PfP initiative in post-Cold War Eastern Europe, the MD and ICI were never conceived of as pathways to full membership, nor do they include the same access to consultations under Article 4 of the Washington Treaty enshrined in the PfP. As a result, incentives for Partners to adapt their security practices to NATO standards have been markedly reduced. In effect, the NATO-Partner relationship in the MD and ICI is subject to some of the same principal-agent problems which beset security force assistance programmes more generally (Biddle et al. 2018).

Taken together, and somewhat resulting from these limitations, NATO Partners in both the MD and the ICI have generally preferred bilateral cooperation with the Alliance over cooperation through their respective partnership frameworks. Political disagreements among different members of both partnership formats are part of the explanation for these limitations. Moreover, the partnership frameworks themselves do not reflect contemporary security dynamics in the region, but are instead based on the political status quo at the time of their foundation. All of this means that NATO is failing to capitalise on one of its greatest strengths—its experience in organising collective security on a regional basis.

NATO should work towards increased cooperation with regional organisations—the LAS, GCC, G5S, AU, and others—to incentivise and promote stronger regional security cooperation. While this is admittedly a long-term process, there is much to gain and very little to lose from reorienting NATO partnerships with MENA countries in this direction. This would involve reorganising existing partnerships into a new framework which better reflects the current security environment, and reinvigorating these frameworks through a stronger emphasis on multilateral cooperation. Current efforts by the US administration to revive the idea of an "Arab NATO" based on cooperation between Gulf countries and Egypt and Jordan—mainly as a tool to counter Iran—could go in such a direction (Smith 2018). There are some encouraging signs that current divisions can be overcome—at least at the level of practical security cooperation. On 12 September 2018, the GCC Chiefs of Defence—significantly including Qatar—met with their Egyptian and Jordanian counterparts as well as with representatives from US Central Command

(CENTCOM) in Kuwait to discuss a deepening of defence cooperation (Al Bawaba 2018). While such initiatives do not preclude bilateral cooperation between the Alliance and specific Partner countries, multilateral cooperation should be a strategic priority for NATO.

The Domestic Picture

All of NATO's partnership programmes—PfP, MD, ICI, Partners across the Globe, as well as the close relations with the EU, the UN, and the OSCE—have served the Alliance in many ways. The 41 official Partner nations serve as essential force multipliers in NATO operations.[6] In fact, these Partners have been critical to the success of some missions. For example, at one point, there were 51 nations represented in ISAF, including all then 28 NATO members and 23 others—most of them NATO Partners. Each nation provided expertise, military forces, funding, and/or other contributions in efforts to modernise Afghanistan and coordinate military operations there. The Alliance also has created several Enhanced Partnership Interoperability Programs with these nations, which primarily train, exercise, and deploy military capabilities with NATO. In addition, at the 2014 Wales Summit, NATO announced a Defence and Related Security Capacity Building Initiative with Georgia, Moldova, and Jordan (NATO 2015).

On the domestic level, NATO has been involved in a number of regional states—mainly in providing educational opportunities and specialised training. These activities, as a rule, are demand-driven—meaning that the content of individual cooperation programmes is determined by Partners. We argue that NATO should revise its "free for all" approach to cooperation with Partners, and should instead utilise the instruments available to the Alliance with strategic oversight. This highlights an inherent tension between the Alliance's emphasis on a demand-driven approach and strategic interests in "capable, credible, legitimate and well-functioning" (security) institutions. Activities related to reforming the security sector—such as NATO's Building Integrity programme—can be perceived as invasive by Partners due to the implications of these activities for domestic balances of power. Given this situation, NATO needs to consider ways to incentivise Partners to make the investment

---

[6] NATO's 41 Partners still include Russia, which is currently not a Partner in good standing. NATO has had no practical cooperation with Russia since April 2014.

necessary to advance in this realm. An important aspect of such an incentive structure would be to increase coherence between Alliance activities and bilateral initiatives by Allies.

From a strategic vantage point, the aim of supporting Partners to become effective security providers implies different things for different Partners, depending primarily on which obstacles a particular Partner Country faces. Afghanistan and Iraq, for example, face different issues than Algeria and Egypt—even though all four countries profit from cooperation with NATO. NATO's current approach to partnership relies to a large extent on Partners themselves choosing which types and areas of cooperation they prefer and on formalising these preferences in a biannual Individual Partnership and Cooperation Programme (IPCP). In this area, NATO's political leaders should take a stronger lead, capitalising on existing bilateral cooperation schemes, and the development of new ones to help guide Partner countries towards the desired end-state. In other words, based on a political vision of security in the MENA, NATO should use its partnership instruments to incentivise Partners to move in the right direction.

A precondition for such an approach is a clearer picture of what effective security provision implies for the structure and capacity of the security sector Partner nations. To put it simply, effective security provision in the MENA is hampered by two different problems: a lack of capacity which prevents the effective provision of security despite best efforts, and deficiencies in security sector governance, which prevents capacities from being deployed efficiently. If states lack capacity, they might be unable to confront domestic or regional security challenges simply because they do not command the human or material resources necessary to do so. On the other hand, if security sectors are governed poorly, while states may well have considerable resources at their disposal, such resources may still be deployed in ways which do not effectively contribute to security provision. The first would constitute a capacity shortfall and to the second would constitute a lack of strategic leadership. In reality, these problems do not exist independently of each other, but are likely to occur simultaneously in different combinations and configurations. On an analytical level, it nevertheless makes sense to examine the two dimensions separately.

Examples which come close to the exemplary type of a capacity shortfall are Afghanistan and Iraq after their recent wars, respectively. In both countries, security institutions had to be built up almost from scratch to enable national security sectors to eventually take over responsibility for security provision. This led to the establishment of the NATO Training Mission in Iraq (NTM-I) after the dissolution of the country's Baathist military upon orders from coalition authorities (Gaub 2016). Given this context, the NTM-I's main mission was to "assist in the development of Iraqi security forces training structures and institutions so that Iraq can build an effective and sustainable capability that addresses the needs of the nation" (SHAPE, n.d.). NATO assistance to Iraq was renewed recently (Emmott and Ali 2018). In Afghanistan, NATO Training Mission in Afghanistan (NTM-A) was set up in 2009 to complement existing capacity-building efforts under US auspices (NATO 2009). Similar NATO-led programmes might be expected to take place in Libya once the situation on the ground allows. The EU-led training of the Libyan coast guard under the auspices of EUNAVFOR Med (Operation Sophia),[7] as well as bilateral efforts with Italy already follow such a pattern (Emmott and Stewart 2017). Moreover, the 2018 Brussels Summit has seen the formal announcement of a new training mission in Iraq (Koehler 2018). All of these activities proceed from the assumption that the Partner countries involved in cooperation with NATO lack specific technical capacities which can be addressed by capacity building and training. The hope underlying such activities is that the strengthening of such capacities will then contribute to domestic stability which will, in turn, increase Alliance security.

On the other side of the spectrum, the effective provision of security can also be hampered by political factors, notably by bad governance of the security sector. The Alliance's Partnership Action Plan on Defence Institution Building (PAP-DIB), which was launched at the 2004 Istanbul Summit, departs from the assertion that "[e]ffective and efficient state defense institutions under civilian and democratic control are fundamental to stability in the Euro-Atlantic area and for international security cooperation" (NATO 2018). This concern with security sector governance is well-founded. Research in civil–military relations and military sociology has long suggested that military effectiveness depends crucially on good governance of the security sector. It has been shown, for example, that the military effectiveness of authoritarian regimes

---

[7] Operation Sophia was originally called European Union Naval Force Mediterranean (EU NAVFOR Med). It is a military operation of the European Union established in April 2015 to neutralise refugee smuggling routes in the Mediterranean.

depends on specific organisational features adopted by armed forces such as merit-based promotion regimes, specific training systems, and information-sharing procedures (Talmadge 2015; Brooks 2006). On a general level, democracies have been found to be more effective militarily because they implement a strict separation of political leadership and military decision-making (Biddle and Long 2004; Reiter and Stam 1998). In short, political meddling in military affairs—through politicised rather than merit-based recruitment and promotion, politicised funding and investment decisions—decreases military effectiveness. The political control of the armed forces by a civilian, rather than military elite, is therefore not just a normative concern, but an important aspect of an effective provision of security.

Moreover, the Alliance does not currently differentiate between different Partner needs. Rather, the 1400 activities contained in the Partnership Cooperation Menu (PCM) are, in principle, open to all Partner countries, even though Individual Partnership and Cooperation Programs are agreed upon with Partner countries. If these partnership activities are to be effective components of a projecting stability agenda, NATO needs to make better use of opportunities to direct cooperation, and to proactively offer bespoke content to specific Partners. In particular, generating capacity without paying attention to governance issues will lead neither to an effective provision of security, nor to security sector reform in the absence of capacity.

A more strategic use of NATO's partnership programmes is predicated upon a detailed needs assessment, framed by an overall understanding of where the Alliance would like Partner countries in the region to move. It is wishful thinking, however, to assume that disparate cooperation activities will somehow automatically lead to an outcome only vaguely defined as "stability." It would be outright foolish to rely on cooperation in the absence of strategy to increase the security of the Alliance.

Counter Arguments: Should NATO Be Doing This?

Of course, in an international alliance that has grown to 29 nations, one cannot expect to achieve consensus easily on matters of grave importance, such as the concepts of projecting stability, enlargement, and out-of-area military operations. As a result, one hears counterarguments to the official line that NATO can pursue both defence and dialogue with equal vigour, or that the two goals of European security and projecting stability are manageable, affordable, and desirable by this political-military alliance of nearly one billion people.

For one thing, the ability to project stability outside NATO's borders must be based on the initial predication of the existence of a Kantian peace in Europe. If the Alliance has to worry about its own borders and the security of its own populations, how can it continue to pursue out-of-area operations and other efforts to project stability abroad? This question has been reinforced by the seeming end of the short peaceful period from 1991 to the resumption of Russian assertiveness starting in 2014.[8] Yet the Alliance has renewed its call for projecting stability, as we have seen in the 2016 Warsaw Summit communiqué, and in documents, speeches, and meetings since. Some members of the Alliance may believe that with the strong response to Russian challenges in Northeastern Europe—including an Enhanced Forward Presence (EFP), forward deployed multinational forces in the Balkans, increased air policing, the creation of new command structures for reinforcements and for the North Atlantic, the enhanced NATO Response Force, and so on—the problem of the Eastern frontier is "fixed." With this challenged sufficiently addressed, some argue, the Alliance can now turn its attention to the South, and projecting stability seems to be the best way to deal with the serious problems arising in the MENA region.

But how can NATO do it all? The Alliance is once again expected to provide significant conventional defence, and nuclear deterrence forces in Europe and the North Atlantic; to perform cooperative security and collective defence missions; and now to project stability to the South. There is little appetite within allied nations for increased defence spending, larger force sizes, or new forays of operational missions in far-away places. The long war in Afghanistan took its toll on popular support for such military operations. At the same time, much of Europe's military force structure and capabilities, as well as America's role in European security, were on a steady decline between 1991 and 2014. The political leadership and the populace both liked the new world, where they did not have to worry about sudden conflict breaking out in their region. But the West also has to respond to a real-world context, which

---

[8] Or perhaps even earlier, such as Putin's speech to the Munich Security Conference, 10 February 2007, or the Russian incursions into Abkhazia and South Ossetia, both in Georgia, in 2008.

sometimes has malevolent actors who *do* want to return to a cold war, or perhaps even a hot conflict.

This philosophical difference between knowing the Alliance needs to provide the forces required to stand up to an adversary, and wishing this was not the case, has created divisions within the Alliance itself. In particular, there is a divide between those who believe the existential threat facing the West comes from a recidivist, nuclear-armed Russia, and those who believe that the more serious and proximate threats are emanating from the South, including terrorism, unchecked migration, and political instability. Without the resources to deal with both, it is disingenuous to proclaim that both are equally important.

There are also divisions within the Alliance over the scope and nature of post-Cold War activities by the Alliance. Indeed, it is true that all nations formally agreed to maintain NATO after the Berlin Wall fell. It is also true that the allure of the Alliance remains strong, as shown by the continuing interest in membership or partnership status by many other countries. But is the alliance overextended? Is it risking its internal integrity in partnering with nations that do not share its Western values? What are NATO's real vital interests? Is the provision of stability one of them? These are questions which have not yet been fully addressed by the member states.

Finally, is NATO really the best organisation for handling such out-of-area missions? Even if the answer is yes, does this imply some sort of moral obligation to act accordingly? Why cannot larger organisations such as the EU, UN or the OSCE be held responsible for projecting stability? Why must a military organisation be in charge?

This last question is the most challenging. Why NATO? If the Alliance genuinely sees NATO as the right organisation to project stability, it still begs an additional question: for what purpose? NATO is a regional security organisation created to ensure the security of its member states in Europe and North America. If Europe is "whole, free, and at peace," does this not suffice? Has not NATO met its charter obligations?

Apparently not. At the time of writing, member states have some 18,000 military personnel in NATO missions around the world: Afghanistan, Kosovo, afloat on the Mediterranean, supporting the African Union, assisting the European Union with the refugee and migration crises, deployed with Patriot missile batteries on the Turkish–Syrian border, forward deployed in the Baltic States and Poland, flying AWACS missions. As Secretary General Stoltenberg noted in 2017:

"NATO is adapting partly by strengthening our collective defense in Europe and partly by stepping up our efforts to project stability to our neighbors" (Stoltenberg 2017). The Alliance, and its national members, want to do both.

The Warsaw Summit declaration amplified this point: "NATO must retain its ability to respond to crises beyond its borders, and remains actively engaged in projecting stability and enhancing international security through working with partners and other international organizations" (NATO 2016). The following questions however for the Alliance remain. How "global" should NATO become? Should it retain its original core functions as a regional organisation created for the collective defence of its homelands? Or should it focus more on out-of-areas missions that fall under the headings of crisis management and collective security? Can it do it all? Should it continue to try? To do both, NATO will need to explicate a number of solid starting points that it seems to be lacking with regard to the concept of projecting stability: a strategy, a clear understanding of its ultimate goals, adequate funding, and the political support of all member states. Without agreement on these starting points, the Alliance will continue to provide grandiose visions without the wherewithal to turn them into reality.

Conclusion: (How) Can We Get There?

In this chapter we have advanced three principal and interrelated points. First, despite the hype surrounding NATO's "new" projecting stability agenda since the 2016 Warsaw Summit, neither the underlying idea nor the phrase itself are new within the Alliance's political discourse. NATO has a 25-year history of projecting stability to the East. Nevertheless, the notion remains ill-defined and needs to be better understood if it is to be useful in guiding Alliance activities in the MENA region and elsewhere. Second, we have outlined how NATO has attempted to project stability to the East and the South, and have questioned the extent to which this overextends Alliance ambitions. Third, we have raised questions about the ability and willingness of the Alliance for taking on this mission. Is NATO really fit for purpose when it comes to projecting stability outside Europe?

These concerns notwithstanding, NATO is currently committed to projecting stability—in addition to collective defence and deterrence. We argue that for this ambition to be successful, a number of preconditions need to be met.

1. *Agree on a clear policy for the Strategic Direction South.* This step is crucial from three interrelated perspectives. Firstly, a policy agreed upon by all 29 Allies will increase the chances that coordination between Alliance activities and initiatives by individual Allies is strengthened. Given different threat assessments and national strategic priorities, full coordination is probably difficult to achieve. Nevertheless, any progress towards coordination would be positive to avoid duplication, and because it would strengthen NATO's credibility in the region. Secondly, a clear policy is an important part of a new public relations strategy for the region. NATO's regional Partners face frequent difficulties in understanding the Alliance's strategic aims—a problem which, combined with a generally sceptical attitude, feeds distrust and misinterpretations about the "real" intentions of the Alliance. A clear strategic approach coupled with an open dialogue process could help address these issues. Third, a coherent policy would give direction to the various activities suggested under the military concept, many of which are already being conducted. In the absence of such guidance, it is difficult to prioritise and to efficiently allocate resources.

2. *Use partnerships strategically.* NATO has long insisted that its partnership programmes be demand-driven. The current military concept mimics this idea.[9] There are two different ways of resolving the inherent tension between a demand-driven approach, and the requirements of a regional strategy. The most radical solution would be to shift from a demand-driven to a conditionality-based approach. This would allow NATO to incentivise what it sees as positive reforms and to target resources where they are most likely to produce favourable outcomes. On the flipside, it might be difficult for Partners to accept such an approach, given the concern that conditionality would encroach upon their sovereignty. A less radical solution would therefore be to cooperate selectively. Here NATO would reinforce cooperation with some Partners and scale back cooperation with others, based on the extent to

---

[9] MC 6055/3, para. 20b.

which individual Partners are willing and able to contribute to the NATO's overall strategic aims. To some extent, this approach is already applied in practical terms, but it would be useful to make it explicit to ensure a proper incentive structure.

References

Aarts, P. (1999). The Middle East: A Region Without Regionalism or the End of Exceptionalism? *Third World Quarterly, 20*(5), 911–925.

Al Bawaba. (2018, September 13). *Egypt, GCC and Jordan Discuss Military Alliance in Kuwait*. https://www.albawaba.com/news/egypt-gcc-and-jordan-discuss-military-alliance-kuwait-1185410. Accessed 23 January 2019.

Asmus, R., Kugler, R., & Larrabee, F. (1993). Building a New NATO. *Foreign Affairs, 72*(4), 28.

Biddle, S., & Long, S. (2004). Democracy and Military Effectiveness: A Deeper Look. *Journal of Conflict Resolution, 48*(4), 525–546.

Biddle, S., Macdonald, J., & Baker, R. (2018). Small Footprint, Small Payoff: The Military Effectiveness of Security Force Assistance. *Journal of Strategic Studies, 41*(1–2), 89–142.

Brooks, R. (2006). An Autocracy at War: Explaining Egypt's Military Effectiveness, 1967 and 1973. *Security Studies, 15*(3), 396–430.

Brownlee, J. (2012). *Democracy Prevention: The Politics of the U.S.-Egyptian Alliance*. Cambridge: Cambridge University Press.

Buzan, B., & Wæver, O. (2003). *Regions and Powers: The Structure of International Security*. Cambridge: Cambridge University Press.

Cook, S. A. (2018, August 31). Putin Is Sneaking up on Europe from the South. *Foreign Policy*. https://foreignpolicy.com/2018/08/31/putin-is-sneaking-up-on-europe-from-the-south/. Accessed 23 January 2019.

Costalli, S. (2017). What Is 'Stability' and How to Achieve It? In S. Lucarelli, A. Marrone, & F. N. Moro (Eds.), *Projecting Stability in an Unstable World* (pp. 25–29). Bologna: Allied Command Transformation, Università di Bologna, Istituto Affari Internazionali.

Dannreuther, R. (1999). Escaping the Enlargement Trap in NATO–Russian Relations. *Survival, 41*(4), 145–164.

de Hoop Scheffer, J. (2006, July 10). *Projecting Stability*. Speech at FRIDE in Madrid. https://www.nato.int/cps/ua/natohq/opinions_22477.htm?selectedLocale=en.

Díaz-Plaja, R. (2018, March 13). Projecting Stability: An Agenda for Action. *NATO Review*. https://www.nato.int/docu/review/2018/also-in-2018/projecting-stability-an-agenda-for-action-nato-partners/en/index.htm. Accessed 23 January 2019.

Emmott, R., & Ali, I. (2018, February 15). At U.S. Urging, NATO Agrees Training Mission in Iraq. *Reuters World News*. https://www.reuters.com/article/us-mideast-crisis-iraq-nato/at-u-s-urging-nato-agrees-training-mission-in-iraq-idUSKCN1FZ1E5. Accessed 23 January 2019.

Emmott, R., & Stewart, P. (2017, February 16). Libya Sends New Request for Military Training to NATO. *Reuters World News*. https://www.reuters.com/article/us-libya-security-nato/libya-sends-new-request-for-military-training-to-nato-idUSKBN15V23B?il=0. Accessed 23 January 2019.

Gaub, F. (2016). *An Unhappy Marriage: Civil–Military Relations in Post-Saddam Iraq*. Regional Insight. Beirut: Carnegie Middle East Center.

Havel, V. (1997, May 13). NATO's Quality of Life. *New York Times*. https://www.nytimes.com/1997/05/13/opinion/nato-s-quality-of-life.html. Accessed 23 January 2019.

Hinnebusch, R. A. (2003). *The International Politics of the Middle East*. Manchester: Manchester University Press.

Hunter, R. E. (1995). Enlargement: Part of a Strategy for Projecting Stability into Central Europe. *NATO Review, 43*(3), 3–8.

International Crisis Group. (2017). *Finding the Right Role for the G5 Sahel Joint Force*. Africa Report No. 258. Brussels: International Crisis Group.

Kaim, M. (2017). *Reforming NATO's Partnerships* (SWP Research Paper RP 1). Berlin: German Institute for International and Security Affairs.

Kamp, K. H. (2018). *Nuclear Reorientation of NATO*. NDC Commentary 01/18. Rome: NATO Defense College.

Koehler, K. (2018). *Projecting Stability in Practice? NATO's New Training Mission in Iraq* (NDC Policy Brief No. 2). Rome: NATO Defense College.

Kroenig, M. (2015). Facing Reality: Getting NATO Ready for a New Cold War. *Survival, 57*(1), 49–70.

Lenderking, T., Cammack, P., Shihabi, A., & Des Roches, D. (2017). The GCC Rift: Regional and Global Implications. *Middle East Policy, 24*(4), 5–28.

Lynch, M. (2016). *The New Arab Wars: Uprisings and Anarchy in the Middle East*. New York: Public Affairs.

Moore, R. R. (2007). *NATO's New Mission: Projecting Stability in a Post-Cold War World*. Westport: Praeger Security International.

NATO. (2009, April 4). *NATO Training Mission—Afghanistan*. https://www.nato.int/cps/en/natolive/news_52802.htm. Accessed 23 January 2019.

NATO. (2010, November 19). *Active Engagement, Modern Defense*. https://www.nato.int/cps/ua/natohq/official_texts_68580.htm. Accessed 23 January 2019.

NATO. (2015, September 5). *Wales Summit Declaration Issued by the Heads of State and Government Participating in the Meeting of the North Atlantic Council in Wales*. https://www.nato.int/cps/en/natohq/official_texts_112964.htm. Accessed 23 January 2019.

NATO. (2016, July 9). *Warsaw Summit Communiqué Issued by the Heads of State and Government Participating in the Meeting of the North Atlantic Council in Warsaw 8–9 July 2016.* https://www.nato.int/cps/en/natohq/official_texts_133169.htm. Accessed 23 January 2019.

NATO. (2017a, October 2). *NATO and MD Partners Meet in Mauritania for the Fifth Mediterranean Dialogue Policy Advisory Group (MD PAG).* https://www.nato.int/cps/en/natohq/news_147563.htm?selectedLocale=en. Accessed 23 January 2019.

NATO. (2017b, May 19). *Relations with Partners Across the Globe.* https://www.nato.int/cps/en/natohq/topics_49188.htm. Accessed 23 January 2019.

NATO. (2018, May 9). *Defence Institution Building.* https://www.nato.int/cps/su/natohq/topics_50083.htm. Accessed 23 January 2019.

Perlmutter, A., & Carpenter, T. G. (1998). NATO's Expensive Trip East: The Folly of Enlargement. *Foreign Affairs, 77*(1), 2–6.

Pinfari, M. (2009). *Nothing but Failure: The Arab League and the Gulf Cooperation Council as Mediators in Middle Eastern Conflicts* (Crisis Sates Working Paper Series 2). London: London School of Economics and Political Science.

Reiter, D., & Stam, A. C. (1998). Democracy and Battlefield Military Effectiveness. *The Journal of Conflict Resolution, 42*(3), 259–277.

Rosenfeld, S. S. (1993, July 2). NATO's Last Chance. *Washington Post.* https://www.washingtonpost.com/archive/opinions/1993/07/02/natos-last-chance/22054ea7-5958-44b0-9e6a-212ee1da51de/?utm_term=.34d6d349cf09. Accessed 23 January 2019.

Rousselet, L. (2017, December 13). *John Manza Gives NATO an 'F' in Projecting Stability.* The German Marshall Fund of the United States (Blog). http://www.gmfus.org/blog/2017/12/13/john-manza-gives-nato-f-projecting-stability. Accessed 23 January 2019.

Samaan, J. L. (2017). *Toward a NATO of the Gulf? The Challenges of Collective Defense Within the GCC.* Carlisle: U.S. Army War College, Strategic Studies Institute.

SHAPE. (n.d.). *NATO Training Mission—Iraq (NTM-I).* Supreme Headquarters Allied Powers Europe. https://shape.nato.int/page136952. Accessed 23 January 2019.

Smith, H. L. (2018, July 30). Donald Trump in Push to Build an Arab NATO. *The Times.* https://www.thetimes.co.uk/article/donald-trump-in-push-to-build-an-arab-nato-sf7qr05gz. Accessed 23 January 2019.

Stoltenberg, J. (2017, March 2). *Projecting Stability Beyond Our Borders.* Speech at the Graduate Institute in Geneva. https://www.nato.int/cps/ic/natohq/opinions_141898.htm.

Talmadge, C. (2015). *The Dictator's Army: Battlefield Effectiveness in Authoritarian Regimes*. Ithaca: Cornell University Press.

Tansey, O., Koehler, K., & Schmotz, A. (2017). Ties to the Rest: Autocratic Linkages and Regime Survival. *Comparative Political Studies, 50*(9), 1221–1254.

Trenin, D. (2013). *The Mythical Alliance: Russia's Syria Policy* (Carnegie Paper). Moscow: Carnegie Moscow Center.

Trenin, D. (2018). *What Is Russia up to in the Middle East?* Cambridge: Polity.

Vito, C. (2015, November 17). *A False Dichotomy: The Choice Between Protecting NATO's Eastern and Southern Flanks*. NATO Association of Canada (Blog). http://natoassociation.ca/a-false-dichotomy-the-choice-between-protecting-natos-eastern-and-southern-flanks/. Accessed 23 January 2019.

Yost, D. S. (1998). The New NATO and Collective Security. *Survival, 40*(2), 135–160.

Young, K. E. (2013). *The Emerging Interventionists of the GCC* (LSE Middle East Centre Paper Series 2). London: London School of Economics and Political Science.

CHAPTER 4

The EU, Resilience and the Southern Neighbourhood After the Arab Uprisings

Emile Badarin and Tobias Schumacher

Resilience is a recurring concept in foreign policy. Since 2015, it has become a guiding principle for EU external action in and towards neighbourhood partner countries. This chapter aims to critically examine and put into perspective the evolution of resilience in EU foreign policy towards the EU's southern periphery, which has been undergoing seismic changes since the emergence of Arab uprisings in 2011. Since then, the trans-nationalisation of negative spill-over effects due to protracted or new conflicts, radicalisation, failing states and stubborn authoritarianism, has intensified the EU's concerns with insecurity and instability in its southern neighbourhood. Volatility in the EU's South has been regularly reproduced as a situation that requires a new EU approach and response. The short-lived popular revolts in 2011 have heightened EU decision-makers' awareness for the multilayered security challenges

E. Badarin (✉) · T. Schumacher
College of Europe, Natolin Campus, Warsaw, Poland
e-mail: emile.badarin@coleurope.eu

T. Schumacher
e-mail: tobias.schumacher@coleurope.eu

© The Author(s) 2020
E. Cusumano and S. Hofmaier (eds.),
Projecting Resilience Across the Mediterranean,
https://doi.org/10.1007/978-3-030-23641-0_4

emanating from Europe's southern periphery, forcing Brussels and the Member States to rethink how to reconcile normative ambitions with hard security challenges—and thus realism-inspired thinking.

Already since the early 1970s, the forerunners of the EU (the European Economic Community and the European Community, respectively) have embarked on various processes destined to design their relationship with Mediterranean countries through several policy frameworks. These include, inter alia, the Global Mediterranean Policy of 1972 (Bicchi 2007), the Euro-Arab Dialogue of 1973 (Allen 1977), the Euro-Mediterranean Partnership (EMP)/Barcelona Process of 1995 (Gillespie 1997; Youngs 2015), the European Neighbourhood Policy (ENP) of 2003/2004 (Schumacher et al. 2017), as well as the Union for the Mediterranean (UfM) of 2008 (Bicchi and Gillespie 2011).

To date, the ENP remains the main framework regulating bilateral relations between the EU and its southern neighbours. It originated in the context of the EU's envisaged 'big bang' enlargement of 2004/2007 and the then realisation that incorporating new members implied the emergence of new neighbours and borders, as well as exposure to previously more distant challenges. In 2002, the United Kingdom and Denmark, two of the initial policy entrepreneurs, proposed an ambitious, differentiated and long-term cooperation framework limited to eastern neighbours such as Belarus, Ukraine and Moldova, while Sweden suggested to include also countries participating in the EMP. This proposition provided the European Commission with the final impetus to develop a policy scheme that would include both eastern as well as southern neighbours.[1]

In anticipation of the EU's upcoming enlargement, formulations such as 'new neighbours' (2002), 'Wider Europe-Neighbourhood' (2003) and the much quoted 'ring of friends' (2003) became parts of the EU's foreign policy discourse. At the time, this discourse was further complemented by the euphemistically articulated objective to make the 2004/2007 enlargement beneficial for both the EU and its new neighbours without generating dividing lines between them (European Commission 2003: 4; European Security Strategy 2003: 7; European Commission 2004: 3).

---

[1] Initially, it was even foreseen to include the Russian Federation in the ENP, though due to the refusal of the former, Russian participation never materialised. Armenia, Azerbaijan and Georgia were added to the ENP only in 2004, thus shortly after the Georgian Rose Revolution.

The EU aimed at achieving these goals by offering its neighbours substantive financial assistance through EU instruments such as the Technical Assistance to the Commonwealth of Independent States (TACIS), the Euro-Mediterranean partnership (MEDA), the European Neighbourhood Partnership Instrument and its successor, the European Neighbourhood Instrument (Maass 2017). Legally, EU-neighbourhood relations became embedded in Association Agreements concluded with most neighbourhood countries (except for Belarus, Azerbaijan and Syria). This was complemented by wide-ranging cooperation (including offers of integration) between the EU and neighbourhood countries in common policy domains such as trade, competition, services, the foreign and security policy, justice, freedom and security.

Indeed, the EU resorted to the ENP in 2011 in response to the Arab uprisings, and subsequent events demonstrate the continuing significance of the ENP framework, despite the many prophecies of doom (Smith 2005). In light of internal (e.g. EU enlargement, the Eurozone crisis, the entering into force of the Lisbon Treaty, etc.) and external developments in the southern neighbourhood, the EU engaged twice in overhauling the ENP. Overwhelmed by regional dynamics, the EU revised the ENP throughout the first months of 2011, though, strictly speaking, this revision was already initiated in the second half of 2010 (Schumacher and Bouris 2017) and thus at a time when Brussels was negotiating an upgrade of bilateral relations with the Tunisian regime of President Zine El Abidine Ben Ali. The revised ENP's ineffectiveness to accommodate the promise of the Arab uprisings and support emerging processes of political liberalisation (European Commission 2011), in conjunction with the outbreak of new conflicts, triggered the second revision of the ENP in 2015. Ever since subsequent events in the southern neighbourhood have put into question the existing orders of regional governance and dramatically altered Brussels' perceptions of the southern neighbourhood from a 'ring of friends' to a 'ring of fire'.

The 2015 review process, drawing on the support of all EU Member States, became a watershed for EU-neighbourhood relations that ushered in the de facto abolition of the EU's long-standing ambition to pursue a values-based agenda in favour of democracy promotion (Delcour 2015). This shift has paved the way for a new framework that focuses primarily on stabilisation, transactionalism and sector-specific cooperation disconnected from the principle of negative conditionality that underpinned (at least discursively) previous editions of the ENP.

What is more is that the 2015 revision of the ENP incorporated resilience-building, albeit vaguely and abruptly, for the first time into the realm of EU foreign policy towards the southern neighbours. Subsequently, a multitude of resilience-related expressions has pervaded EU foreign policy documents, constituting a substantial part of the June 2016 EU Global Strategy for Foreign and Security Policy (EUGS). The latest ENP review was concluded in November 2015, eight months before the adoption of the EUGS. It was, however, closely coordinated with the deliberations leading to the EUGS (European Commission and High Representative of the Union for Foreign Affairs and Security Policy 2017: 14; European Commission 2015: 4; European Union 2016). The EUGS elevated resilience-building to a 'strategic priority' (European Union 2016: 25) in EU external action. Embedded in 'principled pragmatism', the EUGS charts new rules for the EU's engagement in and towards its neighbourhood in conjunction with the ENP.

In this chapter, we argue that the notion of resilience in EU foreign policy towards its southern 'near abroad' is unsettled and continues to undergo a seemingly ever-evolving process of constitution and reconceptualisation. As will be demonstrated, relevant EU foreign policy documents are continually ascribing new notions to resilience and keep upgrading and changing its meaning. This chapter, therefore, adopts a cautious approach and argues that the EU's conception of resilience is work in progress that, first, disguises the EU's struggle to come to terms with the multifaceted fallouts of instability in the southern neighbourhood and, second, downplays Brussels' recent shift from transformative to status quo-oriented aspirations. Consequently, as will be demonstrated, the elusiveness of resilience as a guiding rationale in EU-southern neighbourhood relations, together with ensuing inconsistencies in the practical pursuit of promoting resilience, renders the EU unfit to enhance stabilisation in the southern neighbourhood.

The chapter is structured as follows: it begins by exploring how the notion of resilience was introduced to the ENP framework and subsequently became a foreign policy priority in the context of the EU's ambition to focus on the neighbourhood's stabilisation. The next section presents a critical reading of the conceptual understanding of resilience in EU foreign policy, deemed to be an antidote to most challenges and problems in the neighbourhood. Subsequently, the chapter focuses on the role resilience-building plays in EU peace-building and conflict resolution to safeguard EUrope's own security. The final section provides indicative examples of EU resilience-building in the southern neighbourhood in order to demonstrate the nature and type of interventions EU foreign policy classifies as resilience and generate an advanced understanding of what resilience-building may entail in practice. The last section synthesises the findings and concludes.

THE STABILISATION AGENDA OF THE ENP

In 2003/2004, the EU adopted the European Security Strategy (ESS) (Biscop and Andersson 2007; European Security Strategy 2003) and the Wider Europe strategy (Verheugen 2004; European Commission 2003), both of which converged with the ENP. While the ESS was drafted to set out the EU's global security objectives, it shared with the ENP the aim of offering a blueprint for the future design of the relationship between the EU and its southern neighbours after the 'big bang' enlargement of 2004/2007. Sixteen countries to the east and south of the EU have coalesced into a single geopolitical space, ever since called the European neighbourhood. This neighbourhood is predominantly represented as an unstable space and source of threats to the EU and its Member States (Christou 2010; Verheugen 2004)—a perception that has begun to widely resonate in EU decision-making circles since the outbreak of the war in eastern Ukraine and the persistence of the conflicts in Syria and Libya.

The core objective of the ESS was to 'promote a ring of well-governed countries' in the 'troubled areas' in the EU's neighbourhood (European Security Strategy 2003: 8). Conjointly, both the EES and the ENP provided the EU with discursive reference points to draw a 'ring of friends' around itself and determine its external borders and thus what is foreign (Campbell 1998; Verheugen 2004). The southern segment of this imaginary ring is considered to be 'Europe's main source of security threats, linking the hazards of terrorism, illegal immigration, weapons of mass destruction, and cultural and ideological confrontations' (Verheugen 2004: 3). The ENP's underlying aim was to tackle the threatening and unstable Other(s) by transposing European norms, rules and regulation to neighbourhood countries (Browning and Joeniemmi 2008; Christou 2010; Diez 2005; Meloni 2008; Del Sarto and Schumacher 2005).

Campbell (1998) has cogently displayed the extent to which foreign policy is embedded in the process that constructs the mutually constitutive 'foreign/external' and 'domestic/self' realms (see also Cebeci and Schumacher 2017). Boundary-making and threat externalisation underlie the EU's foreign policy towards southern neighbourhood countries. Furthermore, the temporary fixation of these boundaries is contingent upon processes of enlargement and contraction (as exemplified by the Brexit) as well as EU ambitions to act as a normative empire (Del Sarto 2015). Nowadays, enlargement (Browning and Joeniemmi 2008: 16) and the prospect of contraction, even disintegration (European Union 2016; Tocci 2017), are conceived as potential, yet serious threats for Europe and its ontological security. In this context, the ENP is poised to serve as a tool to define the limits of Europe, blurring the borders (Del Sarto and Schumacher 2005) and establishing a buffer zone around it (Browning and Joeniemmi 2008).

The ideational borderlines between the EU and its southern neighbours seem less porous than those that exist with its eastern neighbours. Ideationally, the South is conceived not only as a constant threat, but also as an 'unreformable' Other that must be excluded and guarded against through 'impermeable' and 'somewhat fixed' borders (Browning and Joeniemmi 2008: 24–26). Walters' (2004: 691–93) analysis of the EU's border-regimes (both visible and invisible) relates to the Euro-Mediterranean frontier as a fixed wall ('limes') that is supposed to delineate the perimeters of the allegedly 'highly organised' space and ward off the disorder emanating from the 'profoundly alien' Other. Therefore, security, migration control, the fight against terrorism, and consequently the management of threats emerging from the southern neighbourhood space have become the key priorities of EU-neighbourhood policies. Indeed, this rationale accentuates the contradiction between the EU's neorealism-inspired hard security considerations and its past liberal and normative discourse.

Despite the reiteration of its concerns with the promotion of democracy, rule of law and human rights in the southern neighbourhoods countries (European Commission 2011), EU policy has de facto increasingly become obsessed with the fight against a multitude of threats and, in recent years, consolidated past practices of prioritising multi-sector cooperation with authoritarian regimes. For example, the agenda of the latest EU-League of Arab States summit in February 2019 in Sharm el-Sheikh, held under the auspices of the Egyptian regime, disposed of any discussions on human rights and democracy while focusing exclusively on multi-sector cooperation in areas of trade, migration and security (Council of the EU 2019). Thus, it blatantly overlooked that, all too often, authoritarian regimes are a source of these challenges rather than credible and legitimate solution providers (Malmvig 2006).

In the context of the EU's foreign policy towards the southern neighbourhood, narratives of external threat and duty/responsibility have underpinned the EU's attempts to export its norms and rules (Christou 2010; Nitoiu 2013). Schumacher (2015) stresses the significance of the value-laden duty narrative and its sub-narratives in guiding EU external relations with its southern neighbours. Through discursive foreign policy practice, the Self, the Other (EU/neighbourhood countries) and their respective spaces (EU/neighbourhood) are continually reconstructed (Pishchikova and Piras 2017). The EUGS has assimilated this logic, declaring that the EU will 'take responsibility' in its 'surrounding regions' and beyond (European Union 2016: 18).

According to the duty/responsibility narrative, the EU has a self-ascribed obligation to promote democracy, peace, human rights, economic growth and well-being in the southern neighbourhood. This narrative dominated the EU foreign policy discourse during the initial response to the Arab uprisings and continued to do so until 2014 (Schumacher 2015). Inspired by Article 8 of the Lisbon Treaty, which stipulates the need to foster 'good neighbourliness', the EU sought to export 'its' norms, values and structures of governance (Hillion 2013; Hanf 2011). Consequently, the revised ENP of 2011 re-consolidated the neoliberal, Washington Consensus-based formula in order to trigger structural changes in neighbouring countries. This practice concurs with the first wave of EU initiatives, such as the EMP, the ESS and the 2003/2004 ENP, all of which embraced the democratic peace paradigm and neoliberal market-based reasoning.

In 2013/2014, however, this formula lost its salience and, ironically, the so-called 'strategic option' to support the Arab uprisings (European Commission 2011: 2) turned out to be rather short-termism, as evidenced by the renewed revision of the ENP in 2014/2015, the adoption of the EUGS in 2016, and the foreign and security policy discourse that ensued. As of late 2015, the 'new' ENP pledges to 'strengthen the resilience of the EU's partners' (European Commission 2015a: 4). More than ever before, stabilisation has become the overarching concept guiding the EU's new strategy for 'security and prosperity' through 'more *effective* partnerships towards a more stable EU Neighbourhood'. This goal has to be achieved mainly by building the 'resilience of

[the] partners' with whom the EU will engage to expand 'cooperation on security' and 'migration-related issues', which, in turn, are supposed to open the doorway into 'a wide range of new areas of cooperation under the ENP' (European External Action Service 2016). Against this backdrop, the subsequent section will, therefore, turn to resilience-building as part of the EU's new stabilisation approach.

Resilience: Curing Instability and Deepening Cooperation in the Southern Neighbourhood?

Within a short period of time, the term 'resilience' has not only made it into the EU's foreign policy discourse, but also became the key paradigm facilitating the stabilisation of the southern neighbourhood. Arguably, it is the most important addition to the ENP. The EUGS pronounces resilience-building as the ultimate priority in EU-Neighbourhood relations. The concept of resilience has its origins in physics and ecology. The former defines it as the 'capacity of a material or a system to return to equilibrium after displacement' (Norris et al. 2008: 127). The ecology literature eschews the idea of equilibrium in favour of adaptation and transformation. It regards resilience in terms of systems' internal ability to absorb shocks, adjust, transform and reorganise in order to continue functioning in disaster and crisis situations (Norris et al. 2008; Walker et al. 2004; Walker and Cooper 2011). As resilience started to find its way into other disciplines, it has since been metaphorically applied to different phenomena and carries different meanings, depending on the area of study. As such, resilience is a newcomer to EU foreign policy and remains in a process of constitution. In order to understand the function of resilience in the EU's foreign policy towards the southern neighbourhood, it is instructive to reflect on some of its core practical entailments and objectives. This also helps evaluate its adequateness for the purported objective of stabilising the southern periphery.

The main purpose of resilience in early EU policies outside the realm of the ENP was to generate 'disaster-resilient' settings and subjects within the broader framework of 'disaster risk reduction' (DRR), mainly in fragile, low-income countries (European Commission 2009: 9). The 2012 EU approach to resilience suggests three ways for building resilience: (1) 'enhancing the entity's strength' to withstand shocks; (2) 'reducing the intensity of the impact'; or (3) applying the two methods at the same time (European Commission 2012: 5). As the second method is untenable in a 'complex, uncertain and contingent' world (European Union 2016), the focus has recently shifted to the first option: boosting entities' 'rapid coping and adaptation mechanisms at local, national and regional level' (European Commission 2012: 5).

At that stage, resilience-building was primarily an add-on to EU humanitarian and development assistance, largely concerned with natural and man-made disasters and humanitarian crises (European Commission 2012, 2013). In 2013, resilience was linked with 'state fragility' and conflicts. State fragility was defined as the 'lack [of] the capacity to carry out basic governance functions to ensure basic service delivery to the population, and to develop mutually constructive relations with society'. Fragile states were considered to be 'more vulnerable to internal or external shocks such as economic crises, conflicts or natural disasters' (European Commission 2013: 1). Accordingly, resilience emerged as a vehicle to stave off fragility abroad.

Throughout the EU's recent foreign policy discourse, resilience has regularly been associated with threat/responsibility narratives, as discussed above. For instance, expressions like 'enhance resilience to disasters', 'disaster-resilient' (European Commission 2009: 3–4), 'reducing risk of crisis' (European Commission 2012: 5), 'building resilience in crisis and risk-prone contexts' (European Commission 2013: 2), or 'conflict-related crises' (Council of the EU 2013: 2) are nowadays readily deployed wherever resilience is mentioned in policy documents relating to the EU's neighbourhood.

In recent years, the EU abandoned its initially optimistic view of the Arab uprisings of 2011 and the supposedly 'strategic option' to support the uprisings' promise to bring about liberty, justice and dignity to societies in the southern neighbourhood (European Commission 2011). The EU interpreted the unfolding events in its southern (and eastern) neighbourhood as phenomena that transformed the space beyond its own borders into a 'ring of fire' and an 'arc of instability' (Bildt 2015; Hahn 2015). Correspondingly, the 'crises narrative' obtained considerable salience in EU foreign and security policy discourses on the South (Schumacher 2016). In 2016, the EUGS scaled-up the crises narrative to include the entire world as a 'complex, uncertain and interconnected' environment abound with rampant contingencies and threats (European Union 2016). This narrative is closely interlinked with the EU's approach to resilience-building, hence the need to embrace insecurity and learn to live with it pro-actively (Duffield 2012; Evans and Reid

2014). In other words, resilience is devoted to the management of risks in the EU's near proximity and further abroad.

In 2012, the European Commission defined resilience as 'the ability of an individual, a household, a community, a country or a region to withstand, adapt and quickly recover from stresses and shocks' (European Commission 2012). The resilience-oriented approach to crises and shocks underlines the positive role the latter may play in instilling reflexive learning, adaptation and better management of resources (Berkes et al. 2008; Walker et al. 2004). In a similar fashion, the EU propagates resilience as an 'opportunity for transformation' (European Commission 2013: 4). Furthermore, resilience is used as an element within the security-development nexus (Duffield 2010) to address fragilities at a lower cost, thereby drawing on the means of the EU and Member States against the backdrop of simultaneously pursued austerity measures (Council of the EU 2013; European Commission 2012). While emphasising the security-development nexus, the EU suggests putting a greater emphasis on resilience to ensure that shocks and crises will not preclude low-income countries from pursuing the path of development and the implementation of the 2030 Agenda for Sustainable Development (European Commission 2017c). On this account, developing and/or southern neighbourhood countries are supposed to cope and manage risks, crises and insecurities single-headedly and continue abiding by bi/multilateral development agreements.

The EU approach to resilience in the southern neighbourhood (and beyond) fails to specify what transformations it entails when applied to foreign policy actions more concretely. The socio-ecology-related literature's understanding of transformability as the capacity to build new structures when previous ones become untenable in the face of shocks (Walker et al. 2004) seems a perfect fit for EU structural foreign policy (Keukeleire and Delreux 2014). Seen this way, crises and insecurities of the Other(s) are considered 'positive' events that open up new opportunities to embed neoliberal structural reforms in cooperation with authoritarian regimes (Amin and El Kenz 2005; Evans and Reid 2014; Walker and Cooper 2011).

Although the term resilience featured nine times in the 2015 edition of the ENP, it acquired elaborate political significance only in the EUGS. The latter has stretched the scope of resilience to include 'all individuals and the whole of society' (European Union 2016: 24). Instead of conveying clarity, the EUGS obscures the meaning and practical implications of resilience, thus letting southern neighbours (and other partners further abroad) incognisant of the practical scope of resilience-building. Rather than defining it, the EUGS notes that a 'resilient society featuring democracy, trust in institutions, and sustainable development lies at the heart of a resilient state' (European Union 2016: 24). Ironically, just a few pages later, the EUGS retracts and restricts the scope of resilience-building to the 'most acute cases' and 'most acute dimensions of fragility '(European Union 2016: 9, 25). Of significance here is the claim that the EU's resilience-building in the southern neighbourhood generates 'long-term social, economic, and political transformation' that includes everyone (European Commission and High Representative of the Union for Foreign Affairs and Security Policy 2017). Yet, down the line, one is struck to find that resilience-building is, first and foremost, concerned with the 'most acute' situations. This deepens the conceptual confusion and tends to signal intra-EU disagreement and lack of direction. When applied to the EU's southern neighbourhood, this poses profound questions regarding agenda- and priority-setting. For example, will priority be given to ongoing territorial conflicts (e.g. in Syria and Libya), to cases of considerable re-authoritarianisation (e.g. in post-2013 Egypt), or will cases of severe forms of human suffering (e.g. Gaza) be prioritised? As a matter of fact, none of these questions was ever considered a priority.

Resilience, Conflict Resolution and Peace-Building

Building resilience to manage the many convoluted conflicts in the southern neighbourhood is the 'central external strategic problem' for the EU (Smith 2016: 451). The HR/VP, Federica Mogherini (cited in European Commission 2017b) emphasised the nexus between resilience and peace-building. As she put it, resilience-building prevents fragile situations 'from turning into new wars, new humanitarian catastrophes, or new refugee crises. This is what we [in the EU] call resilience'. Furthermore, by capitalising on resilience as the only approach 'that can work in the complex world of today' and as 'the European way to peace, security and human development', resilience is placed at a high level of EU foreign policy in general and relations with its southern neighbourhood in particular. The association established between resilience and peace-building has opened new pathways for cooperation between diverse security actors within the framework of the ENP. Security actors such as NATO and the OSCE have also started to employ resilience as a commonly shared paradigm to address security challenges in the southern neighbourhood and boost the 'security and sustainable peace and prosperity' of Europe itself (European Commission 2016a) (on NATO, see chapter by Larsen and Koehler in this volume). What this practically suggests is that inclusive development and societal and state security of southern neighbours are regarded as subordinate to Europe's security and as a means to shore up the security of the European Self.

According to Wagner and Anholt (2016; see also Anholt and Wagner in this volume), the ability of resilience to capture the 'middle ground' between liberal peace-building and democratisation and stabilisation could be a remedy that, in conjunction with sufficient ambiguity, may placate all stakeholders and concerned actors. The indecisiveness of the EU's approach to resilience provides the pretence of engaging in a 'joined-up' approach. In reality, however, it allows each actor to carry on with 'business as usual', thus disguising the EU's own neorealist-inspired actions as part of a larger contribution to resilience-building. This approach not only exacerbates the incoherence of EU foreign policy, but also offers actors a licence to do whatever they please while interpreting their actions as elements of resilience-building. For example, supplying repressive regimes in the southern neighbourhood with military equipment or technologies (which are often used to censor their citizens' online activities) can easily be framed as resilience-building, given that such support would contribute to 'state security'. Likewise, other actors may choose to fund civil rights movements operating against their repressive states on the basis that these states are 'inherently fragile'[2]—and thus non-resilient. In other words, as long as resilience is conceived as a holistic and all-inclusive 'shopping list' of sorts, the EU fosters, rather than reduces, perplexity and distrust at the receiving end of its neighbourhood policies.

As demonstrated above, resilience is prematurely and without any historical foregrounding articulated as a panacea to address the 'root causes' of conflicts, fragility and vulnerability in the southern neighbourhood and further beyond (Council of the EU 2013; European Commission 2013; European Union 2016).[3] While the official EU discourse deploys resilience as a means to tackle a long and a rather erratic list of

[2] The EUGS (European Union 2016: 25) claims that 'repressive states are inherently fragile in the long term'.

[3] Although philosophical research on resilience is lacking, the existing body of literature suggests that resilience relies on the ontological assumption of complex and uncertain world affairs, which cannot be controlled and, therefore, remain insecure. Subsequently, the notion of resilience focuses on human subjectivities as a means to live with dangers and insecurities. (Evans and Reid 2014; Joseph 2013, 2016).

challenges,[4] resilience-building in the southern neighbourhood has not yet addressed any of the factors that triggered the Arab uprisings in 2011 and the subsequent governance-related sources of instability. Thus, resilience, as conceived by the EU, has hitherto fallen short of responding to the core priorities of societies in the southern neighbourhood that continue to revolve, first and foremost, around *hurriyah* and *karamah* (freedom, justice and dignity). Such objectives continue to drive the popular revolts in the South eight years after the outbreak of the 'Arab Spring' as is evidenced by developments in Algeria and Sudan in early 2019.

Moreover, the promotion of resilience in order to stabilise and contribute to conflict resolution and peace-building in the neighbourhood suffers from in-built inconsistencies. First, the EU's conception of resilience lacks a clear definition, let alone a broader philosophical meaning (Joseph 2013). Second, heralding resilience as an all-inclusive framework to tackle the multiple challenges in an unsettled neighbourhood, allows both the EU and its external partners to engage in cherry-picking—a practice that may usher in conflicting outcomes. Third, this approach to resilience comprises inconsistent facets. Consider, for example, the incoherence emerging from accommodating repressive and undemocratic regimes while considering them to be 'inherently fragile' and, therefore, incapable of overcoming societal fragility (European Union 2016: 25). Fourth, resilience is touted as a remedy to address the root causes of conflicts, fragilities and vulnerability. At the same time, however, the EUGS calls for adaptation and coping with problems and conflicts without identifying the means by which to pursue the proposed 'adaption' and 'coping'. Finally, the EUGS regards accession to the EU and 'fair conditionality' as mechanisms to enhance resilience and political liberalisation in neighbourhood countries (European Union 2016: 24), although both were de facto foreclosed by the 2015 ENP.

In sum, the purported unity of action by EU institutions and the Member States—the so-called 'joined-up' approach presented in the EUGS—to diminish incoherence overlooks these in-built incoherencies at the policy level. The ENP has been suffering from the go-alone attitudes of Member States, intra/inter-institutional bickering and turf

---

[4] The list of challenges includes issues such as poverty, vulnerability, fragility, violent conflicts, hybrid threats, climate change, migration, gender inequalities, radicalisation, violent extremism, the building of inclusive societies, sustainable economies, accountable institutions, etc. (European Commission 2013, 2016b, 2017c; European Union 2016).

wars, all of which only confirm the ongoing existence of the much-cited 'capability-expectations gap' (Hill 1993) and 'organized hypocrisy' (Cusumano 2018) in EU foreign policymaking and implementation. This sends conflicting signals which are bound to further undermine the EU's credibility to focus on resilience-building henceforth.

EXAMPLES OF RESILIENCE AND STABILITY-BUILDING IN THE SOUTHERN NEIGHBOURHOOD

This section discusses some examples from the neighbourhood to help establish a preliminary empirical account of the EU's approach to resilience-building by exploring the type of questions it prioritises and deals with. The fact that resilience is a newcomer to EU foreign policy imposes limitations on any practice-based examination. It should, therefore, be underlined that the following discussion explores some *indicative* examples of resilience-building from relevant EU policy frameworks (mainly existing Partnership Priorities (PP) and Single Support Frameworks [SSF]) towards southern neighbourhood countries.

Egypt

While the stability of Egypt, the largest ENP partner country, is deemed critical 'to guarantee long-term stability on both sides of the Mediterranean' (European Council 2017: 1), resilience is absent in the EU-Egypt PP 2017–2020, adopted in June 2017. As stated in the PP, *stability* is 'main strategic objective' of the EU's relationship with Egypt, a country which the EU and the Member States view as 'a key partner to promote peace, and stability in the Southern Neighbourhood' (European Council 2017: 3). Furthermore, the EU-Egypt SSF, adopted on 30 October 2017 and based on the priorities set out in the PP, speaks of 'stabilisation and resilience-building' as the EU's main objectives that shall be achieved by supporting the Egyptian economy and promoting social and development reforms (European Commission 2017a) (for an elaborate account of the case of Egypt, see the chapter by Viceré and Frontini in this volume).

Both frameworks have overlooked the pervasive authoritarian nature of the Egyptian regime and its repressive practices (Human Rights Watch 2018). Throughout the PP and the SSF, Egypt is presented as a democracy in transition, albeit facing 'problems' and challenges (European

Commission 2017a; European Council 2017). From this perspective, the European 'support [to] the country's democratic consolidation' is (supposedly) poised to resolve these challenges and successfully complete the alleged process of democratic transition (European Council 2017: 3). The PP further continues to suggest that the EU and Egypt have a 'shared commitment to the universal values of democracy, the rule of law and the respect for human rights' (European Council 2017: 1). Of significance here is the EU's tacit recognition of excessive restrictions on human rights, political and civil liberties and civil society as if they existed mainly as a result of instability and terrorism and thus independently of autocratic rule. Such an assessment invariably whitewashes the deep-seated authoritarian, military rule in Egypt of any responsibility for instability and radicalisation (Sayigh 2012; Rutherford 2018). From the perspective of Brussels, this legitimates deeper cooperation with Egypt to tackle the 'root causes of terrorism' and 'counter and prevent radicalisation' (European Council 2017: 7) by focusing mainly on resilience-building (European Commission 2016b: 13). This contorted account of the situation in Egypt not only overlooks the inherent fragility of authoritarian states, but also demonstrates a nonchalant shrug on the part of the EU vis-à-vis the fact that authoritarianism and repression are among the root causes of radicalisation and state terror (Ashour 2009).

Lebanon and Jordan

As the Syrian revolt transpired into a full-blown war, many Syrians have sought refuge in neighbouring countries such as Jordan and Lebanon. According to the United Nations High Commissioner for Refugees (UNHCR), Lebanon accommodates approximately one million Syrian refugees, while Jordan hosts 673,000 (UNHCR 2018). By 2014, the so-called 'refugee crisis' narrative was in full swing and refugees were framed as a threat and a source of vulnerability (Holmes and Castañeda 2016). This framing renders them an ideal subject for resilience mediation. Resilience-building in Lebanon and Jordan usually focuses on alleviating the pressure on the limited capacity and resources of both countries to cater to the needs of such a large number of refugees. In this context, the EU focused on contributing to these basic needs and began advocating for 'coping with sudden crises', with a view to 'mitigate their vulnerability' (European Commission 2018b: 2). This is consistent with the EU's neoliberal outsourcing logic which delegates to national governments and local authorities in both Lebanon and Jordan the task of containing refugees within their sovereign borders and preventing them from seeking safe havens in Europe.

In the case of Jordan, low-cost—or 'cost-effective'—contributions to labour market development and basic services delivered to Syrian refugees are classified as resilience-building. For example, the establishment of six new employment centres to match workers with potential jobs, the facilitation of exports of certain Jordanian products to European markets by simplifying pre-existing rules of origin (six factories were granted the authorisation to benefit from this rule), the provision of 'technical assistance and matching' with the EU market to 21 Jordanian factories are among the prime examples currently classified as EU resilience-building (European External Action Service 2017: 3) in the country.

In Lebanon, too, resilience is usually discussed in relation to the Syrian conflict and Syrian refugees. The interventions proposed by the EU rely exclusively on economy-based reasoning and suggest 'improving the economic resilience' of Lebanon to help 'create a climate in which the cost of borrowing to the [Lebanese] Treasury could be significantly lowered' (European Council 2016: 4). Meanwhile, the EU-Lebanon PP stipulate that 'economic disparities' and 'deprived areas' in Lebanon are a 'threat to its stability', and they continue to suggest market-based solutions as a means to building a resilient national economy and reduce sectarian and social tensions (European Council 2016: 6–7). Obviously, this market-based reasoning to resilience seems to de-politicise most of the problems which Lebanon is faced with (on resilience-building in Lebanon, see the chapter by Pounds et al. in this volume).

Palestine

The de-politicising effect of resilience appears more pointedly in the case of Palestine. There, resilience focuses largely on promoting Palestinians living in the so-called 'Area C' (which constitutes 61% of the West Bank and is under full Israeli control) and East Jerusalem to enhance their ability to cope with Israeli occupation and colonialism (European Commission 2018a). However, the means to boost Palestinian 'resilience' pale in the face of the colossal power of the occupier and the relentless expansion of Israeli settlements in violation of international law. Given the Israeli occupation, resilience as a coping strategy for an entity such as Palestine certainly stands no

Table 4.1 EU resilience-building initiatives in the Middle East and North Africa

Country	Examples of EU resilience-building measures
Egypt	Promoting stability, economic and social reforms
Jordan	Supporting the basic needs of Syrian refugees in Jordan; helping open job centres; and simplifying roles of origin
Lebanon	Supporting the basic needs of Syrian refugees in Lebanon; offering market solutions by reducing costs of borrowing funds
Palestine	Promoting Palestinians in Area C of the West Bank and East Jerusalem to cope with Israeli occupation

prospect of success. Moreover, and paradoxically, the EU's resilience approach fails to prioritise Gaza. This neglect comes despite Gaza's immense fragilities, the devastating destruction of its basic infrastructure and continuous de-development. As a matter of fact, according to the UN, Gaza is expected to be 'unlivable by 2020' as a result of three full-scale Israeli military assaults and the imposed blockade since 2007 (United Nations Conference on Trade and Development 2015; Roy 2007) (Table 4.1).

Overall, as far as the above indicative empirical examples of resilience-building in Egypt, Jordan, Lebanon and Palestine demonstrate, the term resilience is used very sparsely and fleetingly in frameworks by the EU and southern ENP partner countries concluded since 2016. This clearly reveals the uncertainty of EU foreign policymakers on how to interpret and then translate their conceptualisation of resilience into concrete action. With such uncertainty, difficult political issues are dodged in favour of supposedly neutral and technical solutions. Arrangements such as the PP and SSF for the period 2017–2020 hardly define the notion of resilience. Instead, they associate resilience with stability, economic and social development, as well as reforms. Simultaneously, resilience measures, as adopted by the EU, all have a focus on private sector development, governance reforms, specific infrastructure projects (energy, environment and water), and the provision of essential basic services for refugees in host countries in the southern neighbourhood. Such interventions resonate strongly with the notion of resilience and in particular with the EU's ambition to pursue low-cost, private sector-driven and responsibility devolution logics. These interventions seem impotent in the face of the political nature and scale of prevailing challenges.

Conclusions

The assumption that the EU has been supporting democracy in its southern neighbourhood, but only suddenly embraced resilience-building as an alternative to ambitious democracy promotion agendas is misleading. As this chapter has demonstrated, the EU's approach of resilience-building mainly is a repackaging of past practices, meant to disguise the continuous support for, and cooperation with, autocratic regimes that regard democracy as their ultimate enemy. As long as the southern neighbourhood is viewed as a 'profoundly alien' space that cannot be democratised (i.e. is 'unreformable'), EU resilience-building, despite its euphemistic rhetoric, will continue to revolve around the perceived need to secure European borders—visible or invisible—with the South. Put differently, the latest shift towards resilience-building in EU foreign policy and external relations remains embedded in past logics of turning the neighbourhood into a security buffer (Browning and Joeniemmi 2008; Del Sarto and Schumacher 2005; Walters 2004).

Portraying resilience as a less ambitious alternative to democracy and human rights promotion is unwarranted and a feeble justification that serves the EU's stability-driven foreign policy. After all, tackling the root causes of conflicts, vulnerabilities, climate change, poverty and other complex challenges is far more ambitious than focusing on democracy promotion alone. Approaching resilience as a form of governmentality (Joseph 2013, 2016, 2018; Evans and Reid 2014) may thus be a useful way to critically understand its operative modes. Besides being seemingly cost-effective, resilience outsources governance responsibility downwards to the unit level (i.e. to individuals, local governments, civil society, the private sector, etc.), in the hope that problems will be addressed locally in a 'peaceful and stable manner', thus preventing negative spill-over effects (European Commission and High Representative of the Union for Foreign Affairs and Security Policy 2017: 3). Obviously, this requires an 'adaptation of *certain* behaviours by *particular* populations' at the micro-level in a way that 'complements the outsourcing logic of neoliberal governance' (Evans and Reid 2014: 9, 16, emphasis in original).

Security, threat and migration management have underpinned the EU's approach to political liberalisation, democratisation, state- and peace-building in the southern neighbourhood already in the past. These elements continue to underlie the EU's resilience-building while tolerating repression, continuous violations of human rights and climates of fear. This approach glosses over political and economic enervations that underlie the multilayered structural crises across the southern neighbourhood. Meanwhile, Article 21(1) of the Treaty on the European Union unambiguously points to 'democracy, the rule of law, the universality and indivisibility of human rights and fundamental freedoms, respect for human dignity, the principles of equality and solidarity' as the guiding principles of EU external action. Thus, embracing resilience is to accept the failure of the liberal project and universality of the EU's grand claims and ambitions towards its southern neighbourhood. Such an acknowledgement, however, comes at a significant political cost that puts into question the fundamental principles—both legal and moral—EU external action is rooted in.

References

Allen, D. (1977). The Euro-Arab Dialogue. *JCMS: Journal of Common Market Studies, 16*(4), 323–342.
Amin, S., & El Kenz, A. (2005). *Europe and the Arab World: Patterns and Prospects for the New Relationship*. London: Zed Books.
Ashour, O. (2009). *The De-Radicalization of Jihadists: Transforming Armed Islamist Movements*. London: Routledge.
Berkes, F., et al. (Eds.). (2008). *Navigating Social-Ecological Systems: Building Resilience for Complexity and Change*. Cambridge: Cambridge University Press.
Bicchi, F. (2007). *European Foreign Policy Making toward the Mediterranean*. Basingstoke: Palgrave Macmillan.
Bicchi, F., & Gillespie, R. (Eds.). (2011). *The Union for the Mediterranean*. London: Routledge.
Bildt, C. (2015). *Europe Surrounded Not by a Ring of Friends—But by a Ring of Fire*. Washington, DC: Center for Strategic and International Studies.
Biscop, S., & Andersson, J. (Eds.). (2007). *The EU and the European Security Strategy: Forging a Global Europe*. London: Routledge.
Browning, C., & Joenniemi, P. (2008). The Geostrategies of the European Neighborhood Policy. *European Journal of International Relations, 14*(3), 519–552.
Campbell, D. (1998). *Writing Security: United States Foreign Policy and the Politics of Identity* (2nd ed.). Manchester: Manchester University Press.
Cebeci, M., & Schumacher, T. (2017). *The EU's Constructions of the Mediterranean (2003–2017)* (No. 3. MEDRESET Working Papers).
Christou, G. (2010). European Union Security Logics to the East: The European Neighborhood Policy and the Eastern Partnership. *European Security, 19*(3), 413–430.

Council of the European Union. (2013, May 28). *Council Conclusions on EU Approach to Resilience: 3241st Foreign Affairs Council Meeting*. Brussels.
Council of the European Union. (2019, February 15). *Sharm El-Sheikh Summit Declaration*. Brussels: European Council.
Del Sarto, R. (2015). Normative Empire Europe: The European Union, Its Borderlands, and the 'Arab Spring'. *Journal of Common Market Studies*, 54(2), 215–232.
Del Sarto, R., & Schumacher, T. (2005). From EMP to ENP: What's at Stake with the European Neighbourhood Policy Towards the Southern Mediterranean. *European Foreign Affairs Review*, 10, 17.
Delcour, L. (2015). *The 2015 ENP Review: Beyond Stocktaking, the Need for a Political Strategy*. CEPOB Policy Brief 1.
Diez, T. (2005). Constructing the Self and Changing Others: Reconstructing 'Normative Power Europe.' *Millennium—Journal of International Studies*, 33(3), 932–955.
Duffield, M. (2010). The Liberal Way of Development and the Development—Security Impasse: Exploring the Global Life-Chance Divide. *Security Dialogue*, 41(1), 53–76.
Duffield, M. (2012). Challenging Environments: Danger, Resilience and the Aid Industry. *Security Dialogue*, 43(5), 475–492.
European Commission. (2003). *Wider Europe—Neighbourhood: A New Framework for Relations with Our Eastern and Southern Neighbours*. COM(2003) 104 final. Brussels: European Commission. http://eeas.europa.eu/archives/docs/enp/pdf/pdf/com03_104_en.pdf.
European Commission. (2004). *On the Commission Proposals for Action Plans under the European Neighbourhood Policy (ENP)*. European Commission, Brussel, December 9. COM(2004) 795 final.
European Commission. (2009, February 23). *EU Strategy for Supporting Disaster Risk Reduction in Developing Countries*. COM(2009) 84 final. Brussels: European Commission. https://ec.europa.eu/europeaid/sites/devco/files/communication-disaster-risk-reduction-20090223_en_3.pdf.
European Commission. (2011, August 2). *A Partnership for Democracy and Shared Prosperity with the Southern Mediterranean*. COM(2011) 200 final. Brussels: European Commission.
European Commission. (2012, October 3). *The EU Approach to Resilience: Learning from Food Security Crises*. COM(2012) 586 final. Brussels: European Commission. http://ec.europa.eu/echo/files/policies/resilience/com_2012_586_resilience_en.pdf.
European Commission. (2013, June 19). *Action Plan for Resilience in Crisis Prone Countries 2013–2020*. SWD(2013) 227 final. Brussels: European Commission. http://ec.europa.eu/echo/files/policies/resilience/com_2013_227_ap_crisis_prone_countries_en.pdf.

European Commission. (2015a, November 18). *Review of the European Neighbourhood Policy.* JOIN(2015) 50 final. Brussels. http://eeas.europa.eu/archives/docs/enp/documents/2015/151118_staff-working-document_en.pdf.

European Commission. (2015b). *The European Agenda on Security.* https://ec.europa.eu/home-affairs/sites/homeaffairs/files/e-library/documents/basic-documents/docs/eu_agenda_on_security_en.pdf.

European Commission. (2016a, July 8). *Joint Declaration by the President of the European Council, the President of the European Commission, and the Secretary General of the North Atlantic Treaty Organization.* Brussels: European Commission. Accessed 30 October 2016.

European Commission. (2016b, April 6). *Joint Framework on Countering Hybrid Threats a European Union Response.* JOIN(2016) 18 final. Brussels: European Commission. https://eur-lex.europa.eu/legal-content/en/TXT/?uri=CELEX%3A52016JC0018.

European Commission. (2017a). *Commission Implementation Decision of 30.10.2017: Adopting a Single Support Framework for European Union Support to Egypt for the Period 2017–2020.* C(2017)7175 final. Brussels: European Commission. https://ec.europa.eu/neighbourhood-enlargement/sites/near/files/single-support-framework-2017-2020-decision_and_annex_egypt.pdf.

European Commission. (2017b, June 7). *EU Presents Its Strategy for More Resilient States and Societies around the World Press Release.* Brussels: European Commission. europa.eu/rapid/press-release_IP-17-1554_en.pdf.

European Commission. (2017c). *The New European Consensus on Development: Our World, Our Dignity, Our Future.* Brussels: European Commission. https://ec.europa.eu/europeaid/sites/devco/files/european-consensus-on-development-final-20170626_en.pdf.

European Commission. (2018a). *New Assistance Package for Palestine: EU Strongly Committed to Support Socio- Economic Revival of East-Jerusalem.* Brussels: European Commission. http://europa.eu/rapid/press-release_IP-18-368_en.htm.

European Commission. (2018b). *Action Document for EU Trust Fund to Be Used for the Decisions of the Operational Board. EU Support for Strengthening the Resilience of Palestine Refugees from Syria, in Jordan and Lebanon.* Ref. Ares(2018)341356. Brussels: European Commission. https://ec.europa.eu/neighbourhood-enlargement/sites/near/files/eutf_madad_action_document_8th_ob_palestinian_refugees_20062018.pdf.

European Commission and High Representative of the Union for Foreign Affairs and Security Policy (2017, June 7). *A Strategic Approach to Resilience in the EU's External Action.* JOIN(2017) 21 final. Brussels: European Commission.

https://eeas.europa.eu/sites/eeas/files/join_2017_21_f1_communication_from_commission_to_inst_en_v7_p1_916039.pdf.

European Council. (2016). *Lebanon-EU Partnership Priorities a Renewed EU—Lebanon Partnership (2016–2020)*. Brussels: European Council. UE-RL 3001/16. https://www.consilium.europa.eu/media/24224/st03001en16 docx.pdf.

European Council. (2017). *EU-Egypt Partnership Priorities 2017–2020*. Brussels: European Council. https://www.consilium.europa.eu/media/23942/eu-egypt.pdf.

European External Action Service. (2016, December 21). *European Neighbourhood Policy (ENP)*. Brussels. https://eeas.europa.eu/diplomatic-network/northern-dimension/330/european-neighbourhood-policy-enp_en.

European External Action Service. (2017). *Annex: Supporting Resilience of Host Countries and Refugees in the Context of the Syrian Crisis: Jordan*. ID: 170406_10. https://eeas.europa.eu/headquarters/headquarters-homepage/24292/supporting-resilience-host-countries-refugees-context-syrian-crisis-jordan_en.

European Security Strategy. (2003, December 12). *European Security Strategy—A Secure Europe in a Better World*. Brussels: European Council.

European Union. (2016). *A Global Strategy for the European Union's Foreign and Security Policy*. https://europa.eu/globalstrategy/sites/globalstrategy/files/regions/files/eugs_review_web_0.pdf.

Evans, B., & Reid, J. (2014). *Resilient Life: The Art of Living Dangerously*. Cambridge: Polity Press.

Gillespie, R. (1997). *The Euro-Mediterranean Partnership: Political and Economic Perspectives*. London: Frank Cass.

Hahn, J. (2015, April 1). *European Neighbourhood Policy Reloaded*. European Commission. https://ec.europa.eu/commission/commissioners/2014-2019/hahn/blog/european-neighbourhood-policy-reloaded_en.

Hanf, D. (2011). *The ENP in the Light of the New 'Neighbourhood Clause' (Article 8 TEU)*. College of Europe.

Hill, C. (1993). Capability-Expectations Gap, or Conceptualizing Europe's International Role. *Journal of Common Market Studies, 3*, 305–328.

Hillion, C. (2013) The EU Neighbourhood Competence Under Article 8 TEU. *Think Global-Act European IV* (pp. 204–214). Paris: Notre Europe-Jacques Delors Institute.

Holmes, S., & Castañeda, H. (2016). Representing the 'European Refugee Crisis' in Germany and Beyond: Deservingness and Difference, Life and Death. *American Ethnologist, 43*(1), 12–24.

Human Rights Watch. (2018). *Country Summary: Egypt*. https://www.hrw.org/sites/default/files/egypt_5.pdf.

Joseph, J. (2013). Resilience as Embedded Neoliberalism: A Governmentality Approach. *Resilience, 1*(1), 38–52.

Joseph, J. (2016). Governing Through Failure and Denial: The New Resilience Agenda. *Millennium, 44*(3), 370–390.

Joseph, J. (2018). *Varieties of Resilience: Studies in Governmentality*. Cambridge: Cambridge University Press.

Keukeleire, S., & Delreux, T. (2014). *The Foreign Policy of the European Union* (2nd ed.). Basingstoke: Palgrave Macmillan.

Maass, A. (2017). Financial Instruments and the European Neighbourhood Policy. In T. Schumacher, A. Marchetti, & T. Demmelhuber (Eds.) (2017), *The Routledge Handbook on the European Neighbourhood Policy* (pp. 234–245). Oxon: Routledge.

Malmvig, H. (2006). Caught Between Cooperation and Democratization: The Barcelona Process and the EU's Double-Discursive Approach. *Journal of International Relations and Development, 9*(4), 343–370.

Meloni, G. (2008), Who Is My Neighbour? In L. Delcour & E. Tulmets (Eds.) *Pioneer Europe: Testing European Foreign Policy in the European Neighbourhood*. Baden-Baden: Nomos.

Nitoiu, C. (2013). The European Public Sphere: Myth, Reality or Aspiration? *Political Studies Review, 11*(1), 26–38.

Norris, F. H., Stevens, S. P., Pfefferbaum, B., Wyche, K. F., & Pfefferbaum, R. L. (2008). Community Resilience as a Metaphor, Theory, Set of Capacities, and Strategy for Disaster Readiness. *American Journal of Community Psychology, 41*(1–2), 127–150.

Pishchikova, K., & Piras, E. (2017). The European Union Global Strategy: What Kind of Foreign Policy Identity? *The International Spectator, 52*(3), 103–120.

Roy, S. (2007). *Failing Peace Gaza and the Palestinian-Israeli Conflict*. London and Ann Arbor, MI: Pluto.

Rutherford, B. (2018). Egypt's New Authoritarianism Under Sisi. *The Middle East Journal, 72*(2), 185–208.

Sayigh, Y. (2012). *Above the State: The Officers' Republic in Egypt*. Washington, DC: Carnegie Middle East Center, Carnegie Endowment for International Peace.

Schumacher, T. (2015). Uncertainty at the EU's Borders: Narratives of EU External Relations in the Revised European Neighbourhood Policy Towards the Southern Borderlands. *European Security, 24*(3), 381–401.

Schumacher, T. (2016). *Back to the Future: The 'New' ENP Towards the Southern Neighbourhood and the End of Ambition*. College of Europe Policy Brief No. 1, Bruges.

Schumacher, T., & Dimitris, B. (Eds.). (2017). *The Revised European Neighbourhood Policy: Continuity and Change in EU Foreign Policy*. Basingstoke: Palgrave Macmillan.

Schumacher, T., Marchetti, A., & Demmelhuber, T. (Eds.). (2017). *The Routledge Handbook on the European Neighbourhood Policy*. Oxon: Routledge.

Smith, K. (2005). The Outsiders: The European Neighbourhood Policy. *International Affairs, 81*(4), 757–773.

Smith, M. (2016). Implementing the Global Strategy Where It Matters Most: The EU's Credibility Deficit and the European Neighbourhood. *Contemporary Security Policy, 37*(3), 446–460.

Tocci, N. (2017). *Framing the EU Global Strategy: A Stronger Europe in a Fragile World*. Basingstoke: Palgrave Macmillan.

UNHCR. (2018, November 12). *Syrian Regional Refugee Response*. UNHCR Operational Portal: Refugee Situations. https://data2.unhcr.org/en/situations/syria/location/36.

United Nations Conference on Trade and Development. (2015). *Report on UNCTAD Assistance to the Palestinian People: Developments in the Economy of the Occupied Palestinian Territory*. https://unctad.org/en/PublicationsLibrary/tdb62d3_en.pdf.

Verheugen, Günter. (2004). *The Wider Europe Matrix*. Brussels: Centre For European Policy Studies.

Wagner, W., & Anholt, R. (2016). Resilience as the EU Global Strategy's New Leitmotif: Pragmatic, Problematic or Promising? *Contemporary Security Policy, 37*(3), 414–430.

Walker, J., & Cooper, M. (2011). Genealogies of Resilience: From Systems Ecology to the Political Economy of Crisis Adaptation. *Security Dialogue, 42*(2), 143–160.

Walker, B., et al. (2004). Resilience, Adaptability and Transformability in Social–Ecological Systems. *Ecology and Society, 9*(2), 1–9.

Walters, W. (2004). The Frontiers of the European Union: A Geostrategic Perspective. *Geopolitics, 9*(3), 674–698.

Youngs, R. (Ed.). (2015). *20 Years of Euro-Mediterranean Relations*. London: Routledge.

CHAPTER 5

EU Counter-Terrorism Cooperation with the Middle East and North Africa

Christian Kaunert, Sarah Léonard and Ori Wertman

Terrorism has been a long-standing concern in most European Union (EU) member states. According to a study conducted by the Pew Research Centre in May 2017, the EU's public is concerned about terrorism to a significant extent, as almost 8% of EU citizens are worried about the rise of Islamic extremism (Abdelsamad 2018). As more than 2400 people have died in terrorist attacks in Europe since 2001 (Berthelet 2017), governments and policy-makers in most EU member states have been urged by their citizens to deliver an adequate response to the terrorist threat (European Parliament 2017: 14). Another concern has been the phenomenon of the lone wolf terrorists. As the development of the internet has enabled bottom-up radicalisation (Abdelsamad

C. Kaunert (✉)
International Centre for Policing and Security, University of South Wales, Pontypridd, Wales, UK
e-mail: christian.kaunert@southwales.ac.uk

S. Léonard
University of the West of England, Bristol, UK

O. Wertman
University of South Wales, Pontypridd, Wales, UK

© The Author(s) 2020
E. Cusumano and S. Hofmaier (eds.),
Projecting Resilience Across the Mediterranean,
https://doi.org/10.1007/978-3-030-23641-0_5

2018), the perpetrators of future attacks no longer need to be recruited by terrorist organisations. Consequently, the assessment that there may be 50,000 radical Islamists in Europe—returning foreign fighters and home-grown radicals—has been heightening concerns that further attacks could be conducted (Paul and Seyrek 2018).

Against this backdrop, terrorism has also been prevalent in the Middle East and North Africa (MENA) region. Today more than ever, as the EU and the MENA region are deeply interdependent and wars and instability in the EU's southern neighbourhood have had negative consequences for Europe, the resilience of MENA states is vital for the security of the EU (Gaub and Popescu 2017: 7–8). As emphasised by Malkki and Sinkkonen (2016: 281), "[t]he idea of 'resilience' features in many counterterrorism strategies that have been written in recent years and it is a term that has been employed by political leaders in the aftermath of terrorist attacks". Furthermore, it is "commonly seen as something inherently positive, something to strive for", although what it exactly means and how it could be measured remain far from clear (Malkki and Sinkkonen 2016: 281). Moreover, although there is a significant connection between the resilience of a state and its counter-terrorism efforts, the connection between resilience-building and counter-terrorism has remained largely unexplored.

The threat of terrorism and the counter-measures against it are not new to the European continent. The 1970s and 1980s saw a significant number of terrorist attacks in several European countries, with more than four hundred victims per year in peak years (Gaub and Pauwels 2017: 4). Nevertheless, although the menace of terrorism was one of the driving forces behind the initiation of some largely informal cooperation in internal security amongst European states in the 1970s, the EU only began to develop its counter-terrorism policy following the terrorist attacks on 9/11 (Argomaniz 2011; Bossong 2013; Kaunert 2010c; Kaunert and Léonard 2019). The EU member states' determination to combat terrorism was increased by their acknowledgment that this threat now had both a multi-faceted character and a transnational scope (Kaunert 2010b; Mahncke and Monar 2006; Spence 2007). The necessity to cooperate amongst EU member states also derived from the perception that, "although some of them may continue to face threats from ethno-nationalist and separatist terrorist groups, they now all faced one major, collective terrorist threat, embodied at the time by al-Qaeda" (Kaunert and Léonard 2019: 273).

Following the terrorist attacks in Madrid (2004) and London (2005), EU member states broadened and strengthened their cooperation by establishing the position of EU Counter-Terrorism Coordinator in March 2004 (Council of the European Union 2004: 14), and adopting the EU Counter-Terrorism Strategy in November 2005 (Council of the European Union 2005). In addition, as policy-makers increasingly realised the strong transnational dimension of the terrorist threat faced by European states, the EU also strived to increase counter-terrorism cooperation with third countries (Kaunert 2010a). In that context, the EU's 2005 Counter-terrorism Strategy highlighted the importance of combating terrorism globally (Council of the European Union 2005: 6). Since then, the EU has consistently sought to forge closer ties with third countries in the fight against terrorism.

Counter-terrorism cooperation with the MENA region is particularly important to the EU for various reasons. In addition to the fact that all countries in this region have been affected by terrorism to various degrees, several terrorist attacks carried out in Europe had significant links to the MENA region. This was already illustrated by the 2004 terrorist attacks in Madrid. The departure of about 5000 Europeans for Syria and Iraq from 2013 onwards and the subsequent attacks carried out in Paris and Brussels by cells comprising terrorists trained in the Middle East have further underlined the connection between security in Europe and the MENA region (Gaub and Pauwels 2017: 4–5). Moreover, changes in the nature of the terrorist groups in the regions surrounding Europe have shaped the evolution of the European response, including a new wave of European counter-terrorism operations. More precisely, EU member states have undertaken a series of military campaigns against terrorist groups in the MENA region since 2012, which represents a major new direction in European security policy (Dworkin 2017).

As the linkages between domestic and external security have been reinforced, European leaders have stressed the necessity of mobilising all the tools at the EU's disposal to tackle internal threats, including those emanating from its neighbourhood (Ioannides 2014). The European Neighbourhood Policy (ENP), which has been developed since 2003 with the main aim of creating a "ring of friends" to the East and the South of the EU in order to stimulate security cooperation, including fighting against terrorism, has been one of these tools (Commission of the European Communities 2003: 4). However, it appears that, in fifteen years, security cooperation in practice has not advanced as much as had been envisaged in the ENP's official documents (Kaunert and Léonard 2011). In addition, since the establishment of the ENP, the EU's neighbourhood has been considerably transformed by political developments and events, such as the Arab Spring, the civil war in Syria, and the war in Ukraine. These events have led some observers to question whether the EU is not surrounded by a "ring of fire" rather than a "ring of friends" (*Economist* 2014). Various terrorist attacks across Europe have further enhanced the importance of the EU's security agenda and highlighted the necessity of fighting terrorism (European Commission 2015: 2).

This chapter examines how the EU has attempted to develop counter-terrorism cooperation with its MENA partners, as well as the results that it has achieved in practice. First, it introduces the security and counter-terrorism policies of the EU and the development of such policies vis-à-vis the MENA region. Subsequently, the chapter explores the evolution of EU-MENA counter-terrorism cooperation, focusing on four dimensions: (1) border controls; (2) countering the financing of terrorism; (3) fostering regional cooperation; and (4) the rule of justice and the protection of human rights. For the purposes of this chapter, counter-terrorism is understood as a broad policy area, which comprises a range of responses across various governmental departments (Keohane 2005), including policing, criminal justice, border controls, the freezing of financial assets, intelligence gathering and, more recently, anti-radicalisation.

The EU's Security and Counter-Terrorism Policies

The EU's counter-terrorism agenda has been to a large extent "crisis-driven" (Argomaniz 2009). In particular, EU counter-terrorism has been heavily influenced by four major shock waves: (1) 9/11; (2) the Madrid and London terrorist attacks; (3) the Syrian Civil War and the rise of Daesh, the phenomenon of foreign terrorist fighters, and the attacks in Paris and Brussels; and (4) the Nice and Berlin attacks, as well as a series of small-scale attacks, highlighting the rise of lone actors and the "weaponisation of ordinary life". Since these shocks were all related to Islamist extremism, Islamic terrorism has been the main focus of EU counter-terrorism efforts (European Parliament 2017: 15). Moreover, although the EU's role in counter-terrorism has significantly grown since 9/11, the EU member states remain the main players in counter-terrorism, with the EU mainly assuming a coordinating role (Abdelsamad 2018). It is noteworthy that various obstacles remain in that respect. These notably include differences in security cultures, which may hamper intelligence-sharing and law enforcement cooperation amongst member states, and limited resources and support for security forces in some EU member states—a weakness that terrorists have exploited (Rotella 2016).

Prior to 11 September 2001, terrorism did not figure prominently on the common EU policy agenda (Kaunert and Léonard 2019), and cooperation in the field of counter-terrorism was largely informal (European Parliament 2017: 16; Torelli 2017: 13). However, shortly after 9/11, the European Council declared that fighting against terrorism was a priority objective for the EU. The Union began to develop an Action Plan on Combating Terrorism (European Council 2001), which recognised the need for the EU to play a greater part in the efforts of the international community to prevent and stabilise regional conflicts (Torelli 2017: 13; European Parliament 2017: 32). The European Security Strategy (ESS), which was adopted in 2003, also highlighted terrorism as a major threat requiring the cooperation of national authorities (Biscop 2008). In that context, the ESS indicated that terrorism should be tackled by using "a mixture of intelligence, police, judicial, military and other means" (European Council 2003: 7). Moreover, the ESS emphasised the necessity for "better coordination between external action and Justice and Home Affairs policies" in the combat against terrorism (European Council 2003: 13).

The terrorist attacks in Madrid in 2004 gave a new impetus to the development of the EU counter-terrorism action. These attacks led to the adoption of various measures, including the strengthening of border controls, judicial cooperation, and information exchange, together with the creation of the post of EU Counter-terrorism Coordinator in 2004. Following the terrorist attacks in London in 2005, an EU Counter-Terrorism Strategy (Council of the European Union 2005) and an EU Strategy for Combating Radicalisation and Recruitment to Terrorism were also adopted (Torelli 2017: 14; European Parliament 2017: 33).

Until 2013, the EU's counter-terrorism agenda did not evolve significantly. The revised ESS (2008) identified "building stability in Europe and beyond" as one of its three strategic goals, to be achieved notably through the promotion of good governance and the development of close and cooperative relations (Biscop 2010). The European Commission also emphasised that "internal security-related priorities should feature in political dialogues with third countries and regional organisations, where appropriate and relevant for combating multiple threats, such as terrorism" (European Commission 2010: 3). In practice, however, a significant divide has remained between the internal and external realms of security in the EU's action, despite a rhetorical commitment to working with third countries in order to tackle various security issues (Ioannides 2014). This is exemplified by the fact that it is only in 2012 that a Common Security and Defence Policy (CSDP) mission—namely the EU Capacity Building Mission in Niger (EUCAP SAHEL Niger)—included a formal counter-terrorism mandate (Council of the European Union 2012, Raineri and Baldaro in this volume), although various official statements from 2001 onwards had acknowledged the important contribution that the CSDP could make to the EU's counter-terrorism efforts (Oliveira Martins and Ferreira-Pereira 2012).

However, the Syrian civil war, the rise of Daesh, and the Paris attacks in 2015 prompted the EU to reconsider its counter-terrorism policies (European Parliament 2017: 34). This is largely because the civil war in Syria attracted about 5000 foreign fighters from the EU, the majority of whom joined extremist groups. It is also estimated that 30% of them have returned to Europe. Whilst not all of these returnees will become terrorists, many of them will have been exposed to sustained radicalisation and violence, and may therefore pose a significant threat to their homeland. This has been illustrated by two major terrorist attacks in France, in January and November 2015, respectively, which involved several terrorists having received training in Yemen and in Syria (European Parliament 2017: 34–35). Thus, as Daesh proved itself even more resolute to directly target Europe by primarily resorting to EU citizens travelling back and forth between Europe and the MENA region, the EU changed its counter-terrorism and de-radicalisation policies in December 2015 (Torelli 2017: 15–16). It was decided to create new criminal offences that address the phenomenon of the foreign terrorist fighters, including receiving terrorist training, travelling and attempting to travel abroad for terrorism, as well as funding or facilitating such journeys (European Parliament 2017: 35). Furthermore, the EU highlighted the importance of "security dialogues" with a range of partners, including neighbouring countries (European Commission 2015: 4).

The attacks in Brussels in March 2016 rapidly appeared to be connected to the above-mentioned international support networks.

Consequently, a sense of urgency to enhance the mechanisms of data exchange and mutual legal assistance grew amongst EU member states. Hence, the EU took further steps in proposing and adopting measures and policies related to the prevention of radicalisation, the detection of travel for suspicious purposes, the criminal justice sector, and cooperation with third countries. The attacks in Nice in July 2016 and Berlin in December 2016 appeared to testify to the phenomenon of the lone wolf (European Parliament 2017: 36).

In 2017, the terrorist attacks in Manchester, London, and Barcelona also intensified the sense of a looming terrorist threat within the EU. As the Union became increasingly aware of the interconnectedness between its own security and that of its neighbours, the European Commission proposed various measures aiming to strengthen counter-terrorism cooperation with third countries, including "the opening of negotiations for agreements between the EU and Algeria, Egypt, Israel, Jordan, Lebanon, Morocco, Tunisia and Turkey on the transfer of personal data between Europol [the EU Agency for Law Enforcement Cooperation] and these countries to prevent and combat terrorism and serious crimes" (European Commission 2017: 2). From an operational viewpoint, the EU's cooperation with countries in the MENA region can be seen as a favourable development (Abdelsamad 2018), although it also raises significant concerns with regard to human rights and data protection, amongst others (Kaunert and Léonard 2011). This has been acknowledged by the EU, which has also sought to support respect for human rights and the rule of law as part of its counter-terrorism cooperation with the MENA countries, as discussed later in this chapter.

The Evolution of EU-MENA Counter-Terrorism Cooperation

For the countries in the EU's southern neighbourhood—the MENA region—terrorism tends to represent an even greater threat than for European states (Gaub and Pauwels 2017: 5). Given its concerns regarding the influence of Daesh and other terrorist organisations in the MENA region, as well as the return of foreign fighters, the EU has a strong interest in understanding security threats that emanate from the MENA region (Dworkin and El-Maliki 2018).

Although European states had already attempted to promote cooperation with the Arab League through the Euro-Arab Dialogue since 1973, it was the 1995 Barcelona Conference that contributed to explicitly integrating counter-terrorism issues within the Euro-Mediterranean Partnership (EMP) framework (Torelli 2017: 20). In order to transform the Mediterranean into a common area of peace, stability, and prosperity, the EMP aimed to strengthen cooperation between the EU and twelve southern Mediterranean countries concerning three key issue areas: (1) political and security, (2) economic and financial, and (3) social, cultural and human (Euro-Mediterranean Partnership 1995). However, concrete cooperation between the two shores remained limited and fluctuant (Torelli 2017: 20). In 2004, in an attempt to address the shortcomings of the EMP, the EU launched the ENP as a complement to the multilateral framework of the Barcelona Process (see Badarin and Schumacher in this volume). Nevertheless, when it comes to counter-terrorism, a systematic analysis of the ENP Action Plans, which are drawn up for every participant in the ENP, reveals that only vague and limited aims have been included in the Action Plans elaborated for the EU's Mediterranean neighbours (MacKenzie et al. 2013; Kaunert and Léonard 2011).

This can be explained by the fact that the EU has been attempting to find an acceptable balance between its security concerns and the need to deal with authoritarian regimes. However, in practice, the EU has tended to prioritise short-term stability over democratic reforms, as it has been perceived to better serve its own security interests (Kaunert and Léonard 2011: 289–290). Nevertheless, the resulting engagement with authoritarian regimes can be argued to have contributed to postponing initiatives that could have addressed radicalisation and terrorism. The EU has preferred not to create possible new tensions by criticising and de-legitimising neighbouring regimes, the very authoritarian nature of which has actually been one of the causes of radicalisation in the region. Thus, the EU has arguably both contributed to the emergence of new forms of radicalisation and largely lost credibility amongst the public within these states, which had hoped that European pressure could eventually lead to more inclusive and democratic processes (Torelli 2017: 21–22).

In 2015, the EU sought to revise its neighbourhood policy, as it attempted to overcome some of the traditional obstacles that had undermined cooperation with the MENA region. This revision essentially involved conducting upgraded security and counter-terrorism dialogues with countries, such as Algeria, Egypt, Iraq, Israel, Jordan, Morocco,

Lebanon, Saudi Arabia, Tunisia and the Gulf Cooperation Council (Torelli 2017: 22–23). Two years later, the European Commission presented a set of operational and practical measures to prevent terrorism and better defend EU citizens, one of which was to enhance multilateral and bilateral counter-terrorism cooperation with third countries, regarded as necessary for strengthening the Union's internal security (European Commission 2017). More recently, in June 2018, the Council approved the Commission's proposal to strengthen Europol's cooperation with third countries in order to fight terrorism and other serious transnational crime more effectively. The negotiating mandates approved by the Council allow the Commission to start talks with eight countries (i.e. Algeria, Egypt, Israel, Jordan, Lebanon, Morocco, Tunisia and Turkey) on behalf of the EU on the exchange of information, including personal data, with Europol (European Commission 2018).

Four Dimensions of EU-MENA Counter-Terrorism Cooperation

EU funding for counter-terrorism efforts and preventing/countering violent extremism (P/CVE), which amounted to approximately 334 million EUR in 2015 and 399 million EUR in 2016, has been largely centred on the MENA region (Gaub and Pauwels 2017: 7). As mentioned above, the EU's counter-terrorism cooperation with its MENA neighbours has arguably focused on four areas: (1) border controls; (2) countering the financing of terrorism; (3) fostering regional cooperation; and (4) strengthening the rule of law and the protection of human rights.

Border Controls

Since terrorist groups take advantage of the challenges inherent to controlling borders in the region in order to escape law enforcement authorities, obtain weapons and generate income through the smuggling of drugs, border control plays an important role in combating terrorism in the southern neighbourhood of the EU. Thus, as the borders in the MENA region have not stopped the flow of fighters travelling to and from Syria and Iraq, the EU has launched several projects aiming to enhance the border control capacities of the states in that region (Gaub and Pauwels 2017: 8).

In 2017, after the EU had declared that it would step up efforts to combat human smuggling and trafficking networks in the central Mediterranean region, it allocated 200 million EUR to the combat against smugglers and traffickers, as well as the management of migration flows (Fiott and Bund 2018: 41). In Tunisia, the EU invested 26 million EUR in 2015 in order to strengthen the Tunisian borders against terrorist infiltration. As a result, Tunisia has strengthened its border management capacities, including the detection of fraudulent documents. In Libya, the EU conducted the EU Integrated Border Management Assistance Mission Libya (EUBAM Libya) between 2013 and 2017 in order to assist the Libyan authorities in border management. With an annual investment of 17 million EUR, it aimed to train and mentor several hundred Libyan officials (see Varvelli and Villa in this volume). In Lebanon, the EU implemented a programme on Integrated Border Management (IBM) in 2012–2018, with an investment of 13.6 million EUR, which focused on securing and controlling borders, document identification, standard operating procedures and contingency planning (see Pounds et al. in this volume). Thus, whilst IBM-related cooperation activities in the region initially centred on stabilising regional security by making it more difficult for Hezbollah—the military wing of which is considered a terrorist organisation by the EU—to access weapons, such activities later refocused on securing Lebanon from infiltration by Islamist fighters from Syria (Gaub and Pauwels 2017: 9–10).

Countering the Financing of Terrorism

Given that terrorist groups in the southern neighbourhood have increasingly diversified their sources of income over the last decade and have gained better access to illicit resources, terrorism and transnational organised crime have become increasingly interconnected. For example, the main sources of income of Daesh were theft and extortion from the territories under its control, kidnapping for ransom, illicit trafficking, fundraising through modern communication networks, and material support from foreign terrorist fighters. Likewise, Al-Qaeda in the Islamic Maghreb (AQIM) has closely cooperated with some of the organised crime networks that are active in the Sahel and the Maghreb. As a consequence, in order to prevent the EU's financial system from being used for money laundering and terrorist financing purposes, the EU adopted the 4th Anti-Money Laundering Directive in May 2015.

In addition, the EU has encouraged member states to provide technical assistance to third countries to help them comply with international Anti-Money Laundering and Countering Financing of Terrorism (AML/CFT) standards. In practice, after it had adopted the Directive, the EU created a blacklist comprising high-risk third countries with deficiencies in combating money laundering and terrorist financing. In 2016, the European Commission also presented an Action Plan to strengthen the fight against the financing of terrorism. The main goals of this plan are to disrupt the revenue sources of terrorist organisations by targeting their capacity to raise funds and to detect and prevent these organisations from moving funds and assets by ensuring that such transactions can be traced and disrupted. Finally, the EU has recently set up the AML/CFT Global Initiative, with an investment of 16 million EUR, to support countries in the MENA region to monitor, disrupt, and deny the financing of terrorism and funds associated with terrorist activity (Gaub and Pauwels 2017: 13–14).

Fostering Regional Cooperation

A significant problem for counter-terrorism initiatives in the MENA has been the lack of security cooperation amongst states in the region, which has provided terrorists with opportunities to move freely between countries, smuggle weapons and launder money undetected. In order to tackle this challenge, the EU has contributed 34 million EUR to two projects in 2005–2019: Euromed Justice, which has aimed to enhance both institutional and administrative capacities in the field of justice, and Euromed Police, which has had the same objectives for the personnel in the internal security sector. In addition, in order to further strengthen its relations with third countries on counter-terrorism, the EU has appointed counter-terrorism and security experts at several of its delegations in the region, including in Tunisia, Morocco, Jordan and Lebanon since 2015. This is an important initiative to foster counter-terrorism cooperation by helping develop mutual trust with local military and law enforcement authorities. In this context, the EU agencies involved in counter-terrorism have also adopted various measures to step up cooperation with MENA states. For instance, since 2015, Eurojust—the European Union's Judicial Cooperation Unit—has striven to extend its network of contact points in the region, including in Lebanon, Jordan, Algeria, Iraq, and with the Palestinian Authority, together with those that have already been appointed in Egypt, Israel, and Tunisia (Gaub and Pauwels 2017: 15–17). As for Europol, it signed a working arrangement with Israel in July 2018, whilst also cooperating with Turkey through a strategic agreement.

Strengthening the Rule of Law and the Protection of Human Rights

Given that terrorism tends to be more prevalent in states characterised by low human rights standards, combating terrorism effectively and protecting human rights are not necessarily two conflicting goals. From that perspective, an effective and rule-of-law compatible criminal justice system plays a crucial role in counter-terrorism efforts. However, the military model of counter-terrorism, in which the state uses military strategies to combat terrorism, often directly undermines the role of the criminal justice system by prioritising operational urgency over the rule of law. In that respect, the Global Counterterrorism Forum (GCTF) (2011: 1), which is a body comprising the EU and 29 member states worldwide, stated in its 2011 Cairo Declaration on Counterterrorism and the Rule of Law that "an effective criminal justice system, fully respectful of human rights and fundamental freedoms, including effective prevention, investigative, and prosecutorial, and judicial capacity" is highly important for the deterrence, disruption, and prevention of terrorist acts.

As a result, the EU has addressed this issue in several of its cooperation programmes with its southern neighbours. The EU notably launched the "Counter-Terrorism in the Middle East and North Africa Region (CT MENA)" project, which provides extensive training opportunities for law-makers, police forces, prosecutors, judges, and other justice sector stakeholders. In Morocco, the EU has allocated 75.5 million EUR for justice sector reforms in order to enhance both judicial independence and the protection of rights and liberties. In Tunisia, the EU funded a 23 million EUR-programme on security sector reform in 2015, which aimed to enhance respect for human rights. In Iraq, the EU invested 12 million EUR for counter-terrorism purposes. These funds have contributed to assisting the Office of the National Security Adviser in the development of a national counter-terrorism strategy and a criminal justice system that respect human rights. The main goal here has been to strengthen the capacity of the Iraqi justice authorities for policy planning and coordination. In Egypt, the EU funded the "Modernisation of the Administration of Justice" programme to the tune of 10 million EUR in 2016. This aimed to improve the rule of law by building administrative capacity and creating a judicial system for minors. In Jordan, the EU has contributed 2.7 million EUR to the improvement of the strategic and operational capacities of the security agencies in order to strengthen their accountability (Gaub and Pauwels 2017: 11–12, 15).

An examination of the EU-MENA counter-terrorism cooperation has therefore shown that, in the allocation of its funding, the EU has largely given priority to strengthening state resilience over societal resilience in the face of the terrorist threat. This is in line with the EU's traditional approach towards the region. It has tended to favour stability, which is seen as guaranteeing security, over change and reforms, which are feared to foster instability in the short term. However, the attempts at also supporting reforms aiming to strengthen the respect for human rights and the rule of law show that the EU has also sought, albeit to a more modest degree, to enhance societal resilience in the MENA region.

Conclusion

Given the transnational nature of the terrorist threat, the EU has sought to develop counter-terrorism cooperation with countries in its neighbourhood. This has been challenging given the persistence of a divide between internal security and external security in the EU's approach. To date, counter-terrorism cooperation between the EU and its southern neighbours has mainly consisted of political dialogue. However, as this chapter has demonstrated, the EU's counter-terrorism cooperation with the MENA countries has also yielded some practical results, especially in areas like border controls, countering the financing of terrorism, fostering regional cooperation, and strengthening the protection of human rights and of the rule of law. In line with the broader EU approach towards the MENA region, counter-terrorism initiatives have tended to prioritise supporting state resilience over fostering societal resilience in the MENA region, although some steps in support of the latter have also been taken through programmes aiming to enhance respect for human rights and the rule of law.

REFERENCES

Abdelsamad, H. (2018). *Terrorism and Counterterrorism in the EU: Overestimated Threat, Oversimplified Approach*. Berlin: Dialogue of Civilizations Research Institute. https://doc-research.org/2018/08/counterterrorism/. Accessed 20 March 2019.

Argomaniz, J. (2009). Post 9/11 Institutionalisation of European Union Counter-Terrorism: Emergence, Acceleration and Inertia. *European Security, 18*(2), 151–172.

Argomaniz, J. (2011). *Post-9/11 European Union Counter-Terrorism: Politics, Polity and Policies*. London: Routledge.

Berthelet, P. (2017). How the European Union Is Making Major Strides Fighting Terrorism. *The Conversation*. https://theconversation.com/how-the-european-union-is-making-major-strides-fighting-terrorism-82866. Accessed 20 March 2019.

Biscop, S. (2008). The European Security Strategy in Context: A Comprehensive Trend. In S. Biscop & J. Anderson (Eds.), *The EU and the European Security Strategy: Forging a Global Europe* (pp. 5–20). London: Routledge.

Biscop, S. (2010). The ENP, Security, and Democracy in the Context of the European Security Strategy. In R. Whitman & S. Wolff (Eds.), *The European Neighbourhood Policy in Perspective: Context, Implementation and Impact* (pp. 73–88). Basingstoke: Palgrave Macmillan.

Bossong, R. (2013). *The Evolution of EU Counter-Terrorism: European Security Policy After 9/11*. London: Routledge.

Commission of the European Communities. (2003). *Communication from the Commission to the Council and the European Parliament: Wider Europe—Neighbourhood: A New Framework for Relations with Our Eastern and Southern Neighbours*. COM (2003) 104. Brussels: Commission of the European Communities.

Council of the European Union. (2004). *Declaration on Combating Terrorism*. 7906/04. Brussels: Council of the European Union.

Council of the European Union. (2005). *The European Union Counter-Terrorism Strategy*. 14469/4/05. Brussels: Council of the European Union.

Council of the European Union. (2012, July 17). Council Decision 2012/392/CFSP of 16 July 2012 on the European Union CSDP Mission in Niger (EUCAP Sahel Niger). *Official Journal of the EU*, L 187/48. Brussels.

Dworkin, A. (2017). *Europe's War on Terror*. London: European Council of Foreign Relations. https://www.ecfr.eu/article/essay_europes_war_on_terror. Accessed 20 March 2019.

Dworkin, A., & El-Maliki, F. Z. (2018). *The Southern Front Line: EU Counter-Terrorism Cooperation with Tunisia and Morocco*. European Council of Foreign Relations.

Economist. (2014, September 20). Europe's Ring of Fire.
Euro-Mediterranean Partnership. (1995, November 27–28). *Final Declaration of the Barcelona Euro-Mediterranean Ministerial Conference of 27 and 28 November 1995 and Its Work Programme.*
European Commission. (2010). *The EU Internal Security Strategy in Action: Five Steps Towards a More Secure Europe.* COM (2010) 673. Brussels: European Commission.
European Commission. (2015). *The European Agenda on Security.* COM (2015) 185. Brussels: European Commission.
European Commission. (2017, October 18). *Security Union: Commission Presents New Measures to Better Protect EU Citizens.* Press Release IP/17/3947.
European Commission. (2018). *Security Union: Strengthening Europol's Cooperation with Third Countries to Fight Terrorism and Serious Organised Crime.*
European Council. (2001). *Conclusions and Plan of Action of the Extraordinary European Council Meeting on 21 September 2001.* SN 140/01.
European Council. (2003, December 12). *A Secure Europe in a Better World—European Security Strategy.*
European Parliament. (2017). *The European Union's Policies on Counter-Terrorism: Relevance, Coherence and Effectiveness.* Study for the LIBE Committee. Directorate-General for Internal Policies, Policy Department Citizens' Rights and Constitutional Affairs.
Fiott, D., & Bund, J. (2018). *EUISS Yearbook of European Security YES 2018.* Paris: European Union Institute for Security Studies. https://www.iss.europa.eu/content/euiss-yearbook-european-security-2018. Accessed 20 March 2019.
Gaub, F., & Pauwels, A. (2017). *Counter-Terrorism Cooperation with the Southern Neighborhood.* European Union Institute for Security Studies.
Gaub, F., & Popescu, N. (2017). *After the EU Global Strategy—Building Resilience.* European Union Institute for Security Studies.
Global Counterterrorism Forum. (2011, September 22). *Cairo Declaration on Counterterrorism and the Rule of Law: Effective Counterterrorism Practice in the Criminal Justice Sector.* https://www.thegctf.org/Portals/1/Documents/Framework%20Documents/A/GCTF-Cairo-Declaration.pdf. Accessed 20 March 2019.
Ioannides, I. (2014). Inside-Out and Outside-In: EU Security in the Neighbourhood. *The International Spectator, 49*(1), 113–132.
Kaunert, C. (2010a). The External Dimension of EU Counter-Terrorism Relations: Competences, Interests, and Institutions. *Terrorism and Political Violence, 22*(1), 41–61.
Kaunert, C. (2010b). Europol and EU Counterterrorism: International Security Actorness in the External Dimension. *Studies in Conflict and Terrorism, 33*(7), 652–671.

Kaunert, C. (2010c). *European Internal Security: Towards Supranational Governance in the Area of Freedom, Security and Justice?* Manchester: Manchester University Press.

Kaunert, C., & Léonard, S. (2011). EU Counterterrorism and the European Neighbourhood Policy: An Appraisal of the Southern Dimension. *Terrorism and Political Violence, 23*(2), 286–309.

Kaunert, C., & Léonard, S. (2019). The Collective Securitisation of Terrorism in the European Union. *West European Politics, 42*(2), 261–277.

Keohane, D. (2005). *The EU and Counter-Terrorism.* London: Centre for European Reform.

League of Arab States. (2014). *Evaluation of European Union Policies Towards the Arab World.* Cairo: League of Arab States.

MacKenzie, A., Kaunert, C., & Léonard, S. (2013). EU Counterterrorism and the Southern Mediterranean Countries After the Arab Spring: New Potential for Cooperation? *Democracy and Security, 9*(1–2), 137–156.

Mahncke, D., & Monar, J. (Eds.). (2006). *International Terrorism: A European Response to a Global Threat?* Brussels: PIE Peter Lang.

Malkki, L., & Sinkkonen, T. (2016). Political Resilience to Terrorism in Europe Introduction to the Special Issue. *Studies in Conflict and Terrorism, 39*(4), 281–291.

Oliveira Martins, B., & Ferreira-Pereira, L. (2012). Stepping Inside? CSDP Missions and EU Counter-Terrorism. *European Security, 21*(4), 537–556.

Paul, A., & Seyrek, D. M. (2018). Two Years After the Brussels Attacks, the Terrorist Threat Remains Very Real. *Euractiv.*

Rotella, S. (2016). How Europe Left Itself Open to Terrorism. *Frontline.* Arlington, VA: Public Broadcasting Service. https://www.pbs.org/wgbh/frontline/article/how-europe-left-itself-open-to-terrorism/. Accessed 20 March 2019.

Spence, D. (Ed.). (2007). *The European Union and Terrorism.* London: John Harper.

Torelli, S. M. (2017). *European Union and the External Dimension of Security: Supporting as a Model in Cooperation* (EuroMeSCo Paper 33). Barcelona: European Institute of the Mediterranean.

CHAPTER 6

Sanctions as a Regional Security Instrument: EU Restrictive Measures Examined

Francesco Giumelli

Building resilience has become one of the objectives of the European Union (EU) in recent years. As discussed in this volume, the EU Global Strategy embeds resilience as one of the main concepts underlying its external action (see chapters by Anholt and Wagner and Badarin and Schumacher). At the same time, the EU has become one of the most active utilisers of sanctions in the international system. Such restrictive measures, as they are known in EU jargon, have been used in crises ranging from the Democratic People's Republic of North Korea (DPRK), to Iran and Venezuela. However, the link between resilience and sanctions has not been examined in detail. Although scholars and policymakers have extensively analysed both the concept of resilience, and of EU sanctions, the role of restrictive measures in strengthening the resilience of the EU's enlarged neighbourhood has not benefited from any systematic analysis.

This chapter discusses whether the EU's utilisation of restrictive measures is compatible with the building of resilient societies, focusing on the EU experience in the Middle East and North Africa (MENA) region.

F. Giumelli (✉)
University of Groningen, Groningen, The Netherlands
e-mail: f.giumelli@rug.nl

© The Author(s) 2020
E. Cusumano and S. Hofmaier (eds.),
Projecting Resilience Across the Mediterranean,
https://doi.org/10.1007/978-3-030-23641-0_6

In general, if resilience is understood as a process by which states and societies are made more resistant to external shocks, then restrictive measures were used to strengthen state and societal resilience. Although their effectiveness has not been achieved to its fullest extent, restrictive measures in the MENA region were designed to assist and support the transition processes to new regimes. This is also due to the evolution of sanctions from comprehensive to targeted. On the one hand, comprehensive sanctions could impair the fostering of resilient societies by undermining the local ownership of institutions and policies, creating anomalous incentives in the allocation of resources, and by favouring one-size-fits-all solutions that counter, rather than contribute to, the achievement of certain objectives. On the other hand, targeted sanctions can be tailored to the needs of local conditions and can be designed to affect discriminately certain actors on the ground only. Additionally, their effects can also be rapidly adjusted to the evolving conditions of a particular crisis. These aspects of targeted sanctions are observable in the four case studies of EU restrictive measures in the MENA region since 2011: Egypt, Tunisia, Syria and Libya. In Egypt, Tunisia and Libya, sanctions were used to sustain the local authorities to consolidate their power after regime change. Conversely, sanctions were adopted to favour the regime transition in Syria and in the first phase of the Libyan crisis.

This chapter is divided into four sections. The first section presents the legal framework of the restrictive measures of the EU. The second section presents the historical record of when and why the EU resorted to sanctions in the past decades. The third section then deals specifically with the four case studies of EU sanctions being imposed on MENA countries. This is followed by a discussion on how the experience of the restrictive measures can be seen through the lenses of resilience. Finally, the conclusion summarises the main findings, and indicates some key weaknesses still impeding the effectiveness of restrictive measures policies of the EU in building resilience in societies beyond its borders.

The Restrictive Measures of the European Union

The Treaty of Rome established the European Economic Community (EEC), and created the conditions for the strong coordination of foreign trade policy by EEC members, but it was only with the Treaty of Maastricht that the EU acquired the possibility of resorting to sanctions as a foreign policy instrument. There are a few notable examples in the pre-Maastricht era when EEC members agreed to impose sanctions collectively. These include the response to the decision of the Soviet Union to establish court-martial in Poland after the repression of the protests organised by Solidarity in 1982, to the decision of Argentina to claim sovereignty over the Malvinas/Falkland Islands and, most notably, to the events in Tiananmen square in 1989 (Kreutz 2005).

The imposition of restrictive measures is normally understood as a measure of common foreign and security (CFSP), but this is not the only way in which sanctions can be adopted. The Council of the European Union (the Council) may decide to impose sanctions in order to transpose decisions made by the United Nations Security Council (UNSC). This has occurred on several occasions since 1993. While such UNSC decisions are transposed under the CFSP legal framework, they are made neither in Brussels nor in the capitals of the member states. There have been occasions where the EU has decided to modify a sanctions regime imposed by the United Nations (UN) either marginally, by adding individuals and entities to the lists as is common in cases of international terrorism, or substantially, such as in the cases of Iran or North Korea. Additionally, it has been noted how "sanction-like" measures are frequently applied by the Council and the European Commission, which do not require the adoption of CSFP decisions. The first of such measures worth noting is the Cotonou Agreement, which outlines the possibility for the EU to suspend aid and other forms of cooperation with signatory states when there are human rights concerns in the partner country as outlined by Article 96 of the Agreement (Giumelli 2013b). Second, others have noted that the suspension of the General System of Preference (GSP) status has been applied according to logic that is normally attributed to foreign policy decisions (Portela 2010). While an argument for including these measures into the study of EU sanctions could be made, this chapter refers exclusively to those restrictive measures imposed formally under the CFSP legal framework.

Sanctions are adopted on the basis of Chapter 2 of the Treaty of the EU, which contains specific provisions on CFSP. In particular, Article 29 of TEU provides the legal bases for Council decisions imposing sanctions. The proposal for new restrictive measures is formally initiated by the High Representative for Foreign Affairs and Security Policy (HR/VP), but several working groups are involved in the process. The Council's Political and Security Committee (PSC) discusses the general lines for CFSP and, as such, considers the opportunity to resort to restrictive measures given the particular context of different political crises. The relevant regional group is consulted for specific knowledge regarding the imposition of new measures and the Working Party of Foreign Relations Counsellors (RELEX), which, since 2004, has been able to convene under the so-called "sanctions" configuration, discusses the legal aspects of the matter. The final decision is taken by the Council of Ministers with unanimity under Chapter 2 of the Treaty of the European Union.

However, restrictive measures are not solely a CFSP matter. The institutional setting of the EU does not allow for such a clear-cut distinction between what falls strictly within the parameters of foreign policy, especially when trade is involved. For instance, among the exclusive competences of the EU vis-à-vis its member states is commercial policy. Consequently, international trade agreements have to be negotiated and signed by the EU only. The functioning of the internal market, which is affected by the implementation of economic sanctions, is a shared competence, which requires EU member states to act upon requests of the EU. Finally, member states have the final word on who is allowed to cross their national borders, which further blurs the borders between foreign and domestic policy.

Thus, resorting to restrictive measures is a unique case in the CFSP landscape which therefore required a more sophisticated elaboration within the Treaty on the Functioning of the European Union (TFEU) and Treaty on EU to be effectively utilised. The legal basis for the interruption of the regular functioning of the EU's economic and financial relations with a third country is provided by Article 215 of the TFEU. This article indicates that when a decision to impose restrictive measures is taken, then the "Council, acting by a qualified majority on a joint proposal from the High Representative of the Union for Foreign Affairs and Security Policy and the Commission, shall adopt the necessary measures" and "shall inform the European Parliament" (Article 215, TFEU). The second paragraph of the article authorises the EU to impose sanctions "against natural or legal persons and groups or non-State entities", but it specifies under Paragraph 3 that such measures "shall include necessary provisions on legal safeguards" (Article 215, TFUE).

Restrictive measures mainly consist of economic boycotts, financial restrictions, travel bans and arms embargoes. Both economic and financial measures are adopted with Council decisions, and are implemented with Council regulations, which have an immediate effect within EU member states and, therefore, firms and companies operating therein have to comply with them. Economic boycotts entail the prohibition of the sale of specific products or services to a targeted country, region, company and/or individual. Financial sanctions involve the freezing of assets and the prohibition of the provision of loans and making payments.

Council decisions imposing arms embargoes and travel bans require further legislation in member states in order to be implemented. Travel bans, which restrict access to the territories of the member states for security reasons, are implemented by member states because the latter remain the final authority over who enters and exits their territory. Arms embargoes prohibit the sale of weapons and related technology or services to individuals, non-state entities and state entities. The prohibition of the sale of arms was initially limited to military goods, but it was soon evident that a number of goods and technologies produced for civilian use could also be utilised to further military objectives. The EU recognised this problem by delegating the final decision to member states, but a list of dual-use goods was adopted in 2009 to harmonise practices (European Union 2009). Exporters who believe that certain goods might fall under such a list need to apply for an export license by the competent national authorities, such as the central bank, or the ministries for economics or foreign affairs.

There are three main documents providing for the use of sanctions by the EU. First, sanctions are imposed according to provisions illustrated in the "Basic Principles" adopted in 2004 (European Union 2004). Second, sanctions are designed and imposed according to ideas policies listed in the "Guidelines" adopted in 2013 in its latest versions (European Union 2012b). This document states that the EU adopts a "targeted" approach, entailing the minimization of sanctions on civilians while increasing the burden on certain actors, namely targeted individuals, political parties, and governmental leaders. Finally, given that imposing sanctions on individuals is extremely detailed, the third document is a set of "Best Practices" for the homogenous implementation of EU decisions across member states (European Union 2016d).

Although CFSP does not fall under the competence of the Court of Justice of the EU, restrictive measures have been increasingly reviewed by the Court in the past years. Shortly after the terrorist attacks of September 11, the case of Nada became the first in a long list of cases to involve people seeking redress from the Court for the undermining of individual freedoms through the implementation of UNSC targeted measures by the EU (Biersteker and Eckert 2009). The Kadi judgements in 2005 and, especially, 2008 were the first ones wherein the Court of the EU decided that restrictive measures, even when imposed by the UNSC, may not be implemented by the EU when such measures constitute a violation of the basic rights ensured by EU law (Larik 2014). Since then, decisions on restrictive measures need to consider the potential infringement of due process principles, such as the right to inform and the effective remedy assigned to listed individuals and entities (Biersteker and Eckert 2009).

When Does the EU Impose Sanctions?

The track record of the EU and sanctions goes back to the Cold War, with the EC sanctions imposed on the Soviet Union (1982), Argentina (1983), and China (1989) (Kreutz 2005). However, imposed sanctions were not legally mandated because the Treaty of Rome and the Single European Act provided mainly for the creation of a common market. Foreign policy was therefore only coordinated outside of the treaties. With the creation of the EU and the "second pillar" of the Maastricht Treaty, EU member states agreed to share the decision-making power on sanctions, and decisions made in Brussels would then become legally binding to all member states with the entry into force of the Maastricht Treaty.

The first years were rather timid when it comes to the adoption of this instrument by the EU. The first legal document imposing restrictive measures was adopted on 28 October 1996 and concerned the imposition of sanctions on Burma/Myanmar (Common Position 635, 1996). Since then, the EU has imposed autonomous sanctions in 33 occasions, including cases in which the EU acted before the UN, such as the cases of South Sudan and Sudan. The European Commission indicates that the EU's wider objectives for the utilisation of sanctions are: promoting international peace and security, preventing conflicts, defending democratic principles and human rights, preventing the proliferation of weapons of mass destruction (WMDs) and fighting terrorism. In previous works, EU sanctions have been classified similarly, as indicated in Table 6.1 (Giumelli 2013a).

The principal category underlying the utilisation of sanctions is human rights promotion. Human rights have been used to justify the

Table 6.1 EU restrictive measures per type of crisis since 1993[b]

Conflict management	Democracy promotion	Non-proliferation	Post-conflict	Terrorism
Afghanistan	Belarus	DPRK	Bosnia & Herzegovina	Libya
DRC	Burundi	Iran	Ivory Coast	Terrorist list
Indonesia	Comoros	Libya	Egypt	
Libya	CAR		FRY	
Sudan	China[a]		FYROM	
South Sudan	Guinea (Conakry)		Guinea	
Transnistria	Guinea-Bissau		ICTY indictees	
Russian Federation	Iran		Libya	
	Myanmar/Burma		Tunisia	
	Nigeria		Zimbabwe	
	Sudan			
	Syria			
	Uzbekistan			
	US			
	Zimbabwe			

[a]The restrictive measures on China are only politically binding
[b]Classification conducted by the author for descriptive purposes only

imposition of sanctions in cases where national authorities were deemed responsible for the violation of human rights of their citizens, such as in the cases of Belarus and Uzbekistan. However, the unlawful overthrow of governments and holding of elections which do not live up to the standards of freeness and fairness have also been reasons to trigger sanctions against individuals and non-state entities in certain countries, such as the Central African Republic and Zimbabwe. Restrictive measures have been adopted to contain the capacities of the DPRK and Iran to develop nuclear programmes and connected to missile technology capability to project their military means to long distances. Sanctions have also been used to manage ongoing conflicts such as in the cases of Transnistria, Libya, the Russian Federation and Syria. The second most frequent utilisation of restrictive measures occur after a conflict has ended. The aim of such sanctions is to contain the activities of *spoilers*, and to consolidate the establishment of new institutions and/or governments. This was the case for Liberia and Ivory Coast, but also for the travel ban and the assets freeze imposed on individuals indicted by the International Criminal Tribunal for the former Yugoslavia (ICTY). In this latter category, there are also sanctions imposed with the objective of assets recovery, specifically relevant for countries in the MENA region such as Egypt and Tunisia. The next section reviews sanctions imposed on countries in the MENA region in order to reflect on the way in which restrictive measures have contributed to the construction of resilient societies in the region.

Stabilising the MENA with Sanctions

The EU has resorted to sanctions in several occasions in the recent past to deal with crises in the MENA region. Whereas Tunisia and Egypt witnessed the EU adopting sanctions to recovery the assets stolen by former leaders as a way to assist the newly established local authorities, in Libya and Syria the EU used restrictive measures to undermine the capabilities of the incumbent regimes of Muamar Gaddafi and Bashar al-Assad.

Assets Recovery in Tunisia and Egypt

The wave of protests in the Arab World began when Mohamed Bouazizi set himself on fire in December 2010, triggering a popular uprising that led to the ousting of the long-term president of Tunisia, Zine El Abidine Ben Ali (International Crisis Group 2011b). The prime minister Mohammed Ghannouchi assumed the leadership of the country when Ben Ali left the country, but the Constitutional Court asked the speaker of the Parliament Fouad Mebazaa to form a new government and organise democratic elections. According to a UN investigative panel, "at least 219 people were killed during the uprising against Ben Ali" (Rifai 2011). A number of international actors imposed sanctions in order to sustain the process of democratisation in Tunisia. The Swiss Government, for instance, froze the funds of Ben Ali in Switzerland.

The EU decided to follow suit by freezing the financial assets of Ben Ali and his wife on 31 January 2011 (European Union 2011a). Later, 48 individuals were blacklisted with the Council Implementing Decision 79 of 4 February 2011. All the 48 individuals were then subjected to a "judicial investigation by the Tunisian authorities in respect of the acquisition of movable and immovable property, the opening of bank accounts and the holding of financial assets in several countries as part of money-laundering operations" (European Union 2011g). These measures amount to a response by the EU of the call for help by Tunisian authorities in trying to recover the assets in the name of, or otherwise associated with, individuals accused of misappropriation. The statement of reasons provided by the EU for the compilation of this list of individuals is as follows:

> Person[s] subject to judicial investigations by the Tunisian authorities for complicity in the misappropriation of public monies by a public officeholder, complicity in the misuse of office by a public office-holder to procure an unjustified advantage for a third party and to cause a loss to the administration, and exerting wrongful influence over a public officeholder with a view to obtaining directly or indirectly an advantage for another person. (European Union 2011a). The 48 individuals initially listed are still listed at the time of the writing of this chapter, and the trial of former President Ben Ali began in May of 2018. (MEE and Agencies 2018)

The departure of Ben Ali from Tunisia sparked a wave of revolts in Egypt that would eventually lead to the deposition of Hosni Mubarak on 11 February 2011 (International Crisis Group 2011a). On 25 January 2011, a series of rallies were organised in many cities in Egypt on the day of commemoration of the police forces. The demonstrations soon escalated into riots and open clashes with the security forces of the regime, with the motto of the people gathered in Tahrir Square becoming "down with Mubarak". With his first address to the nation, Hosni Mubarak decided to change his cabinet as a response to the massive protests of the people and appoint a new vice-president, Omar Suleiman. On 1 February, pressured by hundreds of thousands of protestors in Tahrir Square, and by the return of Mohamed El Baradei, who declared himself available to lead the Egyptian transition to democracy, Mubarak announced that he would not run for President again. However, Mubarak refused to step down. After ten days of continuous protests in Tahrir Square, and many people killed in the clashes with the security forces, President Mubarak resigned on 11 February after 34 years of presidency, and power was turned over to the army. On 21 February, the Council of Ministers affirmed its intention to support "the peaceful and orderly transition to a civilian and democratic government in Egypt based on the rule of law, with full respect for human rights and fundamental freedoms and to support efforts to create an economy which enhances social cohesion and promotes growth" (European Union 2011j). Similar to the case of Tunisia, the EU decided to freeze the assets of "persons having been identified as responsible for misappropriation of Egyptian State funds and who are thus depriving the Egyptian people of the benefits of the sustainable development of their economy and society and undermining the development of democracy in the country" (European Union 2011b). Council Decision 172 of 21 March 2011 identified 19 individuals, including Mubarak himself and his family as targets of this assets freeze (European Union 2011b). Sanctions were renewed and are still in force at the time of writing, but the list has been updated with the removal of six individuals on 21 march 2018 with Council decision 466 (European Union 2018).

In both Tunisia and Egypt, sanctions were imposed immediately after the collapse of the regime, and on a number of individuals that had been accused of stealing from their own countries. The freezing of assets and travel bans concerned 48 individuals in Tunisia and 19 in Egypt, targeting the former presidents, their family members, and their closest associates. In both cases, restrictive measures were imposed against persons having been identified as responsible for "misappropriation of [...] State funds and who are thus depriving the [...] people of the benefits of the sustainable development of their economy and society and undermining the development of democracy in the country" (European Union 2011a, b). In other words, the objective of sanctions was to sustain the newly established national authorities (for a more extensive analysis of Egypt and Tunisia, see the chapter by Amadio Vicere and Frontini in this volume).

Syria

The case of Syria differs from that of Tunisia and Egypt. While protests were sufficient to oust Ben Ali and Mubarak even before sanctions were imposed by the EU, the EU intervened against Bashar al-Assad when he was still in power. Therefore, sanctions were imposed to undermine the national government and favour opposition groups rather than to strengthen national authorities. Possibly, the Council believed that the regime lost legitimacy and, consequently, the opposition constituted the legitimate authority in the region. In any event, the EU resorted to sanctions in response to the violations of human rights committed by the regime and, de facto, targeted the leadership of the legitimate government of Syria.

When protests began in March 2011, the EU intended to open a dialogue with Assad in order to prevent him from using excessive force against his own population. After an initial threat phase, the EU imposed a travel ban on 13 individuals involved in the repression of the civilian population, but Assad was not among them. The EU "condemned the violent repression, including through the use of live ammunition, of peaceful protest in various locations across Syria resulting in the death of several demonstrators, wounded persons and arbitrary detentions, and called on the Syrian security forces to exercise restraint instead of repression" and decided to impose sanctions "against Syria and against persons responsible for the violent repression against the civilian population" (European Union 2011c). After the call for moderation fell on deaf ears, the EU added 23 individuals, including Assad and his closest family members, to the blacklist with Council implementing Decision 302 on 23 May 2011 (European Union 2011f). This list responded to a new phase of sanctions with a clear policy shift from containing Assad's use of repressive violence to regime change in Syria. The number of individuals and entities was expanded to include 66 individuals and entities with Council Decision 522 on 2 September 2011, which also indicated that sanctions should target individuals and entities "benefiting from or supporting the regime, in particular persons and entities financing the regime, or providing logistical support to the regime, in particular the security apparatus, or who undermine the efforts towards a peaceful transition to democracy in Syria" and prohibited "the purchase, import or transport from Syria of crude oil and petroleum products" from 15 November 2011 (European Union 2011d).

The escalation of the crisis in Syria has provided the grounds for further sanctions to be imposed by the EU. The number of gradual addition of individuals to the sanctions list was also justified by the extension of the criteria to be listed, which soon led to the black-listing of the Bank of Syria (European Union 2011e). The embargo on oil was followed by a number of other sectors, such as technologies which could potentially contribute to further internal repression, luxury goods (European Union 2012a), goods of cultural heritage (European Union 2013) and arms.

The Syrian Crisis went through various phases and the restrictive measures were predominantly tailored to address the particular needs of the local situation on the ground, but often were often intended to support (some) opposition to the regime of Bashar al-Assad. For instance, in 2013 the UK pushed for lifting the arms embargo on Syria because the embargo would prevent the EU from selling weapons to the rebels, while the government forces were sustained by other actors in the international system, mainly Russia (Traynor 2013). The current set of sanctions was voted with Council Decision 255 on 1 June 2013, and comprises various measures ranging from the prohibition to purchase oil from Syria, to a ban on dual-use technology, a travel ban, and a freeze of assets of individuals responsible for human rights violations and/or support the government or its policies. Due to the increasing complexity of the crisis, including the direct involvement of Russia and the US, and the intensification of military operations, the sanction's instrument became less relevant. However, the EU continued to add individuals and entities, including the Central Bank of Syria. At the moment of writing, the blacklist included 235 individuals and 66 entities, as well as a number of general provisions.

Libya

The sanctions regime in Libya has been implemented through two different phases. In the first phase, sanctions were designed to sustain the rebellion against the regime of Muammar Gaddafi. In the second phase, sanctions were imposed to sustain the very fragile institutional setting emerging from the political context in Libya after the elections of 2014 (see chapter by Varvelli and Villa in this volume).

In the first phase of the conflict in Libya, the EU imposed restrictive measures as part of a larger strategy aimed at isolating Gaddafi and changing the political leadership. The waves of protests that began in Tunisia in December 2010 also reached Libya in mid-February with a series of protests starting in Benghazi. The violent repression of the government (Adetunji et al. 2011) sparked a strong condemnation from the international community in general and the EU specifically, with a declaration of the HR/VP on 23 February (European Union 2011h) and the conclusions of the extraordinary European Council on 11 March 2011 (European Union 2011i). The UNSC passed Resolution 1970 condemning Libya's behaviour and imposing an arms embargo, a travel ban and an assets freeze, while referring the situation to the International Criminal Court (ICC) (United Nations 2011a). However, Gaddafi's forces made headway in the military operations in Libya, and the balance of the conflict was tilted in his favour. As a consequence, France and the UK above all pressed the UNSC to authorise further measures. The UNSC passed Resolution 1973 which imposed a no-fly zone over Libya and authorised the use of all necessary means to enforce it (United

Nations 2011b). This resolution triggered the military intervention which eventually became NATO operation Unified Protector.

The EU had a multiplier effect on UN strategy, and imposed autonomous sanctions, within the framework specified by UN resolutions, on 28 February with Council Decision 137, a day after the creation of the National Transitional Council of Libya (NTC), and toughened the implementation of sanctions with a provision on vessels inspection. The sanctions list was updated several times with regard to both the travel ban and the assets freeze. In September 2011, the UNSC and the EU delisted a number of entities falling under the control of the rebels, which indicated a clear support of the transition of the regime beyond the rule of Gaddafi (see Council Implementing Decision 521 of 1 September 2011, 543 of 15 September and Council Decision of 22 September). The killing of Gaddafi on 20 October seemed to mark the end of the crisis with the transition of the incumbent government to the NTC and the elections of the General National Congress (GNC) in 2013. The continued sanctions during the transition indicate that sanctions were designed to contain the effects of individuals from the former regime to spoil the consolidation process.

In the second phase, the EU and the UN used restrictive measures to sustain the fragile transition from the regime of Colonel Gaddafi to the institutional setting agreed upon in the Libyan Political Agreement (LPA) of December 2015. In 2014, tensions increased in the country with clashes to conquer Tripoli between the GNC, the forces of General Haftar, and the Islamist and Misrata-based militias. In August 2014, elections took place and the House of Representatives (HoR) was supposed to take over the role previously fulfilled by the GNC. However, the GNC refused to hand over power as a consequence of HoR's decision to establish its headquarter in Tobruk rather than in Benghazi. The Tripoli-based coalition of the GNC, and the Tobruk-based HoR supported by General Haftar, who had been integrated into the Libyan army, became the two main parties in conflict as they both received international recognition. The Libyan Political Agreement (LPA) was signed on 17 December 2015 and it foresaw the creation of a Presidency Council, a Government of National Accord (GNA) and the peaceful co-existence of two legislative bodies, namely, the HoR and a High Council of States, which would have included most members of the GNC. The EU welcomed the signing of the agreement and stood "ready to support the Government of National Accord as soon as it is formed"

(European Union 2015). This position is later affirmed more explicitly in Council Conclusions of 17 and 18 March 2016, in which the Council stated that "[t]he EU stands ready to support the Government of National Accord, as the sole legitimate government of Libya, including, at its request, to restore stability, fight terrorism and manage migration in the central Mediterranean" (European Union 2016b). Since this affirmation, the European Council has taken an interest in Libya only to the extent that it is the location of the threat posed by the Central Mediterranean Route for (irregular) migrants. However, as a number of de facto city-states exist in Libya, such as Sirte, Misrata and Benghazi, the resolution of the crisis is turning out to be extremely complicated.

In this second phase, sanctions reflected both the complexities on the ground and divisions among EU member states, with some countries supporting the government in Tobruk while others supporting the forces in Tripoli. Therefore, since 2014, the sanctions policy was mainly driven by the UN, while the EU limited itself to adjusting the UN regime done before 2015. In July 2015, the Council adopted Decision 1333, which consolidated its previous policy regimes, indicating that sanctions should target persons and entities responsible for the repressive policies of the former regime, and those involved in the misappropriation of funds. However, the EU also managed to expand the sanctions list to include individuals responsible for obstructing the consolidation process and the implementation of the December 2015 agreement. Council Decision 478 on 31 March 2016, for instance, listed an HoR member and two GNC members, and several Council Implementing Decisions targeted vessels accused of illegally exporting oil to other countries.[1] In 2016 and 2017, the EU tasked EUNAVFOR Med Sophia, the naval mission deployed in the Mediterranean to address the migration crisis, with monitoring the UN arms embargo (European Union 2016c) and the illegal trafficking of oil (European Union 2017b). Such measures and other sanctions aimed at undermining Libya's political and security consolidation have been implemented by the UN and transposed by the EU suggesting that sanctions were imposed to support the newly established, although fragile, institutions. For instance, Council Decision 1338 on 17 July 2017 identifies "[t]he smuggling of migrants and trafficking in

---

[1] See European Union (2016a) which will become also a UN indication with UNSCR 2362 of July 2017, and it will be followed by a number of listing of vessels in 2017 and 2018.

human beings" as a factor that "contributes to destabilising the political and security situation in Libya" (European Union 2017a). Such threats to the national authorities are countered with UN and EU sanctions. Even though only a handful of people have been listed, this is the first time that the UN, supported by the EU with Council Implementing Decision 872 of 14 June 2018, reached such a consensus. Another list was added by the Committee later in the year based on an indictment by the Libyan prosecutor general, which can be seen as another move to support the recognised Libyan national authorities.

Sanctions and the Resilience of MENA Countries

Building on the analysis of resilience as conceptualised in the Global Strategy provided by Anholt and Wagner in this volume, resilience aims at strengthening the capacity of national authorities and societies to withstand and adapt to external shocks. This final aim should be achieved by considering the unique particularities of each individual case with a tailor-made approach, rather than applying a one-size-fits-all solution. Resilience-based approaches should be inspired by principled pragmatism, and focus on the need for local ownership.

Within this perspective, the contribution of the use of restrictive measures in building resilience in the MENA region is inextricably linked to the nature of the crises for which sanctions are adopted. In fact, restrictive measures have always been understood as an exceptional measure adopted in extreme circumstances, unlike other foreign policy instruments used in normal situations. While restrictive measures have partly contributed to building resilience in Tunisia and Egypt, but have had much less noticeable impacts in Syria and Libya. When it comes to the imposition of sanctions and the strengthening of state capacity, the necessary premise is to have state institutions in place which can be strengthened. This was certainly the case for Tunisia and Egypt. In Syria and Egypt, by contrast, the situation was different. Restrictive measures in Tunisia and Egypt have been designed to sustain the consolidation process of the regimes after the departure of Ben Ali and Hosni Mubarak respectively. The freeze of assets on former officials was designed to recover the assets allegedly misappropriated enabled by individuals holding positions of particular power in the past. If successful, this policy would secure resources for the newly established governments, weaken the activities of potential *spoilers* to the process, and send a signal to the people that justice for past actions has been achieved.

The same cannot be said in Syria and, to a lesser extent, in Libya. The main difference between these two countries and Tunisia and Egypt is that sanctions were not imposed to sustain the party in power, but rather to weaken the existing and (at least partially) recognised government with the aim to strengthen societal resilience rather than state resilience. In Syria, Assad's government was the target of sanctions a few weeks into the crisis. Consequently, sanctions had the objective of weakening the regime in order to favour the opposition. In Libya too, at least initially, sanctions were imposed to undermine the actions of Gaddafi, who was committed to crushing opposition forces by military means. The utilisation of sanctions to protect human rights against incumbent regimes is less directly linked to the construction of resilient state institution. Rather, it could be linked to the strengthening of societies against human rights violations perpetrated by government authorities, but it is rather unclear how sanctions would contribute to achieve this goal.

This leads the current analysis to the important issue of the involvement of local actors and local context in the imposition of sanctions. In this regard, it can be argued that when sanctions against these countries were imposed, the local context was considered to different degrees. For instance, efforts to establish local ownership is clearly evident in the cases of Tunisia and Egypt. Sanctions were imposed at the request of local authorities and the fate of the sanctioned funds have been determined by the outcome of internal judicial processes, which have been working to identify individual responsibilities in previous regimes. In other words, the decision of resorting to sanctions was almost entirely based on the requests of local governments. When it comes to Syria and Libya, the situation on the ground made the EU pick the side of the rebels against the national authorities, no longer regarded as legitimate. In Syria, sanctions were requested by the rebel/opposition consortium. The case of Libya is even more complex. While in the beginning, the list included individuals belonging to governmental forces only, the complexity of the situation on the ground made it difficult to sustain the legitimate authority emerging from the political agreement in December 2015 to any significant degree. Therefore, restrictive measures followed the principle of local ownership with the formal recognition of the legitimate government, but local complexities and divisions among EU member states hampered any strong efforts to resolve the crisis (see chapter by Varvelli and Villa in this volume).

Finally, the notion of principled pragmatism appears to have inspired decisions taken by the EU in Tunisia and Egypt, while it was less influential in the cases of Syria and Libya. If principled pragmatism is understood as a realistic assessment of the actual possibilities to reach certain normative objectives, then the decision to support the oppositions in both Syria and Libya appears inconsistent. In fact, it is questionable that removing a regime without having alternatives is either principled or pragmatic. On the contrary, the EU limited the objectives of sanctions to achieve something feasible in the cases of Egypt and Tunisia, where principled pragmatism was effectively adopted.

Conclusions

As one of the main foreign policy instruments of the EU, restrictive measures have been used to strengthen the resilience of both states and societies. In its Southern Neighbourhood, the EU has resorted to sanctions aimed at building more resilient societies in Tunisia, Egypt, Syria and Libya. In general, the evolution of sanctions from a comprehensive to targeted nature has created the conditions for their use as a tool for conflict management and, especially, as a post-conflict management tool. Possibly, the ability to engage with internal political dynamics is one of the most important implications of the change in the use of restrictive measures, which has shifted from targeting states to targeting individuals and non-state entities. As a result, sanctions can be used to support the consolidation of new regimes, which in turn strengthens the resilience of states by building local capacities, in several ways. First, sanctions can curtail the capacity of internal actors playing the role of spoilers which may undermine national institutions. This is the case of travel bans and/or freeze of assets that target individuals benefiting from cross-border activities to acquire resources that can be spent in the domestic realm. Second, sanctions can sustain the capacity of state institutions to fulfil judicial functions. For instance, domestic judicial processes can be strengthened by the imposition of sanctions from international actors, so that decisions from local authorities are more likely to produce tangible effects. In general, sanctions do complement the actions of national institutions and, therefore, sanctions work towards building resilience of local institutions to external as well as internal shocks.

However, sanctions are just one of the many, and possibly not the most important, policy instruments at the disposal of policymakers in

Brussels and EU member states. At the very least, a basic foreign policy strategy is built on the carrot and stick principle, so sanctions would only ever constitute one side of the story. On the other side, a careful policy of incentives and aid should also be designed to achieve desired results. The transformative potential of sanctions in building resilient societies should, therefore, not be overestimated.

The understanding that sanctions cannot solve all problems, but that they can contribute to the resilience of state authorities has inspired the approach of the EU in using sanctions in the MENA region in response to the crises in Tunisia, Egypt, Libya and Syria. Especially in the first three cases, restrictive measures were designed with the objective of strengthening the resilience of local states and societies. In Tunisia and Egypt, the EU decided to rely on sanctions after the new regimes were established. After Ben Ali and Hosni Mubarak left power, sanctions were imposed to facilitate the re-appropriation of state funds by targeting individuals under investigation by local authorities for embezzlement. In the case of Libya and Syria, sanctions were initially used to fulfil a more "classical" function of weakening the parties in power. Whereas in the Syrian case a second "phase" never materialised because Assad's regime did not fall, the Libyan case reflects the precedent set by the cases of Tunisia and Egypt, namely, the imposition of restrictive measures to target both potential spoilers of the consolidation of the new regime, and of any activities aimed at circumventing such sanctions. Certainly, the complexity of the situation on the ground does not allow to isolate the impact of sanctions in the evolution of the crisis for analytical purposes, but the development of such policies was premised on the idea of sustaining the consolidation of newly established national authorities.

There are indications that restrictive measures can contribute to the building of resilient states and societies. The EU experience has shown that sanctions can support the capacity of local authorities in their judicial processes, and in thwarting or weakening spoilers. However, sanctions are only part of the story because several other instruments, especially the provision of aid and technical expertise, can have a multiplier effect on the effectiveness of restrictive measures. For instance, the case of Tunisia shows that the policy conditionality embedded within the ENP can complement positively restrictive measures against spoilers. At the same time, intricate conflicts such as in Syria and Libya are extreme cases that should not be taken as reliable pilot to assess the overall effectiveness of restrictive measures in strengthening resilience, especially when it comes to resilient societies. While necessary, sanctions are not in themselves sufficient to strengthen state and, above all, societal resilience. Therefore, further efforts are required, also from analysts and pundits, to identify the most appropriate combination of instruments that need to be adopted in each crisis.

References

Adetunji, J., Beaumont, P., & Chulov, M. (2011). Libya Protests: More than 100 Killed as Army Fires on Unarmed Demonstrators. *The Guardian*.

Biersteker, T. J., & Eckert, S. E. (2009). *Addressing Challenges to Targeted Sanctions: An Update of the 'Watson Report'*. Providence, RI: Watson Institute for International Studies.

European Union. (2004). *'Basic Principles on the Use of Restrictive Measures (Sanctions)' 10198/1/04 (Generic)*. http://register.consilium.europa.eu/doc/srv?l=EN&f=ST%2010198%202004%20REV%201.

European Union. (2009). *Council Regulation (EC) No 428/2009 of 5 May 2009 Setting Up a Community Regime for the Control of Exports, Transfer, Brokering and Transit of Dual-Use Items*. Brussels: Council of the European Union. https://eur-lex.europa.eu/legal-content/EN/TXT/PDF/?uri=CELEX:02009R0428-20171216&from=EN.

European Union. (2011a). *Council Decision 2011/72/CFSP of 31 January 2011 Concerning Restrictive Measures Directed Against Certain Persons and Entities in View of the Situation in Tunisia*. Brussels: The Council of the European Union.

European Union. (2011b). *Council Decision 2011/172/CFSP of 21 March 2011 Concerning Restrictive Measures Directed Against Certain Persons, Entities and Bodies in View of the Situation in Egypt*. Brussels: The Council of the European Union.

European Union. (2011c). *Council Decision 2011/273/CFSP of 9 May 2011 Concerning Restrictive Measures Against Syria*. Brussels: The Council of the European Union.

European Union. (2011d). *Council Decision 2011/522/CFSP of 2 September 2011 Amending Decision 2011/273/CFSP Concerning Restrictive Measures Against Syria*. Brussels: The Council of the European Union.

European Union. (2011e). *Council Decision 2011/684/CFSP of 13 October 2011 Amending Decision 2011/273/CFSP Concerning Restrictive Measures Against Syria*. Brussels: The Council of the European Union.

European Union. (2011f). *Council Implementing Decision 2011/302/CFSP of 23 May 2011 Implementing Decision 2011/273/CFSP Concerning Restrictive Measures Against Syria*. Brussels: The Council of the European Union.

European Union. (2011g). *Council Implementing Decision 2011/79/CFSP of 4 February 2011 Implementing Decision 2011/72/CFSP Concerning Restrictive Measures Directed Against Certain Persons and Entities in View of the Situation in Tunisia*. Brussels: The Council of the European Union.

European Union. (2011h). *Declaration by the High Representative Catherine Ashton on Behalf of the European Union on Libya*. Press Release 36. Brussels: European External Action Service. http://europa.eu/rapid/press-release_PESC-11-36_en.htm.

European Union. (2011i, March 17). *European Council Conclusions*. Brussels: Council of the European Union. http://data.consilium.europa.eu/doc/document/ST-7-2011-INIT/en/pdf.

European Union. (2011j, February 21). *European Council Conclusions*. Brussels: Council of the European Union. https://www.consilium.europa.eu/uedocs/cms_data/docs/pressdata/EN/foraff/119435.pdf.

European Union. (2012a). *Council Decision 2012/206/CFSP of 23 April 2012 Amending Decision 2011/782/CFSP Concerning Restrictive Measures Against Syria*. Brussels: The Council of the European Union.

European Union. (2012b). *'Guidelines on Implementation and Evaluation of Restrictive Measures (Sanctions) in the Framework of the EU Common Foreign and Security Policy' 11205/12 (Generic)*. http://data.consilium.europa.eu/doc/document/ST-11205-2012-COR-2/en/pdf.

European Union. (2013). *Council Decision 2013/760/CFSP of 13 December 2013 Amending Decision 2013/255/CFSP Concerning Restrictive Measures Against Syria*. Brussels: The Council of the European Union.

European Union. (2015, December 17 and 18). *European Council Conclusions*. Brussels: Council of the European Union. http://data.consilium.europa.eu/doc/document/ST-28-2015-INIT/en/pdf.

European Union. (2016a). *Council Implementing Decision (CFSP) 2016/694 of 4 May 2016 Implementing Decision (CFSP) 2015/1333 Concerning Restrictive Measures in View of the Situation in Libya*. Brussels: The Council of the European Union.

European Union. (2016b, March 17 and 18). *European Council Conclusions*. Brussels: Council of the European Union. http://data.consilium.europa.eu/doc/document/ST-12-2016-REV-1/en/pdf.

European Union. (2016c, June 20). *European Council Conclusions*. Brussels: Council of the European Union. https://www.consilium.europa.eu/media/22881/st10495en16.pdf.

European Union. (2016d). *'Restrictive Measures (Sanctions) Update of the EU Best Practices for the Effective Implementation of Restrictive Measures' 15530/16 (Generic)*. http://data.consilium.europa.eu/doc/document/ST-15530-2016-INIT/en/pdf.

European Union. (2017a). *Council Decision 2017/1338/CFSP of 17 July 2017 Amending Decision (CFSP) 2015/1333 Concerning Restrictive Measures in View of the Situation in Libya*. Brussels: The Council of the European Union.

European Union. (2017b). *Council Decision (CFSP) 2017/1385 of 25 July 2017 Amending Decision (CFSP) 2015/778 on a European Union Military Operation in the Southern Central Mediterranean (EUNAVFOR MED Operation SOPHIA)*. Brussels: The Council of the European Union.

European Union. (2018). *Council Decisions (CFSP) 2018/466 of 21 March 2018 Amending Decision 2011/172/CFSP Concerning Restrictive Measures Directed Against Certain Persons, Entities and Bodies in View of the Situation in Egypt*. Brussels: The Council of the European Union.

Giumelli, F. (2013a). *How EU Sanctions Work: A New Narrative* (Chaillot Paper). Paris: EU Institute for Security Studies.

Giumelli, F. (2013b) *The Success of Sanctions: Lessons Learned from the EU Experience*. Book, Whole. Farnham: Ashgate.

International Crisis Group. (2011a). *Popular Protest in North Africa and the Middle East (I): Egypt Victorious?* (Middle East/North Africa Report 101).

International Crisis Group. (2011b). *Popular Protests in North Africa and the Middle East (IV): Tunisia's Way* (Middle East/North Africa Report 106).

Kreutz, J. (2005). *Hard Measures by a Soft Power? Sanctions Policy of the European Union* (Paper 45). Bonn: Bonn International Center for Conversion (BICC). https://www.bicc.de/uploads/tx_bicctools/paper45.pdf.

Larik, J. (2014). The Kadi Saga as a Tale of 'Strict Observance' of International Law: Obligations Under the UN Charter, Targeted Sanctions and Judicial Review in the European Union. *Netherlands International Law Review, 61*(1), 23–42.

MEE and Agencies. (2018, May 29). Tunisia Court Begins First Human Rights Trial Against Former Leader Ben Ali. *Middle East Eye*. https://www.middleeasteye.net/news/tunisia-rights-commission-begins-court-case-against-ben-ali-1936015907.

Portela, C. (2010). *European Union Sanctions and Foreign Policy: When and Why Do They Work*. Oxon: Routledge.

Rifai, R. (2011, January 23). Timeline: Tunisia's Uprising. *Aljazeera*.

Traynor, I. (2013). UK Forces EU to Lift Embargo on Syria Rebel Arms. *The Guardian*.

United Nations. (2011a). *Resolution 1970*. New York: Security Council.

United Nations. (2011b). *Resolution 1973*. New York: Security Council.

CHAPTER 7

European Energy Security and the Resilience of Southern Mediterranean Countries

Luca Franza, Coby van der Linde and Pier Stapersma

INTRODUCTION

The aim of this chapter is to provide a critical overview of energy security issues across the Mediterranean. The inclusion of a chapter dedicated to energy in a volume on security and resilience across the Mediterranean is consistent with the renewed interest in energy security by institutions such as NATO and the European Union (EU).

NATO's role in energy security—first defined at the 2008 Bucharest Summit—has traditionally been centred around support to national authorities in protecting energy infrastructure. In the last decade, energy security has acquired an increasingly prominent role in NATO's agenda and the organisation has been seeking to boost its strategic awareness in this field. Today, NATO recognises energy as a key factor affecting international security and energy security as a key element of resilience.

The EU, which is more directly involved in energy policy-making through a dedicated Directorate-General (DG Energy), has also stepped

L. Franza (✉) · C. van der Linde · P. Stapersma
Clingendael International Energy Programme (CIEP),
The Hague, The Netherlands
e-mail: luca.franza@clingendaelenergy.com

© The Author(s) 2020
E. Cusumano and S. Hofmaier (eds.),
Projecting Resilience Across the Mediterranean,
https://doi.org/10.1007/978-3-030-23641-0_7

up its involvement in energy security issues in the last decade. Alongside affordability and sustainability, security is one of the three pillars of EU energy policy-making. The European Commission released a new Energy Security Strategy in May 2014. Security of supply regulations specific to gas and electricity have also been issued in the last years. The Energy Union policy framework adopted in 2015 emphasised the importance of security, solidarity and diversification of routes, suppliers and sources of energy. The EU is also financing projects that it considers beneficial to energy security.

Both NATO's and the EU's renewed emphasis on energy security appears motivated by growing concerns on Russian gas, in the context of deteriorating political relations. One of the key arguments of this chapter is that other energy security challenges, including those in the Mediterranean region, risk being overshadowed by the current emphasis on Russia.

The first section of this chapter outlines the structural factors that affect energy security in the Southern and Eastern Mediterranean (SEMED)[1] region. This section serves the purpose of highlighting important distinctions among SEMED countries as well as between the SEMED and the wider Middle East and North Africa (MENA) region. The second section offers an analysis of the evolving significance of the SEMED region for Europe's energy security. This analysis focusses on Algeria and Libya, the two net energy-exporting countries in the region. The third section discusses the role of energy in the wider security landscape in the SEMED, as well as the nature of Europe's and NATO's energy security engagement with the region. Finally, the fourth section identifies future opportunities in regional energy relations offered by the SEMED's significant renewable energy production potential. Throughout the chapter, we adopt a broad interpretation of the notion of 'energy security' that goes beyond the military protection of physical assets—incorporating macro-economic, social, and environmental factors. This inclusive approach also resonates in the concept of 'hybrid threat' (Cusumano and Corbe 2018), describing security challenges that combine military and non-military, as well as overt and covert dimensions.

[1] The countries analysed in this chapter are located in full or for the most part outside of Europe and that have a Mediterranean shoreline: Morocco, Algeria, Tunisia, Libya, Egypt, Israel, the Palestinian Territories, Lebanon, Syria and Turkey. This region is referred to as 'Southern and Eastern Mediterranean' or 'SEMED', the acronym adopted by the European Bank for Reconstruction and Development (EBRD).

Energy Security Across the Region

As part of the broader MENA region, Southern and Eastern Mediterranean countries are often grouped together with Gulf countries in energy studies, with the result of analytically important differentiations being lost. The SEMED region is heterogenous when it comes to energy: it includes both oil and gas heavyweights, and countries with some of the highest energy dependency rates in the world. More energy-importing countries are found along the Mediterranean than in the rest of the MENA region. Conversely, the SEMED region overall has a more important role for terrestrial energy transit than the Gulf,[2] although countries across the SEMED region also differ in terms of their strategic value as energy transit corridors. Demography and the level of economic development add further diversity to the picture. All these variables affect the energy security standing of countries in the region on a macro-level.

Table 7.1 provides a synopsis of these variables, illustrating the net energy import position, energy intensity,[3] and carbon intensity[4] of the countries analysed. The first piece of information derived from the synopsis is that the SEMED region is a net *importer* of energy.

The region does nevertheless include two major oil and gas exporters: Algeria and Libya. Figures for Libya are reflective of the instability in the country, as its net energy exports were significantly higher prior to 2011. Egypt, and, to a lesser extent, Syria are relatively important oil and gas producers but also (increasingly) large consumers—which explains their net importer status. Egypt, home to one-third of the region's population, only became a net oil importer in 2006 and a net gas importer in 2012. The case of Egypt is in many ways illustrative of what could happen in other MENA producing countries with fast population growth rates, if measures

---

[2] In the Persian Gulf, hydrocarbons are primarily exported to world markets through coastal terminals.

[3] The indicator Total Primary Energy Supply per Capita (TPES/Pop) shows the energy intensity of the country (in this context, supply needs to be understood as supply *to* the country, so it is in fact an indicator of energy usage rather than production). The indicator 'TPES/GDP', on the other hand, shows the energy intensity of the country's economy.

[4] The indicator 'CO_2/TPES' shows the carbon intensity of the country's energy mix (how much carbon is contained in every unit of energy supplied to the country), 'CO_2/Pop' shows carbon emissions per capita and CO_2/GDP the carbon intensity of the country's economy.

Table 7.1 Key figures on Southern Mediterranean countries

	Population (million)	GDP (billion $)	GDP per capita ($)	Net imports (Mtoe)	TPES/Pop (toe)	TPES/GDP (toe/000 $)	CO_2/TPES (tCO_2/toe)	CO_2/Pop (tCO_2/capita)	CO_2/GDP ($kgCO_2$/$)
Algeria	40.6	196.8	4847	−98.9	1.32	0.27	2.37	3.14	0.65
Egypt	95.7	260.7	2724	19.3	0.90	0.33	2.38	2.14	0.79
Israel	8.5	289.0	34000	15.1	2.69	0.08	2.78	7.46	0.22
Lebanon	6.0	41.9	6983	7.9	1.29	0.19	2.98	3.86	0.55
Libya	6.3	18.8	2984	−14.5	2.39	0.80	2.87	6.88	2.31
Morocco	35.3	114.5	3244	18.6	0.55	0.17	2.84	1.57	0.48
Syria	18.4	15.3	832	5.9	0.54	0.65	2.63	1.42	1.70
Tunisia	11.4	48.6	4263	5.2	0.96	0.23	2.29	2.21	0.52
Turkey	78.2	1122.5	14354	105.7	1.75	0.12	2.48	4.33	0.30
Region	**300.4**	**2108.1**	**7018**	**64.3**	**1.21**	**0.17**	**2.50**	**3.02**	**0.43**
World	**7334**	**75489**	**10293**	/	**1.86**	**0.18**	**2.37**	**4.4**	**0.43**

to keep energy demand in check are not implemented. Conversely, the other countries of the region have traditionally been heavily import-dependent, owing to resource scarcity. Among them, Israel has promising prospects for reducing its import dependency as plans for the exploitation of recent gas findings offshore are quite developed.

Energy intensity also varies across the region. In line with global patterns, more prosperous countries like Israel and Turkey display higher energy consumption rates per capita, but also higher outputs of GDP per input of energy. Unsurprisingly, oil and gas producing countries tend to have the most energy-intensive economies. Decoupling economic growth from energy use is a priority particularly for Syria and Egypt, which have highly energy-intensive economies while being net importers of energy. In the case of Syria, the reconstruction of the economy, if and when the conflict in the country ends, will require entering a new energy-intensive phase of development in parts of the country. In stark contrast with the rest of the MENA region, per capita CO_2 emissions tend to be below the world's average. This is mostly owing to relatively low per capita energy consumption. To the contrary, on average, the carbon intensity of the energy mix is high—particularly in Lebanon and Morocco where imported coal and oil are widely used for power generation. War-torn Libya and Syria are the least efficient in transforming energy inputs into GDP and also have the most carbon-intensive economies.

The Evolving Importance of EU-SEMED Energy Security Relations

Oil and gas exporting countries of the SEMED region have historically played an important role in European energy security. Endowed with sizeable oil and gas reserves and strategically located in Europe's geographical neighbourhood, they have contributed to diversifying the European energy import mix. Algerian gas has also contributed to stimulating competition between gas sources—which has become important for the affordability of the European energy import mix. In turn, Europe is the most important market for SEMED oil and gas, and therefore a key energy security counterpart for oil and gas producing countries in the region.

In the course of the 2010s, however, unprecedented political instability has negatively affected energy supply from the SEMED and the adjacent Sahel and the Middle East regions, more markedly so than in

Table 7.2 Energy disruptions in SEMED countries

Country	Disruptions to energy supplies or energy projects
Algeria	A terrorist attack hitting the In Amenas gas plant results in a temporary 10% gas supply reduction in 2013
Cyprus	Territorial disputes with Turkey complicate plans for offshore gas monetisation
Egypt	Political instability reduces the ability to export oil and gas (stagnant investments, mismanagement of the energy sector); constant attacks on pipelines in the Sinai Peninsula
Israel	Deliberations to monetise gas face a high degree of securitisation, which worsens the investment climate
Libya	Oil production shrinks from approximately 2,000,000 mb/d to 400,000 mb/d as a result of political turmoil beginning in 2011. Non-state actors seize control of oil and gas assets
Syria	The country's oil and gas production is severely hit by the civil war beginning in 2011. Non-state actors seize control of oil and gas assets
Turkey	The reliability of the country as a prospective energy gateway for Europe is disputed as Kurdish fighters repeatedly target pipelines in the South-east of the country and as Turkey-EU relations deteriorate

any other region of the world. Considering that the European energy security discourse is disproportionately focussed on Russia, recognising energy security challenges in the SEMED (Table 7.2) is important, also in light of the continued dependency of Southern European countries on energy supply from the SEMED. The focus of the next sections will be on Algeria and Libya, the region's largest oil and gas producing countries, and its only oil and gas net exporters.

Algeria

Algeria has historically been an important oil supplier for the EU, but its production is declining. Its competitiveness has rested on the size and location of its fields as well as on the high quality of its crude oil. The bulk of Algeria's 12.2 billion barrel oil reserves[5] is concentrated in three large fields in its North-Central and Central-Eastern regions[6]

---

[5] This makes Algeria the 16th country in the world for oil reserves.

[6] Hassi Messaoud, Hassi 'r Mel (also the country's largest gas field) and Ourhoud have combined oil reserves of 9.5 billion barrels (close to 80% of the country's total).

which are now mature.[7] Investments in field expansions and Enhanced Oil Recovery (EOR)[8] have delayed decline for years, but are no longer sufficient. As a result, Algerian production peaked at 2 MMb/d in 2007 and has since then decreased to 1.5 MMb/d (BP 2018). No other major crude oil project is expected to come on stream. Europe's importance for Algerian security of demand, historically high, has been further strengthened by recent developments in international oil markets. This is because, although North America used to be a very important outlet market for Algeria's high-quality 'Sahara Blend'[9] until the 2000s, a lot of Algeria's oil has been rerouted to Europe as a result of the rise in US shale production.[10] Crude oil exports to the EU alone yielded 6 billion USD for Algeria in 2017 (3% of GDP), a notable decline from the 2013–2014 peak (Eurostat 2018). This decline has both volume and price reasons, and the recent recovery of oil prices may bring oil export income up again in 2018. On the other hand, no European country appears disproportionately reliant on Algerian oil.[11] Algeria also has the capacity to refine products, which are mostly consumed domestically. Algeria has multiple coastal terminals to export oil and a pipeline to the Tunisian terminal of La Skhirra, but no oil pipelines cross the Mediterranean (Graph 7.1).

Algeria is also the world's 11th gas reserve holder with 4.3 Tcm of gas underground (BP 2018). Algerian gas production is concentrated in large fields (particularly Hassi 'r Mel), and is on a long-term decline path due to depletion. Gas production has recently increased from 81 Bcm in 2015 to 91 Bcm in 2017, reflecting the beginning of operations in the southwestern fields. This is however only a temporary recovery, as

---

[7] The advanced stage of exploitation of Algerian oil fields is mirrored by Algeria's Reserve-to-Production (R/P) ratio of 21.7—as opposed to a world average of 50.2 and a Middle East average of 71.0.

[8] Enhanced Oil Recovery, a technique used to extract higher quantities of oil from (typically mature) oil fields and involving thermal, chemical or gas injection.

[9] The Sahara Blend is a light crude oil with low sulfur content.

[10] In 2007 Algerian oil exports to the US peaked at 443,000 b/d (EIA).

[11] The largest countries of Europe also feature as the main importers of Algerian crude, implying that Algerian market share is fairly balanced overall across Europe. Besides, intra-European destinations of Algerian oil tend to change quite remarkably from one year to another. In 2016, the main importers were France, Germany, Spain, Italy, The Netherlands and the UK. The majority of EU exports of Algerian Natural Gas Liquids (NGLs) are, on the other hand, structurally directed to The Netherlands.

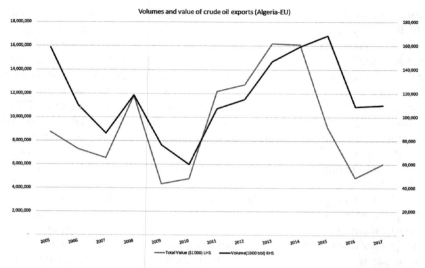

Graph 7.1 Volumes and value of crude oil exports between Algeria and the EU

production from new fields will not offset production decline in legacy fields. One way to reverse this decline would be to tap the country's immense shale gas resources—contained in the Ghadames Basin, which stretches across the Libyan border. However, limited geological survey data, difficulties in attracting foreign investments, and public opposition to shale exploration make this option difficult. Gas is exported via three pipelines (the Maghreb-Europe to Spain via Morocco, the Medgaz directly to Spain, and the Transmed to Italy via Tunisia). In the context of regional instability, it is notable that transit through Morocco and Tunisia has never suffered major setbacks. Even if political relations between Algeria and Morocco have been problematic, the two countries have cooperated effectively on gas trade. Plans to build additional pipelines (the GALSI to Sardinia and the Trans-Saharan project) are stalling due to declining availability of export volumes. Algeria also has two liquefied natural gas (LNG) terminals (Arzew and Skikda), which have now reached full functionality after delays and technical failures.

Absorbing 80% of Algeria's gas exports (BP 2018), the EU has a key role for the North African country's security of demand. Algeria has invested in LNG to diversify demand, but piped volumes remain dominant. Large volumes of Algerian LNG end up in the EU because netbacks are favourable owing to low transportation costs, but Algeria also has the option to ship cargoes elsewhere. Unlike oil, the strategic significance of Algerian gas is geographically localised to Southern Europe, as Italy and Spain absorb the bulk of the volumes (33 Bcm, or 62% of Algeria's total exports [BP 2018]).[12] On the other hand, Algerian gas covers less than 10% of European demand (but 43% of Spanish demand and 26% of Italian demand [BP 2018]). The shortage of South–North transport capacity prevents Central and Northern Europe from tapping Algerian gas.

In Italy, Algeria's main competitor is Russian gas, which balanced Algeria's faltering volumes on a number of occasions. Algeria's flexibility to adjust shipments depending on the buyer's request appears more limited. In recent years, this has not posed problems: when Italy was over-contracted, Algeria agreed to reduce exports owing to its own domestic shortages. Algeria then sold additional output once Italian demand recovered, which coincided with a fortuitous upturn in Algerian production. On the price side, Sonatrach, Algeria's government-owned oil and gas company, has been a staunch defendant of oil indexation. However, Italian importers have obtained a change in pricing terms and Algerian gas now contributes to gas-to-gas competition in the country. In Spain, the main competitor of Algerian gas is LNG.[13] Historically, the Spanish government has been concerned about its exposure to Algerian gas imports—so much that gas supply diversification was codified into law. Diversification away from Algeria has been a key driver of Spanish efforts to build LNG terminals. Price renegotiations are difficult as the Iberian market is not well integrated with the rest of Europe's, which is also an issue for security of supply.

Libya

Libya has historically important energy security links with Europe. Libya has always sold the bulk of its crude oil to European countries (84% in 2014)—among which Italy has been its largest buyer (Eurostat 2018). Major European oil companies, particularly ENI and Total, have huge stakes in the country. With an estimated 48.4 billion barrels, Libya is the world's 10th oil reserve holder (BP 2018). Political complications struck early in the history of the country, whose oil production had already peaked

---

[12] Other countries, such as Portugal and Slovenia, also consume Algerian gas, but in significantly smaller amounts.

[13] Albeit some LNG comes from Algeria, which also owns regasification capacity in Spain.

at 3 MMb/d in the 1960s and subsequently declined due to nationalisation and sanctions hampering investments and procurement. At the onset of the 2011 civil war, the country was producing 1.6 MMb/d (BP 2018). Since then, production has been volatile. After being restored in 2012, it fell again in 2013 with a renewed deterioration in the security environment which witnessed the first deliberate attacks on national oil infrastructure—particularly in the Sirte Basin and in the East. Security remains precarious. Militant groups including the Islamic State (IS) are still active in the Sirte basin. Oil and gas fields, pipelines and export terminals are contested by different factions, notably including the Petroleum Facility Guard (PFG) and pro-Haftar militias. Labour-related protests by local groups and the political struggle to seize control of oil revenues further exacerbate the instability. The fact that prolonged shutdowns have reduced pressure at wells, critical infrastructure has been deeply damaged, and the security environment has further deteriorated, makes it difficult for European countries to count on steady Libyan oil supplies in the short to medium term.

Libya is also a net exporter of gas, albeit at a much smaller scale than neighbouring Algeria. In 2017, its gas reserves and production amounted to 1.4 Tcm (20th largest in the world) and 11.5 Bcm, respectively (BP 2018). Libya consumed 7 Bcm of gas domestically and exported 4.5 Bcm, the entirety of which went to Italy via the Greenstream pipeline, which constitutes a mere 5% of Italian gas consumption (BP 2018). Prior to the civil war, the country used to export small amounts of LNG to Spain, but the liquefaction terminal has been closed due to heavy damage. Pre-war plans to boost natural gas production were expected to result in greater use of gas for power generation, increasing the availability of oil volumes for export. Similar to oil, these plans depend on the country's security environment.

Resilience and New Opportunities

Energy in the SEMED is not only a story of instability, but also a story of resilience. In spite of conflicts and volatility, the oil and gas industry has displayed a high degree of resilience by persisting through highly challenging environments, and by pledging continued investment in exploration and production. The 2010s have not only been marked by instability, but also by the largest gas discovery ever made in the Mediterranean Sea (Zohr). The Eastern Mediterranean is now firmly on the map as one of the world's most promising frontier areas for gas.

Egypt hosts Zohr, a giant field found by ENI in 2015, and already brought on stream. After having been a net exporter of gas, Egypt had to stop its LNG exports via the Idku and Damietta terminals and its piped gas exports to Israel and Jordan via the Arab Gas Pipeline, turning into a net importer in 2012. Booming domestic demand and mismanagement of the energy sector have been responsible for this unfortunate transformation. On the other hand, the introduction of Floating Storage Regasification Unit (FSRU) technology has meant that the country has quickly become able to absorb LNG imports from world markets. With the Zohr discovery, Egypt's position will almost certainly improve. While the domestic market will be prioritised, there will most likely be surpluses of production, which could be liquified in the idle LNG terminals and exported to world markets. Europe would be well positioned to receive Egyptian LNG, owing to low transportation costs. That being said, volumes from Egypt are expected to be destination-flexible, that is, dependent on prices in import markets and Egyptian demand fluctuations.

In the absence of better evacuation routes, Israel plans to ship part of its gas from the Leviathan field to Egypt for internal consumption, but also potentially for liquefaction at Idku and Damietta. The other options on the table to transport Israeli gas out of the region would be a pipeline to Turkey and a pipeline to Greece. The former (Turkey route) would probably be more economical because of its shorter route but plans are complicated by politics, as the infrastructure would either have to cross Lebanese and Syrian waters or Cypriot waters. The latter (Greek route) would be very challenging from an economic and technical point of view. Furthermore, there are doubts that European gas demand (and especially South-eastern European gas demand) will be high enough in the next years to justify such an investment. Because of complicated evacuation plans, and internal pressures to retain gas for national security reasons, Israel has gradually downsized its global gas ambitions. The country seems settled for regional export plans, including exports to Jordan and Egypt. Because the situation is not much easier in Cyprus, where reserves are much smaller and political relations with Turkey are strained, and Lebanon, where exploration is at a much less advanced stage and perceived investment risks are high, Israeli gas liquefied in Egypt may very well be the only volumes of East Mediterranean gas that Europe will ever receive.

In addition to local specificities, there is an overarching reason why new gas projects earmarked for supplying Europe are struggling, namely the reluctance to sign long-term contracts on the part of European buyers. The European gas market architecture has changed so radically in the last decade that deliberate diversification policies based on constructing transaction-specific infrastructure are no longer feasible. Europe has chosen a security-of-supply model which rests on a shorter-term gas-to-gas competition. While this model enables Europe to receive flexible LNG from all around the world, it discourages prospective developers of point-to-point pipelines, who require long-term guarantees, to take investment decisions.

This also explains why conditions for additional supplies through the Southern Gas Corridor (SGC) are not favourable at the moment. It is true that gas from Azerbaijan will flow via the TANAP-TAP system after 2020 because a final investment decision has been made and contracts have been signed. However, it is important to recognise that Azerbaijani volumes will reach flows of 10 Bcm/y—a modest amount compared to the EU's total gas consumption, which amounted to 491 Bcm in 2017 (European Commission 2019), and the quantities envisaged by initial SGC plans. Plans to ship gas to the EU from Iraqi Kurdistan, Iran and Turkmenistan are also on the table, but they are complicated by both economic and geopolitical factors. All this points to the fact that Turkey's role as a major energy gateway for Europe is questionable. Turkey's transit may be limited to Azeri gas shipped via TAP and, possibly, Russian gas rerouted from Ukraine to Turk Stream, a pipeline under the Black Sea that is currently under construction. In such a scenario, the EU would be dependent on Turkish transit for around 5% of its gas consumption around 2020 (assuming stable consumption).

Energy in the Broader Security Landscape and Europe's Policy-Making

The previous sections explain that Southern and Eastern Mediterranean countries have played a historically important role in European security of supply. This role is now being challenged by high domestic demand in the SEMED region, scarce investment signals from Europe and country-specific geopolitical and economic factors. On the other hand, we noted how the energy industry has been resilient in face of a precarious security environment, that energy trade has in some cases cemented cooperation, and finally that new monetisation and trade opportunities have recently arisen.

In addition to these considerations, energy plays a role in SEMED's broader security landscape. Energy trade with Europe has brought sizeable revenues to the oil and gas producing countries in the region. In part, these revenues have been used to finance infrastructure and welfare provisions. Arguably, up until the early 2010s, they have also subdued creeping ethnic, tribal, social and religious tensions, and have consolidated the stability of authoritarian political regimes. Producing countries have been generally unable to translate these revenues into widespread prosperity and sustainable development. The unexpected outbreak of the Libyan civil war in 2011 demonstrated that stability may exist only on the superficial level, and may be hiding brewing tensions.

Persistent problems in SEMED producing countries include high unemployment rates—as the hydrocarbon sector is capital-intensive but not labour-intensive; overreliance on oil and gas revenues—whose volatility is sensitive to international prices beyond SEMED countries' control; and distortions produced by fossil fuel subsidies—including an inefficient use of energy, spiralling demand and smuggling. Smuggling has also increased in the region due to the presence of non-state actors. Although oil and gas have locally been important sources of revenues for terrorist organisations in Libya and Syria, the role of these terrorist organisations in global and even regional oil and gas trade has been, and remains, very marginal.

Looking beyond the large oil and gas exporters, Tunisia and Egypt also experienced political turmoil in which poverty, a lack of jobs and other social issues played a major role. Both countries are now trying to strike a new balance, although the underlying social issues have not been resolved. Morocco has been remarkably stable in the years subsequent to the Arab Spring, although it is now experiencing social unrest in its poorer provinces. Lebanon is most affected by the large influx of Syrian refugees, which are a great burden on the already depressed economy and fragile political balance. The country has also been late to capture the potential of offshore resources and is lagging behind other East Mediterranean countries in creating a proper investment climate. Turkey has played an important role in deciding how to monetise its East Mediterranean gas resources. Turkey is, on the one hand, a potential market, but on the other hand also a political risk if it were to become a transit country for aggregated gas supplies from Egypt and Israel. The politics in the region favours LNG as the best way to monetise the resources and avoid further political complications. The political fragility of the producing countries and uncertainty vis-à-vis European gas demand, where particularly Southern EU countries have suffered from the impact of the financial and economic crisis, have complicated the ability of SEMED countries to reap the benefits of their energy wealth. These countries are therefore demonstrating a cautious approach to the development of East Mediterranean energy resources.

Finally, Europe and NATO's engagement in the region with regard to energy security deserves attention. Assessments of the strategic value of the region for energy differ across Europe. While a priority for Southern European countries, the region does not always receive a lot of attention by other EU Member State, who normally emphasise Russia and the Eastern Neighbourhood. While the EU is a prominent actor in relations between Europe and Russia, energy relations with North African countries are mostly managed bilaterally by Southern European countries. The EU's reluctance to engage more actively with SEMED countries can be explained by several factors.

First, the broader MENA region has long been dominated by US engagement, whose energy priorities left little space for the EU to develop its own policy in SEMED other than through initiatives such as the European Neighbourhood Policy (ENP). For a long time, the US was very sensitive to energy relations that would create exclusive relations and could hinder energy being offered on international markets for the highest bidder. Second, EU's reluctance to follow up on the Moroccan and Turkish accession also played an important role, while France and Italy were also protective of their special interests and role in certain countries in the region against interference from Brussels.

Third, the successful campaign of Eastern European countries to focus energy security discussions on Russia has limited the ability to actively engage in SEMED.

Fourth, the recent attention to climate change made energy policy-making in SEMED also complicated because the EU communicates in terms of backing out of fossil fuels, including natural gas, even though the speed at which this could be realised should not hinder relations with SEMED countries. The uncertainty of EU gas demand did impact the investments in the region to develop the newly discovered offshore resources.

Fifth, the difference in SEMED countries, and the priorities of other security dossiers have played a prominent role in the past 10 years, rendering obsolete energy as a way to build a special relationship and create security of demand and supply. Given the potential of the region to produce renewables, and against the backdrop of growing energy demands in the SEMED countries, competing with exports to the EU and international markets, we conclude that there is room for stepping up political engagement.

WILL OIL AND GAS TRADE GIVE WAY TO A NEW FORM OF ENERGY TRADE?

This chapter highlighted that, in addition to an unstable security environment, a common challenge faced across SEMED countries is a fast-rising domestic energy demand. This is likely to negatively affect the availability of energy exports in future. Contrary to those ambitions and optimistic expectations prevalent in the early 2010s, the transit role of the region is also unlikely to be enhanced substantially in the next decade—for the reasons enumerated above. These points indicate the conclusion that oil and gas trade interdependence between the EU and the SEMED may suffer as a result of instability, lower export availability, doubts on transit, and competition from non-OECD Asia.

Against this background, renewable forms of energy might offer new, interesting opportunities for energy trade—particularly in electricity generated by Concentrated Solar Power (CSP) plants. The long-term potential to convert electricity to tradables, such as hydrogen, or directly export through cross-border electricity interconnectors might lead to a new era in energy relations between SEMED and neighbouring regions. The last section of this chapter focusses on regional renewable energy consumption and production patterns, as well as on potential new trade opportunities.

First of all, it is important to recognise that energy consumption patterns in the region are on the verge of a transformation, as consumption gradually becomes more climate-friendly. SEMED countries signed the Paris Agreement under the United Nations Framework Convention on Climate Change Paris Agreement, and have submitted their National Determined Contributions (NDCs) in the past few years. It is, however, a reasonable assertion that change is not solely driven by the policy choices formulated in the NDCs of countries in the region, but more consequential is technological change resulting from shifting energy policy preferences worldwide (UNFCC 2015).

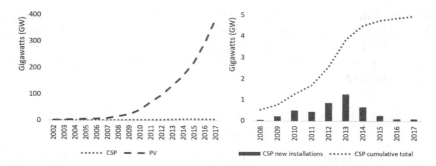

Graph 7.2 Worldwide annual CSP installations and total CSP capacity (left); CSP and PV totals worldwide (right)

Such a change is relevant to the region, for at least two reasons. First, when energy-importing regions move away from the combustion of carbon-intensive fossil fuels, global demand for conventional hydrocarbons exported by some SEMED countries, such as Algeria and Libya, may be affected, potentially with a negative impact on trade balances. Secondly, changing global energy dynamics can create opportunities in the region with respect to exporting clean energy carriers, in efficient, innovative, and perhaps unforeseen ways (Reed 2018).

The potential of renewable energy production in the SEMED is enormous. This is particularly true for electricity generation from solar energy, either using Photovoltaic (PV) technology or CSP technology (see Graph 7.2).[14] Solar energy projects are realised at ever lower

---

[14] It is relevant to distinguish between different categories of solar electricity generating technology, i.e. between Solar Photovoltaics (Solar PV) and CSP. Until about a decade ago, CSP received a lot of attention for its potential to by applied at a large scale (utility scale), while solar PV was particularly popular for smaller-scale (rooftop) applications. In the past ten years, economies of scale in the PV industry have impacted such prospects. Due to noteworthy cost decline in PV modules, utility-scale (ground mounted) PV plants became significantly more attractive. PV projects started to outcompete CSP on a levelised cost basis, and worldwide PV growth outpaced CSP growth (see Graph 7.2). This is not to say that the prospects of CSP have diminished indefinitely. With respect to electricity generation, it is important to recognise both the cost and value sides. CSP often includes integrated energy storage, and consequently delivers electricity in the night following the day, after the sun has set. This benefits consumers, and it can increase the utilisation rate of energy conversion technologies such as electrolysers. Even at a higher relative cost, a CSP project's value proposition could therefore be relatively attractive, compared to a lower cost solar PV project without such storage, depending on the exact context. In any case, when assessing merits of options, it is important to make a fair comparison, taking costs as well as value into consideration.

cost levels (Frankfurt School-UNEP Collaborating Centre 2018). In recent years, PV outcompeted CSP at the global level. PV project costs have declined by 73% since 2010. In 2017, project auctions resulted in record low bids in Argentina, Chile, India and Mexico, but also in MENA countries such as Saudi Arabia, and in Abu Dhabi and Dubai (REN21 2018: 96). Notwithstanding severe competition from PV, sizeable CSP projects were announced and realised in 2018. Projects in the MENA region include the Noor II and III facilities in Morocco (200 and 150 MW), the Ashalim Plot B plant in Israel (121 MW), the Duba 1 ISCC and Waad al Shamal ISCC facilities in Saudi Arabia (43 and 50 MW), and the Shagaya plant in Kuwait (50 MW) (REN21 2018: 101). In the United Arab Emirates, a tender was awarded for the largest CSP facility in the world, which began construction in 2018 (Power Technology 2018). This project illustrates how economies of scale may put CSP back on track again. Construction was started in 2018.

By turning to these renewable energy technologies, serving domestic demand for electricity is relatively easy. Organising clean energy exports may, on the other hand, prove to be more challenging. For clean energy exports to materialise, energy transport infrastructure is required that connects production centres with consumption centres abroad. In some cases, electricity cables from the region into the EU may be a viable option. It remains to be seen, however, whether this would constitute the most effective monetisation model for SEMED resources in every single case.

The challenge here for SEMED countries is that renewable electricity is being increasingly produced locally in European countries, too, and technologies producing electricity in SEMED countries may only provide supplies to EU markets, when local markets are producing abundant electricity supplies. The market value of future electricity exports is difficult to predict. If no long-term contracts are established between buyers (importers) and sellers (exporters), which fits today's paradigm in the liberalised internal EU energy market, market parties and governments will most likely be faced with major market uncertainties. At the same time, SEMED exporters which are dependent on electricity interconnectors for their energy exports cannot easily optimise market value by serving alternative export markets elsewhere in the world (for instance Japan and China).

Converting renewable energy into alternative products and energy carriers prior to exportation could therefore be an attractive alternative. Energy conversion technologies include inter alia: electrolysers that transform electricity into hydrogen (Agora Energiewende 2018) and more advanced approaches to producing clean hydrocarbons required for the aviation and international shipping sectors, and which are essential as chemical feedstock for industries worldwide (IRENA 2018). It is particularly important to stress that such products must ultimately be based on closed carbon cycles to avoid conflict with the long-term ambitions laid out in the Paris Agreement under the United Nations Framework Convention on Climate Change. On the other hand, a preferred option may involve adding value to renewable energy resources in the region before exportation. This option would contribute to local economic development and job creation more than exporting 'raw' electricity through interconnectors. Moreover, converting energy into a set of different energy carriers may contribute more effectively to energy security, as a complex system characterised by multiple technologies for producing, transporting, converting and storing energy is more likely to be more resilient to shocks.

This is where renewable energy production, innovative hydrogen and carbon chemistry, and the closing of carbon cycles could all come together. While transportation of hydrocarbons and CO_2 overseas is well-known territory across the globe, the first pilot project for shipping hydrogen over long distances is under development (ARENA 2018). The SEMED region is a well-positioned resource holder, but the knowledge base and technological potential differ greatly from one country to the other. Regional cooperation—as well as cooperation between potential buyers and sellers—is therefore essential in order to integrate the different options in new value chains, to strengthen the knowledge base further, to scale up technologies, and ultimately to satisfy shifting consumers preferences in established and new markets.

Conclusion

In this chapter, we assessed the role of Southern and East Mediterranean (SEMED) countries in Europe's energy security, as well as the role of energy for security in the SEMED region itself. We also proposed some general observations on Europe's energy security engagement with the region, and highlighted future opportunities for trade in renewable energy.

The two net oil and gas exporting countries of the SEMED region—Algeria and Libya—have historically played a key role in European security of supply, providing diversification and stimulating competition. Italy and Spain, and, to a lesser degree, France, have significantly higher energy security stakes in the region than other EU countries. This is particularly true for natural gas, given the rigidity of pipeline trade compared to the relative ease with which oil flows can be substituted with supplies from other countries. A number of security-related disruptions have hit oil and gas supply from the SEMED region, with a noticeable deterioration since the beginning of the Arab Spring in 2011. A key observation of this chapter is that there have been much more energy supply disruptions in the SEMED region than along the Russian–Ukrainian transit corridor. This is neither reflected in the public debate, nor in the scales of Europe and NATO's energy security engagement towards its southern and eastern neighbourhoods.

The need to balance different policy priorities—ranging from migration to democratisation—makes it difficult for Europe to isolate its regional energy interests pragmatically and act accordingly. Nevertheless, Europe has so far coped relatively well with energy supply interruptions in the region. Alternative oil supplies have been taken from well-supplied global markets. With regard to gas, a combination of weak European demand until 2015, temporarily higher Algerian output following the beginning of operations in its southwestern fields, and higher imports from Russia have balanced supply and demand.

In fact, the biggest challenge to future oil and gas exports from the region may not be related to security, but rather to the spiralling demand for hydrocarbons within the SEMED region. The ubiquity of fossil fuel subsidies has encouraged an inefficient use of energy in hydrocarbon-rich countries. Such inefficiency will restrain the availability of export volumes as fields are mature and no major new investments are expected—with the exception of gas fields in the East Mediterranean, which while locally important, are not expected to deliver massive volumes for Europe. Pipeline projects from the Eastern Mediterranean are complicated by geopolitical factors and by even more serious commercial obstacles, and most notably the fact that Europe is more and more focussed on short-term gas purchases. There is little appetite for long-term commitments and capital-intensive gas projects. This is also likely to limit the importance of Turkey as a future energy gateway to Europe—a sharp contrast to those messages optimistically heralded only a few years ago.

Less exports to Europe means lower revenues for the Algerian and Libyan governments, which—similarly to other countries in the broader MENA region—have to step up their efforts to diversify their economies while making their molecule exports more compatible with the global decarbonisation agenda. As argued in this chapter, the SEMED region's competitive advantage in renewable energy production and potential synergies with Europe may unlock the potential of new energy trade relations in future. This may bring new energy exporters, such as Morocco or Tunisia, onto the scene. Any such transition must be carefully managed because an abrupt interruption of trade would destabilise countries in Europe's Southern Neighbourhood, with undesired consequences for Europe itself. European energy policies should therefore not only focus on increasing the resilience of its energy supplies, but also consider the importance of energy exports to Europe for the economies and societies of SEMED countries.

References

Agora Energiewende. (2018). *The Future Cost of Electricity-Based Synthetic Fuels.* https://www.agora-energiewende.de/fileadmin2/Projekte/2017/SynKost_2050/Agora_SynKost_Study_EN_WEB.pdf. Accessed 20 April 2019.

Australian Renewable Energy Agency (ARENA). (2018, July 27). *Japan's Hydrogen Future May Be Fuelled by Australian Renewables.* https://arena.gov.au/blog/hydrogen-future-australian-renewables/. Accessed 20 April 2019.

British Petroleum (BP). (2018). *Statistical Review of World Energy.* https://www.bp.com/content/dam/bp/business-sites/en/global/corporate/pdfs/energy-economics/statistical-review/bp-stats-review-2018-full-report.pdf. Accessed 20 April 2019.

Cusumano, E., & Corbe, M. (2018). Introduction. In E. Cusumano & M. Corbe (Eds.), *A Civil-Military Response to Hybrid Threats.* Basingstoke: Palgrave.

Energy Information Administration. (Undated). *Algeria Country Profile.* Retrieved in October 2018.

Energy Information Administration. (Undated). *Libya Country Profile.* https://www.eia.gov/beta/international/analysis.php?iso=DZA. Accessed 20 April 2019.

European Commission. (2019). *2018 Quarterly Report on European Gas Markets.*

Eurostat. (2018). *Database on the International Trade in Goods.*

Frankfurt School-UNEP Collaborating Centre. (2018). Global Trends in Renewable Energy Investment 2018. *Frankfurt: School of Finance & Management.* http://www.iberglobal.com/files/2018/renewable_trends.pdf. Accessed 20 April 2019.

International Renewable Energy (IRENA). (2018). *Hydrogen from Renewable Power: Technology Outlook for the Energy Transition.* https://www.irena.org/publications/2018/Sep/Hydrogen-from-renewable-power. Accessed 20 April 2019.

Power Technology. (2018, March 21). *Construction Begins on 700 MW CSP Plant in Dubai.* https://www.power-technology.com/news/construction-begins-700mw-csp-plant-dubai/. Accessed 20 April 2019.

Reed, S. (2018, February 15). From Oil to Solar: Saudi Arabia Plots a Shift to Renewables. *New York Times.* https://www.nytimes.com/2018/02/05/business/energy-environment/saudi-arabia-solar-renewables.html. Accessed 20 April 2019.

Renewable Energy Policy Network for the 21st Century (REN21). (2018). *Renewables 2018 Global Status Report.* http://www.ren21.net/wp-content/uploads/2018/06/17-8652_GSR2018_FullReport_web_final_.pdf. Accessed 20 April 2019.

United Nations Framework Convention on Climate Change (UNFCC) Secretariat. (2015). *Mission Innovation: Clean Energy.*

CHAPTER 8

Libya: From Regime Change to State-Building

Matteo Villa and Arturo Varvelli

More than seven years have passed since the insurgency that toppled the regime of Muammar Gaddafi in Libya, and prospects for peace and stability in the country still remain dim. The clashes, starting in April 2019 for control over the western part of the country, which have already caused over 300 casualties and displaced over 35,000 persons at the time of writing, are a case in point. As the literature on regime transitions shows, it is almost impossible to formulate precise forecasts in the context of crisis. Nevertheless, the past offers many insights to understand the situation on the ground, and opens up a small window onto the future trajectory of the country.

In this chapter, we start by sketching out a historical overview of the relations between Libya and Western countries belonging to NATO and the EU. We then discuss regime change and state building in Libya since 2011. As regards to regime change, we propose an in-depth analysis of the NATO-led Operation Unified Protector (OUP), which had a major role in unseating Gaddafi from power in 2011. We argue that, given the

M. Villa (✉) · A. Varvelli
Italian Institute for International Political Studies (ISPI), Milan, Italy
e-mail: matteo.villa@ispionline.it

many political, logistical, and tactical peculiarities of the intervention in Libya, it is hard to draw a clear assessment of whether NATO's intervention aimed at regime change per se.

Moving on to state building, we track some of the main political evolutions in the country between 2012 and 2018. Our main argument is that attempts at state building disregarded or glossed over the most delicate phases of nation building, which are especially crucial for a country that has never shared a common sense of belonging and purpose like Libya. The lack of meaningful EU support in the formal transition process in 2011–2014 and the negative influence of a number of external actors after the situation started precipitating in 2014 hindered an already fragile transition.

We argue that, since 2014, the two main obstacles to the sustainable pacification of the country are that external actors focus on supporting their preferred factions instead of the whole peace process, and that almost all of them attempt to exclude particularly important domestic players, namely the leaders of dominant militias. In light of all this, we conclude by offering some tentative recommendations for viable paths forward for the stabilisation of the country.

West-Libya Relations: A Fraught Conundrum

For better and for worse, at least since the end of the Second World War, Libya has been a crucial piece in the Mediterranean power game. Libya's oil wealth, coupled with its central geopolitical position in North Africa, has always made the country strategically important for Europe. However, deepening relations between Western countries and Libya has proven far more difficult than with most other North African countries. In fact, after the 1969 *coup d'état* that brought him to power, Muhammad Gaddafi proved to be a very difficult partner to deal with, and Libya has been the bogeyman of the Euroatlantic community for decades.

Gaddafi's strand of Arab and Islamic socialism combined with a strong anticolonial sentiment to set his regime against most Western countries right from the beginning. Just a few years after his rise to power, Gaddafi expelled all Italians (nationals of the former colonial power) residing on Libyan territory, threw out most Western oil firms by nationalising the oil sector, and evicted US and UK troops from military bases on Libyan territory. Gaddafi's Libya was considered a controversial partner even closer to home. Relationships with Egypt deteriorated since the 1970s, until the two countries severed their diplomatic ties completely in 1979 after Cairo signed a peace treaty with Israel. Several other Arab and African countries maintained tense and erratic relations with Gaddafi, a leader whose ambitions often provided him with more enemies than friends—as exemplified by the Chadian–Libyan border conflict between 1978 and 1987.

Gaddafi's enmity with the West was often perceived as a thorn in the flesh by strategists devising foreign and security policies for the EU and NATO. Even when relations between the states on the northern and southern shores of the Mediterranean intensified in the 1990s, Libya lagged behind. The role of Gaddafi's Libya as a state sponsor of terrorism, already epitomised by its direct financing of the Provisional Irish Republican Army and the Popular Front for the Liberation of Palestine, peaked in the late 1980s. In 1986, Libya was a prime suspect for the bombing of a discotheque in Berlin. In response to the bombing, the US launched a one-day air strike against the country (Operation El Dorado Canyon) causing at least 60 Libyan casualties. Libyan officials were also involved in the bombing of two airplanes: the 1988 Pan Am 103, which crashed into residential areas of the Scottish city of Lockerbie, and the 1989 UTA Flight 772 that came down over the Ténéré desert in Niger. These two bombings, the resulting investigations, and the diplomatic action taken by the US, the UK, and France in the UN Security Council (UNSC) resulted in sanctions being imposed on Libya in 1992.

Since the mid-1990s, however, Libya's defeat in the war with Chad, and the end of the Cold War left Gaddafi even more isolated within the international community. At the same time, the economic malaise associated with a prolonged period of low oil prices (1983–1999) caused increasing domestic unrest, especially in the eastern region of Cyrenaica. These developments compelled Gaddafi to embark on a cautious but steady attempt to restore relations with the West. As a result, UN sanctions against Libya were lifted in 1999, when the country gained observer status in the EU-led Barcelona Process, which had already begun in 1995 for most other countries in the MENA region (see chapter by Badarin and Schumacher in this volume). Also in 1999, the Sirte Declaration established the African Union (AU), with Gaddafi playing a prominent role both in its initial creation and in the first steps of the fledgling organisation. The thaw in relations with Western countries continued into the early 2000s, enshrined in the construction and commissioning of a natural gas pipeline, the Greenstream, connecting Libya to Italy. Finally, in 2003, UN sanctions were lifted after Libya officially acknowledged its responsibility for the Lockerbie bombing, and after Gaddafi made an emphatic commitment to giving up the pursuit of weapons of mass destruction in December of that year.

From then on, Libya was included in the EU Neighbourhood Policy, a framework of good neighbourly relations between the EU and neighbouring countries. However, formal cooperation between Libya and the EU brought few results if any at all. In reality, Gaddafi was a major opponent of the creation of the Union for the Mediterranean (UfM) in 2008—at the time, the most ambitious project aimed at bringing together all of the countries bordering the Mediterranean into one forum. Gaddafi denounced the initiative as a "new form of 'colonialism' perpetrated by the Europeans" (Varvelli 2008). While Libya's inclusion in multilateral forums proved impossible during this period, bilateral relations somewhat improved, sometimes markedly, with a number of European countries. In 2006, the US re-established full diplomatic relations with the country, reopening its embassy in Tripoli, and removing Libya from the list of states sponsors of terrorism. In 2008, Italy and Libya signed the Treaty on Friendship, Partnership and Cooperation (Klepp 2010), which included a clause committing Italy to pay Libya EUR 5 billion over 25 years as reparations for its colonial past. The following year, Gaddafi visited Italy for the first time since he came to power. However, in hindsight, all these efforts at re-establishing relations between Gaddafi and Western powers proved fleeting, as protests swept the Arab world in 2011.

The 2011 NATO Intervention in Libya

Since the start of the Libyan crisis in 2011, the role of EU and NATO countries has been criticised as inconsistent and contradictory. Western countries disagreed on how to solve the crisis, and their collective response to the crisis proved timely, but not always coordinated. The EU as a whole remained silent when protests in eastern Libya erupted in mid-February 2011, while the UK and France quickly positioned themselves as supporters of the revolution. London and Paris urged the international community, and especially the NATO Alliance, to take a tough stance. Their push for establishing a no-fly zone (NFZ), and proposals to provide the rebels with aerial support, were met with an initial reluctance in the US by the Obama administration, with vocal opposition by the Italian and German governments, and criticism by other NATO countries, especially Turkey (Lizza 2011; see also chapter by Larsen and Koehler of this volume).

Ultimately, NATO's intervention in the region was hailed by many as a success. The Alliance was able to reverse the balance of forces on the ground, with Gaddafi's regime falling just a few months after the start of operations, no NATO casualties were inflicted by the Libyan armed forces, and a novel way to use aviation to achieve strategic objectives was successfully implemented. On the other hand, some claimed that the NATO intervention was a failure, pointing at Libya's subsequent descent into division and civil war. In this section, we aim to show that these sweeping positions should be the subject of a much more nuanced analysis, and that there are a number of takeaways that need closer scrutiny by researchers and policymakers alike.

After protests broke out in Libya in February 2011, rebel forces started to organise themselves and took control of a number of cities, especially in the eastern region of Cyrenaica. However, Gaddafi's forces rapidly reorganised, and in early March were making rapid gains along the coastal corridor linking Tripoli to the west with Bengasi and Tobruk to the east. Meanwhile, debate raged on between countries supporting some sort of military intervention, such as France and the UK, those arguing for caution such as the US, Germany, and Italy, and those opposing intervention to a greater or lesser extent, such as China, Russia, and Turkey.

By mid-March, Gaddafi's forces had retaken control of most cities along the route towards Bengasi, and were preparing to enter the city, where the headquarters of the rebels had been temporarily established. However, provocative words by Gaddafi raised fears of a massive retaliation against rebel forces and civilians as soon as the regime's troops had quelled the rebellion, which gave those supporting intervention the necessary justification to convince key decision-makers in NATO countries. Meanwhile, support for an intervention spread to other governments in the MENA region, including Arab countries.

The breakthrough came on 17 March 2011, when the UNSC approved Res. 1973/2011. Proposed by France, the UK, and Lebanon, the resolution gained 10 votes in favour, and 5 abstentions (including China, Russia, and Germany—the latter held a rotating seat as a non-permanent member at the time). The resolution explicitly referenced Chapter 7 of the UN Charter, which allows for necessary action, including the use of force, to be taken against any "threat to peace, breach of the peace, or act of aggression". Essentially, the Resolution contained three key elements:

1. It demanded "the immediate establishment of a cease-fire and a complete end to violence and all attacks against, and abuses of, civilians";
2. It authorised the international community ("Member states… acting nationally or through regional organizations or arrangements") to take "all necessary measures…to protect civilians and civilian populated areas…while excluding a foreign occupation force". For these purposes, arming anti-Gaddafi forces was legalised, de facto suspending the UN-sanctioned arms embargo against the whole country put in place by Res. 1970/2011 of 22 February; and
3. It established a NFZ, with "a ban on all flights in the airspace" of Libya, authorising UN members to enforce it.

The US, the UK, France, and Canada launched coordinated but autonomous military operations on 19 March in order to enforce the NFZ. Four days later, NATO launched its own operation, OUP. Three of the four autonomous national operations already in place were unified under NATO command on 31 March, while Canada maintained its operational autonomy. Formally, OUP (23 March–31 October 2011) had three main aims:

1. To enforce an arms embargo in the Mediterranean sea, in order to avoid any transfer of arms to the Libyan regime, pursuant to UNSC Res. 1970/2011;
2. To enforce the NFZ; and
3. To conduct air and naval strikes against Gaddafi's forces involved in attacks against civilians or threatening to do so.

The third objective especially shows that the official mandate of OUP went beyond the mere establishment of a NFZ. This broader mandate was enabled by the wording of UNSC Res. 1973/2011, which left much to interpretation in its request to protect civilians involved in the fighting between the regime and the rebels in Libya and only explicitly excluded the sending of a "foreign occupation force".

The core element of OUP was initially a relatively small, multinational air campaign (Mueller 2015). But the objective of the campaign gradually shifted: in the very first weeks, between mid-March and early April, the aim was to incapacitate the air and ground forces available to Gaddafi's regime. Having achieved this first goal in just a few weeks, at a meeting in Berlin on 14 April 2011, NATO Foreign Ministers and non-NATO partners participating in the operation decided to continue the operation until all attacks against civilians and populated areas ceased and Gaddafi's regime consented to the "safe and unhindered humanitarian access to all the people of Libya in need of assistance" (NATO 2011a). While formally remaining within the UN mandate, the goal of continuing operations until "all attacks" against civilians had ceased implied providing rebel forces with effective and continuous air support. In fact, the need to protect civilians acted as the primary political justification for the continuation of NATO's aerial campaign almost indefinitely—most likely, with the decisive victory of one of the two parties and a sufficiently prolonged and credible ceasefire.

After the liberation of Tripoli on 22 August 2011, NATO's Secretary General reiterated the need for continued NATO involvement in the region to protect the Libyan people (NATO 2011b). A similar political rationale was echoed as NATO heads of state and government convened in Paris on 1 September for the "Friends of Libya" summit. On 16 September, as rebels were now consolidating their presence in the rest of the country, UNSC Res. 2009/2011 created the UN Support Mission in Libya (UNSMIL), a political mission aimed at supporting the National Transitional Council (under which banner the rebels had formally grouped as an alternative to the Gaddafi regime), and at rebuilding the rule of law and state institutions. Finally, with Gaddafi's capture and death on 20 October, the North Atlantic Council decided to terminate OUP by the end of the month, having achieved the implicit objective of regime change in Libya. Subsequently, UNSC Res. 2016/2011 stated that the provisions calling for an intervention within UNSC 1973/2011 would be terminated at midnight of 31 October, thus bringing to an end the UN mandate to intervene militarily in Libya.

The key elements of OUP reviewed in the aforementioned section call for a number of considerations. First, the operation was a success from a tactical and strategic standpoint. At its peak, the mission involved around 8000 military personnel, 21 maritime vessels and 250 aircrafts. NATO allies carried out more than 26,000 air sorties, an average of over 120 per day. 42% of these were air raids, which damaged or destroyed around 6000 military targets. In all this, the coalition recorded no military casualties directly related to the fighting. The rapid reversal of fortunes for the Gaddafi's regime, and the negligible number of casualties suffered by the Coalition helped keep controversies to a minimum. In the US, even tepid public support for the intervention (just 47% of respondents sided in its favour) did not lead to a politicisation of the operation (Pew Research Center 2011). This situation was almost a polar opposite to what Americans experienced with Afghanistan since 2001 and Iraq since 2003, where support for the interventions was very high, albeit it declined rapidly in the months and years after the initial deployment.

The second noteworthy point is that, despite its limited scope compared to other missions, even Unified Protector exposed itself to accusations of "mission creep". Was the mission's purpose limited to protecting civilians and avoiding a massacre, or was overthrowing Gaddafi in fact the undeclared objective? Moreover, did the unstated purpose of the mission even extend beyond regime change, to not only remove Gaddafi and his allies, but to also replace the closed autocracy with a functioning democracy, possibly aligned to Western interests in Libya (Zenko 2016)? It is possible to argue that the objective of the mission implicitly shifted after the first few weeks. Initially limited to keeping Gaddafi's forces out of Benghazi and other previously rebel-held cities along the eastern coast, Unified Protector eventually started providing outright aerial support for rebel advances towards Tripoli.

Regardless of the mission's purpose, the nature of the implementation of the NFZ was an important innovation in war tactics. Before Libya, NFZs had been enforced in just two other cases: over Bosnia (1992–1995), and over Iraq (1991–2003). However, the NFZ enforced over Libya was very different from these previous two missions: it did not solely entail a coercive effort to keep the target country's air force from flying over certain areas, but also included a proactive attempt to incapacitate the Libyan air force, grounding all enemy airplanes. This meant that operations extended far beyond mere aerial interdiction, and entered the domain of an air bombing campaign. After all, it was evident from the start that a "classic" NFZ would have not have made much of a difference in strategic terms. This was because Gaddafi was mostly advancing towards rebel-held areas by using ground troops. His aviation's air strikes, while important in lowering the morale of the rebels and to speed up the advance, were not essential to maintaining superiority on the ground.

Furthermore, the mission would have not been possible without such a strong international backing, especially by the UN and regional non-NATO allies. Regarding the UN, a number of major NATO countries were unwilling to intervene without first securing a strong backing by the UNSC. The conflict of interest was evident, as three out of five permanent members are NATO allies (US, UK, and France), and two of them strongly supported a military intervention in Libya. UNSC Res. 1973/2011, which called for the intervention, is reminiscent of the 1990–1991 Gulf War, when UNSC Res. 678/1990 set a deadline for the withdrawal of Iraqi troops from Kuwait and empowered states to use all necessary means to enforce this decision after the deadline had expired. These two UN-sanctioned interventions can be contrasted with the NATO-led intervention in Kosovo in 1999. In the latter, the intervention had not been backed by a UNSC resolution, which caused major criticism for NATO's air campaign over the Federal Republic of Yugoslavia. Only ex post, after hostilities had ended, did the UN certify what was already de facto a reality on the ground—i.e. the separation between Kosovo and the Federal Republic of Yugoslavia—by establishing a peacekeeping mission (UNMIK) with UNSC Res. 1244/1999 on 10 June 1999. Despite the similarities, the parallels between the UN backing of an intervention in Kuwait in 1990–1991, and in Libya in 2011 should not be overemphasised. One of the most noteworthy differences is that, in 1990, the Soviet Union's vote in favour of, and China's abstention from UNSC Res. 678/1990 resulted from a series of international political dynamics that were absent in Libya. The vote of the Soviet Union was largely influenced by the fact that the country was rapidly disintegrating, while China decided to abstain in the shadow of the Tiananmen incident. In 2011, instead, China and Russia were much more stable, and their veto could have easily called into question NATO allies' decision to intervene. In such circumstances, why did Russia and China not vote against the resolution? Two factors may have been at play. First, despite the fact that Gaddafi's Libya was experiencing a tentative thaw in diplomatic relations before the unrest spread to the country in February 2011, the level of isolation of the Iraqi and Libyan regimes at the time of the interventions is comparable, especially after Gaddafi continued to blame the attempted insurrection on Western interference and employed harsh, vengeful rhetoric against the domestic opposition. Also, the perception of a "wave" of unrest and revolutions spreading throughout the entire MENA region (the so-called Arab Spring) might have convinced some key actors, such as France, to change their expected behaviour to favour an intervention. Similar perceptions of such a wave of unrest held by the Russians and Chinese might have also convinced them that opposing an intervention would have isolated their countries as well.

The role of regional (non-NATO) allies was also crucial. Western countries, especially the US, had expressed reservations towards an intervention that was not backed by at least some regional (preferably Arab and Muslim) countries (Hastings 2011). Given the military interventions in Afghanistan and Iraq, the US had no appetite to open up a third front of active involvement at the risk of affecting its relations with other MENA countries. Luckily for NATO, there was no lack of such regional support, which further indicates Gaddafi's isolation. The Gulf Cooperation Council stepped into endorse the establishment of a NFZ in early March. Even more important was the unprecedented move by the Arab League, which voted to support the NFZ on 12 March, offering a de facto endorsement of armed intervention against one of its own members. Finally, a number of countries in the region (Qatar, the United Arab Emirates, Saudi Arabia, Jordan, and Egypt) decided to take an active part in the operations, in close cooperation with the NATO command. All this contributed to tipping the scale of many sceptical Western governments towards an intervention, and gave much broader legitimacy and support to planned operations.

This nuanced view of the international context leading up to the intervention calls for a closer examination of the relations between NATO countries. In particular, the flurry of debates among the allies in the weeks leading up to UNSC Res. 1973/2011 and to the start of OUP shows that the Alliance's cohesion was tested more than once. Article 5 of the North Atlantic Treaty on collective self-defence has never been invoked to support missions within the territory of an Ally. NATO military missions have in fact always been implemented "out of area" in Bosnia, Kosovo, Afghanistan, the Mediterranean Sea, the Gulf of Aden, and so on.

Member states' interests inevitably become all the more divergent when NATO operations move away from core areas of cooperation, shifting from collective self-defence to force projection abroad. In the Libyan case, there were two main fault lines (Lindström and Zetterlund 2012). The first ran between those European allies who favoured a rapid intervention (France and the UK), those who were far more cautious

(Italy, Germany, and the US), and those who—at least initially—vocally opposed the intervention (Germany and Turkey). The second fault line concerned the type of approach to be pursued, dividing countries favouring national missions only loosely coordinated at the multilateral level (France and Canada), and those favouring NATO-led approach (the US, Germany, and Italy). Divergences continued throughout the campaign, with Italy, Germany, and the US continuing to lobby for a more prudent approach in the choice of targets for the air raids.

From a broader, institutional perspective, there has been some debate on whether the Libya intervention sanctioned the final transformation of NATO from a defensive pact to an "expeditionary force" for out-of-area operations (Hallams and Schreer 2012; Cavanagh Hodge 2013). In light of our analysis, two points stand out. On the one hand, far from being a fully fledged expeditionary force, NATO's operation in Libya was limited to an aerial operation and a naval embargo, with no boots on the ground, which served to assuage the fears of some allies (including the US), both in terms of domestic legitimacy and ownership over the transition and stabilisation period following the end of combat operations. On the other hand, a number of conditions had to be fulfilled before the operation could garner enough support among the Allies. This bodes ill for any future and more complex operation requiring more than just aerial support in order to succeed.

Finally, the counterfactual debate on what would have happened had foreign actors refrained from intervening in Libya is likely to continue for years. Whereas some claim that without the intervention, Gaddafi's forces would have reacted brutally against its citizens, and especially against rebels (Hamid 2016), others claim that NATO intervention was unwarranted (Kuperman 2015). The latter group looks at the current situation of prolonged instability in the country, and argues that without external interventions either Gaddafi would have swiftly regained control of the situation, or a new domestic compromise (with a rebel-held government or a government of national accord (GNA)) would have succeeded in stabilising the country.

Both scenarios appear unrealistic, however. When NATO countries did make the decision to intervene, the situation in Libya already seemed highly compromised. Even if Gaddafi would have managed to retake Benghazi and quash dissent there, insurgencies in the east of the country would have arguably continued to spread, leading to a prolonged standoff and a fragmentation of the country similar to the one we are experiencing today.

2012–Present: The Obstacles to State-Building

It was already clear in 2011 that the coalition of anti-Gaddafi forces that had coalesced around the National Transitional Council was a highly heterogeneous ensemble of diverse groups rather than a united opposition, and that almost all that kept it together was the common goal of ousting Gaddafi.

Attempts at a swift transition proved too fast for such a fractious country, as grudges between different armed groups resurfaced. Three elections—for the General National Congress (GNC) in 2012, the Libyan Constitutional Assembly in February 2014, and the Libyan House of Representatives in June 2014—only served to deepen existing divisions instead of bridging them. The phase of "nation building", which involves not only the setting up political institutions, but during which a national reconciliation dialogue takes place, encouraging the formation of a common history with which the vast majority of the population of a country can identify, was skipped or glossed over as formal steps were prioritised. Nation building should have been recognised as particularly crucial for a country that, for decades, was held together more by the autocratic rule of its leader and the relatively high well-being that the redistribution of oil rents allowed to its citizens, than by an actual sense of common belonging and purpose (Varvelli and Mezran 2012; Villa 2012).

In spite of such evident difficulties, after the end of the civil war in 2011, the interest of most European countries in the Libyan crisis sharply decreased (Toaldo 2017). EU powers' relative indifference to the evolution of the situation in Libya between 2011 and 2014 was the result of two main factors. First, the overall situation in the country seemed sufficiently stable and on a path to improvement from an outside perspective. After Gaddafi's defeat, the National Transitional Council quickly named an interim government. On 7 July 2012, the first parliamentary elections since the fall of Gaddafi were held. With a high turnout and a poor result for the Islamist parties, the prospect for successful regime change appeared not too distant. Moreover, a decrease in migratory flows towards Europe in 2012 reinforced the perception that the country was stable, while simultaneously removing one of the European governments' main reasons for concern. Second, between 2012 and 2014, Europe was focused on its internal problems: the Greek crisis and its contagion, the start of a double-dip recession accompanied by high unemployment rates, and the opening up of a rift between pro- and anti-austerity countries. According to the fall 2012 Eurobarometer, back then the first priority for

European citizens was unemployment, followed by the economic situation and rising prices (European Commission 2012).

The challenging situation within European borders and the relatively stable situation in Libya, combined with the divergent strategic interests of the main European countries involved (especially between France and Italy), all contributed to divert attention away from the North African country. Europeans did not feel the need to find a common ground to help Libya stabilise and rebuild. Despite the murder of the American ambassador in Benghazi on 11 September 2012, the European position remained unchanged.

However, by the end of 2013, the situation in Libya had worsened. First, the GNC, whose mandate was set to expire in February 2014, unilaterally extended its tenure, unleashing a hostile reaction from the population. In an increasingly tense atmosphere, Libyan Prime Minister Ali Zeidan was ousted and replaced by Abdullah al-Thani in March 2013. Shortly thereafter, on 16 May, General Khalifa Haftar launched Operation Dignity, which aimed at eradicating terrorist groups from Benghazi, thus further complicating the picture. In the same month the EU, in an attempt to bridge its internal differences, sent its Special Representative for the Southern Mediterranean Region Bernardino León to Tripoli as the EU Special Envoy to Libya. His meeting with al-Thani, however, produced limited results.

In the meantime, a new round of elections for the new House of Representatives (HoR) was held on 25 June 2014. Unlike previous rounds, turnout amounted to a meagre 18%, with Islamist factions again largely underrepresented (Eljarh 2014). A deteriorating security situation in Tripoli pushed the newly reappointed Prime Minister, Abdullah al-Thani, to select Tobruk, replacing Tripoli as the institutional seat of the Libyan head of state. The same held true for the new HoR, which, according to the amended constitutional declaration, was supposed to meet in Benghazi. In Tripoli, the same blocs that had lost the election in June decided to form an independent government with Omar al-Hassi as prime minister. This schism occurred for two main reasons. On the one hand, the creation of the Libya Dawn Coalition[1] changed the balance of power in Tripoli and, on the other, the HoR split between those

---

[1] The Libyan Dawn Coalition was created to oppose Operation Dignity and included Islamist and revolutionary factions in Tripoli, the city-state of Misrata and various cities in western Libya.

who relocated to Tobruk and those who boycotted this decision. In the summer of 2014, spreading violence in the country led to the evacuation of foreign staff from most embassies, the relocation of the EU Border Assistance Mission (EUBAM) to Tunisia, and the temporary withdrawal of UNSMIL staff. It was only after the summer of 2014 that the approach of EU countries started to change.

Since 2014, European countries have been able to coordinate their agendas by kick-starting and supporting the political process, resulting in the Skhirat agreement in December 2015. International reconciliation efforts began in September 2014, led by UN Special Representative Bernardino León. Since the beginning of León's mandate, the EU and its five most important members states (Germany, France, the UK, Italy and Spain) put pressure on Libyan parties to reach an agreement. Despite fierce disagreement among Libyan factions—so strong as to prompt al-Thani to ask General Haftar to advance and reconquer Tripoli—the peace process backed by the EU gained traction.

The year of 2015 saw two diverging developments shed an uncertain light on the future of Libya. On the one hand, the weakening of the Libya Dawn coalition, with some militias beginning to support UN and EU mediation efforts, appeared to clear the way for national reconciliation. On the other, there were growing fears in European capitals due to a rapid increase of migrants arriving to Europe from Libya (and, also in 2015, from Turkey to Greece), and the appearance of Islamic State affiliates in Libya, particularly in Derna and Sirte. This persuaded European countries to work more quickly to solve the Libyan impasse. Europe and Europeans viewed the southern Mediterranean predominantly through the prism of illegal migration, framed as a national security threat (see chapter by Del Valle in this volume). In fact, immigration became the most pressing concern among European citizens, and the EU's inability to solve the crisis contributed to the wave of Euroscepticism and national-populism the EU is still experiencing to this day (European Commission 2015). These difficulties gave further impetus for European action towards Libya. Moreover, many factors forced Libyans themselves to recognise that a reconciliation agreement was necessary: chronic instability, coupled with low international oil prices since mid-2014, had by then led to a critical economic situation, with real GDP shrinking by more than one-third in just two years between 2013 and 2014.

Thanks to European resolve and León's actions, during the summer of 2015, the two parliaments began to meet regularly, prompting some optimism in European capitals. León and European leaders pushed Libyans to reach an agreement based on the expansion of the presidential council to nine members—thus making it more inclusive—under the leadership of Fayez al-Serraj. Moreover, France, Germany, Italy, the UK, and the US set up an informal contact group and released periodic joint statements backing UN mediation and Fayez al-Serraj's General National Accord (GNA).

In spite of such initiatives, the embarrassing exit of León from the negotiating process in November 2015 raised many doubts about the possibility of reaching an agreement. In fact, it emerged that, during his mandate, León had received and accepted a job offer from the United Arab Emirates, a country that had frequently violated the international arms embargo imposed on Libya. Moreover, in e-mails disclosed by *The Guardian*, León expressed his will to weaken the alliance between Tripoli and Misrata and his favouring of the House of Representative (HoR) in Tobruk (Ramesh 2015).

León's successor, Martin Kobler, sought to change the negotiating approach by enlarging the support base of the deal, but European countries lost patience and pushed for an agreement as soon as possible. On 17 December 2015, representatives of the two parliaments, as well as of political parties, civil society, and local governments, signed the Skhirat Agreement in Morocco (the agreement was not voted on by any of the two Parliaments). As per UNSC Res. 2259, this political agreement was based on an institutional system "in which a collective presidency (the PC) acted as head of state while a cabinet, the Government of National Accord (GNA), had to be approved by the HoR. The GNC was meant to become the High Council of State with consultative powers and a role in co-appointing with the HoR holders of major offices." The UNSC unanimously approved the deal on 23 December, and the EU foreign ministers promised to grant EUR 100 million to Libya following the formation of a government in January 2016.

The unexpected exit of León evidences both the EU's inability to find a viable resolution to the crisis and the negative influence of other external powers. In particular, most of the regional and international actors involved operated under the impression that they would be able to direct the revolution towards their preferred political outcomes. It could even be said that the current balance of power among the principal local actors (militias, parties, municipalities, etc.) starkly mirrors the interests of global and regional powers and their attempts at influencing the situation.

Table 8.1 Timeline of the Libyan crisis

Date	Event
February 2011	Violent protests break out in Benghazi, spreading to other cities. **First civil war** starts
March 2011	UNSC authorises the no-fly zone over Libya NATO starts operation Unified Protector. Arab countries join in the operation, and the Arab League endorses it
August 2011	Rebels enter Tripoli. Gaddafi goes into hiding
October 2011	Gaddafi captured and killed. The National Transitional Council (NTC) declares Libya "liberated". **First civil war** ends
January–March 2012	Clashes between former rebels in Benghazi. Requests for more autonomy by Cyrenaica
July–August 2012	Elections for the General National Congress (GNC). NTC hands over power to GNC
February 2014	After Constitutional Assembly election, mandate of the GNC expires, but the Congress refuses to disband. Protests start
May 2014	**Second civil war** starts. Khalifa Haftar launches military assault against 'militant Islamist groups' in Benghazi. Haftar tries to capture parliamentary building
June 2014	Parliamentary elections (just 18% turnout) amid violence
January 2015	Partial ceasefire between Haftar's Libyan National Army (LNA) and the Tripoli-based militia alliance
February 2015	Islamic State (IS) beheads 21 Egyptian Christians in Derna. Egypt bombs the city. IS expands control over Sirte
December 2015	Tobruk's House of Representatives (HoR) and Tripoli's GNC sign the Skhirat agreement, paving the way for a Government of National Accord (GNA)
January 2016	GNA constituted in Tunisia, but neither Tripoli nor Tobruk recognise its authority. IS moves eastwards towards Tobruk
March 2016	GNA moved to Tripoli by boat. Attempts to establish its authority by securing the support of main militias
September 2016	LNA seizes key oil terminals in Cyrenaica
December 2016	IS militants expelled from Sirte
July 2017	IS expelled from Benghazi after 3 years of fighting
July 2018	LNA forces retake Derna. IS loses almost all territorial control in the country
September 2018	Fighting between rival militias flares up in Tripoli
April 2019	LNA gains control of most of the Tripolitania, surrounding Tripoli

External pressures have been further mounting since 2016, due to growing political and military activism of Russia, Egypt, and the United Arab Emirates. Military and diplomatic actions by these countries have thus far achieved two conflicting results. On the one hand, they contributed to the resumption of negotiations that had otherwise reached a dead end. On the other hand, they strengthened Haftar vis-à-vis Serraj, bolstering the former's leading role in any future political scenario for the country. It is not surprising that these external actors carved out a key role for themselves following a backing-off of Western powers from any significant influence in Libya's future. In early 2019, renewed violent confrontations between Haftar-led militias and the UN-recognised government escalated to unseen levels, with Haftar attempting to gain control of the whole of the country and, in particular, its capital city. The role of external actors came again into focus during this time, as Haftar's offensive started just a few days after the General had visited Saudi Arabia and the country had apparently promised support for Haftar's push. It was also alleged that Haftar's allies were attacking Tripoli by relying on arms provided by Egypt, UAE, and Saudi Arabia.

The timeline below summarises the main events occurring in Libya from 2011 to December 2018 (Table 8.1).

THE FUTURE OF LIBYA: A VIABLE, REALISTIC PATH TO STABILISATION

Most attempts to return stability to Libya in the post-Gaddafi era have failed to contribute significantly to the pacification, unification, and the socio-political and institutional consolidation of the country. The reasons behind these failed attempts are complex and largely due to Libya's multiple identities and loyalties (regionalism, localism, tribalism), its acute political polarisation and, above all, the disruptive role of international actors (including European countries).

Libya now appears as a patchy collection of hundreds of militias, mainly divided, albeit not exclusively, into two coalitions: the first centres around the GNA led by Fayez al-Sarraj supported by the United Nations and the EU, and the second centres around Field Marshal Khalifa Haftar and the parliament in Tobruk. It appears increasingly evident that no meaningful steps forward can be made on the path towards a future of stability for the country where: (a) foreign powers continue to favour specific sides in the conflict instead of reaching positions of compromise; and (b) those stakeholders that have been sidelined from the peace process—namely, powerful militias with sufficient military and political leverage at the local level—are not brought to the table.

Attempts to involve these militias in the reconstruction of the Libyan state was made, particularly during the Ali Zeidan period, but with little success. This was due in most part to the fact that attempts to integrate the militias into the police or the armed forces occurred only at the technical, rather than the political level. There has been no real attempt at a disarmament, demobilisation and reintegration programme (DDR) to restore the state's legitimate monopoly on the use of force. In particular, armed groups have been disincentivised to disarm, by not being offered the prospect of entering into a reintegration process that satisfies not only the social and economic needs of individual ex-combatant, but also the political needs of militias.

The narrative often used to describe the issue of armed groups is of little use, since, quite unrealistically, it tends to consider these actors as a single bloc, rejecting them in their entirety as criminal groups and threats to the state. Furthermore, this narrative does not take into account the broad legitimacy that, at times, militias enjoy within their local communities. Actors such as Hezbollah, the FARC, or the Tamil Tigers, are or were organised as separate entities from and in opposition to, the state, largely as a result of local demands and the grievances of the communities they (claim to) represent. At the same time, having established their own parallel institutions, these actors have intentionally provided state-like functions—even if not over the entire national territory—and have thus become key interlocutors in the peace process (Alaaldin 2018).

Furthermore, the exclusion of militias from negotiations essentially rejects a proper understanding of the reality on the ground. In several cases, armed non-state actors have replaced the state in the provision of services and security. To maintain that militias can only oppose and disrupt attempts at restoring stability is misleading: if well managed, competition between state and non-state actors can lead to co-option, and the actions of militias may contribute positively to state objectives, for example by countering other militias that are openly and stubbornly anti-state.

In light of these considerations, the formal involvement of militias in negotiations should be returned to the core of any attempt at international mediation in Libya. This process should aim at transforming militias from mostly military actors into political actors, and from local into national actors. Until today, the negotiations under the auspices of the UN have avoided taking such actions. This has opened up even more room for external actors with specific interests to deal with selected militias, alone and secretively. Therefore, attempts at involving militias in the peace process could ensure that no crucial actor is left behind while, at the same time, reducing the leverage of those foreign actors whose goal it is to keep the country divided. The fact that the fighting for the territorial control of the Tripolitania rages on at the time of writing forcefully shows that a sustainable solution for a united Libya must include the construction of a web of alliances with militias. A progressive disarmament and reintegration goal should remain a long-term goal, but only be implemented after stabilisation will have been secured by ensuring the participation of militia into a collective effort to preserve peace and security in the country.

The fact that militias play a key role in illicit trafficking/smuggling (of oil, weapons, drugs, migrants, etc.) leads to a further consideration: in order to combat illicit trafficking, the militias must be provided with alternative sources of financing. Serious reflection is required on which mechanisms for redistributing hydrocarbon revenues in the country should be pursued. Libya is a rentier state, which bases its revenues almost exclusively on sales of oil and gas (see chapter by Franza et al. of this volume). Moreover, it should not be forgotten that, despite the current crisis, Libya remains potentially one of Africa's richest countries.

Finally, an effective combination of EU and NATO activities could contribute to the stability of the Southern Mediterranean, including Libya. NATO holds the most significant force projection and deterrence capabilities in the region and beyond and could leverage more effectively the influence that comes from such a position. The EU, meanwhile, is the most important trade and development cooperation partner by far. However, meaningful contributions to stability from either the EU, NATO, or a cooperation between the two can only be achieved when internal divergences between members are overcome, and the two institutions manage to speak (and act) with a single voice. As shown throughout this chapter, differences between NATO members hindered the capacity to act in the first weeks of the Libyan conflict, but were effectively overcome thanks to a mix of internal diplomacy and developments on the ground. On the other hand, a rift between EU members (especially between Italy and France) continued to hinder the peace process, and could even be considered as one of the factors fuelling the continuation of the second Libyan civil war. With this in mind, one example of effective EU–NATO cooperation that helped stabilise the situation in the Central Mediterranean is operation EUNAVFOR MED Sophia's close partnership with the Allied Maritime Command in Naples, Strategic direction south hub, and NATO operation Sea Guardian. Wider and deeper EU-NATO deconfliction and coordination be needed in order to contribute to stabilise Libya and the wider Southern Mediterranean region.

In conclusion, in the case of Libya, a significant part of internal and external actors' interests in the country hinges upon the control of hydrocarbon revenues. However, this reality has not been matched by sufficient discussions of the issue throughout peace negotiations. While not surprising, given the sensitivity of the topic, there is room to discuss how to make the redistribution of revenues smarter and more effective. Redistribution has the power to provide citizens with basic welfare and reactivate economically productive activities. In the long term, it could replace the black economy with formal activities, producing a mitigating effect on illicit trafficking, and making local communities recognise the benefits of the rentier state.[2] It is therefore clear that security and economy must go hand in hand with the process of reconstructing the Libyan state.

References

Alaaldin, R. (2018). Armed Groups, Governance and the Future of the Middle East. In A. Colombo & P. Magri (Eds.), *ISPI Annual Report 2018: Global Scenarios and Italy*. Milano: Ledizioni.

Cavanagh Hodge, C. (2013). Full Circle: Two Decades of NATO Intervention. *Journal of Transatlantic Studies, 11*(4), 350–367.

Eljarh, M. (2014, July 22). Libya's Islamists Go for Broke. *Foreign Policy*.

European Commission. (2012). Standard Eurobarometer. 78.

---

[2] For instance, the predominant narrative portrays the smuggling of migrants as highly profitable for criminal organisations. On the contrary, evidence shows that, despite the fact that migrant smuggling revenues are concentrated and "unbalanced" towards a small group of people in the country, their size is not such as to structurally change the local economy, and oil revenues could easily replace the revenues lost from the lack of migrants smuggling. In concrete terms, UNODC estimates that in 2016 each migrant paid about USD 3000 to leave Libya by sea (UNODC [2018], *Global Study on Smuggling of Migrants*, United Nations Publications, June 2018). This is equivalent to no more than USD 490 million in the peak year (about 162,000 people arrived in Italy in 2016 upon leaving Libya). By comparison, assuming an oil production at 1 million barrels per day, and a price of $70.2 per barrel (Brent price on 11 November 2018), current oil revenues exceed $25.6 billion. In sum, the smuggling of migrants from Libya equates to less than 2% of total oil revenues.

European Commission. (2015). Standard Eurobarometer. 84.
Hallams, E., & Schreer, B. (2012). Towards a 'Post-American' Alliance? NATO Burden-Sharing After Libya. *International Affairs, 88*(2), 313–327.
Hamid, S. (2016, April 12). Everyone Says the Libya Intervention Was a Failure: They're Wrong. *Brookings Institute.*
Hastings, M. (2011, October 27). Inside Obama's War Room. *Rolling Stone.*
Klepp, S. (2010). Italy and Its Libyan Cooperation Program: Pioneer of the European Union's Refugee Policy? In J. P. Cassarino (Ed.), *Unbalanced Reciprocities: Cooperation on Readmission in the Euro-Mediterranean Area,* pp. 77–93. Washington: MEI.
Kuperman, A. J. (2015, March/April). Obama's Libya Debacle: How a Well-Meaning Intervention Ended in Failure. *Foreign Affairs, 94,* 66–77.
Lindström, M., & Zetterlund, K. (2012). *Setting the Stage for the Military Intervention in Libya.* Stockholm: Försvarsdepartementet/Ministry of Defence.
Lizza, R. (2011, May 2). The Consequentialist. *The New Yorker.*
Mueller, K. P. (Ed.). (2015). *Precision and Purpose—Airpower in the Libyan Civil War.* Santa Monica: RAND.
NATO. (2011a, April 14). Statement on Libya.
NATO. (2011b, August 22). Statement by the NATO Secretary General on the Situation in Libya.
Pew Research Center. (2011, March 14). Public Wary of Military Intervention in Libya.
Ramesh, R. (2015, November 4). UN Libya Envoy Accepts £1,000-a-day Job from Backer of One Side in Civil War. *The Guardian.*
Toaldo, M. (2017). Europe: Carving Out a New Role. In K. Mezran & A. Varvelli (Eds.), *Foreign Actors in Libya's Crisis.* Milan: Ledizioni.
Varvelli, A. (2008). *L'Italia, la Libia e l'indebolimento del rapporto privilegiato* (ISPI Policy Brief 97).
Varvelli, A., & Mezran, K. (Eds.). (2012). *Libia. Fine o rinascita di una nazione?* Roma: Donzelli.
Villa, M. (2012). L'insostenibile peso della rendita e la sorte del regime di Gheddafi in Libia. In A. Varvelli & K. Mezran (Eds.), *Libia. Fine o rinascita di una nazione?* Roma: Donzelli.
Zenko, M. (2016, March 22). The Big Lie About the Libyan War. *Foreign Policy.*

CHAPTER 9

Resilience to What? EU Capacity-Building Missions in the Sahel

Luca Raineri and Edoardo Baldaro

The Sahel states, and Mali and Niger in particular, are often considered to be the quintessential embodiment of state fragility. Since the concept was popularised in policy literature, these countries have consistently ranked in the 'alert' category of the fragile states index (Fund for Peace 2018), at the very bottom of the United Nations Development Programme (UNDP) human development index (UNDP 2018), and in the lowest percentile of the World Bank's World Governance Indicators for political stability (World Bank 2018).

Although the concept of state fragility remains essentially contested (Newman 2009), recent studies (OECD 2008, 2013) have clarified its content in dialectic opposition to the notion of state resilience. Such a conceptual framing builds on the idea that the capacity of states to withstand internal or external shocks—such as economic crises, political transitions, and natural disasters—can be expressed along a continuum

L. Raineri (✉)
Sant'Anna School of Advanced Studies, Pisa, Italy
e-mail: luca.raineri@santannapisa.it

E. Baldaro
University of Naples "L'Orientale", Naples, Italy

© The Author(s) 2020
E. Cusumano and S. Hofmaier (eds.),
Projecting Resilience Across the Mediterranean,
https://doi.org/10.1007/978-3-030-23641-0_9

stretching from resilience, on the one hand, to vulnerability and collapse, on the other. From this perspective, 'fragility' indicates a state's tendency towards the latter end of such spectrum.

This conceptualisation has spilled over the disciplinary boundaries of development scholarship and practice, as state fragility becomes increasingly perceived as a threat to international peace and security (World Bank 2011). Consequently, the promotion of resilience is increasingly regarded as a recipe for stability and ranked as a security priority. The EU Global Strategy's (EUGS) (European Union 2016) insistence on resilience provides a perfect illustration of this trend. In particular, the EUGS places significant emphasis on the need to promote resilience in countries adjacent to EU's Neighbourhood. Since these ideas were articulated at a moment of increasing European engagement in the Sahel (Venturi 2017), it is tempting to read between the lines an implicit reference to European security strategies in the region.

However, in spite of its increasing prominence, the notion of resilience maintains a significant degree of vagueness. The EUGS does not elaborate on the concept and limits itself to a minimalist definition: resilience is 'the ability of states and societies to reform, thus withstanding and recovering from internal and external crises' (EU Commission 2016: 23). The EUGS enumerates many different policy tools and strategies to promote and maintain resilience including, inter alia: the support to accountable governance; the fight against terrorism and organised crime; the protection of human rights; the reform of the justice, security and defence sectors; building rule-of-law capacity. Such an all-encompassing conception of resilience may represent a deliberate choice of maintaining 'constructive ambiguity' (Rayroux 2014) in order to accommodate diverging interpretations and priorities. It also allows for tailor-made, context-sensitive solutions to be developed depending on circumstantial needs. Nevertheless, this ambiguity runs the risk of diluting the analytical value of the notion of resilience. Conceptual opacity may lead to equivocal interpretations, mis-specified strategies, and generic templates which fail to provide proper guidance to policy implementation and which increase the risk of inaccurate programming.

In the case of the Sahel, subsequent policy documents further specify the EU' strategy of promoting resilience in the region. The Sahel Regional Action Plan 2015–2020 (Council of the EU 2016) updates the Strategy for Security and Development in the Sahel (Council of the EU 2011) in light of the crises in Libya and in Mali that have erupted since, and identifies preventing radicalisation as the EU's first priority in the region. Moreover, in late 2016, the annual report on the Sahel Regional Action Plan (EEAS 2016) further clarified the need to adapt EU action to 'the political priorities of the EU, notably following the EU mobilization against irregular migration and related trafficking'. Building on these policy documents, one may conclude that the EU intends to promote resilience in the Sahel by reinforcing the capacity of Sahelian states to tackle, first and foremost, radicalisation towards violent extremism, and irregular migration.

Such goals are obviously worthwhile, and in line with the EUGS. However, one may contend that this approach conveys an implicit choice to lay emphasis on the destabilising potential of external stressors, such as radicalisation and irregular migration, rather than on the institutional fragilities that are characteristic of Sahel states. That is to say, this approach assumes that exogenous security contingencies of unprecedented scale threaten to overwhelm the weak defences of Sahel states, like a sudden tsunami inundating a shoreline. This chapter aims to critically analyse such a framing by questioning the assumed exogenous nature of the shocks that threaten the resilience of Sahelian states. We argue that it is not so much the magnitude of external contingencies such as radicalisation and irregular migration that draws attention to the fragility of the Sahel states. On the contrary, it is the inherent fragility of these states that makes security contingencies worrisome, irrespective of their size. Put otherwise, and expanding on the simile above, one does not need a tsunami to threaten the stability of a sandcastle. From this perspective, strengthening the resilience of Sahel states to withstand internal and external shocks would require state-building more than capacity-building, and therefore a more comprehensive and longer-term engagement and not only circumscribed measures in the security sector.

To substantiate our argument, we provide a detailed analysis of the Common Defence and Security Policy (CSDP) missions launched by the European Union in the Sahel. These include European Union Capacity Building Mission (EUCAP) Sahel Niger, EUCAP Sahel Mali, and European Union Training Mission (EUTM) Mali. While the EU makes clear that CSDP is only one of the tools through which it intends to promote resilience in the regions beyond the European neighbourhood, alongside development and diplomacy (EU Commission 2016), we argue that CSDP missions constitute the most prominent implementation of EU *security* policies, and therefore illustrate well how resilience is operationalised in practice. On the one hand, the increasing convergence towards a regional coordinated strategy (Council of the EU 2017a) provides the ground for comparisons and allows us to study the three missions within a unitary framework. On the other hand, the diversity of the missions analysed, including military and civilian operations with different mandates in different countries and with different degrees of successfulness, provides cases varied enough to uphold nuanced interpretations.

Building on this framework, we first introduce and analyse the mixed performances of the missions in order of their 'seniority', before inferring the commonalities and divergences of the missions and examining the shared context of their origin. We argue that the exogeneity and size of the external shocks identified may be overestimated, and conclude with an overall assessment of the EU strategy to promote resilience in the Sahel through capacity-building in the security sector.

EUCAP Sahel Niger: Stability as Migration Management?

Since late 2011, the collapse of the Gaddafi regime and the panic about the destabilising potential of the inflows of combatants and smuggled weapons from Libya (De Tessières 2018) alarmed Niger and its international partners. The EU promptly launched 'quick-impact' projects aimed at reabsorbing the Nigerien diaspora returning from Libya, and at the same time began to plan a CSDP mission for a longer-term response to the crisis. Following the request of Nigerien authorities, on 16 July 2012, the Council of the EU eventually authorised the deployment of EUCAP Sahel Niger, a civilian non-executive CSDP mission mandated to support the capacity-building of the Nigerien security sector. In particular, the mission was requested to build on Niger's own Security and Development Strategy—adopted in 2011 and largely inspired by the EU Strategy for Security and Development in the Sahel—in order to promote 'the development of an integrated, multidisciplinary, coherent, sustainable, and human rights-based approach among the various Nigerien security actors in the fight against terrorism and organised crime' (Council of the EU 2012). The specific activities to support these objectives included training, advice, and capacity-building in the fields of rule-of-law, criminal investigation, forensic techniques, and intelligence. Furthermore, the mandate emphasised the need for a 'comprehensive regional and international coordination in the fight against terrorism and organised crime'. In accordance with the geographic articulation of the

EU Strategy for Security and Development in the Sahel, the mission consequently established liaison officers in Mali and Mauritania.

EUCAP Sahel Niger initially had a relatively small budget of 8.7 million euros, and a limited time period of 12 months. In the following years, subsequent Council Decisions prolonged the mission until July 2016 while leaving the mandate and the budget substantially unchanged. However, the worsening of the Libyan crisis had altered the strategic environment of EUCAP Sahel Niger, and of the country more generally. Most notably, the deterioration of the rule-of-law and border management in Libya led to large-scale mixed migratory flows from Africa to Europe. Due to its strategic position and porous borders, Niger became a hub of northbound human smuggling (Reitano 2015), prompting the EU to request the cooperation of Nigerien authorities to curb irregular migration. The emergence of new priorities thus stimulated a reconsideration of EUCAP Sahel Niger's original mandate. However, while the fight against terrorism and organised crime enumerated in the mission's original mandate built on Niger's own security priorities, migration had always represented less a threat than a source of resilience for the country (Raineri 2018). Facing some initial hesitations, the simultaneous introduction of generous aid packages and more stringent conditionalities tied to the EU migration agenda probably contributed to ensuring Niger's compliance with the new European priorities. Hence, in April 2016 EUCAP Sahel Niger established a permanent field office in Agadez with a view to increasing its assistance to the Nigerien regions most severely hit by irregular migration and smuggling. In July 2016, the mission's mandate was renewed with the addition of a new objective: assisting the Nigerien authorities and security forces to better control migration flows and combat irregular migration and associated criminal activity more effectively. To this end, the Council also authorised a significant budget increase to 26.3 million euros. Lastly, in September 2018, the Council extended the mandate of EUCAP Sahel Niger for an additional two years, further increasing the budget to 63.4 million euros. While the new mandate reiterates the same objectives of strengthening the Nigerien security forces' capacity to fight terrorism and organised crime, it also preludes to a progressive phasing out of the mission, and is more focused on ensuring sustainability through training of the trainers and mentorship.

Throughout its long-running existence, EUCAP Sahel Niger was significantly enlarged from around 50 to more than 200 officers, and its personnel has contributed to the training of approximately 12,000 members of the Niger's internal security forces, armed forces and judiciary (EEAS 2018b). To ensure projects' sustainability, training has also been accompanied by the provision of teaching modules for the security forces' academies, the training of trainers, the upgrading training facilities, and the delivery of non-lethal border-management equipment.

The results of these efforts have been mixed, although the perplexing lack of an effective impact assessment mechanism makes more accurate conclusions unavailable. However, some promising achievements are noteworthy. EUCAP Sahel Niger has successfully assisted Nigerien authorities in elaborating appropriate legal frameworks, procedures and operating strategies, including the Internal Security Strategy, the National Border Policy, and the National Security Strategy (the latter being still ongoing). This Strategy was adopted in September 2017, and provides an underlying shared framework to ensure interoperability and coordination across different security actors. Recent surveys also suggest that Niger's internal security forces far exceed those of neighbouring countries in their intelligence and forensic capacities (Desmarais 2018), in which EUCAP Sahel Niger has invested significantly. Lastly, one may also attribute the relative restraint and discipline demonstrated by the Nigerien security forces to EUCAP Sahel Niger's close monitoring (Frowd and Sandor 2018).

On the other hand, the adoption of a rigid top-down approach from Brussels has had a negative impact on the flexibility, conflict- and context-sensitivity of EUCAP Sahel Niger. In particular, the establishment of a EUCAP Sahel field office in the volatile region of Agadez stirred considerable scepticism because it allegedly entailed considerable economic and political costs while its benefits remained elusive (Molenaar et al. 2017). Local observers contend that the field office appeared to address Niger's security needs less than those of European leaders, eager to show to their anxious constituencies the implementation of a securitised approach to migration based on muscular measures. This highlights a troubling disconnect between rhetoric, intentions and capabilities of European responses to security crises, possibly going beyond the single case of Niger (Ivaschenko-Stadnik et al. 2017; Cusumano 2018). At the institutional level, EUCAP Sahel Niger seems to have been unable to effectively tackle the corruption, nepotism, and patronage politics characterising Niger's security sector. These issues do not only entail ethical concerns, but also contribute directly to fostering radicalisation and terrorism (UNDP 2017), irregular migration (Raineri 2018), arms smuggling (De Tessières 2018) and organised crime. EUCAP Sahel Niger does not have a comprehensive security sector reform (SSR) mandate, but the inability to address the structural weaknesses of Niger's security apparatus runs the risk of increasing the resilience of the security threats instead of the security sector.

EUTM Mali: The Sisyphean Reform of the Malian Military

In October 2012, when an institutional crisis in the South and a jihadist insurgency in the North were still ravaging Mali, the UN Security Council called upon

> Member States, regional and international organizations, including the African Union and the European Union, to provide as soon as possible coordinated assistance, expertise, training and capacity-building support to the Armed and Security Forces of Mali, consistent with their domestic requirements, in order to restore the authority of the State of Mali over its entire national territory, to uphold the unity and territorial integrity of Mali and to reduce the threat posed by AQIM [Al-Qaeda in the Islamic Maghreb] and affiliated groups. (UNSC 2012)

On this basis, the EU then prepared a crisis management concept with a view to planning the deployment of a CSDP military assistance operation. When a French-led international military operation expelled the jihadist groups from towns in Northern Mali in early 2013, a request by the Malian authorities provided the legal basis for the EU to launch a training military mission in the country. EUTM was then deployed in February 2013 with an initial mandate of 15 months and a budget of 12.3 million euros. The mission was tasked with providing training and support to the Malian armed forces, especially in the fields of command-and-control, logistics, and applicable international law. Within this framework, EUTM also contributed to training armed battalions for immediate redeployment in the North, with a view to helping Mali restore state sovereignty throughout its territory.

In subsequent years, EUTM's mandate was repeatedly extended and expanded. In May 2014, the mission was renewed for another 24 months, and its budget increased accordingly. In May 2016, the third mandate introduced a greater focus on decentralised training, the training of trainers, and leadership skills, allegedly with the goal of fostering ownership and context-sensitivity. It also enlarged the geographical area of operation to Central Mali, as a result of the jihadist insurgency spilling over to the regions of Mopti and Ségou. Finally, in May 2018, the fourth mandate added the further objective of supporting the operational of the G5 Sahel Joint Force,[1] and to this end provided a substantial increase of the mission budget to approximately 60 million euros. Throughout this time, the training personnel of the mission had also increased from 200 to approximately 400 officers.

Since the first deployment, about half of the Malian armed forces have gone through the training provided for by EUTM (EEAS 2018a). This is a considerable achievement, especially if one considers the fast pace of recruitments within the Malian armed forces in the last years (Lebovich 2018). However, the empirical ascertainment of the mission's actual impact is still lagging behind. In 2014 the Malian armed forces, including those units recently trained by EUTM, performed very poorly during the clashes against non-state armed groups in Kidal and lost control of the town. While the Malian armed forces are still struggling to restore the unity and territorial integrity of Mali, allegations of very serious misconduct and human rights abuses against civilians perpetrated by the Malian military are beginning to surface (HRW 2017; ISS 2016; MINUSMA 2018).

The inherent limits of EUTM can contribute to explaining these disappointing results. Observers have noticed the prevalence of a top-down approach and the limited coordination with other military missions in Mali, such as the French operation *Barkhane* and the United Nations Multidimensional Integrated Stabilization Mission in Mali (MINUSMA). Combined with the lack of appropriate needs-assessment and monitoring tools, these factors may have constrained the flexibility, adaptability, and context-sensitivity of EUTM, and therefore limited its impact on the ground (Bøås et al. 2018). At the same time, EUTM's short-term mandates focused on stabilisation are at odds with the longer-term engagement that would be required to carry out a sustainable SSR, and leave more structural issues unaddressed (Tull 2017). In the last decades, in fact, issues of widespread corruption, opacity in personnel recruitment and equipment procurement, and political interferences have considerably undermined the capabilities and morale of the Malian army,

---

[1] The G5 Sahel Joint Force is a joint military and security project implemented by the five countries of the G5 Sahel (Mauritania, Mali, Niger, Burkina Faso and Chad). It would create a regional force able to fight against the transnational threats of terrorism, organised crime, and irregular migrations currently affecting the Sahel.

and contributed to eroding the broader legitimacy of the state and its security apparatus (Bergamaschi 2014; Briscoe 2014; MacLahlan 2015).

These tendencies risk being further exacerbated by the adoption of the Military Orientation and Programming Law (LOPM) in 2015, which EUTM allegedly contributed to drafting in a substantive way. The LOPM provides a two-digit allocation of the national budget to the security sector, with a considerable increase of the military expenditures of more than 40% (Berghezan 2016) for the period 2015–2019. This is expected to enhance the capabilities of Malian army to fight non-state armed groups and terrorists. According to the law, Mali will invest 350 million USD per year in the defence sector, out of a total state budget of approximately 3 billion USD per year.[2] In April 2018, the Prime Minister of Mali further specified that the overall security sector absorbs up to 22% of the state budget of Mali (Ahmed 2018). A financial boost may indeed be warranted to strengthen the capabilities of the Malian armed forces, and their resilience to external threats such as insurgents and jihadists. However, building on lessons learnt from past SSR programmes worldwide (De Boer and Bosetti 2015), these measures risk being ineffective and even counterproductive unless clear oversight mechanisms are introduced to ensure transparency and accountability. In a notoriously opaque sector such as defence policies, additional resources may be easily diverted and squandered to fuel criminal interests, patronage politics, and corruption. Such misuses risk fermenting into social tensions like those that precipitated the collapse of the Malian state in 2012, well before rebel and terrorist armed groups occupied the North (Raineri 2016). It is unclear to what extent the LOPM incorporates such a system of checks and oversight, but the corruption scandals involving Malian armed forces in recent years provide limited room for optimism.

One may therefore conclude that EUTM's emphasis on building the capacity of the Malian army to fight external enemies such as terrorists and insurgents may be insufficient. Acknowledging local responsibilities and the institutional fragilities characterising the Malian military may well be politically costly, but it has better chances to succeed in strengthening the resilience of the Malian army and state more generally, than underwriting the illusive projection of the problem outside of the geographic and institutional boundaries of the state.

[2] On the whole, however, Malian state budget is largely dependent on foreign donors (see Bergamaschi 2014).

EUCAP Sahel Mali: Dealing with Delegitimised Institutions

Following the Council decision of 14 April 2014, EUCAP Sahel Mali was officially launched on 15 January 2015, with an initial mandate of one year and a financial budget of 11.4 million euros, which followed a preliminary funding of 5.5 million euros allocated for the period April 2014–January 2015 (Council of the EU 2015). Since its inception, EUCAP Sahel Mali was aimed at 'supporting reform in Mali', complementing the 'military training mission EUTM and the EU's broader engagement in Mali' (Council of the EU 2014a).

As in the case of EUTM, the launch of EUCAP Sahel Mali followed an official request by the Malian authorities. In general terms, '[t]he mission provides experts in strategic advice and training to the Malian Police, Gendarmerie and National Guard and the relevant ministries in order to support reform in the security sector' (EUCAP 2018). Accordingly, the initial mandate indicated four main goals for the mission, mainly focused on the necessity of starting a process of deep reform of the internal security apparatus, and on the redeployment of internal security forces in the northern regions (Council of the EU 2014b). These objectives prioritised the need to re-establish the basic functions and capacities of the Malian security forces, and were elaborated when the north still represented the main challenge to the full restoration of the internal sovereignty in Mali. It is not surprising then, that at the moment of renewing the mission's mandate, the Council opted to add new duties and goals to EUCAP, more aligned with the situation on the ground, and more consistent with the EU's changing priorities in the region.[3] In particular, in the new mandate—extending the mission until January 2019 with an initial budget of 29.7 million euros (Council of the EU 2017b)—two new priorities have been introduced: supporting Mali in managing its borders and the migration flows, and strengthening the Malian internal security forces' capacities in their fight against terrorist and criminal groups. At the same time, EUCAP was also requested to both expand and deepen its geographical focus. On the one hand, the mission should support regionalisation by inserting liaison officers in other G5 Sahel countries and favouring exchanges among G5 Sahel's

---

[3] As we have shown in the previous paragraph, the same move also affected the evolution of the mandate of EUTM.

internal security forces. On the other hand, EUCAP should bolster its presence in the country by deploying advice and training in the other Malian regions (EUCAP 2018). Moreover, the new mandate includes a reference to the 'Accord for Peace and Reconciliation', the peace agreement signed in 2015 with most of the northern insurgent groups, which foresees a broad reform of the internal security forces (Bagayoko 2018).

As a non-combat mission, EUCAP Sahel Mali follows three main lines of operation for implementing its mandate, namely through training, strategic advice, and cooperation and coordination. In quantitative terms, figures seem to suggest that EUCAP's training programmes are quite successful. Following the principle of 'training the trainers' in order to further local ownership and increase context-sensitiveness, EUCAP had by October 2017 trained 3400 officials, offering classes on topics that go from professional methods to human rights issues (Bøås et al. 2018). In a similar vein, human resources management, command structure, and internal monitoring are at the centre of the advising activities, implemented with the Ministry of Defence (leading the Gendarmerie and the National Guard) and the Ministry of Internal Security (in charge of the Police) (Bagayoko 2018). Finally, cooperation and coordination are interwoven at three levels. EUCAP should foster cooperation among the different ministries involved in Malian internal security, while coordinating its action with EUTM, MINUSMA, and other international actors. Moreover, EUCAP is now a pivotal actor in the regionalising process of the EU's strategy. In particular, two main initiatives epitomise this new task contained in the mandate. On the one hand, EUCAP supports the *Groupe d'Action Rapide - Surveillance et Intervention au Sahel* (GAR-SI SAHEL) programme, a project that should create and train multinational border-management units of the Gendarmerie, formed by recruits coming from the five countries of the G5. On the other hand, a Regional Coordination Cell has been created within EUCAP, in order to provide the mission with a permanent structure in charge of the supervision and the coordination of the European security actions towards the region (Bagayoko 2018; Bøås et al. 2018).

As of the two principal limitations of EUCAP Sahel Mali, the dysfunctionality of local partners, and the intrinsic tensions within the mission's mandate are noteworthy. With reference to the former, it is worth noting here that the Malian internal security apparatus has a long history of unachieved reforms. The last example, the Orientation and Programming of Internal Security Law (*Projet de Loi d'Orientation et de*

Programmation sur la Sécurité Intérieure [LOPSI]), should mirror the LOPM, by mobilising more than 650 million euros with the support and the advice of external partners, but it is still blocked by a lack of political agreement among central authorities (Bagayoko 2018). In the meantime, the Police and the Gendarmerie face legitimacy problems. These institutions, along with the judiciary, continue to be perceived as the most corrupted elements of the state apparatus (Mali-Mètre 2017). Even more worrisome, it is almost impossible to receive reliable figures on the effective number of policemen and gendarmes employed by the respective ministries, as some official sources calculate that the Malian security forces are formed by 13,000 units, while others reduce this number to less than 10,000 units (Bagayoko 2018; Bøås et al. 2018). These facts are well known by EUCAP staff, who are also aware of their inability to address this issue: as observed by an EU official, 'ethics is a big problem… until they don't have decent salaries we can do as many trainings as we want, that is not gonna change things'.[4]

At the same time, the expansion of the mandate could multiply tensions and even contradictions within EUCAP's initiatives. The fight against terrorism and organised crime, a coordinated and regionalised action for border and migration management, and the absorption of northern fighters in the internal security apparatus, seem to compose the three sides of an 'impossible triangle'. Malian authorities lack control over approximately two-thirds of the country, and strategies and allegiances of the different socio-economic and armed groups change and evolve according to the contingent opportunities (Sandor 2017). Consequently, pursuing one goal risks endangering policy advancement in the other domains. On the other hand, EUCAP is more and more burdened by the increasing expectations and sense of urgency coming from Brussels, in particular with regard to the need to find quick-fix solutions to the security situation in the centre of the country. This creates clear tensions with the potential long-term engagement of EUCAP, and exacerbates the risk of furthering corruption and the mismanagement of aid, by pushing the absorption capacity of the Malian security sector to the limits.[5]

---

[4] Interview with EU Officer held in Bamako in November 2017 in the framework of EUNPACK project.

[5] Interview with EU Officer held in Bamako in November 2017 in the framework of EUNPACK project.

Table 9.1 CSDP missions in the Sahel

Mission	Launching date	Budget	Personnel	Mandate
EUCAP Sahel Niger	16 July 2012	63.4 million euro (since September 2018)	200 officers	1. Supporting capacity-building of the Nigerien security forces 2. Assisting Nigerien security forces in fighting terrorism and organised crime 3. Assisting Nigerien authorities to better control migration flows
EUTM Mali	17 January 2013	60 million euro (since May 2018)	400 officers	1. Training and support to the Malian armed forces 2. Favouring the redeployment of the Malian army in the North and the center of the country 3. Supporting the operationalisation of the G5 Sahel Joint Force
EUCAP Sahel Mali	14 April 2014	29.7 million euro (since January 2017)	100 officers (June 2016)	1. Supporting the reform and the redeployment in the North of the Malian internal security forces 2. Supporting Mali in fighting terrorism and organised crime 3. Supporting Mali in managing borders and migration flows 4. Regionalising EU's action

In conclusion, as for EUTM, only a long-term and conflict-sensitive engagement appears as the solution, for allowing EUCAP Sahel Mali to have a positive impact in advancing resilience within the Malian internal security sector (Table 9.1).

Conclusion

The analysis of EU-CSDP missions in Niger and Mali suggests that the European strategy to project resilience in the Sahel features a markedly outward orientation. Emphasising the regional dimension may foster coordination and avoid costly overlaps, but at the same time risks shifting the focus away from the national problems. Nevertheless, leaving the institutional fragilities of Sahelian states unaddressed and unresolved undermines the potential impact of EU efforts to promote resilience through capacity-building in the security sector.

In the same vein, EU strategies convey an implicit externalisation of the threats that resilience-building measures are designed to tackle. Radicalisation and terrorism, organised crime and human smuggling, are presented as exogenous shocks inflicted upon Sahel states. This assumption is questionable on at least two grounds: it is based on an uncritical partition between inside and outside that assumes the exogeneity of the threats and the morality of state order, and it overestimates the impact of regional dynamics on local affairs. A case in point is the view underpinning EU Sahel strategies that the collapse of the state apparatuses in Libya triggered the destabilisation of the entire region by unleashing uncontrolled flows of weapons, terrorists, and migrants across porous borders. While this fear may have been warranted at the very beginning of the Libyan crisis in 2011, the evidence made available by subsequent studies necessitates a more nuanced assessment. Most weapons stolen from Gaddafi's arsenal remained in Libya to meet a soaring local demand, while non-state armed groups in the Sahel region—including rebels and terrorists—have sourced their weapons directly from Mali's and Niger's national stockpiles, either by theft or by informal transactions (Anders 2015; CAR 2016; De Tessières 2018). From this perspective, arms smuggling is less of an exogenous problem than one may be tempted to think, with the corruption of security forces representing an *endogenous* source of fragility that should not be underestimated. Similarly, a growing body of literature provides convincing evidence that radicalisation and terrorism in the Sahel to a large extent are not due to contagion from foreign ideas and foreign fighters, but are a home-grown reaction to abuses by the security forces that exacerbate local tensions (ISS 2016; UNDP 2017; Pérouse de Montclos 2018). Furthermore, the sociology of Sahel societies suggests that even organised crime is not alien to, but deeply embedded within, the local states' apparatuses through 'big men' networks of patronage politics. These collusions underpin the infrastructure of smuggling in both Mali (Molenaar and Van Damme 2017) and Niger (Raineri 2018), and contribute to explaining irregular migration patterns in the region better than security contingencies in Libya alone.

Building on these observations, one may be tempted to speculate that Sahel states may not share the objective of having an efficient, modern, and independent security sector (Tull 2017). The revenues of extralegal economies and the fear of military coups—which have been frequent both in Mali and Niger—may explain why political elites in Bamako and in Niamey prefer to keep the security sector under control by perpetuating the prevailing logic of patronage. Paradoxically, under the ambiguous umbrella of resilience-building, the interests of local leaders may be in alignment with EU security ambitions in the Sahel. This can contribute to clarifying the significant degree of acceptance of short-term, 'light-footprint' interventions focusing on building the capacity of local security forces to tackle external enemies, even when other security priorities may be more compelling. On the other hand, it helps to explain the otherwise puzzling lack of adequate monitoring and evaluation mechanisms, in the absence of which the assumption that more training and budget increases the resilience of Niger's and Mali's security forces cannot be disputed.

In conclusion, the constant renewal of the mandates of the three CSDP missions demonstrates an increasing European interest in managing the destabilising dynamics afflicting the Sahel Region. Moreover, since the approval of the first European strategy for the Sahel, the region has represented a veritable 'laboratory of experimentation', where the EU has tested and implemented its renewed strategic concept and approach to crisis and conflict (Lopez Lucia 2017). To a certain extent, the development of the European action towards the Sahel exemplifies the wider change, which is currently redefining the European approach to crisis- and conflict-management. While the 2011 Strategy for Security and Development in the Sahel anticipated the main principles expressed in the 2014 EU's comprehensive approach, and reiterated the centrality of the so-called security-development-good governance nexus, the 2015 Sahel Regional Action Plan expresses the shift towards a more security-focused action for spreading stability and resilience, which trumps longer term engagements to development and state-building (Venturi 2017). These dynamics are directly affecting the CSDP missions in the area. As we have shown in this chapter in fact, the three missions tend to suffer from similar problems, that are weakening their efficacy and which have not been solved by the expansion of each mission's budgets and mandates. An implicit tension exists between Brussels perceptions and the need for a quick result and the complexities of the realities of the ground. Both in Mali and Niger, real and long-term solutions to instability and insecurity can come only from a deep reform of local institutions, or to a lesser extent, from a better assessment of the local will and capacity to absorb external resources and practices.

In this sense, it is advisable for the European Union to better ensure that a comprehensive approach to security and context-sensitive analysis underpin resilience-building measures in the Sahel. In the short term, this entails the adoption of monitoring and evaluation mechanisms common to the three CSDP missions, so as to better assess the potentials but also the unintended consequences of EU action. In the longer term instead, factoring local needs and societal claims in resilience-building measures could discourage rent-seeking and free-riding by enhancing accountability and sustainability in external security strategies. On the other hand, stronger synergies should be created between the CSDP missions and other European actors working at the political or development level, as a way to further coordination and enhance threat- and context-assessment capacities. In a context characterised by different and interlinked institutional, socio-political and economic crises, it would be worthwhile for the EU to act in a comprehensive manner, valorising and integrating its different instruments and sectors of expertise: resilience in the Sahel would be fostered by implementing a truly integrated and sustainable approach, able to take into consideration the different fragilities and challenges which are shaping the local and the regional environments.

References

Ahmed, B. (2018, April 23). Mali: l'intégration des ex-rebelles est une question «résolue», affirme le Premier ministre. *Jeune Afrique*.

Anders, H. (2015). Expanding Arsenals: Insurgents Arms in Northern Mali. In Small Arms Survey (Ed.), *Weapons and the World*. Cambridge: Cambridge University Press.

Bagayoko, N. (2018). *Le processus de réforme du secteur de la sécurité au Mali* (A Stabilizing Mali Report). Montreal: Centre FrancoPaix en Résolution des conflits et Missions de paix.

Bergamaschi, I. (2014). The Fall of a Donor Darling: The Role of Aid in Mali's Crisis. *The Journal of Modern African Studies, 52*(3), 347–378.

Berghezan, G. (2016, June). *Dépenses militaires et importations d'armes dans cinq États ouest-africains.* Note d'analyse du GRIP. Bruxelles.

Bøås, M., Diallo, A., Drange, B., Kvamme, F., & Stambøl, E. (2018, January). *The Implementation of EU Crisis Response in Mali* (EUNPACK Working Paper D.7.4). Brussels.

Briscoe, I. (2014). *Crime After Jihad: Armed Groups, the State, and Illicit Business in Post-Conflict Mali.* The Hague: Clingendael Report.

Conflict Armament Research (CAR). (2016). *Investigating Cross-Border Weapon Transfers in the Sahel.* London: Conflict Armament Research (CAR).

Council of the EU. (2011, March 21). *Council Conclusions on a European Union Strategy for Security and Development in the Sahel.* Brussels.

Council of the EU. (2012, July 16). *Council Decision 2012/392/CFSP on the European Union CSDP Mission in Niger (EUCAP Sahel Niger).* Brussels.

Council of the EU. (2014a, April 15). *Council Press Release 8773/14 on EUCAP Sahel Mali: EU Support Mission for Internal Security in Mali Established.* Luxembourg.

Council of the EU. (2014b, April 15). *Council Decision 2014/219/CFSP on the European Union CSDP Mission in Mali (EUCAP Sahel Mali).* Brussels.

Council of the EU. (2015, January 13). *Council Decision 2014/2019/CFSP Launching the European Union CSDP Mission in Mali (EUCAP Sahel Mali) and Amending Decision 2014/219/CFS.* Brussels.

Council of the EU. (2016, June 20). *Council Conclusions on the Sahel.* Luxembourg.

Council of the EU. (2017a, June 20). *Council Decision 2017/1102/CFSP, Amending Decision 2014/219/CFSP on the European Union CSDP Mission in Mali (EUCAP Sahel Mali).* Brussels.

Council of the EU. (2017b, January 11). *Council Press Release 8/17 on EUCAP Sahel Mali: Mission Extended for Two Years, €29.7 Million Budget Adopted.* Luxembourg.

Cusumano, E. (2018). Migrant Rescue as Organized Hypocrisy: EU Maritime Missions Offshore Libya Between Humanitarianism and Border Control. *Cooperation and Conflict, 54*, 1–22.

De Boer, J., & Bosetti, L. (2015). *The Crime-Conflict 'Nexus': State of the Evidence* (Research Paper 4). Tokyo: United Nations University Centre for Policy.

De Tessières, S. (2018). *At the Crossroads of Sahelian Conflicts: Insecurity, Terrorism, and Arms Trafficking in Niger.* Geneva: Small Arms Survey.

Desmarais, A. (2018, June). *Le monitoring des armes au Sahel. Les institutions forensiques nationales.* Geneva: Small Arms Survey.

EEAS—European External Action Service. (2016, December 23). *Annual Report on the Sahel Regional Action Plan*. Brussels.
EEAS—European External Action Service. (2018a, July 31). *EUTM Mali Fact-Sheet*. Bamako.
EEAS—European External Action Service. (2018b, August). *Civilian Mission EUCAP Sahel Nigerfact-Sheet*. Niamey.
EUCAP Sahel Mali. (2018). *About Us*. https://eucap-sahel-mali.eu/about_en.html.
European Union. (2016, June). *Shared Vision, Common Action: A Stronger Europe: A Global Strategy for the European Union's Foreign and Security Policy*. Brussels.
Frowd, P., & Sandor, A. (2018). Militarism and Its Limits: Sociological Insights on Security Assemblages in the Sahel. *Security Dialogue, 49*(1), 70–82.
Fund for Peace. (2018). *Fragile State Index Annual Report*. Washington, DC. http://fundforpeace.org/fsi/2018/04/24/fragile-states-index-2018-annual-report/.
HRW—Human Rights Watch. (2017). *Mali: Recrudescence des abus commis par les groups islamistes et du banditisme*.
ISS—Institute for Security Studies. (2016, August). *Mali's Young Jihadists* (Policy Brief 89). Pretoria/Dakar.
Ivaschenko-Stadnik, K., Petrov, R., Raineri, L., Rieker, P., Russo, A., & Strazzari, F. (2017, March). *How the EU Is Facing Crises in Its Neighbourhood: Evidence from Libya and Ukraine* (EUNPACK Working Paper D.6.1). Brussels.
Lebovich, A. (2018). *Halting Ambitions: EU Migration and Security Policy in the Sahel* (ECFR Policy Brief 266).
Lopez Lucia, E. (2017). Performing EU Agency by Experimenting the "Comprehensive Approach": The European Union Sahel Strategy. *Journal of Contemporary African Studies, 35*(4), 451–468.
MacLachlan, K. (2015, August). *Security Assistance, Corruption and Fragile Environments: Exploring the Case of Mali 2001–2012*. London, UK: Transparency International.
Mali-Mètre. (2017). *Enquête d'Opinion: 'Que pensent les Malien(ne)s?' Friedrich Ebert Stiftung Research Pool*.
MINUSMA. (2018, February). *Droits de l'homme et processus de paix au Mali: Janvier 2016–Juin 2017*. Bamako.
Molenaar, F., Ursu, A., Tinni, B., Hoffmann, A., & Meester, J. (2017). *A Line in the Sand Roadmap for Sustainable Migration Management in Agadez* (Clingendael Report).
Molenaar, F., & Van Damme, T. (2017). *Irregular Migration and Human Smuggling Networks in Mali* (Clingendael Report).
Newman, E. (2009). Failed States and International Order: Constructing a Post-Westphalian World. *Contemporary Security Policy, 30*(3), 421–443.

OECD—Organisation for Economic Co-operation and Development. (2008). Concepts and Dilemmas of State-Building in Fragile Situations: From Fragility to Resilience (OECD/DAC Discussion Paper). *OECD Journal on Development, 9*(3), 61–148.

OECD—Organisation for Economic Co-operation and Development. (2013). *Fragile States 2013: Resource Flows and Trends in a Shifting World*. Paris: OECD.

Pérouse de Montclos, M.-A. (2018). *L'Afrique, nouvelle frontière du djihad?* Paris: La Découverte.

Raineri, L. (2016). Mali: The Short-Sightedness of Donor-Driven Peacebuilding. *Journal of Peacebuilding and Development, 11*(1), 88–92.

Raineri, L. (2018). Human Smuggling Across Niger: State-Sponsored Protection Rackets and Contradictory Security Imperatives. *The Journal of Modern African Studies, 56*(1), 63–86.

Rayroux, A. (2014). Speaking EU Defence at Home: Contentious Discourses and Constructive Ambiguity. *Cooperation and Conflict, 49*(3), 386–405.

Reitano, T. (2015). A Perilous but Profitable Crossing: The Changing Nature of Migrant Smuggling Through Sub-Saharan Africa to Europe and EU Migration Policy (2012–2015). *The European Review of Organised Crime, 2*(1), 1–23.

Sandor, A. (2017). *Insecurity, the Breakdown of Social Trust, and Armed Actor Governance in Central and Northern Mali* (A Stabilizing Mali Report). Montréal: Centre FrancoPaix en Résolution des conflits et Missions de paix.

Tull, D. (2017). *Mali, the G5 and Security Sector Assistance: Political Obstacles to Effective Cooperation*. SWP Comments.

UNDP—United Nations Development Programme. (2017). *Journey to Extremism in Africa*.

UNDP—United Nations Development Programme. (2018). *Human Development Index*.

UNSC—United Nations Security Council. (2012, October 12). *Resolution 2071*. New York.

Venturi, B. (2017, December). *The EU and the Sahel: A Laboratory of Experimentation for the Security–Migration–Development Nexus* (IAI Working Papers 17[38]). Rome.

World Bank. (2011). *World Development Report: Conflict, Security, and Development*. Washington, DC: World Bank.

World Bank. (2018). *Worldwide Governance Indicators*. Washington, DC. http://info.worldbank.org/governance/wgi/#reports.

CHAPTER 10

Resilience and Conflict Resolution: UN Peacekeeping in Mali

Chiara Ruffa, Sebastiaan Rietjens and Emma Nygren

INTRODUCTION

State fragility in the Sahel region has triggered a renewed interest of the United Nations (UN) to build resilience in the region. Resilience-building efforts look for existing strengths to allow individuals, communities, and societies to overcome and address security threats by building their own capacities. In contrast to what happened in other regions, however, UN efforts for building resilience in the Sahel were immediately connected to large-scale external security responses. The UN introduced the concept of resilience in the Sahel as early as 2014. At first, improving resilience was understood to be key to conflict prevention, and efforts were made to promote resilience with softer, political

---

C. Ruffa (✉)
Swedish Defence University, Stockholm, Sweden

Uppsala University, Uppsala, Sweden

S. Rietjens
Netherlands Defence Academy, Breda, The Netherlands

E. Nygren
Department of Peace and Conflict, Uppsala University, Uppsala, Sweden

© The Author(s) 2020
E. Cusumano and S. Hofmaier (eds.),
Projecting Resilience Across the Mediterranean,
https://doi.org/10.1007/978-3-030-23641-0_10

means. The Department of Political Affairs launched a much-acclaimed United Nations Integrated Strategy for the Sahel, endorsed by the UN Security Council in June 2013 (UNSC 534/2013). The strategy entailed 'life-saving activities that meet immediate needs, while building the resilience of people and communities as part of a long-term development agenda' (UN 2019a). To achieve such an objective, the UN pursued 'good offices to mobilise political will and resources to address the challenges in the region' (UN 2019a). The strategy explicitly aimed at building resilience through both capacity-building and political inclusion. Notwithstanding the seemingly broader focus, increasing resilience has from the start focused on security, and the capacity-building component of the strategy has focused overwhelmingly on strengthening border management capabilities. As it can be read in the strategy, 'collaborative management of borders is not only about constraining the activities of criminals and terrorists, but also about giving opportunity to legitimate economic activity' (UN 2019a). The political inclusion component of the strategy focuses on 'supporting vulnerable households and promoting food and nutritional security, while also building capacity for long term resilience' (UN 2019a). As of 2016, the UN Department of Political Affairs (DPA) merged the Office of the Special Envoy to the Sahel with the United Nations Office for West Africa, creating the United Nations Office for West Africa and the Sahel.

While the office continues to focus implicitly on resilience, the increasing insecurity in the region has triggered a more widespread emphasis on insecurity. This has meant that DPA efforts have become first accompanied and then surpassed by the activities of the Department of Peacekeeping Operations (DPKO). DPKO has become one of the main actors in the region after launching the United Nations Multidimensional Integrated Stabilisation Mission in Mali (MINUSMA), combined with the corresponding marginalisation of DPA. With the reinforced strategy in the Sahel, the UN renewed its engagement in the region in 2014. Mali, with its chronic instability, became a central component of the renewed strategy (on the EU approach to the Sahel region, see chapter by Raineri and Baldaro in this volume). With troops from 52 contributing countries deployed, MINUSMA is one of the largest, most diverse, and most complex UN missions ever launched. This mission is an especially important case for the study of how UN peacekeeping operations can foster resilience because it contains all the key prerequisites: MINUSMA has a complex, multidimensional mandate that does not only focus on security and it explicitly states among its objectives the necessity of supporting reconstruction and reconciliation (although it does not explicitly refer to intelligence). MINUSMA also follows a recent turn to introduce intelligence in UN peacekeeping (Shetler-Jones 2008).

Not only does the mission contain several ambitious objectives in its mandate. MINUSMA is also one of the most innovative missions in terms of structure and personnel. After a period of inactivity, several western European countries have now stepped up their contribution to UN missions and deployed innovative capabilities to Mali including special forces, fighting helicopters as well as a large intelligence contingent (Karlsrud and Smith 2015; Karlsrud and Osland 2016; Rietjens and Ruffa 2019; Van Willigen 2016). Its multidimensional and integrated mandate includes the protection of civilians and the strengthening of state capacity. In its recent report on the UN mission in Mali, the UN Secretary General stressed once again the UN's emphasis on resilience by 'supporting Mali in the reconstitution of its armed forces, promoting development and strengthening resilience, as well as ensuring the Joint Force of the Group of Five for the Sahel (G5), comprising of Burkina Faso, Mauritania, Mali, Niger and Chad, is provided with sufficient resources to be an effective instrument in restoring stability in the Sahel' (Reliefweb 2018). While resilience was not explicitly mentioned in the mandate authorising the mission, it is the most common *leitmotif* of any UN document concerning Mali, and is framed as a key instrument to the resolution of conflict. While the focus on resilience remained, the very nature and structure of MINUSMA made it almost impossible to build it. In other words, the UN mission in Mali became key for the UN to build resilience in the Sahel as Mali was identified as a key area of insecurity in the whole region. Yet, the mission's architecture remains overwhelmingly focused on security and military objectives, which ultimately inhibit the building of resilience and trigger widespread incoherence.

This chapter draws on MINUSMA as a source of insights into the UN's role in relation to building resilience in the Sahel and beyond. We structure our chapter into three parts. First, we provide some context for how the conflict in Mali unfolded and where the necessity to build resilience comes from. Second, we discuss the ambitions set by the UN mission and its role in building resilience. Finally, we draw some conclusions for building resilience via UN peacekeeping and beyond.

Conflict and State Breakdown in Mali and Beyond

When discussing resilience in Mali much focus has been laid on resilience towards environmental disasters, such as droughts (Gressly 2013). The UN and other aid organisations focused on five humanitarian priorities: food insecurity, malnutrition, consequences from conflicts, epidemics, and natural disasters (UNOCHA 2014). At the annual session of Peacebuilding Commission in 2018, Deputy Security-General Amina J. Mohammed said that achieving peace in the Sahel region requires tackling the root causes, found in discrimination, human rights violations, weak governance, conflict and impact of climate change (UN 2018). On the same note, the G5 Sahel group has been seen as a catalyst of resilience in and of itself. Save the Children wrote in 2012 a report on ending the everyday emergency through resilience in the Sahel (Gubbels 2012). They take their own perspective on resilience defining it as efforts to decrease malnutrition and act earlier on the early warnings to a faster recovery and development (Gubbels 2012).

In order to understand how the UN is building resilience in Mali through peacekeeping, we need to first discuss what resilience is designed to protect against, that is what kind of shocks Mali has gone through. The conflict in Mali should be seen as deriving from lasting structural conditions, such as weak state institutions, ineffective governance, fragile social cohesion, and severe inequalities, coupled with the effects of environmental degradation, climate change, and economic shocks (Lotze 2015). The current conflict goes back to the collapse of the Gaddafi regime. The Malian government has continually neglected the Northern regions of Mali, a legacy that dates back to colonialism. Since independence, the Touaregs living in the northern parts of Mali have organised several rebellions striving to acquire independence of the northern regions (region of Azawad). The failure of these rebellions led many Touaregs to voluntary join Gaddafi's militias in Libya. In exchange for serving in the Libyan leader's security forces, the Touaregs received military training and weapons (Chauzal and Van Damme 2015). When Gaddafi's regime fell in 2011, most Tuareg returned to northern Mali to face disappointment and frustration with the state of governance and development in the region. Soon after, the National Movement of the Liberation of Azawad (MNLA) was founded in October 2011. In parallel to these events, an armed rebellion pushed the Malian Defence and Security Forces (MDSF) out of their main locations by the end of January 2012 (Lotze 2015). Growing discontent among the MDSF of the government's response in dealing with the rebellion in the north finally led to a *coup d'état* in March 2012. The coup leaders ousted the government, suspended the constitution, and created the National Committee for the Rehabilitation of Democracy and the Restoration of the State. However, because the military was focused on consolidating the coup, efforts to contain the rebellion in the north were abandoned. Several rebel groups did at this point work together taking advantage of the situation by launching an offensive campaign with the intent to expand the area under their control. By the end of April 2012, the northern cities of Aguelhoc, Lere, Tinzaouantene, Tessalit, Kidal, Timbukto, and Gao were all controlled by MNLA. However, this was also to be the beginning of internal fighting among the Touareg, some of whom joined the newly founded group Ansar Dine, a religious rebel group striving to implement sharia law in the region of Azawad (Chauzal and Van Damme 2015). The MNLA proclaimed the independence of the 'Republic of Azawad', and declared the end of its military offensive. The coup was widely condemned and a series of sanctions were imposed on its leaders. Moreover, the Economic Community of West African States (ECOWAS) deployed a mediation team tasked with finding a political solution to the crisis. MNLA's military successes pressured the coup leaders to enter into dialogue with ECOWAS which quickly established the basis of a transitional government. On 20 August 2012, a government of National Unity was formed (Lotze 2015). However, the conflict kept escalating due to the split of MNLA and Ansar Dine and the founding of Al-Qaida Organisation in the Islamic Maghreb (AQIM) and Movement for Unity and Jihad in West Africa. By the end of July 2012, the jihadist armed groups had taken control of most northern cities. As a consequence of renewed fighting, the region experienced a significant increase in the number of human rights abuses and forced displacements. Mali became even more torn apart. While Islamic groups controlled the northern territories and installed sharia law, a military junta was installed in its capital Bamako and called for revenge on the northern Islamic groups. This dire situation was widely seen as the peak of failed national unity in Mali.

In the face of these developments, the United Nations Security Council authorised the deployment of the African-led International

Support Mission in Mali (AFISMA) on 20 December 2012. AFISMA's mandate was primarily to enforce peace and support the recovery of government control in northern Mali and, when possible, transition to stabilisation activities (United Nations 2012). The total approved mission strength surpassed 9500 personnel (8859 military, 590 police, and 171 civilian). In January 2013, while the African Union (AU) and ECOWAS prepared for the deployment of AFISMA, the Islamic movements mounted another military offensive and advanced to towns in central Mali. The transitional government, fearing that the armed groups could soon get to Bamako, requested French military support. In the next few days, France launched Operation Serval, which initially comprised of 2400 troops (Boeke and Scuurman 2015). With the support of Malian and Chadian forces, and the MNLA, the French managed to push the Islamic movements out of the major population centres (Lotze 2015). Meanwhile, France argued for the transition of AFISMA into a UN peacekeeping operation. The transitional government, ECOWAS, and the AU endorsed the proposal, and, on 25 April 2013 the UN Security Council approved the establishment of the MINUSMA.

BUILDING RESILIENCE IN MALI? UN PEACEKEEPING

MINUSMA was launched to take over AFISMA's responsibilities on 1 July 2013 (UN 2013). The Security Council also authorised France to maintain a parallel counter-terrorism force in Mali, also mandated to support MINUSMA if necessary. MINUSMA is one of the most complex operations ever undertaken by the UN. The mission's mandate included the (1) stabilisation of key population centres and support for the re-establishment of State authority throughout the country; (2) support for the implementation of the transitional road map, including the national political dialogue and the electoral process; (3) protection of civilians and UN personnel; (4) support for humanitarian assistance; (5) support for cultural preservation; and (6) support for national and international justice (UN 2013: 7–8). While no reference was made to the term 'resilience', it was clear that part of the challenge was to 'support', as extensively emphasised by the mandate, post-conflict reconstruction and the ability of institutions and society not to fall back into conflict.

The mission is dispersed throughout large parts of the country, from the capital Bamako in the south to Timbuktu in the west and Kidal in the northern part. The mission has faced many challenges, including terrorist attacks, ambushes and improvised explosives devices (IED), and UN camps and convoys of peacekeepers were attacked multiple times (Security Council Report 2019b). This made MINUSMA the deadliest UN peacekeeping operation in UN history (BBC 2015).

African troop- and police-contributing countries (T/PCCs) deployed most of the uniformed personnel in Mali. By the end of October 2018, a total of 9506 troops and police personnel came from African TCCs (UN 2018). Among the African troop-contributing countries, ten ECOWAS countries contributed to significant troops contingents. In addition to African troops, MINUSMA marked a European return to UN peacekeeping operations (Karlsrud and Smith 2015). By the end of October 2018, European countries provided 1220 uniformed personnel deployed in command and staff positions, as well as intelligence, surveillance, and reconnaissance units, unmanned and unarmed aerial systems, transport and attack helicopters, and fixed-wing transport aircraft (Karlsrud and Smith 2015; UN 2018). During the same period, Asian TCCs contributed 2837 uniformed personnel, including traditional contributors, such as Bangladesh, Nepal, and Sri Lanka, but also unusual providers of combat troops, such as China (UN 2018). The military part of MINUSMA is called upon to monitor disputed borders, monitor and observe peace processes, provide security, assist in-country military personnel with training and support, support ex-combatants, and protect civilians. This makes the military an essential part in promoting resilience. The next section zooms in on how the MINUSMA force fostered the building of resilience and what challenges they were confronted with. In doing so, we specifically focus on one subset of MINUSMA's force, i.e. the intelligence organisation in the period 2014–2016. If an actor knows what threats to expect, in terms of e.g. size, impact and origin, it becomes better able to anticipate and focus its activities to counter these threats. This makes intelligence a crucial element in building resilience.

MINUSMA Contribution to Building Resilience[1]

The main unit within MINUSMA's intelligence organisation was ASIFU, the All Sources Information Fusion Unit (ASIFU). Upon request of Under-Secretary-General for Peacekeeping Hervé Ladsous,

---

[1] This section relies on empirical material collected for Rietjens and Ruffa (2019).

ASIFU had to strengthen the regular intelligence structure of MINUSMA's force, as intelligence capabilities in previous UN operations were considered insufficient (see, e.g., Dorn 2010). ASIFU consisted of a headquarters in Bamako of approximately 90 persons as well as two subunits: (1) a multinational Intelligence Surveillance and Reconnaissance (ISR) company of approximately 65 people under Dutch command in sector East (Gao) and (2) a Swedish ISR Taskforce of approximately 200 people in sector West (Timbuktu).

ASIFU's task was to 'contribute especially to traditionally non-military intelligence analysis, such as illegal trafficking and narcotics trade; ethnic dynamics and tribal tensions; corruption and bad governance within Mali and MINUSMA area of interest'.[2] In addition, ASIFU emphasised intelligence at the mid and long term, i.e. at least three months ahead.

In addition to ASIFU, MINUSMA had regular intelligence branches at the different hierarchical levels, i.e. an S2 branch operated at the battalion level, a G2 branch at the brigade level and a U2 branch operated at MINUSMA headquarters. These regular branches focused on short-term security-related intelligence. However, during large periods MINUSMA's regular intelligence branches fell short of providing security-related intelligence as they did not have the personnel (both in quality and quantity) and equipment (both in terms of collection as well as processing and analysis). Although ASIFU was pressured to step in and fill the gap, it refused to do this and largely maintained its original way of operating. As a result, ASIFU's intelligence products became rather detached from the Force Commander's main interest and were therefore only used to a limited extent in the decision-making process of the military component of MINUSMA. This disconnect indirectly undermined the mission's ability to build resilience.

The problems encountered become even more critical as ASIFU was struggling with retrieving information from the locals. In Rietjens and Ruffa (2019), we find that 'ASIFU['s] peculiar placement in the command structure was to strictly separate western intelligence capabilities from the other UN contributors' capabilities'. The reason for such separation was to strengthen (information) security and counterintelligence

---

[2] PowerPoint presentation by representative of UN Department of Peacekeeping Operations, Carlisle Barracks, United States, 28 January 2015.

since 'intelligence is a trust sport, which you only play with those you trust'.[3] Also, the specific military command culture of their country of origins was perceived as problematic:

> It seems that in the West African military culture the role of intelligence is very different from ours. The role of intelligence is to find out little things for the commander when asked, often focusing on events that have already occurred, but not to present information proactively because that would imply that the commander did not have the right information or that he should act which, both of which are not desirable for these commanders.[4]

Notwithstanding these problems, most European military peacekeepers lacked strong connections to the local culture (see also Elron et al. 1999; Rubinstein et al. 2008). In many cases, European soldiers lacked an awareness of the complexity of the conflict, the history of Mali and the ethnic sensitivities there. European troops' insufficient cultural awareness negatively influenced their possibility to retrieve intelligence, as they were not fully able to unravel the dynamics of the environment in order to address the information requirements they were tasked with. To the contrary, many of the African units mastered some of the local languages and had in-depth socio-cultural intelligence towards the local population in Mali (Danish Institute of International Affairs 2017).

Looking at MINUSMA as a whole, one observes that MINUSMA has a hierarchical structure in which the civilian and military components operated in stovepipes (Lucius and Rietjens 2016; Metcalfe et al. 2012; Rietjens 2017; Rietjens and Dorn 2017; Rousseau 2006; Soeters and Heeren-Bogers 2013; Ruffa and Vennesson 2014). On the one hand, UN civilian officials were directed by two deputy Special Representatives of the Secretary General (SRSGs), the chief of staff (in the case of JMAC, JOC, and UNDSS) or the police commissioner (in the case of UNPOL) and emphasised the political and reconstruction processes. On the other hand, the UN military component was tasked with the security aspects of the mission and its force commander directed all the military assets.

---

[3] Interviews with military representatives of the intelligence staff at the UN headquarters (U2) and ASIFU headquarters by one of the authors.
[4] Interview with the chief of the all source intelligence cell of the ISR Company by one of the authors.

In the beginning, the civilian and military components lacked the necessary structure to communicate efficiently with each other. In an effort of improving the coordination and clarification of each unit's mission, Joint Coordination Board (JCB) was installed in 2015. Weekly meetings were held which overall 'streamlined the intelligence gathering process in Mali' (Duursma 2018: 452; for a more general discussion Paris 2009). However, as the JCB was a coordinating body only, it had no directive powers, which clearly limited its effectiveness, and indirectly the building up of resilience.

In addition to these issues related to MINUSMA's organisational structure, many of the civilian organisations saw the military peacekeepers as a threat to their perceived impartiality and therefore their own security. This was because MINUSMA had openly taken an official pro-governmental stance and was actively supported by France. As a result, many of the organisations were very hesitant to share information with MINUSMA's intelligence units. In his research on civil–military communication in Gao, Van der West (2016: 33) noted that:

> One respondent of the ISR Company went to visit the UNOCHA office the day after a demonstration against MINUSMA took place in Gao and said the following: 'And I arrived at United Nations Office of the Coordination for Humanitarian Affairs (UNOCHA), and they directly told us that they were not very keen on us visiting them, out of their own interest. In order to not be identified with the military part of the UN'.

Concluding Remarks: Give Resilience a Chance?

From our first exploratory analysis, it seems obvious that MINUSMA falls short of building resilience due to several reasons. Resilience is usually defined as a society's ability to resist and recover from shocks. The particular case of MINUSMA is an interesting example in two ways. As one of the most ambitious peacekeeping missions ever launched, MINUSMA is also one of the most likely to be able to build resilience (Levy 2008). However, the scale of the operation heightened the lack of coordination and incoherence that our chapter has sought to unveil. Probably because of its high level of ambition, MINUSMA has not sufficed in strengthening state resilience, let alone societal resilience.

Challenges and opportunities of building resilience should be placed in the broader context of the MINUSMA mission set-up. Peacekeeping actors should strive to better integrate their approaches and activities while maintaining their individual identities as well as their right to take independent decisions (De Coning and Friis 2011). A first challenge to address in order to enhance peacekeeping operations' ability to strengthen resilience is to improve linkages (e.g. making more extensive use of liaison officers) between military intelligence capacities and the main force. This mirrors a major need to strive to improve coherence in UN missions (Campbell 2008; Campbell and Kaspersen 2008). Second, it would be important to further integrate or at least more clearly define the relationships between the regular intelligence branches and ASIFU. Finally, the UN and the international community at large should think about how to better integrate high-tech capabilities within a generally low-tech environment (see, e.g., Dorn 2016), while avoiding the recreation of divisive practices of exclusions based on technological divides. While greater diversity in UN peacekeeping has undeniable advantages in terms of legitimacy and representativeness (Ruffa 2014, 2017, 2018; Saideman and Auerswald 2014; Russo and Cesarani 2017), the recent return of European troops to UN peacekeeping in Africa begs the question of how to strike the correct balance between these two dynamics (Nilsson and Zetterlund 2016).

We find that addressing this topic more openly could be especially useful for building resilience. In a way, MINUSMA has engaged in an impressive effort to build resilience through peacekeeping. Its mandate is broader and more all-encompassing than most UN peacekeeping mandates ever conceived. Yet, what is missing is a more development-focused approach with extensive coordination between military, humanitarian aid and development cooperation providers. Such coordination, however, has to be respectful of these actors' mutual differences. As a recent report from the International Peace Institute suggests, '[r]esearchers suggested that the Malian government should pursue reform more inclusively in the center of the country, while USAID, the European Union, and other development actors could further support peacebuilding programmes that build on local resilience and leverage potential bridges among communities' (International Peace Institute 2018). In other words, the key to building resilience in Mali seems to be adopting a clearer focus and including a broader range of both external and internal actors. As in many other contexts, what the international community still seems to fail to recognise is that resilience has to be built at the micro- and local-level. Having a broader peacekeeping mission will not suffice: more actors, both local and international, should be included to build resilience from the bottom-up. Recent work has pointed at the importance of building peace from the bottom up (Autesserre 2014a, b, 2019). Building resilience from the bottom up in order to enhance the chance of durable peace, however, can only be achieved by first establishing minimal security conditions, echoing the classical tensions between humanitarian and developmental approaches (Donini 2011; Friis 2012). The ongoing debate within the peacekeeping literature should address more explicitly the notion of resilience, which is line with the more recent micro-turn in the study of peacekeeping missions (Bove et al., forthcoming; Fjelde et al. 2019; Hultman et al. 2013, 2014) and in stark contrast with previous approaches (Fortna 2008).

Peacekeeping forces with offensive mandates might not be the best-suited actors to increase resilience in fragile states. At the same time, ambitious and multidimensional mandates, with some elements of enforcement, may be the only way to improve volatile security conditions. While resilience has the advantage of drawing the international community's attention on the necessity to listen to local needs, more needs to be done to develop instruments and processes that can make resilience a viable conceptual tool that the UN can use to build peace in Mali, the Sahel, and beyond.

References

Autesserre, S. (2014a). Going Micro: Emerging and Future Peacekeeping Research. *International Peacekeeping, 21*(4), 492–500.
Autesserre, S. (2014b). *Peaceland: Conflict Resolution and the Everyday Politics of International Intervention.* Cambridge: Cambridge University Press.
Autesserre, S. (2019, January/February). The Crisis of Peacekeeping: Why the UN Can't End Wars. *Foreign Affairs.*
BBC. (2015, November 20). *World's Most Dangerous Peacekeeping Mission.*
Boeke, S., & Scuurman, B. (2015). Operation Serval: The Strategic Analysis of the French Intervention in Mali: 2013–2014. *Journal of Strategic Studies, 38*(6), 801–825.
Bove, V., Ruffa, C., & Ruggeri, A. (Forthcoming). *Why and How Peacekeeping Composition Matters.* Oxford University Press.
Campbell, S. P. (2008). (Dis)integration, Incoherence and Complexity in UN Post-conflict Interventions. *International Peacekeeping, 15*(4), 556–569.

Campbell, S. P., & Kaspersen, A. T. (2008). The UN's Reforms: Confronting Integration Barriers'. *International Peacekeeping*, 15(4), 470–485.

Chauzal, G., & Van Damme, T. (2015). *The Roots of Mali's Conflict: Moving Beyond the 2012 Crisis* (CRU Report). Netherlands Institute of International Relations Clingendael.

Danish Institute of International Studies. (2017). *African Peacekeepers in Mali*. Copenhagen: DIIS.

De Coning, C., & Friis, K. (2011). Coherence and Coordination: The Limits of the Comprehensive Approach. *Journal of International Peacekeeping*, 15(1), 243–272.

Donini, A. (2011). Between a Rock and a Hard Place: Integration or Independence of Humanitarian Action. *International Review of the Red Cross*, 93(881), 141–157.

Dorn, A. W. (2010). United Nations Peacekeeping Intelligence. In L. K. Johnson (Ed.), *Oxford Handbook of National Security Intelligence* (pp. 275–295). Oxford: Oxford University Press.

Dorn, A. W. (2016). *Smart Peacekeeping: Toward Tech-Enabled UN Operations*. New York: International Peace Institute.

Duursma, A. (2018). Information Processing Challenges in Peacekeeping Operations: A Case Study on Peacekeeping Information Collection Efforts in Mali. *International Peacekeeping*, 25(3), 446–468.

Elron, E., Shamir, B., & Ben-Ari, E. (1999). Why Don't They Fight Each Other? Cultural Diversity and Operational Unity in Multinational Forces. *Armed Forces & Society*, 26(1), 73–97.

Fjelde, H., Hultman, L., & Nilsson, D. (2019). Protection Through Presence: UN Peacekeeping and the Costs of Targeting Civilians. *International Organization*, 73(1), 103–113.

Fortna, V. P. (2008). *Does Peacekeeping Work? Shaping Belligerents' Choices After Civil War*. Princeton: Princeton University Press.

Friis, K. (2012). Which Afghanistan? Military, Humanitarian, and State-Building Identities in the Afghan Theater. *Security Studies*, 21(2), 266–300.

Gressly, D. (2013). How to Build Resilience in the Sahel. *The Guardian*.

Gubbels, P. (2012). *Ending the Everyday Emergency: Resilience and Children in the Sahel*. https://www.preventionweb.net/publications/view/27663.

Hultman, L., Kathman, J., & Shannon, M. (2013). United Nations Peacekeeping and Civilian Protection in Civil War. *American Journal of Political Science*, 57(4), 875–891.

Hultman, L., Kathman, J., & Shannon, M. (2014). Beyond Keeping Peace: United Nations Effectiveness in the Midst of Fighting. *American Political Science Review*, 108(4), 737–753.

International Peace Institute. (2018). *Threats and Drivers of Mass Atrocities in Mali*. https://www.ipinst.org/2018/06/threats-and-drivers-of-mass-atrocity-in-mali.

Karlsrud, J., & Osland, K. M. (2016). Between Self-Interest and Solidarity: Norway's Return to UN Peacekeeping? *International Peacekeeping, 23*(5), 784–803.

Karlsrud, J., & Smith, A. C. (2015). *Europe's Return to UN Peacekeeping in Africa? Lessons from Mali* (Providing for Peacekeeping No. 11). New York: International Peace Institute.

Levy, J. S. (2008). Case Studies: Types, Designs, and Logics of Inference. *Conflict Management and Peace Science, 25*(1), 1–18.

Lotze, W. (2015). United Nations Multidimensional Integrated Stabilization Mission in Mali (MINUSMA). In J. Koops, T. Tardy, N. MacQueen, & P. Williams (Eds.), *The Oxford Handbook of United Nations Peacekeeping Operation*. Oxford: Oxford University Press. https://doi.org/10.1093/oxfordhb/9780199686049.013.72.

Lucius, G., & Rietjens, S. J. H. (2016). *Effective Civil-Military Interaction in Peace Operations—Theory and Practice*. Berlin: Springer.

Metcalfe, V., Haysom, S., & Gordon, S. (2012). *Trends and Challenges in Humanitarian Civil-Military Coordination: A Review of the Literature* (HPG Working Paper).

Nilsson, C., & Zetterlund, K. (2016). Sweden and the UN: A Rekindled Partnership for Peacekeeping? *International Peacekeeping, 23*(5), 762–783. https://doi.org/10.1080/13533312.2016.1235097.

Paris, R. (2009). Understanding the 'Coordination Problem' in Postwar Statebuilding. In D. Paris & T. D. Sisk (Eds.), *The Dilemmas of Statebuilding: Confronting the Contradictions of Postwar Peace Operations* (pp. 53–78). Abingdon: Routledge.

Reliefweb. (2018). *Report of the Secretary-General on the situation in Mali (S/2018/541)*. https://reliefweb.int/report/mali/report-secretary-general-situation-mali-s2018541.

Rietjens, S. J. H. (2017). Lifting the Fog of Hybrid War? UN Environmental Understanding in Mali. In E. Cusumano & M. Corbe (Eds.), *A Civil-Military Response to Hybrid Threats* (pp. 181–197). Palgrave: Basingstoke.

Rietjens, S. J. H., & Dorn, A. W. (2017). The Evolution of Peacekeeping Intelligence. In E. Braat, F. Baudet, & J. van Woensel (Eds.), *Between Learning and Law: Perspectives on Military Intelligence from the First World War to Mali* (pp. 197–220). The Hague: Asser Press.

Rietjens, S., & Ruffa, C. (2019). Understanding Coherence in UN Peacekeeping: A Conceptual Framework. *International Peacekeeping, 26*(4), 383–407. https://doi.org/10.1080/13533312.2019.1596742.

Rousseau, D. M. (2006). Is There Such a Thing as Evidence-Based Management? *Academy of Management Review, 31*(2), 256–269.

Rubinstein, R. A., Keller, D. M., & Scherger, M. E. (2008). Culture and Interoperability in Integrated Missions. *International Peacekeeping, 15*(4), 540–555.

Ruffa, C. (2014). What Peacekeepers Think and Do: An Exploratory Study of Ghanaian, Korean, French and Italian Soldiers in the UN Mission in Lebanon. *Armed Forces and Society*, 40(2), 199–225.

Ruffa, C. (2017). Military Cultures and Force Employment in Peace Operations. *Security Studies*, 26(3), 391–422.

Ruffa, C. (2018). *Military Cultures in Peace and Stability Operations*. Philadelphia: University of Pennsylvania Press.

Ruffa, C., & Vennesson, P. (2014). Fighting and Helping? A Historical-Institutionalist Explanation of NGO-Military Relations. *Security Studies*, 23(3), 582–621.

Russo, M., & Cesarani, M. (2017). Strategic Alliance Success Factors: A Literature Review on Alliance Lifecycle. *International Journal of Business Administration*, 8(3), 1–9.

Saideman, S. M., & Auerswald, D. P. (2014). *NATO in Afghanistan*. Princeton: Princeton University Press.

Shetler-Jones, P. (2008). Intelligence in Integrated UN Peacekeeping Missions: The Joint Mission Analysis Centre. *International Peacekeeping*, 15(4), 517–527.

Soeters, J. M. M. L., & Heeren-Bogers, J. (2013). The Quest for 'Evidence-Based Soldiering'. In H. Amersfoort, R. Moelker, J. M. M. L. Soeters, & D. Verweij (Eds.), *The Armed Forces: Towards a Post-Interventionist Era?* (pp. 117–129). Berlin: Springer.

United Nations. (2012, December 20). *Security Council Resolution 2085: Adopted at 6898th Meeting*. New York, NY: United Nations Security Council.

United Nations. (2013, April 25). *Resolution 2100 (2013): Adopted by the Security Council at Its 6952nd Meeting*. New York, NY: United Nations Security Council.

United Nations. (2014). UNOCHA. Sahel Humanitarian Response Plan 2014.

United Nations. (2018). *Building Climate Resilience and Peace, Go Hand in Hand for Africa's Sahel*. https://news.un.org/en/node/1025671/building-climate-resilience-and-peace-go-hand-in-hand-for-africas-sahel-un-forum-2. Accessed 20 March 2019.

United Nations. (2019a). *The Sahel*. https://www.un.org/undpa/en/africa/sahel.

United Nations. (2019b). *Security Council Report, 2019*. Mali: Chronology of Events.

Van Willigen, N. (2016). A Dutch Return to UN Peacekeeping? *International Peacekeeping*, 23(5), 702–720.

Van der West, K. (2016). *Civil-Military Communications Within Integrated United Nations Peacekeeping: The Interaction Between the Dutch Military and Civil United Nations Entities During the MINUSMA-Mission in Gao (Mali)* (Master thesis). Groningen: University of Groningen.

CHAPTER 11

Resilience in the Eye of the Storm: Capacity-Building in Lebanon

Nick Pounds and Rudolf Keijzer

Despite having undergone a bloody, sectarian civil war, domination by Syria, invasion by Israel, and the highest (per capita) inflow of refugees in the world, Lebanon has—aside from the reappearance of minor sectarian conflict—avoided contagion from the wave of rebellion and violence that has characterised the Southern and Eastern Mediterranean regions over the last few years. This enduring stability is even more remarkable since Lebanon is an integral part of the battleground between Middle Eastern regional powers, and both Iran and Saudi Arabia have clients on Lebanese soil (Danahar 2015; Tholens 2017). Hence, a study of the Lebanese case can shed light on the underpinnings of resilience, providing crucial insights into how to effectively enable the development of resilient states and societies in the region. Specifically, we argue that the seven baseline

---

N. Pounds (✉)
Independent Consultant, Sheborne, UK

R. Keijzer
Consultancy for Resilience and Sustainable Stability,
Rotterdam, The Netherlands

requirements identified by NATO as the underpinnings as societal resilience cannot serve as a blueprint for the stabilisation of Lebanon, which entails focusing on other priorities, such as addressing economic inequalities and curbing other countries' meddling into Lebanese internal politics.

To understand the apparent resilience of Lebanon, this chapter will explore the empirical nature of resilience, and the role that the international community—in particular NATO, the EU and their member states—play in enhancing resilience in the region. It does so by first establishing a baseline outlining the historical, political, regional, social and security factors that have shaped the Lebanese context. The following section then reviews the foundations of resilience, and the fragilities that challenge these foundations. The ensuing section summarises relevant policies and activities undertaken by NATO, the EU, the UN and their member states. The final section recommends some policy priorities on which the EU and NATO should focus over the next few years.

The Lebanese Historical, Cultural, and Geopolitical Context

Today's Lebanon is the *Grand Liban* created by France in September 1920, a mainly mountainous country with a surface area of 10,452 square kilometres, bounded by Syria in the north and the east, and Israel to the south. Geopolitically it is a borderland: control over its territory has been contested throughout history, leading to wide ethnic, cultural, and religious diversity within the population.

Since gaining independence in 1943, and a brief period of peace and economic prosperity, Lebanon has been plagued by conflict. As Van Veen (2015) and others have argued, an influx of Palestinian fighters in the late 1960s triggered a contest between Lebanese elites, which culminated in a civil war. The outcome was occupation of the north by Syria, invasion of the south by Israel, and sectarian conflict which continued intermittently until 1990, when the Taif Accord was agreed. The Taif Accord enshrines a consociational,[1] power-sharing agreement that

---

[1] Practically, this means that leading political representatives of the parties that represent the country's larger sectarian groups have tended to govern on the basis of a power-sharing formula. This consists of a mix of predefined formal rights that protect sectarian interests and give sectarian groups a fixed stake in government, and informal flexibility in terms of the actual interpretation and utiliza-tion of these rights to exert influence (Van Veen 2015).

assigns equal sectarian representation in parliament and public institutions (Geha 2015). Even then, sporadic violence continued until 1991, when the Government began to exert control, and militias were demobilised, with the notable exceptions of Hezbollah and the Israeli-backed Army of South Lebanon (SLA). This long period of conflict and occupation polarised Lebanese society along sectarian lines, weakened the Government's authority, hampered economic development, and created significant levels of poverty and inequality.

Recent History

Whilst the Taif Accord ended the excesses of the civil war, Lebanon continued to suffer from political violence, especially in the Israeli-occupied South, where, with backing from Syria and Iran, Hezbollah emerged as the main resistance movement. In early 1999, fighting escalated as Hezbollah staged attacks on Israeli forces and the SLA. Israel retaliated against Hezbollah strongholds and expanded air strikes beyond its so-called 'security zone'. In May 2000, Israel conducted a rapid withdrawal from Lebanon, in compliance with UN Security Council (UNSC) Resolution 425, leaving the SLA to disintegrate. Nevertheless, Hezbollah and Israeli forces continued to exchange fire in the border area, leading to another invasion by Israel in 2006. Hezbollah resisted by using a sophisticated hybrid mix of guerrilla warfare against the occupying forces and a campaign of rocket bombardment against northern Israel, resulting in casualties and disruption, with the aim to influence Israeli public against the occupation. In August 2006, the UNSC unanimously approved Resolution 1701, which called for an end of hostilities. The resolution called for a withdrawal of Israeli troops from Lebanon, the deployment of the Lebanese Armed Forces (LAF) to the South, an enlarged United Nations Interim Force in Lebanon (UNIFIL) and the disarmament of Hezbollah, in accordance with an earlier resolution.[2] The LAF were subsequently deployed in southern Lebanon, and, in October 2006 most Israeli troops withdrew. This purported victory over Israeli aggression had served to consolidate the position of Hezbollah which, with backing from Iran, had become a powerful political and military entity within Lebanon.

---

[2] UNSCR 1559, adopted in September 2004, called for the disbanding and disarmament of all Lebanese and non-Lebanese militias.

Meanwhile, following the so-called 'Cedar Revolution', Syria had withdrawn all its military forces from Lebanon by the end of April 2005, setting the stage for the formation of the two political factions that still dominate Lebanon's contemporary politics—the predominantly Shia, pro-Syrian, March 8 and the predominantly Sunni, pro-Saudi, March 14 party alliances. In the background, Hezbollah has a strong influence on the government and its own security forces, leading some to suggest the term 'hybrid sovereignty' to describe the coexistence of non-state and state forms of authority (Tholens 2017). The fact that Hezbollah has links to Iran, is listed as a terrorist organisation by every Western country, and is engaged in a conflict with Israel, further complicated international engagement with and assistance to Lebanon.

Despite UNSC Resolution 1701, neither the Lebanese government nor UNIFIL have attempted to disarm Hezbollah and perhaps with good reason. A 2007 LAF operation to dismantle the Palestinian Fatah al-Islam militia, followed by a Lebanese government attempt to reduce Hezbollah's military capabilities, sparked clashes between the March 8 and March 14 alliances which, in May 2008, brought about renewed factional violence. Fighting was quickly halted by an internationally sponsored and regionally administered agreement between the Lebanese Government and opposition forces (Geha 2015), but the fragility of the political settlement at the heart of the Lebanese state was exposed.

Since 2011, Lebanon has been under pressure from the ongoing Syrian civil war, which prompted both cross-border ideological contagion and an influx of over a million registered Syrian refugees. These factors are compounded by the competing geopolitical ambitions of regional powers. Whilst Hezbollah operates under Iranian direction in support of the Assad regime and broader Iranian ambitions in the region, supported also by Russia, Saudi Arabia seeks to challenge the status of Hezbollah within Lebanon, through its clients in the March 14 faction.[3]

Political and Social Structures

Religious communities in the Ottoman Empire were largely autonomous in matters of personal status and were at times treated as corporations for tax and public security matters. Membership of a millet, as these

---

[3] The 2017 resignation announcement of the Sunni Prime minister Saad Hariri, whilst visiting Saudi Arabia, is a good example of this.

religious communities were called under Ottoman law, gave individuals citizenship. This arrangement was employed in the founding of the modern state of Lebanon, imbuing Lebanese politics with its sectarian nature, closely connecting religion with civic affairs, and turning the size and competing influence of the various religious groups into matters of overriding political importance (Saliba 2010).

The constitution of 1926 and subsequent amendments define Lebanon as an independent republic. Executive power is vested in a president (elected by the legislature for six years) with a prime minister and a cabinet chosen by the president but responsible to the legislature. Under an unwritten agreement, made at the time of the National Covenant of 1943, but enshrined in the Taif Accord, the president of Lebanon must be a Maronite Christian, the prime minister a Sunni Muslim, and the speaker of parliament a Shia Muslim. A Christian majority in the legislature must also be maintained.[4] Van Veen (2015) noted that sectarian loyalties tend to trump national interest, an observation supported by findings from a recent study (Cammett et al. 2018) which suggests that shared religious identity between candidates and citizens is the most important driver of political support in Lebanon—even beyond vote-buying and other clientelist practices of outreach routinely employed by parties and politicians.

Estimates of the total population of Lebanon vary between 4.5 and 6.5 million, of which approximately 40.5% are Christian, 27% Sunni, 27% Shia and 5.4% Druze (CIA Factbook). However, such population distributions by sect are unreliable since the last formal population census was performed under the French mandate in 1932. More than 220,000 Palestinians live in Lebanese refugee camps, whilst 40,000 Iraqi refugees and at least 100,000 foreign workers, mostly from African and Asian countries, also reside in Lebanon (Cherri et al. 2016). Like other states in the region, it is generally estimated that over half the population is under the age of 30 (CIA Factbook; Cordesman 2017). Also significant is a large diaspora, estimated by the Lebanese government to be around 15 million (Pukas 2018), with significant political and economic influence (Hourani 2007).

---

[4] The denominational composition of the legislature following the 1989 Taif Accord is: 34 Maronites, 27 Sunni, 27 Shia, 14 Greek Orthodox, 8 Greek Catholics, 8 Druzes, 5 Armenian Orthodox, 2 Alaouites, 1 Armenian Catholic, 1 Protestant, and 1 Christian Minorities.

Security Forces

Formally, the state's security organisations are: the LAF—reporting to the Ministry of Defence; the Internal Security Forces (essentially the police service) and the General Security Directorate—reporting to the Ministry of Interior and Municipalities; and the State Security Directorate—reporting directly to the offices of the president and the prime minister. Civil Defence and Customs Administration are also considered part of the security sector. However, the actual security sector is far more complex, including not just the armed wings of various sectarian-based political parties (in particular Hezbollah), but also a range of semi-sectarian civil society actors, families, clans and tribes, and the private sector (Geha 2015).

As the national security forces—like all public bodies in Lebanon—have sectarian and clientelist affiliation reflecting the power-sharing constitutional formula, they suffer from a significant weakness at the institutional level. This institutional weakness leads to a lack of political consensus on the role, composition, leadership and interaction of the various security forces, and the lack of any formal National Security Policy. Syrian influence, up to 2005, led to state security institutions being underfinanced, understaffed and subject to the political influence of pro-Syrian elites, resulting in a legacy of ageing equipment and highly centralised, bureaucratic, Soviet-style modalities used by Syrian military forces (Osman and Kassis 2014; Van Veen 2015).

CHALLENGES TO RESILIENCE IN LEBANON

Resilience is usually defined as the ability to avoid and withstand shocks, and is closely related to stability, which, although subject to academic debate, is generally accepted to begin with the effectiveness and legitimacy of a government, which is strongly influenced by cultural and societal norms (Pounds et al. 2018; Anholt and Wagner in this volume). Despite intense regional instability and the meddling in domestic Lebanese politics by regional powers, largely ineffective state institutions, and a sectarian-dominated political system, Lebanon has remained stable. This stability may have primarily resulted from the horror of civil war, still fresh in the minds of the older population, and the ability of a consociational government to provide some assurances to all sects. On the other hand, all aspects of fragility identified by OECD (2018)[5] are apparent in the country, and the extent to which Lebanon could withstand further shocks in its current state is questionable.

In 2016, NATO agreed on seven baseline requirements for national resilience against which member states could measure their level of (civil) preparedness: assured continuity of government and critical services; resilient energy supplies; stable food and water resources; functioning civilian communications and transport systems; and the ability to deal effectively with mass movement of people and with casualties (NATO 2018a). However, reference to the Lebanese context quickly shows that the country continues to function as a state, despite the absence of, or weakness in, most of these requirements. This state of affairs raises questions about the relevance of such requirements when seeking to promote resilience in Lebanon's unstable region. This section shows that in Lebanon and perhaps other states on the EU/NATO southern border, as well as some NATO members, the key factors to be addressed to effectively enhance resilience are not those identified in current NATO policy. Rather, poor governance with external interference, a weak economy, and threats to societal and individual stability are more relevant factors for the effective projection of resilience.

Government Effectiveness

Regardless of ideological and cultural factors, for most citizens, the principle measure of any government's effectiveness is its provision of fair and effective security, justice and public services,[6] underpinned by the existence of economic opportunities. Indeed, a recent, comprehensive review of trends and data in the Middle East and North Africa (Cordesman 2017) identified that poor governance and corruption correlates closely with instability and violence as much as religious or sectarian divisions. In this regard, recent international assessments rank Lebanon in the bottom 25–50% of states in terms of general

---

[5] Thinking on State Fragility is evolving, with both traditionalist and critical academic schools. OECD in its recent Fragility Index reports has adopted an central position reflecting the Copenhagen School which considers Political, Security, Social, Economic, and environmental factors.

[6] As first defined by Rousseau in his 'Discourse on Political Economy and the Social Contract'.

governance,[7] and one of the lowest in the Arab World in terms of competitiveness (World Bank 2018; Schwab 2018).

A recent international Monetary Fund (IMF) report (2018) warned that Lebanon's debt is unsustainable at 150% of GDP, and set to rise rapidly, without adjustment. In parallel, a World Economic Forum report (Schwab 2018) ranks Lebanon 95th out of 140 countries worldwide in quality of infrastructure. This statistic is important because there exists a strong correlation between the level of economic development in a country and the quality of its infrastructure (Sanchez 2018). Whilst the dilapidated state of Lebanon's infrastructure and services is primarily a result of many years of governmental neglect, the stress generated by massive refugee flows has exacerbated the problem, which should be recognised and reflected in EU support to the country (Saloukh 2018a). However, in addition to political concerns, financial mismanagement is an obstacle to international investment. Various measurements—such as Transparency International's corruption index from and the WEF's prevalence of irregular payments and bribes index—place Lebanon in the lowest 14% of countries worldwide in terms of corruption, transparency, and accountability. Without the governance reforms demanded at the Economic Conference for Development through Reforms with the Private Sector (CEDRE) conference in Paris in April 2018, significant international investments will be hard to encourage, and the economy will continue to languish.

The Lebanese State's capacity to govern effectively is hampered by political deadlock as well as economic constraints. At the state level, national institutions have been described as 'locked in the delicate politico-sectarian system set out in the Taif peace agreement' (Tholens 2017). The result is an increasing reliance on security governance as the main manifestation of the state, but security is strongly linked with sectarian affiliation to elite individuals and parties, who share local and national power. This, in turn, results in weakness at the institutional level, with multiple authorities jostling for power, and various legal ambiguities which enshrine sectarian representation. The final consequence is a lack of consensus on the role, composition,

---

[7]'Governance consists of the traditions and institutions by which authority in a country is exercised. This includes the process by which governments are selected, monitored and replaced; the capacity of the government to effectively formulate and implement sound policies; and the respect of citizens and the state for the institutions that govern economic and social interactions among them' (World Bank 2018).

leadership and interaction of the various security forces, which inhibits their ability to act impartially and effectively respond to security demands (Osman and Kassis 2014; Geha 2015).

Government Legitimacy

Political settlements generally have two dimensions: a horizontal dimension (concerning power-sharing between elites) and a vertical dimension (an agreement between elites and the population on the responsibilities and limits of power) (Beetham 1991). In the consociational Lebanese government structure, enabling any stakeholder easily to play a spoiler role, elites are organised on a sectarian basis and politics is dominated by sectarian loyalties and clientelist networks. Within this arrangement, elites seek to maintain or increase their relative power and secure advantages for both their internal constituencies and their regional sponsors (Saloukh 2018b; Atallah 2017).

The delicate Lebanese political balance deteriorated after the 2011 Arab uprisings, leading domestic politics to become gridlocked as Lebanon's weak government struggled to reconcile competing interests. Parliamentary elections were cancelled in 2013 as parliament extended its term three times, whilst the government failed to address deep crises in the provision of basic public services, from electricity to waste disposal. Although no serious calls for regime change have emerged, public trust in the government is at its lowest point since Syria controlled Lebanon (Muhana 2017). The state is therefore particularly vulnerable to meddling and the sort of disinformation that Russia—now active in this region—has employed elsewhere. A recent survey indicated that, sectarian divisions notwithstanding, there are substantial levels of public trust and confidence in the security forces. However, such levels vary significantly across agencies and regions, and, to a lesser degree, across ethnic and religious groups (Geha 2015). Notably, the LAF—which presents itself as cross sectarian and is regarded as one of the most effective state institutions—recorded the highest levels of trust, with over 80% nationally.

Individual and Societal Resilience

Most states are reliant to some degree on social, cultural and ideological factors to promote stability (Pounds et al. 2018; OECD 2018). Where central government is weak or fractured, as it is in Lebanon, individual and societal resilience becomes crucial for withstanding future shocks. However, long-standing confessional identification and mistrust, magnified during the Lebanese civil war and fuelled by the conflict in Syria, continue to fester to this day, reinforcing the sectarian nature of Lebanese society, heightening its susceptibility to shocks or occasional outbursts of violence,[8] and allowing interference from regional powers. Furthermore, a large part of the population is under economic pressure and reliant on support from the international diaspora.

For a long time, poverty in Lebanon remained largely hidden but since 2011, the influx of refugees from Syria has brought the issue into sharp focus (Kukrety 2016). The outdated but most recent nationwide survey, the 'Living Conditions and Household Budget Survey', was conducted by the Government and UNDP over a decade ago (2004–2005). This survey showed that 28.5% of the population were living in poverty and eight per cent were in extreme poverty, with the North, South and Beka'a Valley being the poorest regions (UNDP 2016). The situation has worsened significantly since then, with the global economic crisis of 2008, the Syria crisis, and an ongoing internal political stalemate. A recent survey placed Lebanon 6th worst worldwide in terms of wealth inequality, with 64% of the population having wealth of less than USD 10,000, a situation which continues to worsen (Credit Suisse 2014). As was identified by UNDP (2016) this inequality, combined with variations in poverty relating to sectarian and regional divides, places strain on relations between communities and provides opportunity for spoilers to exploit ethnic and confessional tensions.

The surge of refugees fleeing the war in Syria has aggravated social tensions and poverty in regions of Lebanon with a history of fragile public services provision, where large numbers of Syrian refugees are present. A national poll in 2013 indicated most interviewees believed that refugees were threatening national stability and security, taking jobs from the local population and benefiting from international aid in an unfair manner (Mahdi 2017; Kukrety 2016). With the crisis in its seventh year, attitudes towards hosting Syrian refugees have hardened. Uncertainty over the length of the conflict in Syria, overstretched services, high levels of unemployment (particularly amongst the younger population), and

---

[8] Most recently in 2014 between Sunni and Alaouites in Tripoli.

intercommunal friction have fuelled concern that resident population has exceeded the state's capacity and brought pressure to repatriate Syrian refugees (Cherri et al. 2016; Stel and Meijden 2018).[9]

ENHANCING RESILIENCE IN LEBANON: EXISTING INITIATIVES

In light of the challenges identified above, this section outlines relevant interventions to date, with an emphasis on NATO, the EU and some of the bilateral activities between Lebanon and member states of EU and NATO. Projecting stability in neighbouring regions is one of the priorities underpinning NATO–EU cooperation, set out in a joint declaration signed at the Warsaw Summit in July 2016. The two organisations outlined areas for strengthened cooperation in view of common challenges to the east and south, including countering hybrid threats and enhancing resilience. Due to the significant role of the UN in Lebanon, and the fact that much EU and bilateral funding is channeled via the UN system, its role will also be reviewed in this section.

NATO

At the Warsaw Summit in 2016, NATO Allies committed to contribute more funds to project stability and strengthen security outside NATO territory in the belief that, 'if NATO's neighbours are more stable, NATO is more secure' (NATO 2018a, b; see chapter by Larsen and Koehler in this volume). In its Strategic Direction South initiative for the Middle East and North Africa, NATO focused on building partnerships with regional powers, through associations such as its Mediterranean Dialogue and the Istanbul Cooperation Initiative. Moreover, a south-facing Regional Hub has recently been established in Naples, centring its efforts on 'connecting, consulting and coordinating' with a range of actors, to better understand the challenges and opportunities to NATO's south (NSDS 2018). Strategic Direction South notwithstanding, there is currently no NATO-Lebanon partnership. It has been argued that Lebanon is difficult for NATO due to the hybrid political infrastructure

---

[9] Lebanon's only formal policy document on the Syrian refugee crisis, is the October 2014 Syrian Displacement Policy, which calls for encouraging refugees to leave Lebanon 'by all possible means'.

and Hezbollah's activity in the region, as well as regional grievances, linked to US support for Israel. However, as demonstrated below, bilateral engagement by some member states, especially the US, indicates that Hezbollah and support to Israel are not insurmountable obstacles. Such initiatives suggest that NATO's limited success in engaging with Lebanon results primarily from NATO's policy and structure, which follow pre-defined and pre-decided military response plans to crises and require broad political consensus for activities that are not pre-planned and approved. This lack of flexibility is the major challenge to be addressed by NATO to project resilience and prevent crises to its south, and particularly in the case of Lebanon.

The EU

In 2016, the EU adopted a new Global Strategy on Foreign and Security Policy (Global Strategy), which requires members to make bigger contributions to collective security, and implies close cooperation with NATO (European Union 2017a; see chapters by Anholt and Wagner in this volume):

> The Global Strategy's push for a European Union of security and defence, in complementarity with NATO and all our partners, anticipated the debate on military burden-sharing across the Atlantic. (Mogherini 2018)

The EU is represented in Lebanon by a delegation that supports and encourages the country to fulfil its international obligations and implement an ambitious agenda of political, economic, and social reforms. The delegation has four main tasks: to represent EU interests, promote cooperation with and amongst EU Member States in Lebanon, support the reform agenda of the Lebanese government, and to ensure that EU cooperation benefits those most in need. The EU-Lebanon partnership, signed under the framework of the EU Neighbourhood Policy (ENP, see chapter by Badarin and Schumacher, in this volume), is defined by an Association Agreement signed in 2006, followed by an EU-Lebanon Action Plan formulated in 2007 and revised in 2016. In 2016, EU and Lebanon adopted Partnership Priorities for the years 2016–2020, which set a strategic agenda in line with the priorities of the ENP and the EU's Global Strategy. The identified Partnership Priorities include: security and countering terrorism, governance and the rule of law, fostering growth and job opportunities, and migration and mobility (Council of the

EU 2016; EU 2017b, 2018). However, the hybrid political landscape in Lebanon, and in particular, the dual role of Hezbollah as a militant group and a political party, poses difficulties for EU engagement and has been part of the reason why EU policy has oscillated between a normative and a realist agenda (Seeberg 2009). This ambivalence has ultimately undermined the effectiveness of the ENP framework and the ability of the EU to stabilise the situation in Lebanon (and beyond) through conflict resolution (Ovádek and Wouters 2017). The priorities of transparency, accountability, and the fight against corruption, as agreed in 2016 should steer programmes. Unfortunately, whilst policy objectives are clear, a proper overview of projects delivered is not available and reference to priority setting cannot be found in EU's open reporting.

The EU currently allocates a total assistance budget (2017–2020, grants and loans) of more than EUR 2.2 billion to Lebanon. Mainly through the UN, the EU supports Lebanon to tackle the negative consequences of the large number of refugees with humanitarian aid, as well as basic services, for example education, to both refugees and vulnerable Lebanese communities. Efforts to reform key sectors such as security, justice, and good governance, are particularly encouraged since they all support sustainable growth and are aimed at reducing regional disparities in Lebanon (EU 2017b). The European Neighbourhood Instrument (ENI), which has an indicative budget in Lebanon of EUR 200 million (2017–2020), is the key financial instrument for cooperation with the country. At the CEDRE Conference in Paris, the EU announced a package of up to EUR 150 million, which were conditional upon reforms, to support the Lebanese economy which, in turn, could generate up to EUR 1.5 billion loans for Lebanon until 2020. Furthermore, in relation to the refugee crisis, at the UN-EU-led Brussels I Conference (April 2017, USD 6 billion pledged) and at the Brussels II Conference (April 2018, USD 4.4 billion pledged), the EU and the international community renewed their support for Syria, Lebanon, Turkey and Jordan. A transparent overview of the amount of EU-allocated or spent money in Lebanon is not available, due to different reporting mechanisms within the EU, and lack of information sharing via open reporting.

The UN

The UN has a long history and complex structure within Lebanon, where it operates through 23 Agencies, Funds and Programmes, UNIFIL, and a Political Mission (the Office of the UN Special

Coordinator for Lebanon) with approximately 2500 civilian staff and 10,000 peacekeepers. As mentioned above, UNIFIL, which was launched in 1978, is still trying to accomplish its goals. With Israeli troops on one side of the border and Hezbollah on the other, enduring peace remains fragile if not illusory (Jett 2017).

The UN and the Government of Lebanon have agreed on a 2017–2020 strategy to promote a secure, stable, and prosperous country. The three pillars of the UN Strategic Framework (UNSF) are thus: the Peace and Security Group, led by the office of the United Nations Special Coordinator for Lebanon (UNSCOL); the Governance and Political Stability Group, led by United Nations Development Program (UNDP) and the Socio-Economic Development Group, led by the Resident Coordinator's Office (RCO). The outcomes of this strategic framework cannot yet be assessed as the reports for 2017 are not yet available.

In parallel, the Lebanon Crisis Response Plan (LCRP), which covers the period of 2017–2020, and focusses on the refugee crisis, was agreed with the Government. The LCRP is the Lebanon chapter of the Regional Refugee and Resilience Plan 2017–2018 (3RP), led by UNHCR and UNDP, and aims to achieve a more stable Lebanon and peaceful coexistence between the Lebanese host society and vulnerable refugee communities. The LCRP follows the UN standard sectoral approach, guided broadly by the UN Millennium Goals, and is not specifically tailored to the domestic Lebanese institutions or its institutional needs, which ultimately leads to major challenges to an effective and sustained engagement of Lebanese institutions.

The Bilateral Cooperation of EU/NATO MEMBERS

Whilst EU and NATO-led initiatives have proved slow in delivery, partner nations have taken their own initiatives. For example, despite the regional difficulties encountered by NATO, the US has provided more than USD 2 billion in bilateral foreign assistance to Lebanon since 2006, with support for Lebanon's state institutions and security agencies as the principal beneficiaries. In addition, the US has provided Lebanon with nearly USD 1.8 billion in humanitarian assistance since the start of the Syrian crisis. Since 2006, the US has also awarded over USD 1.7 billion in security assistance to the LAF. The Netherlands too funds several projects, both directly and indirectly, via the EU and UN, including security-related integrated border management and civil-military cooperation programmes. In 2018, Lebanon was designated as a focus country for Dutch foreign policy and will receive assistance for around EUR 200 million for the period 2018–2021. The UK has a Conflict Stability and Security Fund project worth GBP 22.6m over three years, and supports LAF plans to secure the border between Lebanon and Syria.

The Civil Military Cooperation Centre of Excellence (CCOE)—which is NATO accredited but bilaterally funded by individual member states—has been involved in the Dutch project to develop LAF's Civil Military Cooperation (CIMIC) capability and had a very positive result so far, as highlighted at the CIMIC community of interest conference in Rome in May 2018 (CCOE 2018). This engagement also allows lessons learned, especially on how to counter hybrid threats, to be fed into the NATO community, highlighting the potential for NATO to draw on its Centres of Excellence (COEs) for mutually beneficial engagement in Lebanon.

This section described the policies of the key organisations and countries represented and operating in Lebanon. Whilst policies abound, executing them is a major challenge. This is primarily due to the reason that, whereas NATO—to a large extent—relies on the EU, the EU implements its priorities mainly via the UN system, which, in turn, is institutionally geared towards developing countries and crisis response. More flexible, bilateral efforts seem to be more successful but lack mutual coordination.

Enhancing Resilience in Lebanon: The Way Ahead

The Lebanese context shows that the underpinnings of resilience relate more closely to the criteria outlined by the OECD criteria and the EU Global Strategy's aim of 'fighting poverty and inequality, so that over time home-grown positive change can emerge' (Rehrl 2017: 32), rather than the criteria set out in NATO policy.

Existing policies and programmes, together with the political sensitivities that constrain direct NATO engagement, suggest the need for the EU to take the lead—in partnership with the UN—to establish effective, locally owned forms of international community engagement. In light of the provision of the NATO–EU declaration signed in Warsaw in July 2016; however, there remains scope for NATO actions aimed at enhancing security governance and enhancing Lebanon's resilience.

Despite the EU's Association Agreement and Action Plan, and the UN's Strategic Framework, there is to date scant evidence of any significant or tangible impact of international communities activities' on the problems faced by many Lebanese people. This suggests a need for a sharper focus on results and locally owned initiatives. On top of this, there is a need for concerted political action by all parties to mitigate regional interference in Lebanese political affairs. Therefore, whilst addressing the need for more effective governance, the immediate priorities for intervention by the EU, NATO, and their member states should include:

1. Greater emphasis on addressing poverty and inequality in Lebanese communities, whilst seeking to mitigate the malign societal influences of sectarianism and clientelism. Coordinating with the UN to more effectively provide wider access to services, in particular: water, electricity, sanitation, and education.
2. Improving and reforming the capabilities of the security sector.
3. Working with the UN and national governments within the region to facilitate the early return or resettlement of Syrian refugees.
4. Using coordinated political and economic leverage to dissuade regional and global actors from interfering in internal Lebanese politics. This may facilitate the proper engagement of Hezbollah within the Lebanese state.

These priorities are elaborated below.

Poverty, Inequality and Provision of Public Services

Given the considerable levels of funding allocated by EU, to support the needs of both refugees and Lebanese born communities, in parallel with similar initiatives by the UN, it would be reasonable to expect some noticeable impact on poverty, inequality and the provision of basic services. However, as outlined above, independent surveys continue to report high levels of poverty, an absence of access to basic services in many communities, and widespread perceptions of unfair prioritisation, particularly in favour of refugees. One of the tasks set out for the EU Delegation is to ensure that EU cooperation benefits those most in need. In a complex socio-economic environment, distorted by sectarianism and clientelism, coupled with multiple donors and civil society implementing partners, robust coordination and programme management and greater transparency, are essential to effectively address poverty, inequality, and the provision of basic services. Rather than developing new initiatives, the priority should be the empowerment of government initiatives, a better management of existing programmes, and greater transparency regarding outputs, to prevent misperceptions and misinformation.

Security Sector Reform

Security should the natural sector for NATO intervention through capacity-building initiatives aimed at reforming the sectarian and clientelist tendencies of the security sector. The above-mentioned constraints; however, continue to inhibit NATO initiatives, suggesting the need to continue relying on bilateral forms of cooperation. Given that, bilateral assistance is not well coordinated, NATO's Southern Hub could, perhaps, serve as a platform to improve this, together with COEs' initiatives.

Return or Resettlement of Syrian Refugees

Regardless of developments within Lebanon, the country's resilience will remain ephemeral until issues arising from the civil war in Syria and political interference by Saudi Arabia, Iran and potentially Russia, are mitigated or countered. NATO, the EU and their member states have enough diplomatic influence and economic power to address these issues, if sufficient political will exists. With the long war in Syria reaching its end game, the emphasis of EU aid to refugees should shift from to encouraging and enabling their voluntary repatriation. Whilst repatriation—an issue raised by the Lebanese representatives at the Brussels talks—would likely meet resistance from refugees and humanitarian organisations in the short term, it would be in the interests of all parties that Syrians return to start rebuilding their lives and their shattered state, as well as to relieve the intolerable pressure on the overburdened Lebanese state and society. The EU and NATO should explore means to guarantee the security to Syrian returnees, which could be established as a condition to provide the international aid that will surely be needed to rebuild Syria.

Third-Party Intervention in Lebanese Politics

Mitigating or ending the impact of the struggle between Iranian and Saudi interests in Lebanon's internal politics would have enormous benefit on the inter-factional strains within Lebanese society, thus improving resilience and reducing the possibility for Russia to act as a spoiler, once a stabilisation of Syria in line with Moscow's ambition has been completed. At the heart of this is the close relationship between Iran and Hezbollah, which infuriates the Saudis, preoccupies Israel, and hampers engagement by Western actors. A combination of international engagement with Hezbollah and a coordinated use of political and economic influence on regional powers is probably the only pragmatic approach to this issue. The EU and NATO, although theoretically well-placed to lead this approach, may have difficulty in achieving internal political consensus. Consequently, concerted bilateral action by a coalition of willing member states may be a more realistic ambition.

Conclusions

The capacity of the Lebanese state to govern effectively is hampered by political deadlock, inherent in the consociational model of Lebanese government, and by economic constraints, which make individual and societal resilience indivisible from the resilience of the state. Whilst measures to unlock the political deadlock and improve governance are essential for stability and prosperity, these will take time. Therefore, in the short term, international intervention should also seek to strengthen societal resilience by addressing poverty and inequality, factionalism and clientelism, and the extreme challenges arising from the presence of a disproportionately high number of refugees.

By combining their efforts, the EU and NATO are well-placed to support Lebanon in building its resilience in the face of the political, economic and security challenges it faces. The EU Global Strategy fits well with the problems identified, particularly regarding the challenges to cultural and societal resilience. However, NATO can also contribute through the expertise of its COEs and member states. The EU should use its influence to free Lebanese internal politics from regional interference and find ways to disengage Hezbollah from Iranian influence by facilitating its engagement within the Lebanese state.

There is widespread pressure for reforming and restructuring Lebanese governance as part of the agreement to finance its development plans, and with good reason. The communiqué from the 2018 CEDRE conference in Paris stated:

Regarding structural reforms, the Lebanese government stressed that fighting corruption, strengthening governance and accountability, including public finance management, modernizing procurement rules, reforming customs and improving public investment management are of utmost importance.

Whilst such an undertaking is welcome, Western countries should not assume their own governance models to be the blueprint (OECD 2018). Notwithstanding its inefficacy, consociational politics is deeply rooted in the history and culture of Lebanon and may be part of the explanation why, despite all its problems, the Lebanese state was not consumed by the wave of violent unrest that swept the rest of the region. Thus, the challenge is to reform the state bureaucracy and the interaction between elites, without damaging a political settlement which, in spite of all its limitations, appears to have sheltered Lebanon from the storm that has engulfed other Middle Eastern countries.

REFERENCES

Atallah, S. (2017). *Lebanon's Political Stability Collides with Geopolitical Realities*. Lebanese Centre for Policy Studies. https://www.lcps-lebanon.org/featuredArticle.php?id=127. Accessed 20 March 2019.

Beetham, D. (1991). *The Legitimation of Power*. Basingstoke: Palgrave.

Cammett, M., Kruszewska, D., & Atallah, S. (2018). *What Lebanon's Elections Can Teach Us About the Importance of Religion in Elections*. LCPS Analysis. https://www.lcps-lebanon.org/featuredArticle.php?id=151. Accessed 20 March 2019.

CCOE. (2018, May 14–16). *NATO CIMIC Community of Interest Conference*. Rome: NATO Defence College. https://www.cimic-coe.org/products/conceptual-design/coic-2018/. Accessed 20 March 2019.

Cherri, Z., González, P. A., & Delgado, R. C. (2016). The Lebanese-Syrian Crisis: Impact of Influx of Syrian Refugees to an Already Weak State. *Risk Management and Health Care Policy, 9*, 165–172.

CIA. (Undated). *The World Factbook*. https://www.cia.gov/library/publications/the-world-factbook/. Accessed 10 April 2018.

Cordesman, A. A. H. (2017). *Tracking the Trends and Numbers: Islam, Terrorism, Stability and Conflict in the Middle East*. Center for International and Strategic Studies. https://www.csis.org/analysis/tracking-trends-and-numbers-islam-terrorism-stability-and-conflict-middle-east. Accessed 20 March 2019.

Council of the European Union. (2016, November 11). *Decision No 1/2016 of the EU-Lebanon Association Council Agreeing on EU-Lebanon Partnership Priorities*. Brussels.

Credit Suisse. (2014). *Global Wealth Data Book 2014*. Zurich: Credit Suisse.

Danahar, P. (2015). *The New Middle East: The World After the Arab Spring*. London: Bloomsbury.

European Union. (2017a, May 15). *Handbook the Common Security and Defence Policy of the European Union* (3rd ed.). Brussels.

European Union. (2017b, June 23). *Final Joint Staff Working Document Report on EU-LEBANON Relations in the Framework of the Revised ENP*. Brussels.

European Union. (2018). *European Neighbourhood Policy and Enlargement Negotiations*. https://ec.europa.eu/neighbourhood-enlargement/neighbourhood/countries/lebanon_en. Accessed 20 March 2019.

Geha, C. (2015). *Citizens' Perceptions of Security Institutions in Lebanon* (International Alert Background Paper). https://www.international-alert.org/publications. Accessed 20 March 2019.

Hourani, G. (2007). *Lebanese Diaspora and Homeland Relations*. Paper Prepared for the Forced Migration & Refugee Studies Program at the American University in Cairo. http://schools.aucegypt.edu/GAPP/cmrs/Documents/Guitahourani.pdf.

IMF—International Monetary Fund. (2018). *Lebanon: Staff Concluding Statement of the 2018 Article IV Mission*. http://www.imf.org/en/News/Articles/2018/02/12/ms021218-lebanon-staff-concluding-statement-of-the-2018-article-iv-mission. Accessed 20 March 2019.

Jett, D. (2017, September 26). The Future of UN Peacekeepers in Lebanon. *Foreign Affairs*.

Kukrety, N. (2016). *Poverty, Inequality and Social Protection in Lebanon* (OXFAM Research Report). https://www.oxfam.org/en/research/poverty-inequality-and-social-protection-lebanon. Accessed 20 March 2019.

Mahdi, D. (2017). *Understanding Refugee Politics in Lebanon and Calls for Repatriation* (Lebanese Centre for Policy Studies Brief 30). https://www.lcps-lebanon.org/publication.php?id=314&category=700&title=700. Accessed 20 March 2019.

Mogherini, F. (2018). The EU Global Strategy at 1—Personal Message by Federica Mogherini.

Muhana, E. (2017, June 29). Is Lebanon's New Electoral System a Path Out of Sectarianism? *The New Yorker*.

NATO. (2018a). *Resilience and Article 3*. https://www.nato.int/cps/ie/natohq/topics_132722.htm. Accessed 20 March 2019.

NATO. (2018b). *Projecting Stability, an Agenda for NATO Partners*. https://www.nato.int/docu/review/2018/Also-in-2018/projecting-stability-an-agenda-for-action-nato-partners/EN/index.htm. Accessed 20 March 2019.

NSDS. (2018). *NSDS Hub, Projecting Stability.* https://www.thesouthernhub.org/. Accessed 20 March 2019.

OECD. (2018). *States of Fragility 2018.* Paris: OECD Publishing.

Osman, Z., & Kassis, S. (2014). *Security Sector Overview: Final Report Providing Overview of Lebanese Security Sector.* Beirut: International Alert.

Ovádek, M., & Wouters, J. (2017). *Differentiation in Disguise? EU Instruments of Bi-lateral Cooperation in the Southern Neighbourhood* (Working Paper No. 186). Leuven Centre for Global Governance Studies—Institute for International Law, KU Leuven.

Pounds, N., El Alam, I., & Keijzer, R. (2018). A Military Contribution to State Resilience: Afghanistan and Lebanon. In E. Cusumano & M. Corbe (Eds.), *A Civil-Military Response to Hybrid Threats.* Cham: Palgrave Macmillan.

Pukas, A. (2018). *Lebanese Across the Globe: How the Country's International Community Came to Be.* Artictle in the Arab News. http://www.arabnews.com/node/1296211/middle-east. Accessed 20 March 2019.

Rehrl, J. (Ed.). (2017). *Handbook on CSDP: The Common Security and Defence Policy of the European Union* (3rd ed.). Vienna: Federal Ministry of Defence and Sports of the Republic of Austria.

Saliba, I. (2010). *Lebanon: Constitutional Law and the Political Rights of Religious Communities.* Legal Report—The Law Library of Congress. https://www.loc.gov/law/help/lebanon-constitutional-law.php. Accessed 20 March 2019.

Saloukh, B. F. (2018a). *Romanticising Paris IV.* Lebanese Centre for Policy Studies Analysis. https://www.lcps-lebanon.org/featuredArticle.php?id=137. Accessed 20 March 2019.

Saloukh, B. F. (2018b). *The Pleasures of Sectarianism.* Lebanese Centre for Policy Studies Analysis. https://www.lcps-lebanon.org/featuredArticle.ph'p?id=131. Accessed 20 March 2019.

Sanchez, D. G. (2018). *Fighting Corruption to Ensure High-Quality Infrastructure Investment.* Lebanese Centre for Policy Studies Analysis. https://www.lcps-lebanon.org/featuredArticle.php?id=138. Accessed 20 March 2019.

Schwab, K. (Ed.). (2018). *The Global Competitiveness Report 2018.* Geneva: World Economic Forum.

Seeberg, P. (2009). The EU as a Realist Actor in Normative Clothes: EU Democracy Promotion in Lebanon and the European Neighbourhood Policy. *Democratization, 16*(1), 81–99.

Stel, N., & Meijden, A. (2018). *Lebanon's Eviction of Syrian Refugees and the Threat of De Facto Refoulement.* Lebanese Centre for Policy Studies Analysis. http://www.lcps-lebanon.org/featuredArticle.php?id=188. Accessed 20 March 2019.

Tholens, S. (2017). Border Management in an Era of 'Statebuilding Lite': Security Assistance and Lebanon's Hybrid Sovereignty. *International Affairs, 93*(4), 865–882.

UNDP—United Nations Development Programme. (2016). *Rapid Poverty Assessment in Lebanon for 2016*. http://www.lb.undp.org/content/lebanon/en/home/Response_to_the_Syrian_Crisis/successstories/Rapid-Poverty-Assessment-in-Lebanon-for-2016.html. Accessed 20 March 2019.

Van Veen, E. (2015). *Elites, Power and Security. How the Organization of Security in Lebanon Serves Elite Interests* (Clingendael Conflict Research Unit Report).

World Bank. 'Worldwide Governance Indicators'. http://info.worldbank.org/governance/wgi/#home. Accessed 20 March 2019.

CHAPTER 12

The Horn of Africa: NATO and the EU as Partners Against Pirates

Stefano Ruzza

Introduction

The first decade of the twenty-first century bore witness to a substantial increase in maritime piracy, especially in waters off the Horn of Africa. This upsurge in maritime crime seriously threatened both economic interests and the freedom of the seas. It should suffice to mention that traffic through the Suez Canal is extremely relevant for worldwide trade, and vessels transiting in or out of it must navigate through the areas of water easily affected by Somali-based piracy, which soon also acquired the capabilities to launch attacks up to several hundred miles away from East African coasts. The international community mobilised in an attempt to contain and tackle the latest manifestation of this old-fashioned threat.

This chapter analyses the international response to Somali-based piracy by investigating the following questions. First, was such a response successful in generating resilience, or, to state this differently, did it guarantee the continuity of maritime traffic through the affected area first, and then manage to contain and reduce piracy thereafter? Second, if the international response was successful in putting the threat back into

S. Ruzza (✉)
Department of Cultures, Politics and Society, University of Turin, Turin, Italy

© The Author(s) 2020
E. Cusumano and S. Hofmaier (eds.),
Projecting Resilience Across the Mediterranean,
https://doi.org/10.1007/978-3-030-23641-0_12

check, what were the reasons for its success? Third, who took most of the effort, why and how? As it will be explicated in this chapter, the international response to Somali-based piracy has been very effective, and succeeded in generating resilience in the face of a rapidly escalating threat thanks to the high level of cooperation between relevant stakeholders. More generally, this case shows the relevance and impact of broad and deep cooperation, both among military and between civil and military, to counter wicked problems (such as piracy) and to enhance resilience.

The three guiding questions are addressed through the following structure. The next section focuses on Somali-based piracy, considering its roots and assessing its scale and impact. It is followed by a section dedicated to the international response to Somali piracy, which evaluates the naval missions deployed in the Gulf of Aden and Western Indian Ocean, as well as the other policy tools constituted a part of what became an articulated governance mechanism to fight piracy. The fourth section analyses the international response, recognising the particular relevance of cooperation for the overall success of the operation. The last section is dedicated to the conclusions, recalling the main findings of the chapter.

THE RISE OF SOMALI PIRACY

Piracy is legally distinguished from 'armed robbery at sea' in that, whereas the former occurs on international waters, the latter occurs in waters under the jurisdiction of a specific state.[1] For instance, most cases of maritime crime in the Gulf of Guinea belong to the category of armed robbery at sea. However, the distinction between piracy proper and robbery had little meaning when applied to the Somali context, given the protracted ineffectiveness affecting the Somali Government and the attached inability to police its waters. Since this chapter focuses on Somali maritime crime, the word 'piracy' is used to refer indistinguishably to attacks occurring both inside and outside of territorial waters.

---

[1] Piracy is defined by art. 101 of the United Nations Convention of the Law of the Sea (UNCLOS), while the definition of armed robbery at sea can be found in IMO Resolution A.1025 (26), 2010, "Code of Practice for the Investigation of Crimes of Piracy and Armed Robbery Against Ships".

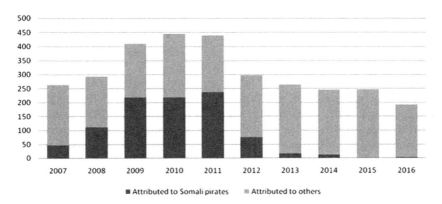

Graph 12.1 Number of pirate attacks per year, 2008–2016 (*Source* Adaptation from IMB)

Somali piracy grew fast throughout the first decade of the twenty-first century, pushing upward the number of attacks recorded worldwide, and constituting about half of the global number of attacks between 2009 and 2011 (see Graph 12.1). From a global average of 250 reported attacks per year between 2005 and 2007 (IMB 2010), the figure continuously increased, reaching its peak in 2010 and 2011, then starting to decline due to the international response. Somali piracy contributed significantly to the 70% increase in global piracy between 2007 and 2010. Attacks related to Somali pirates boomed in 2008: they tripled compared to figures in 2007, and again doubled in 2009. In 2008 and 2009, attacks in the Gulf of Aden area were reported to have occurred on average every 30 hours (Chalk 2016: 123).

The roots of Somali piracy date back well before 2008 and origins that can be traced to a variety of reasons, among which the collapse of the Somali state in 1991 is often emphasised (Chalk 2010). As state capacities dissolved, Somali authorities were unable to patrol territorial waters and therefore unable to prevent and punish activities such as illegal fishing and dumping of dangerous waste. Both these happened to a substantial extent, depleting fisheries and thus affecting local livelihoods. Fishers first tried to dissuade fish-stealers and waste-dumpers, and then imposed a 'tax' levy on them as a form of compensation. Escalating from these beginnings, piracy was born and justified as a mean to recapture resources in the face of impoverished livelihoods, mainly through the seizing of foreign vessels and their release following the payment of a ransom. Not surprisingly, pirates often perceived and presented themselves as the 'Somali coast guard' (Hari 2009; Marchal 2011; Bueger 2013).

The surge in the activity of Somali pirates visible from 2009 onward can be linked to the collapse of the security apparatus created by the informal government of the Puntland region. After the disintegration of the Somali state, Puntland managed to reorganise far more effectively than the rest of the country. This was due to a substantial investment by the Puntland informal government in policing and border guard activities. However, in 2008 Puntland found itself unable to pay for its security apparatus, leading much of its personnel to resort to other means of sustenance such as piracy (Hansen 2009: 30–34; Kinsey et al. 2009; Marchal 2011: 38).

Slow ships, cruising at 15 knots or less, with low freeboards and lacking defences have been particularly vulnerable to Somali pirates, but it is well known that larger ships have also been the repeated target of successful attacks. Vessels employed by the World Food Programme (WFP) to deliver humanitarian aid to Somalia were no exception to this. The famous incident involving the US-flagged Maersk Alabama, from which captain Richard Phillips was kidnapped in 2009, was tasked with a WFP mission at the time. In late 2007, the WFP sent out a call for protection of its convoys, receiving a positive response initially from a number of Western states (Canada, Denmark, France, and The Netherlands), and then from NATO, which in turn launched two ad hoc, brief missions which were implemented consecutively between October 2008 and August 2009, Allied Provider and Allied Protector (Bridger 2013: 2; World Food Programme 2008; NATO 2016).

Somali pirates resorted systematically to kidnap and ransom, placing themselves at the forefront of this particular business. In 2012 Somali pirates held 589 hostages, 349 of whom were captured in the same year, whereas in Western Africa, kidnapped seafarers amounted only to 206 in the same period (Oceans Beyond Piracy 2013). The World Bank calculated that, between April 2005 and December 2012, Somali pirates hijacked 179 ships, collecting between 339 and USD 413 million in ransoms (World Bank 2013). Peter Chalk estimated that ransom sums between 2008 and 2013 ranged between USD 1 and 12 million each, up from an average of USD 150,000 in 2005 (Oceans Beyond Piracy 2011; Chalk 2016). The extensive use of the kidnap-and-ransom business model implies that Somali pirates tended to limit damages to ships, as well as the murder of seafarers, making it comparatively less violent than its Western African equivalent. Nonetheless, a relatively high incidence of deaths occurred due to the sheer scale of Somali piracy and to the use of hostages as human shields during rescue attempts (Chalk 2010: 93; Oceans Beyond Piracy 2013). Notwithstanding its relatively limited level of violence, given its magnitude and its ability to threaten naval traffic through the Suez Canal—a chokepoint of global importance—Somali piracy had a serious economic impact on the international shipping industry. The 'Oceans Beyond Piracy' organisation, a spinoff of the One Earth Future Foundation, was created in 2010 and attempted to estimate the direct and indirect costs of Somali piracy on an annual base. Such costs were estimated to have peaked in 2010 at around USD seven billion, and reaching close to six billions in 2012, but halving down to three in 2013, and then stabilising at around 1.5 billion for the years from 2015 onward (Oceans Beyond Piracy 2018a).

The International Response to Somali Piracy

The threat posed to the freedom of the seas by Somali piracy pushed the international community to devise a response, yet reactions to Somali piracy were limited and ad hoc up until 2008. In 2005, Italy was the first country to deploy a military frigate in a counter-piracy mission in the Gulf of Aden (Cusumano and Ruzza 2015), but the boom of piracy off the coasts of Somalia in 2008 called for more substantial and coordinated international efforts. Starting in June 2008 with Security Council Resolution 1816, the UN enacted a number of acts condemning piracy and allowing states to enter Somalia territorial waters in order to fight piracy and armed robbery at sea (United Nations 2008a).

On this legislative base, a Maritime Security Patrol Area (MSPA) was established in August 2008 by the Combined Maritime Forces (CMF), a US-led, multinational naval partnership (Sterling 2009; US Navy 2009a). Coordination between CMF and the private shipping industry was possible through both the United Kingdom Marine Trade Operations (UKMTO) and the United States Maritime Liaison Office (MARLO). Those are respectively Royal Navy and US Navy capabilities to facilitate the exchange of information between UK/US military assets and private maritime interests at large (Clark 2009; Gortney 2009). Along with these first efforts and the two aforementioned ad hoc NATO missions (Allied Provider and Allied Protector), several countries initiated their own counter-piracy missions in the Gulf of Aden area, including China, India, Iran, Russia and Saudi Arabia (Bridger 2013: 2; Gortney 2009: 3). Moreover, the EU Military Staff (EUMS) launched a Naval Coordination Cell (NAVCO), in the attempt to fill a gap in coordination between those demanding security against Somali piracy (private parties, as well as organisations such as the WFP or the African Union) and security suppliers active in the region (EU NAVCO 2008). From these beginnings were developed three major international naval missions, also known as the 'Big Three', which together assumed the largest share of military counter-piracy endeavours against Somali piracy. The 'Big Three' include EUNAVFOR Atalanta, Combined Task Force 151 (CTF-151), and NATO Ocean Shield.

EUNAVFOR Atalanta was established in December 2008, and is still running at the time of writing. Its mandate was extended in 2016 to last until December 2018. The number of vessels deployed within the framework of Atalanta varied, reflecting the degree of pirate activity: up to ten vessels at the beginning of the mission, decreasing to just two more recently (EUNAVFOR 2018). EUNAVFOR also established the Maritime Security Centre—Horn of Africa (MSCHOA), a platform open to the shipping industry to register the transit or presence of their vessels in the waters affected by Somali piracy (defined as the 'high risk area' or HRA). This allows EUNAVFOR, and by extension, all the other active counter-piracy missions, to gain an overview of maritime traffic in the region, and hence to be able to calibrate efforts to counter piracy. MSCHOA acts as a coordinating centre as well, directing the deployment of EUNAVFOR assets and other multilateral missions present in the region (CTF-151 and NATO Ocean Shield), in case of an emergency. Last but not least, MSCHOA also provides a channel to relay piracy alerts and counter-piracy guidance to civilian vessels in transit through the HRA (Garrun 2011; EUNAVFOR 2018).

The European Union (EU) also launched in the following years two others Common Security and Defence Policy (CDSP) missions aimed at tackling Somali piracy in a more comprehensive fashion, as a part of the EU's integrated approach to the Horn of Africa. These missions are EUTM Somalia and EUCAP Somalia (the latter was known as EUCAP Nestor until 2015). The former was established in April 2010, and was tasked to train, mentor, and advise the Somali National Armed Forces (SNAF), with the aim of strengthening local state institutions and the overall security condition in Somalia. The mission was extended in 2016 to last until the end of 2018, reaching its fifth mandate, with a budget close to EUR 27 billion between 2017 and 2018. Twelve EU member states have contributed troops to EUTM Somalia (2018). In July 2012, the EU also launched EUCAP Nestor, a civilian mission supporting Horn of Africa countries to develop self-sustaining capacities in maritime security, with a special focus on coast guard forces. After a strategic revision at the end of 2015, the mission was refocused to Somalia only, and was relabelled EUCAP Somalia. At the time of writing, EUCAP Somalia is still active, and had an allocated budget of EUR 27 million in 2018, with eight contributing countries (EUCAP Somalia 2018). While the root causes of piracy off of the coast of Somalia have not been eliminated, it is important to remark that, to complement its overall counter-piracy strategy, the EU acted not with the sole aim of guaranteeing freedom of navigation in the region, but also to generate autonomous security capabilities in the Horn of Africa (and particularly in Somalia) through these missions.

Moving to the second-initiated of the 'Big Three', Combined Task Force 151 (CTF-151) was launched in January 2009 by the CMF. When the MSPA was established, counter-piracy activities were conducted *ad interim* by CTF-150, an anti-terrorism naval mission active under the CMF. CTF-151 was then supposed to take over the counter-piracy function carried out temporarily by CTF-150. CTF-151's mandate was enumerated as follows:

> In accordance with UNSC Resolutions, and in cooperation with non-member forces, CTF 151's mission is to disrupt piracy and armed robbery at sea and to engage with regional and other partners to build capacity and improve relevant capabilities in order to protect global maritime commerce and secure freedom of navigation. […] In conjunction with the North Atlantic Treaty Organisation (NATO) and the European Union Naval Force Somalia (EUNAVFOR), and together with independently deployed naval ships, CTF-151 helps to patrol the Internationally Recommended Transit Corridor (IRTC) in the Gulf Aden. (Combined Maritime Forces 2016)

CTF-151's mandate demonstrates the relevance of cooperation with EU, NATO, independent naval missions, and regional partners. The creation of a specific ad hoc counter-piracy mission in the form of CTF-151 clarified the respective mandates of CTF-150 and CTF-151 (anti-terrorism for the former, counter-piracy for the latter) and generated the possibility of catering to a broader audience of potential partners, which may not be interested in fighting terrorism, but are willing to tackle piracy. Although EUNAVFOR Atalanta and the later-launched NATO Ocean Shield were never closed to cooperation from non-EU and non-NATO states (as each had contributions from non-member countries), the establishment of CTF-151 provided an extra venue for non-Western governments to provide support to counter-piracy activities, drawing from the thirty-plus membership of CMF. Apart from the EU and NATO members, Japan, Korea, Pakistan, Singapore, and Thailand, among others, contributed to CTF-151.

In 2008, shortly before the launch of CTF-151, CMF also helped in the establishment of the Shared Awareness and Deconfliction (SHADE) working group to facilitate coordination between stakeholders involved or interested in counter-piracy activities in the waters affected by Somali piracy (Gortney 2009: 13; Weitz 2011: 157–158). SHADE does not coordinate naval operations, but rather provides a platform to deconflict activities, to avoid duplication of efforts, and to share information. Meetings are held in Bahrain and have been chaired, on a rotational basis, by CMF, EUNAVFOR, and NATO, with the latter joining after the inception of its own naval operations in 2009. SHADE meetings are open to independent naval missions, international organisations, Interpol, and the maritime industry. Throughout the years, countries such as China, India, Japan, Russia, and South Korea participated in SHADE meetings and activities (Clark 2009; Oceans Beyond Piracy 2018c).

SHADE suggested to incorporate the Fleet Exercise Web (FEXWEB), an unclassified internet forum hosted by EUNAVFOR, as a tool to share information between nations or coalitions engaged in counter-piracy. The rationale for this proposal was to be found in the need to have a platform accessible to all interested parties and able to overcome the inability of different communication systems (from EU and NATO, as well as from specific countries) to talk to each other. The use of FEXWEB later evolved into the creation of 'Mercury', a neutral platform allowing easy exchange of information such as the position of assets or incident reports (Gortney 2009: 13; Garrun 2011; Gebhard and Smith 2015). In early 2009, through the SHADE mechanism, the CMF also promulgated its cooperation with the EU and the UKMTO to create an IRTC for civilian vessels transiting in the area, in order to complement the MSPA and make transit as secure as possible (Clark 2009; Gortney 2009).

The creation of SHADE shortly preceded the founding of the Contact Group on Piracy off the Coast of Somalia (CGPCS), which was established in January 2009, pursuant to United Nations Security Council (UNSC) Resolution 1851. Whereas UNSC Resolution 1816 authorised naval forces to enter Somali waters to combat piracy for six months, Resolution 1851 provided the legal base for a long time effort (United Nations 2008a, b). The CGPCS is an international forum open to all stakeholders interested in countering piracy, whether public or private, single or grouped into organisations. To date, nearly eighty countries and several international organisations have participated in the Contact Group, including the African Union, the Arab League, the EU, the International Maritime Organization (IMO), NATO, and various departments and agencies of the United Nations. Besides having regular plenary sessions (often held at the headquarters of the United Nations), the CGCPS runs its technical activities through a number of working groups, which in turn keep the links with mechanisms such as SHADE. While CGPCS and SHADE activities are coordinated, the two remain separate entities. Whereas the former has a more distinct political nature, concerned with the governance of counter-piracy activities in general, the latter focuses on practical implementation, acting at the operational level (Cardiff University et al. 2018; US Department of State 2017). Within this general framework, MSCHOA keeps the operational channel of communications open with civilian vessels in transit in or about to transit through the HRA, while Mercury provides a common platform for stakeholders to communicate.

The latest of the 'Big Three' missions to begin its operations was NATO Ocean Shield, established in August 2009. Given the decrease in the incidents related to Somali piracy, the mission was terminated in December 2016 (NATO 2016). Ocean Shield deployed a total of 68 vessels on a rotational basis, at a peak of seven operating on the seas, down to just one during periods of lowest activity (Allied Maritime Command 2016). The NATO mission was the smallest of the 'Big Three': according to Oceans Beyond Piracy (2018b), in 2017, it had just two ships assigned which spent 91 days on patrol, whereas CTF-151 has a total of over 1000 days, and EUNAVFOR reached 1756 days. However, NATO has not stopped altogether its counter-piracy efforts. It maintains situational awareness in the HRA, and upkeeps its links with other stakeholders engaged in the contrast of piracy (NATO 2016).

Table 12.1 The 'Big Three' counter-piracy naval missions

Mission	EUNAVFOR Atalanta	CTF-151	NATO Ocean Shield
Lead organisation	EU	CMF	NATO
Starting date	December 2008	January 2009	August 2009
Closing date	Ongoing	Ongoing	December 2016
Relevant related initiatives	MSCHOA Mercury EUTM Somalia EUCAP Nestor/ Somalia	MSPA SHADE ITRC	Preceded by missions Allied Provider (October–December 2008) and Allied Protector (March–August 2009)

The private shipping industry had a major role in countering piracy as well. Apart from coordinating with the different mechanisms constituting part of the governance system devised to counter Somali piracy, it actively provided situational awareness through the Piracy Reporting Centre in Malaysia. This Centre was founded and operated by the International Maritime Bureau (IMB), a branch of the International Chamber of Commerce (ICC) tasked with countering maritime crime. Moreover, the downward trend in pirate attacks visible from 2012 (see Table 12.1) was not exclusively due to concerted military efforts. While the deployment of multilateral naval missions played an important role in curbing piracy off the Horn of Africa, first and foremost by disrupting attacks, there was another relevant factor that made a difference, as the international shipping industry, previously sceptical about the use of armed guards onboard merchant vessels, changed its stance. Up until its third edition, the counter-piracy Best Management Practices (BMPs), promoted by the shipping industry and addressed to shipowners, encouraged a reliance on unarmed defence measures while discouraging the use of armed guards. This approach was revised in 2011, a year in which Somali-based piracy attacks reached its peak. The fourth iteration of the BMPs opened up to the use of armed guards as an integrative security measure. The IMO subsequently endorsed this policy change. It is worthwhile noting that many European countries revised their laws and regulations in 2011 in order to allow shipowners flying European flags to employ armed guards onboard civilian vessels. Following this legislative reform and general change in attitude, the use of armed guards on a ship transiting through the HRA became widespread (Oceans Beyond

Piracy 2012: 17; Cusumano and Ruzza 2018a, b). The combination of naval missions and armed guards onboard merchant ships was ultimately effective in drastically cutting down the incidence of piracy in the region between the Gulf of Aden and the Western Indian Ocean.

Concerted Efforts: Enhancing Resilience to Piracy

Between 2008 and 2011, the global governance of counter-piracy activities reached its maturity. This governance framework emerged as a complex and multifaceted apparatus, where new initiatives complemented existing ones. CGPCS, SHADE, MSCHOA and Mercury constituted an integrated system able to generate and enact new policies, direct and deconflict resources, coordinate with the shipping industry down to individual vessels, and quickly share information. The 'Big Three' multilateral naval missions assured the constant presence of navies in the HRA, undertaking patrolling and guaranteeing sufficiently rapid response times, while the presence of armed guards onboard merchant vessels provided the first layer of defence. The MSPA and the IRTC provided means to keep the civilian traffic in the HRA manageable from the military standpoint, and to secure it from the civilian one. The activities of naval missions and armed teams were complemented in a comprehensive perspective by the two CSDP missions operating in Somalia with the aim generating self-sustaining security capabilities in the area. Finally, the shipping industry contributed too, not only by coordinating with existing governance mechanisms, but also by feeding its own inputs and by crafting new policies. The introduction of practices allowing for and regulating the use of armed guards onboard merchant vessels is the most relevant example of such shipping-initiated policies.

The inevitable question is: has this framework been successful? Or to put it differently: was this set of actors and measures able to generate resilience to piracy, a threat that emerged rapidly and which substantially affected global (economic) interests? The analysis conducted in this chapter clearly suggests a positive answer. Resilience can be defined as the ability to absorb and recover from a shock. Available data shows that maritime traffic through the Gulf of Aden was heavily impacted by Somali piracy, with the peak of attacks and economic damage reached between 2008 and 2012. Yet, maritime trade was able to continue, and, as soon as the international response gained full strength, the number of attacks steadily declined, quickly returning to pre-2005 levels, and reaching zero in 2016. It can therefore be stated with confidence that the policies enacted to counter Somali piracy are an example of an effective attempt to enhance the resilience of shipping to maritime crime.

The question that follows from this observation is: what allowed such a successful case of resilience to come into being? It is impossible not to notice that cooperation—both among different public actors and between public and private actors—played a prominent role in the fight against Somali piracy. Cooperation has been broad, involving a substantial number of stakeholders, and assuming various forms, which ranged from a reiteration of existing alliance mechanisms to unprecedented, ad hoc networks of actors. It may be argued that cooperation has been favoured because protecting maritime trade is a shared interest, and that countering piracy is a common concern. Protecting maritime trade and fighting piracy are more than open-ended concepts, they are indeed inclusive interests, which affect a number of parties, and hence are able to solicit a broad and positive response. Traditionally, pirates are defined as *hostis humani generis*, 'enemies of humankind', in par with slave owners (Stiles 2008). From this, it follows that a substantial rise in piracy can generate a strong common reaction.

Focusing more specifically on the policies enacted from 2008 onward, the willingness to crystallise the opportunity for cooperation generated by the existence of an international norm against pirates, can be observed in the prompt establishment of CTF-151. Its predecessor, CTF-150, was not meant to fight piracy specifically, and undertook such a task *ad interim*, just to address the emergency. But as an anti-terrorism mission, CTF-150 had limited potential to fully mobilise all the parties with an interest in countering piracy. The establishment of CTF-151 made the intended means and goals of both missions clearer. This allowed not only for a clarification of operational roles and mobilisation of more pertinent assets, but also for a broadening of cooperation by fully integrating partners interested in counter-piracy rather than in anti-terrorism. This contributed to clarifying the purely counter-piracy scope and purpose of the SHADE mechanism, as well as of any initiatives stemming from or supported by it, and to avoiding the transmission of any mixed message about their intent.

Given the prominent role that cooperation had in ensuring that the struggle against Somali piracy was successful, it is important to analyse this cooperation in-depth. In order to do that, it is worth examining who took on the largest share of the burden and to interrogate why they did so. It is immediately evident that the greatest part of the effort has been either sustained or otherwise incentivised by the Euro-Atlantic community. Material interests were far from irrelevant. Collectively, EU member states plus Norway controlled about 40% of the world mercantile fleet by gross tonnage in 2011, a share that remained steady in the following years (UNCTAD 2011; Oxford Economics 2015). The biggest worldwide container operator, Maersk, is based in Denmark, and the second and the third largest, MSC and CMA, are also both headquartered in Europe. In 2012, the shipping industry located in EU member states plus Norway had an overall direct economic impact of EUR 56 billion, an indirect impact of a EUR 59 billion, and an induced impact of EUR 30 billion, totalling EUR 145 billion of economic activity (Goodwin 2016). In comparison, the United States controlled only 3.7% of the worldwide mercantile fleet by gross tonnage in 2011 (UNCTAD 2011). However, US foreign trade rates constitute around 15% of global maritime trade in metric tonnes, and in 2011 about 47% of US foreign trade (in value) was moved by maritime vessels, while 22% of trade cargo (in value) consisted of fuel and oil, making these the most important commodities for both imports and exports (Chambers and Liu 2012: 2; US Department of Transportation 2013: 6–7). As these figures demonstrate, the West had a major material interest in leading the way against Somali piracy, given how much the European economy benefits from maritime trade, and how much the US economy depends on it. But on the top of this, Western countries in general and the United States in particular have also traditionally been defenders of the freedom of the seas. Hence, it could be argued that protecting maritime trade was also geared to maintaining hegemonic status in the international order (Cusumano and Ruzza 2018b).

Even if the West had substantial interests at stake, it is important to note that the second largest global power—China—also had reasons for serious concern. The mercantile fleet controlled by China plus Hong Kong in 2011 amounted to close to 12% of the worldwide total, and Chinese container operators were already in the global top ten at that time (UNCTAD 2011). Fifteen ships flying China's flag were attacked between 2008 and 2012, not to mention Chinese-controlled vessels flying a different flag (IMB 2012). Hence, quite unsurprisingly, China launched its own counter-piracy mission in 2008, deploying and maintaining its own independent three-ship force (complemented by a team of special forces) in the HRA. The mission is still running at the time of writing, and, over the course of ten years, has protected about 6400 transits (Scimia 2018). Congruently with its narrative of 'peaceful rise', China's missions were coordinated with Western-created infrastructure, most notably in the framework of the SHADE mechanism (Erickson and Strange 2013). This allowed China to protect its own material interest while minimising its efforts, and avoiding a confrontation with the West. The commander of CMF at the peak of counter-piracy operations, Vice Admiral William Gortney, reported that all the forces engaged in counter-piracy operations in the HRA, whether Western-affiliated or not, kept regular communications with CMF, avoiding incidents and opened up to cooperation whenever possible. His words parallel those of Rear Admiral Terence McKinght, the first commander of CTF-151, who expressed a similar degree of satisfaction (Gortney 2009: 12–13; US Navy 2009b).

Conclusions

From a comprehensive perspective, the 'Big Three' naval missions (lead respectively by the EU, CMF, and NATO), the overall counter-piracy governance mechanism (CGPCS, SHADE, MSCHOA, and Mercury), private sector involvement (visible not only through the coordination of efforts and the sharing of information, but also through the deployment of armed teams onboard merchant vessels), and the two CDSP missions (EUTM Somalia and EUCAP Nestor/Somalia) can be grouped together within a larger attempt aimed not only at countering piracy, but also aimed at increasing the resilience of states concerned by piracy. This is a rather large group that includes shipping states economically impacted by piracy as well as the shipping industry, but also the states where piracy is hosted (Somalia first and foremost) and those with shores facing on the HRA (from India to Yemen).

Regarding counter-piracy efforts, this chapter set out to explore the following questions. First, has the struggle against Somali piracy been a successful case of resilience projection? Second, if so what accounts for its effectiveness? Third, who took the largest share of the counter-piracy efforts, why did they do so, and how did it operate in order to create resilience? The answers to the first two questions have already been provided. The international response to Somali-based piracy has been effective because it succeeded in generating solid resilience in the face of a rapidly escalating threat. The main reason for such a success can be traced to substantial cooperation among stakeholders. The proper framing of counter-piracy activities, as well as the creation of formal and informal mechanisms and channels for cooperation, coordination, and information sharing, allowed the broadest and deepest engagement of civilian and military parties, whether they were already parties to a previously existing coalition or not.

The third question investigates the actual dynamics behind this success. Due to both material concerns and considerations of status, the EU, NATO, and the United States assumed a larger share of the burden, as they deployed material assets and acted as the promoter and facilitator of several joint initiatives. Intra-Western cooperation was particularly extensive. To some extent, this may be considered a natural outcome, as the West already had structures in place designed to ease cooperation in the face of shared security concerns, NATO being the first and foremost of such structures. However, it has to be noted that cooperation reached unprecedented levels as new coordination mechanisms (such as SHADE) were created over time, and instruments to overcome limits to interoperability (like Mercury) were quickly devised and put into action. Furthermore, cooperation was gradually extended beyond existing structures and partnerships, by involving both the private sector and non-Western countries (some of them through CTF-151, and others through mechanisms such as SHADE). In sum, increasing intra-Western cooperation generated platforms that stretched the boundaries of already existing Western alliances. This was eased by the adoption of a narrative that relies on the international norm against piracy.

The experiences drawn by the fight against Somali piracy can help in facing future crises. The SHADE format, for instance, has already been replicated to address the issue of migration across the Mediterranean, with the creation of the SHADE MED (on civil-military cooperation in the Mediterranean, see chapter by Del Valle in this volume). In full analogy with its predecessor aimed at countering piracy, the SHADE MED is defined as a 'forum where representatives from nations and organisations interested in or impacted by the migratory phenomenon in the Mediterranean basin can meet to de-conflict and coordinate their Maritime Security Operations by sharing situational awareness, assessment of the evolution of trends and best practices' (EUNAVFOR MED 2018). The first meeting of SHADE MED, held in 2015, saw the participation of delegates from states, international organisations, and private parties, variously interested in and concerned by the migration phenomenon (EUNAVFOR MED 2015).

There are three key lessons that can be learned from the fight against Somali piracy. Such lessons can provide policy suggestions extending beyond the case analysed here. The first is the relevance of framing. The clearer the common threat, and the lesser the confusion or overlap with other already existing missions or mandates, the larger the potential for cooperation. The change of pace intrinsic in the creation of specific anti-piracy multinational missions has made this evident. As an anti-terrorism mission, CTF-150 surely had the capabilities to counter pirates materially, yet it is only with the creation of CTF-151 that the preconditions for the creations of new channels and venues for cooperation were created. The second is the importance of creating ad hoc, specialised forums. The SHADE format generated a new platform for deconflicting and optimising efforts, and, even if its inception was promoted by Western organisations, it was not perceived as a partisan institution. The combination of these two factors managed to bring all the parties with a stake in countering piracy in the HRA to the table. The third lesson relates to the importance of creating channels of communications, such as the Mercury system, that allow information to be shared easily. Even in the face of political sensitivities or interoperability limits, these systems can increase informal exchanges which in turn allow for informal cooperation and for mutual trust to be enhanced.

References

Allied Maritime Command. (2016). *Operation Ocean Shield: Participating Forces*. http://www.mc.nato.int/missions/operation-ocean-shield/participating-forces.aspx. Accessed 20 March 2019.

Bridger, J. M. (2013, September). *Safe Seas at What Price? The Costs, Benefits and Future of NATO's Operation Ocean Shield* (NATO Research Paper [95]). www.ndc.nato.int/download/downloads.php?icode=386. Accessed 20 March 2019.

Bueger, C. (2013). Practice, Pirates and Coast Guards: The Grand Narrative of Somali Piracy. *Third World Quarterly, 34*(10), 1811–1827.

Cardiff University, European Union Institute of Security Studies, and Oceans Beyond Piracy. (2018). *Lessons from Piracy*. http://www.lessonsfrompiracy.net. Accessed 20 March 2019.

Chalk, P. (2010). Piracy Off the Horn of Africa: Scope, Dimensions, Causes and Responses. *Brown Journal of International Affairs, 16*(2), 89–108.

Chalk, P. (2016). The Privatization of Counter-Piracy: Implications for Order at Sea. In S. Ruzza, A. P. Jakobi, & C. Geisler (Eds.), *Non-state Challenges in a Re-ordered World* (pp. 122–138). Abingdon and New York, NY: Routledge.

Chambers, M., & Liu, M. (2012). *Maritime Trade and Transportation by the Numbers*. US Department of Transportation, Bureau of Transportation Statistics. https://www.rita.dot.gov/bts/sites/rita.dot.gov.bts/files/publications/by_the_numbers/maritime_trade_and_transportation/pdf/entire.pdf. Accessed 20 March 2019.

Clark, A. (2009, June 4). *Counter Piracy Operations, Challenges, Shortfalls and Lessons Learned*. Combined Maritime Forces.

Combined Maritime Forces. (2016). https://combinedmaritimeforces.com. Accessed 20 March 2019.

Cusumano, E., & Ruzza, S. (2015). Contractors as a Second Best Option: The Italian Hybrid Approach to Maritime Security. *Ocean Development & International Law, 46*(2), 111–122.

Cusumano, E., & Ruzza, S. (2018a). Security Privatisation at Sea: Piracy and the Commercialisation of Vessel Protection. *International Relations, 32*(1), 80–103.

Cusumano, E., & Ruzza, S. (2018b). United States Anti-piracy Policies: Between Military Missions and Private Sector Responsabilization. In M. Clementi, M. Dian, & B. Pisciotta (Eds.), *US Foreign Policy in a Challenging World: Building Order on Shifting Foundations* (pp. 63–81). Cham: Springer.

Erickson, A., & Strange, A. (2013, November 1). China and the International Antipiracy Effort. *The Diplomat*. http://thediplomat.com/2013/11/china-and-the-international-antipiracy-effort/. Accessed 20 March 2019.

EUCAP Somalia. (2018). https://www.eucap-som.eu/about-us/. Accessed 20 March 2019.

EU NAVCO. (2008, October 15). *European Union Initiatives in Support of Implementation of UNSCR 1816*. Brussels.

EUNAVFOR. (2018). http://eunavfor.eu. Accessed 20 March 2019.

EUNAVFOR MED. (2015, November 26). *First Shared Awareness and De-confliction (SHADE) Meeting for the Mediterranean Sea*. Press Release 04/15. Rome.

EUNAVFOR MED. (2018). https://www.operationsophia.eu/. Accessed 20 March 2019.

EUTM Somalia. (2018). https://www.eutm-somalia.eu. Accessed 28 September 2018.

Garrun, D. (2011, November 23). *How to Catch a Pirate—Cooperation Is Key*. Naval Technology. https://www.naval-technology.com/features/featurehow-to-catch-a-pirate-cooperation-is-key/. Accessed 20 March 2019.

Gebhard, C., & Smith, S. J. (2015). The Two Faces of EU-NATO Cooperation: Counter-Piracy Operations Off the Somali Coast. *Cooperation and Conflict, 50*(1), 107–127.

Goodwin, A. P. (2016, December 1). *The Economic Value of Shipping and Maritime Activity in Europe*. Oxford Economics. Accessed 20 March 2019.

Gortney, W. E. (2009). *Statement of Vice Admiral William E. Gortney, US Navy Commander, US Naval Forces Central Command, Before the House Armed Services Committee on Counter-Piracy Operations in the US Central Command Area of Operations.* https://www.marad.dot.gov/wp-content/uploads/pdf/HOA_Statement-Vice_Adm_William_Gortney-USNavy.pdf. Accessed 28 September 2018.

Hansen, S. J. (2009). *Piracy in the Greater Gulf of Aden: Myths, Misconceptions and Remedies* (NIBR Report 2009:29). Oslo: NIBR.

Hari, J. (2009, April 13). You Are Being Lied to About Pirates. *The Huffington Post.* http://www.huffingtonpost.com/johann-hari/you-are-being-lied-to-abo_b_155147.html. Accessed 20 March 2019.

International Maritime Bureau (IMB). (2008, 2009, 2010, 2011, 2012, 2013, 2014, 2015, 2016 and 2017). *Piracy and Armed Robbery Against Ships.*

International Maritime Organization (IMO). (2010). *Resolution A.1025 (26), Code of Practice for the Investigation of Crimes of Piracy and Armed Robbery Against Ships.* London.

Kinsey, C. P., Hansen, S. J., & Franklin, G. (2009). The Impact of Private Security Companies on Somalia's Governance Networks. *Review of International Affairs, 22*(1), 147–161.

Marchal, R. (2011). Somali Piracy: The Local Context of an International Obsession. *Humanity, 2*(1), 31–50.

NATO. (2016, December 19). *Counter-Piracy Operations.* http://www.nato.int/cps/en/natohq/topics_48815.htm. Accessed 20 March 2019.

Oceans Beyond Piracy. (2011). *The Economic Cost of Maritime Piracy 2010.* One Earth Future Foundation.

Oceans Beyond Piracy. (2012). *The Economic Cost of Somali Piracy 2011.* One Earth Future Foundation.

Oceans Beyond Piracy. (2013). *The Human Cost of Maritime Piracy 2012.* One Earth Future Foundation.

Oceans Beyond Piracy. (2018a). *The State of Maritime Piracy 2017.* One Earth Future Foundation.

Oceans Beyond Piracy. (2018b). *The State of Maritime Piracy 2017: Piracy and Armed Robbery Against Ships in East Africa 2017.* One Earth Future Foundation. http://oceansbeyondpiracy.org/reports/sop/east-africa. Accessed 28 September 2018.

Oceans Beyond Piracy. (2018c). *Shared Awareness and Deconfliction.* One Earth Future Foundation. http://oceansbeyondpiracy.org/matrix/shared-awareness-and-deconfliction-shade. Accessed 20 March 2019.

Oxford Economics. (2015, February). *The Economic Value of the EU Shipping Industry—Update.* https://www.oxfordeconomics.com/my-oxford/projects/294334. Accessed 20 March 2019.

Scimia, E. (2018, January 8). Anti-piracy Mission Helps China Develop Its Blue-Water Navy. *Asia Times.* http://www.atimes.com/anti-piracy-mission-helps-china-develop-blue-water-navy/. Accessed 20 March 2019.

Sterling, J. (2009). Navy Creates Force Devoted to Fighting Piracy. *CNN.* http://edition.cnn.com/2009/WORLD/africa/01/08/piracy.task.force/index.html?iref=newssearch. Accessed 23 December 2016.

Stiles, K. (2008). Banning Piracy: The State Monopoly on Military Force. In W. Sandholtz & K. Stiles (Eds.), *International Norms and Cycles of Change.* Oxford and New York, NY: Oxford University Press.

United Nations. (1982). *United Nations Convention on the Law of the Sea (UNCLOS).* Montego Bay.

United Nations. (2008a, June 2). *Security Council Condemns Acts of Piracy, Armed Robbery Off Somalia's Coast, Authorizes for Six Months 'All Necessary Means' to Repress Such Acts.* https://www.un.org/press/en/2008/sc9344.doc.htm. Accessed 20 March 2019.

United Nations. (2008b, December 16). *Security Council Authorizes States to Use Land-Based Operations in Somalia as a Part of Fight Against Piracy Off Coast.* https://www.un.org/press/en/2008/sc9541.doc.htm. Accessed 20 March 2019.

United Nations Conference on Trade and Development—UNCTAD. (2011). *Review of Maritime Transport 2011.* Geneva and New York.

US Department of State. (2017, January 20). *Contact Group on Piracy off the Coast of Somalia.* https://www.state.gov/t/pm/rls/fs/2017/266864.htm. Accessed 20 March 2019.

US Department of Transportation, Maritime Administration. (2013). *2011 US Water Transportation Statistical Snapshot.* https://www.marad.dot.gov/wp-content/uploads/pdf/US_Water_Transportation_Statistical_snapshot.pdf. Accessed 20 March 2019.

US Navy. (2009a). *New Counter-Piracy Task Force Established.* http://www.navy.mil/submit/display.asp?story_id=41687. Accessed 23 December 2016

US Navy. (2009b). *USS Boxer Becomes Flagship for CTF 151.* http://www.navy.mil/submit/display.asp?story_id=43303. Accessed 20 March 2019.

Weitz, R. (2011). *War and Governance: International Security in a Changing World Order.* Santa Barbara, CA: Praeger.

World Bank. (2013). *Pirate Trails: Tracking the Illicit Financial Flows from Piracy Off the Horn of Africa.* A World Bank Study. Washington, DC: World Bank.

World Food Programme—WFP. (2008). *NATO Escort to VFP Vessels.* https://www.wfp.org/sites/default/files/wfp191852.pdf. Accessed 20 March 2019.

CHAPTER 13

Paths to Resilience: Examining EU and NATO Responses to the Tunisian and Egyptian Political Transitions

Maria Giulia Amadio Viceré and Andrea Frontini

INTRODUCTION

The unfolding of the Arab uprising has shown that enhancing the ability of countries affected by regime change to face crises is necessary for the European Union (EU) and the North Atlantic Treaty Organization (NATO or Atlantic Alliance) to ensure the stability of the European neighbourhood. This chapter aims at shedding light on EU and NATO policies, and on their efforts to project resilience in the Southern Mediterranean region. This is achieved by analysing those paths to resilience the EU and NATO chose to support, taking stock of past policies in this area, and assessing how the differing strategies adopted towards the Tunisian and Egyptian political transitions led to different results. Thus, even though Tunisia and Egypt were both subject to authoritarian rule, the 2011 crises took divergent trajectories in the two countries. Despite

M. G. Amadio Viceré (✉)
LUISS University, Rome, Italy

A. Frontini
Formerly European Policy Centre, Trieste, Italy

© The Author(s) 2020
E. Cusumano and S. Hofmaier (eds.),
Projecting Resilience Across the Mediterranean,
https://doi.org/10.1007/978-3-030-23641-0_13

the persistence of socio-economic hardship and continued terrorist threats, transition to democracy in Tunisia seems to be heading toward consolidation. On the contrary, Egypt has returned to a non-democratic regime. Given the importance of Tunisia and Egypt for the stability, and hence the security, of the broader Middle East and North Africa (MENA) region, these countries constitute suitable case studies for examining transatlantic democracy promotion strategies in the region (Hassan 2015). Furthermore, the Arab uprisings and subsequent regime changes represented the most significant test for the EU after the Lisbon Treaty (2009), and the innovations it introduced in EU foreign policy (Amadio Viceré 2018). An examination of the cases at hand may also shed light on the inter- and intra-institutional practices of the EU and NATO.

The political transitions in Egypt and Tunisia arose from democratising pressures which had been suffocated by decades of authoritarian resilience (Pace and Cavatorta 2012). And yet the Euro-Atlantic diplomacy's response to such transitions sought to ensure stability in North Africa by enhancing state resilience at the expense of broader societal resilience. Why was that so? Indeed, EU and NATO policies interacted with the countries' structural and cultural specificities (Nassif 2018; Stepan 2018), while adapting to the conditions on the ground as the events unfolded. Nevertheless, unlike scholarly works conceiving the EU as an ethical, normative power (Aggestam 2008; Manners 2002; Whitman 2011), and in line with more critical approaches (Bicchi 2006; Diez 2013; Fisher Onar and Nicolaidis 2013; Nicolaidis and Howe 2002), this contribution shows that, as the response capabilities of the EU and NATO were challenged, both organisations focused on avoiding the risk of state failure rather than fostering an all-encompassing democratisation process.

The remainder of the chapter is structured as follows. The first section offers an overview of the origins and development of the Tunisian crisis and assesses EU and NATO responses to the Tunisian political transition between late 2010 and the first anniversary of the EU Global Strategy (EUGS; June 2017), presented by the High Representative of the Union for Foreign Affairs and Security Policy (HR/VP), Federica Mogherini, in June 2016 (EEAS 2016b). The second section outlines the roots and evolution of the Egyptian crisis, and examines EU and NATO policies towards the Egyptian transition, from the deposition of President Hosni Mubarak until summer 2017. Finally, the chapter draws some conclusions from the analysis.

Projecting Resilience in Tunisia

The Tunisian upheaval was a momentous political breakthrough. Not only did it reshape the country's domestic politics, but it also influenced the broader wave of unrest that shook up MENA countries. A number of key economic and social factors contributed to this unrest, undermining the legitimacy and effectiveness of the regime (Kerrou 2017). These include low growth, stagnating domestic and foreign investments, high youth unemployment, corruption of public authorities, and a generally weak rule of law. Events began to unfold in December 2010 (BBC 2017), when Mohamed Bouazizi, a university graduate working as a fruit seller in the town of Sidi Bouzid, burnt himself to protest high unemployment and police violence. Bouzid's dramatic deed, leading to his death in hospital a few weeks later, resonated among many Tunisians as a symbol of political martyrdom, driving massive demonstrations against the two-decade-old authoritarian regime of President Ben Ali. Despite the initial abrupt suppression by the security forces, the mobilisation soon reached Tunis, forcing Ben Ali to flee to Saudi Arabia in January 2011, and leading to the resignation of Prime Minister Mohamed Ghannouchi the following month. Amid early episodes of violence, the Tunisian political transition led to the establishment of a new regime. A 'Higher Authority for the Realisation of the Objectives of the Revolution, Political Reform and Democratic Transition' was created and an Assembly, in charge of drafting a new Constitution, was elected in October 2011.

Cooperation between the new political forces, in particular the majoritarian moderate Islamist movement, Ennahdha, and secular parties such as Ettaktol, immediately proved uneasy. This led to occasional stalemates in the drafting of the constitutional text, and to a rise in ideological polarisation across the country. Domestic tensions and armed clashes, which also involved Salafists and loyalists of the old regime, reached a climax between February and July 2013, with the assassination of opposition leaders Chokri Belaid and Mohamed Brahimi. These tensions forced Ennahdha to agree to an interim government (*The Telegraph* 2011). Despite continuing unrest, including terrorist attacks, Tunisia's first free parliamentary elections were held in October 2014, and won by the Nidaa Tounes bloc. The latter was headed by Beji Caid Essebsi, who was elected President and has been leading the country until the present. The country's difficult transition towards a fully functioning democratic regime has been further complicated in the past few years by a multitude of unresolved socio-economic challenges. Such challenges are compounded by heightened security threats (Kerrou 2017) such as smuggling activities by criminal organisations, as well as terrorist threats inside the country (e.g. the 2015 Bardo Museum attack) and along its borders (see chapter by Léonard and Kaunert in this volume). In addition to this, Tunisia has been the largest exporter of foreign fighters to Syria and Iraq (Council of Europe 2017).

The Tunisian Political Transition: The EU Response

The unexpected outbreak and subsequent development of the Tunisian revolution had a defining impact on EU policy towards the country, and the MENA region more broadly. The Tunisian uprising challenged old foreign policy assumptions and prompted a reformulation of the overarching priorities and practical approaches of EU institutions and Member States. In many respects, Tunisia played a key role in shaping the EU's early cooperation with its Southern Neighbourhood. In fact, this was the first country to sign an Association Agreement with the bloc in 1998 and an Action Plan seven years later (EEAS 2018). Within the 1995 Euro-Mediterranean Partnership (the Barcelona Process), EU–Tunisia cooperation was established with the objective of promoting sustainable development (Ayadi and Sessa 2016; see chapter by Badarin and Schumacher in this volume). Such cooperation was built on political dialogue as well as on economic and financial collaboration. However, the EU's cooperation with the Ben Ali regime in Tunis soon became pragmatic and transactional, in line with the EU's general approach towards authoritarian regimes in the MENA region before the Arab uprisings. Under the assumption that neoliberal economic development and political change would ultimately coincide (Pace 2014), Brussels fostered the region's resilience by focusing on its security and stability rather than promoting democracy and human rights to the full (Bicchi 2009). Creating a free-trade area as a means to achieve peace and stability in the Arab world was already central to the Barcelona Process. Yet this approach was further enshrined in the 2003 European Security Strategy (EU 2003), which neglected the issue of political democratisation in MENA countries. The same was true for the European Neighbourhood Policy (ENP 2004)/Union for the Mediterranean (2005), which pursued democracy promotion through the narrow perspective of economic relations (Pace 2009). Consequently, the EU pushed for trade liberalisation and structural modernisation at the local level, along with security cooperation focussing on illegal migration and organised crime. By contrast, minimal attention was paid to the issues of rule of law and human rights in the country (Ayadi and Sessa 2016).

The overthrow of Ben Ali and the beginning of a tumultuous and uncertain political transition in Tunisia challenged existing EU policy in the region. Brussels' response had to navigate through disagreements among Member States over the dynamics and actors at play in the country. The French Government's initial pro-regime stance (*The Guardian* 2011), and the difficulty of EU institutions to quickly adapt their policy toolbox to rapidly evolving events and crises are a case in point (Echagüe et al. 2011). However, diverging preferences amongst Member States within the Foreign Affairs Council were soon overcome by a wide consensus on the need to support the transition (Council of the European Union 2011). Ultimately, the EU attempted to embrace democratisation (Dandashly 2015) rather than continue to maintain an 'authoritarian resilience' (Pace and Cavatorta 2012: 125) in Tunisia. Thus, the revision of the ENP (25 May 2011) introduced the concept of 'deep and sustainable democracy', envisaged new funds for civil society, and linked such funds to a conditionality approach entailing the three key areas of action of 'money, market and mobility' (Echagüe et al. 2011; see chapter by Badarin and Schumacher in this volume). Moreover, the EU supported the Tunisian path towards democracy through a range of tools and platforms under the umbrella of the SPRING Programme in late 2011. Brussels' prioritisation of a peaceful and pluralistic transition in Tunisia also took the form of high-level visits and technical missions advising the country's new authorities on the formation of a post-revolutionary regime, including the establishment of control authorities, the drafting of the constitution, and the conduct of free and fair elections (Ayadi and Sessa 2016). These policy initiatives were coupled with the announcement of a Privileged Partnership in 2012, which paved the way to starting negotiations for a Deep and Comprehensive Free Trade Agreement (DCFTA), and the setting up of a Mobility Partnership.

Despite the occasional stalemate brought by the political, security and socio-economic challenges affecting the country's stability, EU attempts to project societal and state resilience in Tunisia have been persistent in the past six years (Ayadi and Sessa 2016). In more recent times, however, the EU's priorities towards the Southern neighbourhood have been shifting towards a more distinctive focus on security. The 2016 EUGS enshrined such a shift by adopting 'principled pragmatism' as a guiding concept of EU foreign policy (see chapter by Anholt and Wagner in this volume). Moreover, the EUGS explicitly introduced the notion of 'state and societal resilience', to be fostered in order to enhance the EU's prevention and early warning capacity vis-à-vis any further instability (Colombo et al. 2018).

Although hailed in the EUGS as a 'prosperous, peaceful and stable democracy' (EEAS 2016b), a joint Communication by the HR/VP and the Commission in September 2016 acknowledged that 'the Tunisian transition is fragile and faces serious risks' (High Representative and European Commission 2016: 2). According to the Communication, this is due to continuing terrorist threats, insufficient political resolve to fully implement key provisions of the new Constitution, and multiple weaknesses affecting the Tunisian economy. Against this background and in the context of the EUGS' implementation, EU policies on Tunisia have been re-centred on promoting the country's stability and security. This includes, in particular, the fight against terrorism, radicalisation, irregular migration and organised crime, as well as the strengthening of the Union's role as Tunisia's main trade partner via a renewed emphasis on the DCFTA negotiations (Dandashly 2015; see chapter by Léonard and Kaunert in this volume).

NATO's Response

Compared with Tunisia's decade-old cooperation with the EU, NATO's role in the country has been far less comprehensive and visible. This is due to both the history and politics of security cooperation between the West and the MENA region. The Cold War had made the Southern Mediterranean less relevant for NATO, given the imperative of territorial deterrence against the perceived Soviet threat in Central and Eastern Europe. Although Middle Eastern crises in the 1960s and 1970s, particularly the Arab-Israeli wars, contributed to a greater awareness of the rising strategic importance of the region, the 'Soviet prism' still dominated NATO's strategic planning and security projection (Gaub 2012). In this context, the Atlantic Alliance's[1] relations with Tunisia in the

---

[1] Hereinafter simply the Alliance.

almost fifty years that followed the signing of the 1949 Washington Treaty were virtually non-existent (see chapter by Larsen and Koehler in this volume).

The situation began to evolve with the end of the Cold War. The ensuing period of optimism over the transatlantic security environment, and the prospects for improved north–south relations in the Mediterranean—a political priority long pursued by NATO's Southern European Members like France, Italy and Spain (Reichborn-Kjennerud 2013)—prompted NATO to launch the Mediterranean Dialogue (MD) in 1994 (NATO 2015).[2]

Within this framework, NATO–Tunisia bilateral cooperation until the 2011 regime change focussed on the fight against terrorism, military cooperation, scientific and technological collaboration, and public diplomacy (NATO 2007). Nevertheless, while the break-up of diplomatic relations between Tunisia and Israel in 2000 contributed to making MD's multilateral approach largely unsuccessful (Filípková et al. 2012), the pre-2011 cooperation between NATO and Tunisia remained at the level of diplomatic dialogue and trust-building exercises. This lack of success was compounded by the broader constraints affecting the MD during that period. Such constraints included NATO's historically negative image in the country and the region at large; its limited understanding of local and regional complexities (Gaub 2012); and the high degree of suspicion by the Ben Ali regime vis-à-vis potential interferences by Western partners in defence and security (Hanlon 2012).

The political transition beginning in 2011 caused a stalemate in the cooperation between Tunisia and NATO. On the one hand, the legitimacy and effectiveness of the Alliance's traditional interlocutors of the armed forces and security apparatuses were deeply challenged by the outbreak of protests. On the other hand, despite the logistical support Tunisia regularly offered to anti-Ghaddafi insurgents, NATO's decision to launch Operation Unified Protector in Libya between February and October 2011 was not welcomed by the new political leadership in Tunis (Filípková et al. 2012) due to fears of violence spillovers across the border. Such fears notwithstanding, a meaningful dialogue resumed in

---

[2] The MD pursued three main goals: achieving better mutual understanding—the political dimension; contributing to regional security and stability—the practical dimension; and dispelling misconceptions about NATO—the public diplomacy dimension (Lesser et al. 2018).

2014, with the signing of a new Individual Partnership and Cooperation Programme centred on counter-terrorism and border security. Several factors drove the resumed cooperation between the Alliance and Tunisia. Firstly, the consolidation of the country's political leadership. Secondly, a deteriorating domestic and regional security landscape exacerbated by jihadist terrorism and the presence of foreign fighters, protracted civil war in Libya, state fragility in Algeria; and migration pressures from the Sahel. Finally, the push by NATO's Southern European Members to lessen the Alliance's focus on deterring Russia following the 2013 Ukraine crisis (Bianchi et al. 2017). The creation of the NATO Strategic Direction South, Hub in Naples (Italy), aimed at sharing information on regional security between Allies and Partners, epitomises this last aspect (NATO 2017b). Another milestone in Tunisia–NATO *rapprochement* was reached a year later with the visit of Prime Minister Habib Essid to the Alliance's Headquarters in Brussels to discuss further cooperation (Profazio 2018). Consequently, in the 2018 Brussels Summit Declaration, NATO Members announced new Defence and Related Security Capacity Building measures to further assist Tunisia in the areas of cyber defence, countering the use of improvised explosive devices, and the promotion of transparency in resource management (NATO 2018b).

Projecting Resilience in Egypt

When the first upheavals against the regime started in Cairo on 25 January 2011, Hosni Mubarak had been President for almost 30 years. Under his authoritarian rule, Egypt had been suffering from poor rule of law (Pace 2009), deteriorating socio-economic conditions and human rights' violations (El-Ghazaly et al. 2011). As the conflict between the military and the opposition deepened, the protests in Tahrir Square led to Mubarak's deposition. Presidential powers were assumed by the Supreme Council of the Armed Forces (SCAF) on 13 February 2011. Although slow political change, violent repression of dissent and human rights' violations characterised the immediate aftermath of the President's ousting (Freedom House 2013), a second phase in the political transition seemed to begin in 2012 with the coming into power of the Muslim Brotherhood (Voltolini and Colombo 2018). Almost one year after Egyptians had taken to the streets, the Islamist Freedom and Justice Party (FJP) scored a major victory in the parliamentary elections of 21 January 2012. Not long afterwards, on 24 June the Muslim

Brotherhood's candidate, Mohammed Morsi, became the first democratically elected president in modern Egyptian history. Yet Morsi fell short of many citizens' expectations of genuine democratisation. At the end of December 2012, he attempted to introduce a decree promoting the exclusion of democratic control over presidential decisions, which was subsequently withdrawn due to popular protests. The rule of the Muslim Brotherhood also led to further polarisation of the Egyptian society (Dandashly 2015). The fracture between religious and secular forces became all the more evident in late 2012, when the government proposed a constitution which would substantially limit the freedoms of speech and assembly (Albrecht 2013). In fact, even though the new Egyptian constitutional text had been approved in a referendum on 15 and 22 December 2012, violent clashes between protesters and governmental forces followed its introduction.

Eventually, taking advantage of popular discontent and anti-government demonstrations, the Egyptian armed forces, guided by Army Chief Abdul Fattah al-Sisi, overthrew Morsi on 3 July 2013. From that moment on, Egypt began its path towards military authoritarianism. While the transitional authorities proposed a roadmap envisaging the constitution's revision and new parliamentary and presidential elections in 2014 (Ahram Online 2013), repression of the Muslim Brotherhood started immediately after the military coup (Ardovini 2017). By the end of 2013, the army-backed government had declared the Muslim Brotherhood a terrorist group (Bradley and El-Ghobashy 2013). Later on, Al-Sisi's new constitution essentially banned religious parties in the country and envisaged increased military control over the government (18 January 2014; Arafa 2012). The advent of the new Egyptian regime was finally formalised in the presidential elections of May 2014, when the former Army Chief obtained 93.3% of the votes in an electoral ballot harshly criticised for the repression of the opposition voices (Azeem 2014). Since then, political repression and violence have escalated in Egypt, essentially casting a shadow over hopes for democratic reforms (Freedom House 2018).

The Egyptian Political Transition: The EU's Response

Despite Egypt being an authoritarian regime, the EU had maintained bilateral relations with Cairo during Mubarak's long mandate to serve its interests in the region, including cooperation on migration, counter-terrorism, and the Middle East Peace Process (Hassan 2015). The outbreak of protests and the violent repression of demonstrators frustrated the alignment amongst the EU and its Member States on the strategies adopted towards Egypt until that moment. Although all Member States were initially reluctant to side with anti-government demonstrations (Reuters 2011), a cleavage soon emerged between Northern and Southern European countries on how to handle the Egyptian political transition. While the former, particularly the UK, supported the resignation of the Egyptian President and the creation of a military-led transitory government (Waterfield 2011), the latter, headed by Italy, insisted on the relevance of Mubarak's regime in containing the spreading of Islamic extremism and in preventing mass influxes of migrants (El Pais 2011). To be sure, similarly to the Tunisian case, the EU reacted to the ousting of Mubarak by institutionalising the SPRING Programme. This Programme involved: expanding the mandates of the European Bank of Investment and the Neighbourhood Investment Facility; creating new policy instruments, such as the European Endowment for Democracy and the Civil Society Facility; and revising the ENP. However, concrete changes remained limited and EU efforts at democracy promotion in Egypt continued to be dominated by 'security concerns as a response to the threat of instability' (Dandashly 2018: 37; see also Noutcheva 2015).

After the victory of FJP's and the election of Morsi, EU Member States were divided among those, such as Germany and the UK, who feared the possibility of Egypt turning into an Islamist regime and the potential ensuing implications on the Arab country's relations with Israel (Hague 2013; Steinberg 2015), and those, such as France, who were keener to accept the election results after the tension triggered by their initial reluctance towards the Arab turmoil (Daguzan 2013). Eventually, as the security conditions in Libya worsened and the fear of an instability contagion in neighbouring Egypt increased,[3] the EU continued to seek to avoid state failure by ensuring socio-economic prosperity in the country (Amadio Viceré and Fabbrini 2017). During the Muslim Brotherhood's rule, besides the DCFTA negotiation, the European Commission offered Egypt the opportunity to further develop trade relations, and increase macro-financial assistance and budget support (European Commission, The President 2012). The creation of an EU–Egypt Task Force, intended to enhance aid coordination between

---

[3] At the time, the EU fear of the spread of Islamic extremism in the region originated from the murder of the American Ambassador to Libya, Christopher Steven, by militiamen in Benghazi on 11 September 2012.

the EU with third-countries' private and public sectors, constituted an exception to this trend (Huber 2013). Nonetheless, its implementation proved difficult, as shown by the EU's inability to prevent the Egyptian government from excluding human rights groups from a Task Force meeting (ECFR 2013; 13–14 November 2012).

In reaction to Morsi's presidential decree and to the new Egyptian constitution, the European Parliament went as far as to demand a suspension of economic support to Cairo in March 2013 (European Parliament 2013). Meanwhile, several EU programmes devoted to civil society organisations were cancelled due to a lack of commitment by Egyptian authorities (Pinfari 2013). The EU did, however, prioritise security concerns in its response to the July 2013 regime change. Whilst some national representatives had voiced their discontent towards Morsi's deposition (CBC 2013), EU Member States and institutions all avoided the use of the word 'coup'. In spite of the army's violent political repression, EU representatives soon established bilateral diplomatic relations with Al-Sisi. To be sure, the EU decided to suspend a transfer of military equipment that could potentially be employed to repress civilians in August 2013 (Council of the EU, FAC 2013). Yet, as the then HR/VP Catherine Ashton put it, Brussels continued to offer 'support' and 'help' to Egypt, but abstained from any 'interference' (High Representative 2013: 1).

The EU's strategy to stabilise Egypt through its new regime, notwithstanding its crackdown on opposition forces and minorities, persisted as time went by. Although some criticism of Al-Sisi's constitution was raised by the European Parliament (6 February 204; European Parliament 2014), EU Member States welcomed its introduction and stated their intention to continue assisting the Egyptian people (Council of the EU, FAC 2014). As for the victory of the Army Chief at the presidential elections, the EU congratulated Al-Sisi for having guaranteed peace and order during the voting period (EU 2014). While the military regime consolidated itself, the EU continued to fund socio-economic initiatives and began revising the ENP. Although still focusing on the understanding that economic growth would lead to a stabilisation of the neighbourhood, contrary to its 2011 predecessor, the 2015 ENP did not aim at fostering substantive democratic reforms. Instead, it identified trade, energy security, transports, mobility and security as priorities, and acknowledged the unwillingness of some countries to abide to EU values (Poli 2016).

Under the label of 'principled pragmatism', such an approach was reiterated in the 2016 EUGS. Rather than emphasising the need for democratisation, the official document considered the increase of societal resilience as the most effective response to repressive states (EEAS 2016a). While resilience building was embedded in one of the five lines of action identified in the October 2016 Roadmap on the Follow-Up to the Strategy (EEAS 2016b), a Joint Communication by the HR and the Commission in June 2017 reiterated the importance of socio-economic development for enhancing broader societal resilience in authoritarian contexts (High Representative and European Commission 2017). The same objectives are enumerated within the framework of the implementation of the EUGS and the EU–Egypt partnership priorities for 2017–2020 which cover three main areas: socio-economic development, 'with a view to building a *stable* and prosperous Egypt'; foreign policy cooperation aimed at the '*stabilising*' the MENA region; and 'enhancing the *stability* of Egypt' as a 'modern and democratic state', while cooperating with it on security, terrorism and migration *[italics added]* (Council of the EU 2017).

NATO's Response

When the 2011 revolt began, Cairo was NATO's most relevant partner in the region. While Egypt was one of the first countries to be involved in the 1994 Mediterranean Dialogue, its ties with the Alliance were further developed in 2007 through an Individual Cooperation Programme (ICP). In exchange for its cooperation, Egypt received technical assistance and training from NATO Members (Orfy 2010). While cooperative security was defined as one of the Alliance's main objectives in its 2010 Strategic Concept (NATO 2010), the majority of its collaboration with this country was of a technical and military nature and, therefore generally insufficient at the political level (Gaub 2012; see also chapter by Larsen and Koehler in this volume).

NATO did not distance itself much from the EU in its response to the events in Egypt. Initially, its reaction towards the Egyptian uprising was cautious because of the country's strategic relevance for the Alliance. Whereas NATO's Southern European Members felt particularly exposed to irregular migration and religious extremism, the US, who had been establishing a politico-strategic partnership with Egypt since the late 1970s (Scharp 2011; Mcinerney 2010), feared the impact on Israel's security and energy flows (Isaac 2011). Eventually, despite initial reluctance to side with anti-government forces, NATO Secretary General Anders Fogh Rasmussen welcomed Mubarak's decision to resign by stressing the relevance of a 'speedy, orderly and peaceful transition to democracy' (BBC 2011).

In a similar way to the EU, and in line with its core mission and approach to this area, the Alliance reacted to the Egyptian uprising by focusing on regional insecurity and state failure rather than on substantive democratic reforms. In April 2011, NATO offered MENA countries new terms of cooperation, hitherto reserved for Euro-Atlantic partners (Reichborn-Kjennerud 2013). Such terms included 'enhanced political consultation on security issues of common concern'; 'strengthened practical cooperation'; and 'support for defence education, training and capacity building, within existing resources' (NATO 2011: 2). Hence, in the words of Rasmussen (2011: 1), the Arab uprisings had 'shown the importance of intensifying political dialogue' to achieve 'lasting stability, security and prosperity across North Africa and the Middle East'. Furthermore, notwithstanding the SCAF's violent repression and persistent human rights' violations, in December 2011 NATO foreign ministers declared their readiness to consider new requests from MENA countries within the MD for partnership and cooperation for the reform of the security and defence sectors (NATO 2011).

The Alliance's approach did not change with the Muslim Brotherhood's coming into power. Shortly after the FJP's victory, in recognising a 'time of unprecedented change in the Mediterranean and broader Middle East', NATO heads of state and government reiterated their commitment to strengthening and developing partnership relations with countries in the region to achieve 'security and stability' (NATO 2012; Chicago Summit, May 2012). Thus, despite continuous civil unrest in the country, NATO continued to support Morsi's regime through training programmes (NATO 2014a). When the Egyptian army overthrew President Morsi in 2013, NATO Members 'raised concerns over Mediterranean instability', and declared that NATO would watch Egypt closely (Euractiv 2013). Indeed, 'growing instability' in the MENA region and its implications for the peace and security of the Euro-Atlantic area were among the main issues discussed at the NATO Summit in Wales on 5 September 2014. On that occasion, NATO Members reiterated their 'support to the legitimate aspirations of the people', while stressing their intention to 'explore options for possible

NATO assistance to bilateral and international efforts to promote stability' (NATO 2014b). Thus in 2014, in the framework of the MD, the Netherlands offered the Egyptian military technical and material training (NATO 2016a).

At the 2016 NATO Summit in Warsaw, NATO heads of state and government committed to 'remain actively engaged in projecting stability and enhancing international security', by deepening political dialogue and enhancing practical cooperation with its partners, including Egypt. Such practical cooperation involved increased 'support in the areas of counter-terrorism, small arms and light weapons, counter-improvised explosive devices, and military border security' (NATO 2016b). While the formalisation of the Alliance's partnership with Al-Sisi's military regime occurred with the establishment of an Egyptian diplomatic mission to NATO (2017a), such a commitment resulted in the participation of Egypt in NATO-led political dialogue and the provision of material support and training throughout 2017 (NATO 2018a).

Conclusions

Significant differences exist between EU and NATO, particularly with regard to their structural characteristics and the final objectives they pursue. While the EU is a political system characterised both by supranational and intergovernmental features, NATO is an intergovernmental, security organisation with a prominently military profile. Furthermore, although most EU Member States are also part of NATO, the latter includes the US, Canada and Turkey as well. In spite of these obvious organisational differences, and of the presence of the US as a driving power within the Alliance, EU and NATO responses to the Arab uprisings essentially coincided. Indeed, while the EU initially revised its approach by focusing on the development of substantive democracy through socio-economic reforms, NATO shifted towards enhanced political cooperation with Tunisia and Egypt in the immediate aftermath of their regime changes. Still, as time went by, the policies followed by the two organisations ultimately overlapped. As the EU and NATO focused on avoiding the risk of state failure, they both essentially enhanced state resilience at the expense of the broader societal resilience.

Resilience has become a political 'mantra' underpinning Euro-Atlantic diplomacy in the Southern neighbourhood in the post-Arab uprising. In this context, however, particular emphasis has been placed on the need to increase the resilience of state institutions, whether democratic or not, rather than addressing the root causes of the general absences of societal resilience in the region. EU and NATO have primarily addressed the symptoms of local instability, but largely neglected the long-term causes of insecurity in Tunisia and Egypt. While the former include terrorism, organised crime and human trafficking, the latter mostly consist of domestic socio-economic challenges. All this considered, it is reasonable to argue that the chapter's findings raise an important theoretical challenge for the concept of normative power Europe and, more in general for the qualifying features of the EU international identity compared to other actors (see Manners 2002).

A reshaping of the pattern of resilience fostered by the EU and NATO in Tunisia and Egypt, as well as of the wider MENA region, is undoubtedly necessary. Such a revision would require the adoption of a more holistic notion of national and regional security, which should reach beyond the traditional parameters of institutional stability and effectiveness, and encompass measures targeting socio-economic and human security matters. Certainly, the EUGS' recent differentiation among state and societal resilience is a step in this direction. However, such approach has not been fully implemented yet in the MENA region. In the cases under consideration, for instance, a predominant focus on pursuing EU's member states' interests on security, migration and trade, has hindered the EU's stated objective of increasing both state and societal resilience in these countries.

Given the persisting security challenges in the Southern Mediterranean area, the convergence of priorities between the EU and NATO is likely to continue in the future (Lesser et al. 2018). As the cases of Tunisia and Egypt demonstrate, if an effective principle for dividing labour among the two organisations continues to be missing, rather than to a virtuous integration of efforts in the Southern Mediterranean region, such convergence in projecting resilience risks to lead to an inefficient duplication. A possible way forward could build upon the 2016 Warsaw Joint Declaration and its follow-up developments, in order to frame a solid coordination mechanism between the two organisations in countering regional insecurity. On the one hand, this could include a more regular use of joint analysis and information-sharing on potential threats to states and societies. On the other hand, the definition of a clear and sustainable division of labour in military and civilian security cooperation with local partners should be fostered through enhanced dialogue and coordination on the ground between EU Delegations and NATO Contact Point Embassies, aimed at both preventing or in tackling domestic and regional security crises.

References

Aggestam, L. (2008). Introduction: Ethical Power Europe? *International Affairs, 84*(1), 1–11.
Ahram Online. (2013, July 3). *Egypt Military Unveils Transitional Roadmap.* http://english.ahram.org.eg/News/75631.aspx. Accessed 11 November 2018.
Albrecht, H. (2013, January 25). *Egypt's 2012 Constitution: Devil in the Details, Not in Religion* (Peace Brief 139). United States Institute of Peace. https://www.files.ethz.ch/isn/159373/PB139.pdf. Accessed 11 November 2018.
Amadio Viceré, M. G. (2018). *The High Representative and EU Foreign Policy Integration: A Comparative Study of Kosovo and Ukraine.* Basingstoke: Palgrave Macmillan.
Amadio Viceré, M. G., & Fabbrini, S. (2017). Assessing the High Representative's Role in Egypt During the Arab Spring. *The International Spectator, 52*(3), 64–82.
Arafa, M. A. (2012). Whither Egypt? Against Religious Fascism and Legal Authoritarianism: Pure Revolution, Popular Coup, or a Military Coup d'etat. *Indiana International and Comparative Law Review, 24*(4), 859–897.
Ardovini, L. (2017). The Politicisation of Sectarianism in Egypt: 'Creating an Enemy' the State vs. the Ikhwan. *Global Discourse, 6*(4), 579–600.
Ayadi, R., & Sessa, E. (2016, June). *EU Policies in Tunisia Before and After the Revolution: Study for the Foreign Affairs Committee (AFET) of the European Parliament EP/EXPO/B/AFET/2015/04.* Brussels. http://www.europarl.europa.eu/RegData/etudes/STUD/2016/578002/EXPO_STU%282016%29578002_EN.pdf. Accessed 11 November 2018.
Azeem, Z. (2014, May 26). Egypt's Vote for Repression. *Al Monitor.* https://www.al-monitor.com/pulse/originals/2014/05/egypt-elections-al-si-si-strongman-political-repression-votes.html#. Accessed 11 November 2018.
BBC. (2011, February). *Hosni Mubarak Resigns: World Reaction.* https://www.bbc.com/news/world-middle-east-12435738. Accessed 11 November 2018.
BBC. (2017, November 1). *Tunisia Profile—Timeline.* https://www.bbc.co.uk/news/world-africa-14107720. Accessed 11 November 2018.
Bianchi, M., Lasconjarias, G., & Marrone, A. (2017, July). *Projecting Stability in NATO's Southern Neighbourhood* (NDC Conference Report). NATO Defense College (NDC). http://www.ndc.nato.int/news/news.php?icode=1076. Accessed 11 November 2018.
Bicchi, F. (2006). 'Our Size Fits All': Normative Power Europe and the Mediterranean. *Journal of European Public Policy, 13*(2), 286–303.

Bicchi, F. (2009). Democracy Assistance in the Mediterranean: An Overview. *Mediterranean Politics, 14*(1), 61–78.

Bradley, M., & El-Ghobashy, T. (2013, December 25). Egypt Declares Muslim Brotherhood a Terrorist Organization. *The Wall Street Journal.* http://www.wsj.com/articles/SB10001424052702303799404579280260534285946. Accessed 11 November 2018.

CBC News. (2013, July 5). *World Leaders Put Egypt on Notice Over Democracy.* http://www.cbc.ca/news/world/world-leaders-put-egypt-on-notice-over-democracy-1.1347854. Accessed 11 November 2018.

CBC News. (2014, February 10). *Council Conclusions on Egypt.* Brussels. http://www.consilium.europa.eu/uedocs/cms_data/docs/pressdata/EN/foraff/140971.pdf. Accessed 11 November 2018.

Colombo, S., Dessì, A., & Ntousas, V. (Eds.). (2018). *The EU, Resilience and the MENA Region.* Brussels: Foundation for European Progressive Studies (FEPS); Rome: Istituto Affari Internazionali (IAI). http://www.iai.it/en/pubblicazioni/eu-resilience-and-mena-region. Accessed 11 November 2018.

Council of Europe. (2017, February). *Terrorism: Tunisia Fears the Return of Foreign Fighters.* https://www.coe.int/en/web/corruption/bilateral-activities/ukraine/-/asset_publisher/plqBCeLYiBJQ/content/terrorism-tunisia-fears-the-return-of-foreign-fighters?inheritRedirect=false. Accessed 11 November 2018.

Council of the EU. (2011, January 31). *Council Conclusions on Tunisia.* Brussels. https://www.consilium.europa.eu/uedocs/cms_data/docs/pressdata/EN/foraff/119051.pdf. Accessed 11 November 2018.

Council of the EU. (2017, June 16). *Association Between the European Union and Egypt.* Brussels. http://www.consilium.europa.eu/media/23942/eu-egypt.pdf. Accessed 11 November 2018.

Council of the EU, Foreign Affairs Council. (2013, August 21). *Council Conclusions on Egypt.* Brussels. http://trade.ec.europa.eu/doclib/docs/2013/september/tradoc_151710.pdf. Accessed 11 November 2018.

Daguzan, J. F. (2013). France and Islamist Movements: A Long Non-dialogue. In L. Vidino (Ed.), *The West and the Muslim Brotherhood After the Arab Spring.* Dubai: Al Mesbar Studies and Research Centre and Foreign Policy Research Institute. https://www.fpri.org/docs/201303.west_and_the_muslim_brotherhood_after_the_arab_spring.pdf. Accessed 11 November 2018.

Dandashly, A. (2015). The EU Response to Regime Change: In the Wake of the Arab Revolt: Differential Implementation. *Journal of European integration, 37*(1), 37–56.

Dandashly, A. (2018). EU Democracy Promotion and the Dominance of the Security-Stability Nexus. *Mediterranean Politics, 23*(1), 62–82.

Diez, T. (2013). Normative Power as Hegemony. *Cooperation and Conflict, 48*(2), 194–210.

Echagüe, A., Michou, H., & Mikail, B. (2011). Europe and the Arab Uprisings: EU Vision Versus Member State Action. *Mediterranean Politics,* 16(2), 329–335.

El-Ghazaly, S., Evers, E., & Shebaya, S. (2011). Entrenching Poverty in Egypt: Human Rights Violations that Contributed to the January 25 Revolution. *Yale Human Rights and Development Journal,* 14(2), 132–144.

El Pais. (2011, January 31). *Shame on Europe.* http://elpais.com/elpais/2011/01/31/inenglish/1296454847_850210.html. Accessed 11 November 2018.

EEAS—European External Action Service. (2016a, June 28). *Shared Vision, Common Action: A Stronger Europe: A Global Strategy for the European Union's Foreign and Security Policy.* Brussels. http://eeas.europa.eu/archives/docs/top_stories/pdf/eugs_review_web.pdf. Accessed 11 November 2018.

EEAS—European External Action Service. (2016b, September 16). *Roadmap on The Follow-Up to the EU Global Strategy.* Bratislava. https://club.bruxelles2.eu/wpcontent/uploads/2016/09/feuilleroute-strategieglobale@ue160922.pdf. Accessed 11 November 2018.

EEAS—European External Action Service. (2018). *Relations Between the EU and Tunisia.* https://eeas.europa.eu/headquarters/headquarters-homepage_en/16047/Relations%20between%20the%20EU%20and%20Tunisia. Accessed 11 November 2018.

Euractiv. (2013, July 31). *EU's Top Diplomat Endeavours to Resolve Egypt Crisis amid NATO Concerns.* https://www.euractiv.com/section/global-europe/news/eu-s-top-diplomat-endeavours-to-resolve-egypt-crisis-amid-nato-concerns/. Accessed 11 November 2018.

European Council on Foreign Relations. (2013). *Middle East and North Africa in European Foreign Policy Scorecard 2012.* http://www.ecfr.eu/scorecard/2013/mena/56. Accessed 11 November 2018.

European Parliament. (2013, March 14). *Situation in Egypt.* Strasbourg. http://www.europarl.europa.eu/sides/getDoc.do?pubRef=-//EP//TEXT+TA+P7-TA-2013-0095+0+DOC+XML+V0//EN. Accessed 11 November 2018.

European Parliament. (2014, February 6). *Resolution on the Situation in Egypt* (2014/2532 (RSP)). http://www.europarl.europa.eu/oeil/popups/summary.do?id=1336888&t=d&l=en. Accessed 11 November 2018.

European Union. (2003, December). *A Secure Europe in a Better World: European Security Strategy.* Brussels. https://europa.eu/globalstrategy/en/european-security-strategy-secure-europe-better-world. Accessed 11 November 2018.

European Union. (2014, June 5). *Declaration on Behalf of the European Union on the Presidential Elections in Egypt* (10649/1/14 REV 1). Brussels. http://www.consilium.europa.eu/uedocs/cms_Data/docs/pressdata/EN/foraff/143096.pdf. Accessed 11 November 2018.

Filípková, L., et al. (2012). *NATO and the Arab Spring: Challenge to Cooperation, Opportunity for Action?* (Association for International Affairs

Policy Paper 1/2012). http://www.amo.cz/en/prague-transatlantic-talks-en/nato-and-the-arab-spring-challenge-to-cooperation-opportunity-for-action-2/. Accessed 11 November 2018.

Fisher Onar, N., & Nicolaidis, K. (2013). The Decentring Agenda: Europe as a Post-Colonial Power. *Cooperation and Conflict, 48*(2), 283–303.

Freedom House. (2013, August 9). *Timeline of Human Rights Violations in Egypt Since the Fall of Mubarak*. https://freedomhouse.org/article/timeline-human-rights-violations-egypt-fall-mubarak. Accessed 11 November 2018.

Freedom House. (2018). *Egypt Profile*. https://freedomhouse.org/report/freedom-world/2018/Egypt. Accessed 11 November 2018.

Gaub, F. (2012). *Against All Odds: Relations Between NATO and the MENA Region*. U.S. Army War College Strategic Studies Institute. https://ssi.armywarcollege.edu/pubs/display.cfm?pubID=1112. Accessed 11 November 2018.

Hague, F. (2013). International Policy Responses to Change in the Arab World. In L. Vidino (Ed.), *The West and the Muslim Brotherhood After the Arab Spring*. Dubai: Al Mesbar Studies and Research Centre and Foreign Policy Research Institute. https://www.fpri.org/docs/201303.west_and_the_muslim_brotherhood_after_the_arab_spring.pdf. Accessed 11 November 2018.

Hanlon, Q. (2012). *The Prospects for Security Sector Reform in Tunisia: A Year After the Revolution*. Strategic Studies Institute. https://issat.dcaf.ch/sqi/Learn/Resource-Library/Policy-and-Research-Papers/The-Prospects-for-Security-Sector-Reform-in-Tunisia-A-Year-After-the-Revolution. Accessed 11 November 2018.

Hassan, O. (2015). Underminig the Transatlantic Democracy Agenda? The Arab Spring and Saudi Arabia's Counteracting Democracy Strategy. *Democratization, 22*(3), 479–495.

High Representative and European Commission. (2016, September 29). *Strengthening EU Support for Tunisia*. Brussels. https://eeas.europa.eu/sites/eeas/files/communication_from_commission_to_inst_en_v6_p1_859678-2.pdf. Accessed 11 November 2018.

High Representative and European Commission. (2017, June 7). *A Strategic Approach to Resilience in the EU's External Action*. Brussels. https://ec.europa.eu/europeaid/2017-joint-communication-strategic-approach-resilience-eus-externalaction_en. Accessed 11 November 2018.

High Representative of the Union for Foreign Affairs and Security Policy. (2013, September 11). *Speech by EU High Representative Catherine Ashton to the European Parliament on the situation in Egypt* (A 454/13). Brussels. http://europa.eu/rapid/press-release_SPEECH-13-689_en.htm. Accessed 11 November 2018.

Huber, D. (2013). US and EU Human Rights and Democracy Promotion Since the Arab Spring. Rethinking Its Content, Targets and Instruments. *The International Spectator, 48*(3), 98–112.

Isaac, S. K. (2011, March). NATO and Middle East and North Africa (MENA) Security: Prospects for Burden Sharing (NATO Defence College Forum Paper). https://www.files.ethz.ch/isn/128708/fp_16.pdf. Accessed 11 November 2018.

Kerrou, M. (2017, November). *Challenges and Stakes of State and Societal Resilience in Tunisia* (IAI Working Paper 17/31). Istituto Affari Internazionali and Foundation for European Progressive Studies (FEPS). http://www.iai.it/sites/default/files/iaiwp1731.pdf. Accessed 11 November 2018.

Lesser, I., Brandsma, C., Basagni, L., & Lété, B. (2018, June). The Future of NATO's Mediterranean Dialogue—Perspectives on Security, Strategy and Partnership. *The German Marshall Fund of the United States.* http://www.gmfus.org/publications/future-natos-mediterranean-dialogue. Accessed 11 November 2018.

Manners, I. (2002). Normative Power Europe: A Contradiction in Terms? *Journal of Common Market Studies, 40*(2), 235–258.

Mcinerney, S. (2010, April 7). *Redirection of U.S. Democracy Assistance in Egypt Is Raising Questions About the Obama Administration's Interest in Democracy Promotion.* Carnegie Foundation. https://carnegieendowment.org/sada/40530. Accessed 11 November 2018.

Nassif, H. B. (2018). Patterns of Civil-Military Relations and Their Legacies for Democratization: Egypt Versus Tunisia. In A. Stepan (Ed.), *Democratic Transition in the Muslim World: A Global Perspective.* New York: Columbia University Press.

Nicolaidis, K., & Howe, R. (2002). 'This Is my EUtopia …': Narrative as Power. *Journal of Common Market Studies, 40*(4), 767–792.

North Atlantic Treaty Organisation (NATO). (2007, June). *Discours du Secrétaire général délégué Alessandro Minuto Rizzo à la conférence du Dialogue méditerranéen.* https://www.nato.int/cps/en/natohq/opinions_8774.htm?selectedLocale=fr. Accessed 11 November 2018.

North Atlantic Treaty Organisation (NATO). (2010, November 19). *NATO's New Strategic Concept.* https://www.nato.int/strategic-concept/. Accessed 11 November 2018.

North Atlantic Treaty Organisation (NATO). (2011, December 7). *Final Statement.* https://www.nato.int/cps/en/natohq/official_texts_81943.htm?mode=pressrelease. Accessed 11 November 2018.

North Atlantic Treaty Organisation (NATO). (2012, May 20). *Chicago Summit Declaration.* https://www.nato.int/cps/en/natohq/official_texts_87593.htm?selectedLocale=en. Accessed 11 November 2018.

North Atlantic Treaty Organisation (NATO). (2014a, January 27). *The Secretary General's Annual Report 2013.* Brussels. https://www.nato.int/cps/en/natohq/opinions_106247.htm?selectedLocale=en. Accessed 11 November 2018.

North Atlantic Treaty Organisation (NATO). (2014b, September 5). *Wales Summit Declaration*. https://www.nato.int/cps/ic/natohq/official_texts_112964.htm. Accessed 11 November 2018.

North Atlantic Treaty Organisation (NATO). (2015, February). *NATO Mediterranean Dialogue*. Brussels. https://www.nato.int/cps/en/natohq/topics_60021.htm. Accessed 11 November 2018.

North Atlantic Treaty Organisation (NATO). (2016a, February 11). *The Secretary General's Annual Report 2015*. Brussels. https://www.nato.int/cps/en/natohq/topics_127529.htm. Accessed 11 November 2018.

North Atlantic Treaty Organisation (NATO). (2016b, July 9). *Warsaw Summit Communiqué*. https://www.nato.int/cps/en/natohq/official_texts_133169.htm. Accessed 11 November 2018.

North Atlantic Treaty Organisation (NATO). (2017a, March 15). *Egypt Appoints Ambassador to NATO*. http://www.atlanticcouncil.org/blogs/natosource/egypt-appoints-ambassador-to-nato. Accessed 11 November 2018.

North Atlantic Treaty Organisation (NATO). (2017b, September 5). *NATO Strategic Direction South Hub Inaugurated*. https://www.nato.int/cps/ic/natohq/news_146835.htm. Accessed 11 November 2018.

North Atlantic Treaty Organisation (NATO). (2018a, March 15). *The Secretary General's Annual Report 2017*. Brussels. https://www.nato.int/cps/en/natohq/topics_152773.htm. Accessed 11 November 2018.

North Atlantic Treaty Organisation (NATO). (2018b, July 11). *Brussels Summit Declaration*. Brussels. https://www.nato.int/cps/en/natohq/official_texts_156624.htm. Accessed 11 November 2018.

Noutcheva, G. (2015). Institutional Governance of European Neighbourhood Policy in the Wake of the Arab Spring. *Journal of European Integration, 37*(1), 19–36.

Orfy, M. M. (2010). *NATO and the Middle East: The Geopolitical Context Post-9/11*. Abingdon: Routledge.

Pace, M. (2009). Paradoxes and Contradictions in EU Democracy Promotion in the Mediterranean: The Limits of EU Normative Power. *Democratization, 16*(1), 39–58.

Pace, M. (2014). The EU's Interpretation of the 'Arab Uprisings': Understanding the Different Visions About Democratic Change in EU-MENA Relations. *Journal of Common Market Studies, 52*(5), 969–984.

Pace, M., & Cavatorta, F. (2012). The Arab Uprisings in Theoretical Perspective—An Introduction. *Mediterranean Politics, 17*(2), 125–138.

Pinfari, M. (2013). The EU, Egypt and Morsi's Rise and Fall: 'Strategic Patience' and Its Discontents. *Mediterranean Politics, 18*(3), 460–466.

Poli, S. (2016). La revisione della politica europea di vicinato. *European Papers, 1*(1), 263–274.

President of the European Commission. (2012, September 13). *Statement by President Barroso following His Meeting with Mr Mohamed Morsi, President of Egypt* (SPEECH/12/596). Brussels. http://europa.eu/rapid/press-release_SPEECH-12-602_en.htm?locale=en.

Profazio, U. (2018, April 6). *Tunisia's Reluctant Partnership with NATO*. International Institute for Strategic Studies. https://www.iiss.org/blogs/analysis/2018/04/tunisia-reluctant-partnership-nato. Accessed 11 November 2018.

Rasmussen, A. F. (2011, May 31). NATO and the Arab Spring. *The New York Times*. https://www.nytimes.com/2011/06/01/opinion/01iht-edrasmussen01.html. Accessed 11 November 2018.

Reichborn-Kjennerud, E. (2013). *NATO in the "New" MENA Region: Competing Priorities Amidst Diverging Interests and Financial Austerity*. Norwegian Institute of International Affairs. https://www.nupi.no/en/Publications/CRIStin-Pub/NATO-in-the-New-MENA-Region. Accessed 11 November 2018.

Reuters. (2011, January 31). *Factbox—International Reaction to Crisis in Egypt*. http://www.reuters.com/article/uk-egypt-world-idUKTRE70U2KK20110131. Accessed 11 November 2018.

Scharp, J. M. (2011, January 28). *Egypt: Background and U.S. Relations*. Congressional Research Service. http://www.voltairenet.org/IMG/pdf/Egypt_Background_and_U-S-_Relations.pdf. Accessed 11 November 2018.

Steinberg, G. (2015, January 19). Germany and the Muslim Brotherhood. *Al-Mesbar Center*. https://www.fpri.org/docs/chapters/201303.west_and_the_muslim_brotherhood_after_the_arab_spring.chapter5.pdf. Accessed 11 November 2018.

Stepan, A. (2018). Introduction. In A. Stepan (Ed.), *Democratic Transition in the Muslim World: A Global Perspective*. New York: Columbia University Press.

The Guardian. (2011, February 27). French Foreign Minister Resigns.

The Telegraph. (2011, November 22). *Tunisia's Coalition Agrees New Posts as It Forms Interim Government*. https://www.telegraph.co.uk/news/worldnews/africaandindianocean/tunisia/8906335/Tunisias-coalition-agrees-new-posts-as-it-forms-interim-government.html. Accessed 11 November 2018.

Voltolini, B., & Colombo, S. (2018). The EU and Islamist parties in Tunisia and Egypt After the Arab Uprisings: A Story of Selective Engagement. *Mediterranean Politics, 23*(1), 83–102.

Waterfield, B. (2011, February 4). Egypt Crisis: David Cameron Reprimands Baroness Ashton at EU summit. *The Telegraph*. http://www.telegraph.co.uk/news/worldnews/africaandindianocean/egypt/8303929/Egypt-crisisDavid-Cameron-reprimands-Baroness-Ashton-at-EU-summit.html. Accessed 11 November 2018.

Whitman, R. (Ed.). (2011). *Normative Power Europe Empirical and Theoretical Perspectives*. Basingstoke: Palgrave Macmillan.

CHAPTER 14

Civil-Military Cooperation in the Mediterranean Sea: Lessons Not Learnt

Hernan del Valle

INTRODUCTION

On Sunday 10 June 2018 the interior minister of Italy, Matteo Salvini, sent shockwaves through Europe by blocking the MS Aquarius from docking at Italian ports. The Aquarius, a vessel run by the non-governmental organisations (NGOs) Médecins Sans Frontières (MSF) and SoS Méditerranée (SoS Med), was carrying 629 asylum seekers and migrants rescued the night before in international waters off the coast of Libya.

It was the first time in years that Italian authorities had denied people rescued at sea the possibility of disembarking on Italian territory. Malta, the other geographically close European country, also denied the Aquarius access to its ports. The ship was left stranded at sea while European leaders pointed fingers at each other. The world media reported widely on this political stalemate, while supplies on board the overcrowded ship started to run out and anxiety grew amongst the crew. The diplomatic crisis was solved when the prime minister of Spain offered a safe port. Sailing all the way to Spain made no sense from an operational perspective, but it was the only option left. After enduring

H. del Valle (✉)
Harvard University, Cambridge, MA, USA

© The Author(s) 2020
E. Cusumano and S. Hofmaier (eds.),
Projecting Resilience Across the Mediterranean,
https://doi.org/10.1007/978-3-030-23641-0_14

a gruelling journey of 800 nautical miles in bad weather conditions, the exhausted men, women, and children finally reached Valencia on June 17th after more than one week adrift at sea.

In the weeks that followed, tension at the southern European maritime border grew as the Italian government continued to crack down on migrants and those rescuing them. The Aquarius was refused access to Italian ports once again in August, after rescuing 141 people. The British overseas territory of Gibraltar, where the Aquarius was legally registered, revoked the ship's registration and withdrew its flag, forcing MSF and SoS Med to cease its operations for almost three weeks until an alternative registration in Panama could be arranged.

Since 2014, Italian authorities had provided the operational space for NGOs to run search and rescue (SAR) operations in the central Mediterranean. Under the direction of the Maritime Rescue and Coordination Center (MRCC) in Rome, tens of thousands of people had been rescued from overcrowded and flimsy boats, and brought to safe ports in Sicily and the Italian peninsula. At the peak of the operation in mid-2017, more than 10 NGO-run boats were operating at sea, cooperating actively with the Italian Coast Guard to save lives. Only a year later, the political tide had shifted dramatically. The public discourse had become increasingly hostile towards NGOs SAR operations. Several ships had been impounded by the police at Italian ports or had stopped operating due to fear of criminalization. NGO personnel were being prosecuted in Italian courts. The Aquarius was the only NGO-run boat still operating.

The final blow came on 22 September 2018, when the Aquarius received a message from the Panama Maritime Authority (PMA) stating that "unfortunately" it was "necessary that Aquarius be excluded from (its) registry" because it had become a "political problem against the Panamanian government and the Panamanian fleet that arrive to European ports [sic]" (MSF 2018a). Under political pressure, the ship was once again stripped of its flag. The Aquarius was rendered stateless, undocumented, deprived from diplomatic protection, and vulnerable to administrative sanctions. With the Aquarius temporarily immobilised in the French port of Marseille, SoS Med and MSF launched a public campaign to persuade states worldwide to provide a flag to the ship. No government stepped up. In November, the Public Prosecutor's office in Catania issued an order to impound the Aquarius and placed its captain, NGO personnel, and shipping agents under investigation for alleged irregularities in the disposal of waste generated on board. MSF and SoS Med denounced the case as politically motivated, explained that throughout the operation the Aquarius had followed the standard waste management procedures required by Italian port authorities, and announced their intention to fight the charges in court (MSF 2018b). Marred by legal, political and administrative harassment, the last NGO-run boat had finally been forced to stop. Civilian-led rescue operations at sea were ground to a halt. What had happened?

As Head of Advocacy and Communications for Médecins Sans Frontières (MSF), I have been directly involved in planning and implementing rescue missions in the Mediterranean between 2015 and 2018. Drawing on first-hand experience of the organisation's decision-making and its engagement with government officials and policymakers, this article discusses the complex relationship between NGOs and civilian and military authorities at the maritime border between Europe (Italy) and North Africa. It describes how the initial cooperation on search and rescue (SAR) operations in the Central Mediterranean changed as the political objectives of European governments shifted along with the mood of their electorates. Through this experience, I explore the shifting function of maritime SAR within the broader European system of border control. I will show how the operational space for NGOs to cooperate with the MRCC and Italian Coast Guard to save lives was progressively reduced as Italian authorities adopted measures to subordinate SAR to the political objective of stemming immigration into Europe.

This paper is divided in three parts. Section one, "The Framing of Migration as a Threat in Contemporary Europe", provides the policy background against which civilian-led SAR operations to assist asylum seekers and migrants emerged. It offers a brief overview of the processes of securitisation and militarisation of migration management over the past three decades, and outlines governments' efforts to ensure the private sector and civil society contribute to border management strategies.

Section two, "The Rise and Fall of Civilian-Led Migrant Rescue in the Mediterranean", offers an overview of civilian-led SAR operations between the years 2014 and 2018. It shows how initial cooperation between Italian authorities and SAR NGOs turned from a joint effort to save lives into the persecution of NGOs for aiding illegal immigration. This section tracks the expansion of the NGO SAR efforts and the subsequent government crackdown in light of the shifting of political objectives and the growth in anti-immigration rhetoric across Europe.

Section three, "Analysis and Conclusions", lays out the lessons not yet learnt on civil-military cooperation, which, in the context of the Southern European border, resulted in the criminalisation of SAR NGOs, a reduction of the operational effectiveness of maritime rescue missions, and an increased risk of loss of migrants' lives. This final section outlines the human costs of migration deterrence and the challenges ahead for humanitarian NGOs and civil society organisations which assist refugees and migrants at the European border.

The Framing of Migration as a Threat in Contemporary Europe

The Securitization and Militarization of Migration Management

The social construction of migratory movements as a threat to the political order in Europe has contributed to a process of securitisation and militarisation of migration management over the past three decades (Bigo 1994; Huysmans 2000; Bourbeau 2015). To protect the perceived interests of the European Union (EU), a variety of physical, legal, and administrative barriers have been put in place to limit the arrival of asylum seekers and migrants from the Global South. The consensus on the legitimacy of increasingly unequal mobility rights across European borders has been gradually built around three sets of arguments.

First, the narrative that has developed in Europe since the early 1990s has framed asylum seekers and migrants as competing with native Europeans for limited jobs and as a burden on states in times of scarcity. In its moderate version, this narrative invokes the notions of European identity and belonging to argue that the welfare state has a responsibility to categorically prioritise 'its own people' over new arrivals (Faist 1995). A more extreme version of this narrative, defined as 'welfare chauvinism' (Huysmans 2000), frames asylum seekers and migrants as illegitimate recipients who claim benefits from a system to which they should not be entitled as *foreigners* and *outsiders*. This narrative effectively places notions of cultural identity or ethnic origin above traditional social policy criteria of allocating state resources according to need. Even if more sophisticated economic and social analyses have shown that both legal and illegal migration have been a significant contributing factor to the economy of Europe for decades, the construction of asylum seekers and migrants as outsiders who constitute an economic burden has become an article of faith, and continues to shape both media accounts and policy responses (Papademetriou 2006; Acosta and Wiesbrock 2015; Matthijs et al. 2015).

Second, the arrival of asylum seekers and migrants stokes fears of an existential threat to the essence of Europe. A close look at different versions of this argument reveals a real anxiety, although how that European essence is defined varies greatly across Europe. Some extreme groups unambiguously allude to the ethnic and racial origin of newcomers, which confirms the weight of racism as a force that continues to structure the discourse around migration in Europe (Lentin 2008). Other anti-immigration narratives emphasise religious and cultural differences, decrying the tensions created by multiculturalism and the dangers for a Europe demographically 'submerged' by a migratory wave which will destroy national identity (RT France 2018). All these narratives share the common thread of articulating asylum seekers and migrants as outsiders, and a threat to the political order and wellbeing of Europeans. As such, it has been successfully exploited by anti-immigration groups to single out people from Africa and the Middle East as undesirable aliens. Even if demographic data shows that the number of refugees and migrants arriving in Europe remains negligible vis-à-vis the total population, the reaction against diversity and multiculturalism remains a powerful driver of policy formation. The need to limit the arrival of new immigrants and impose on those already in Europe the duty to assimilate has become a policy priority.

Finally, refugees and migrants are framed as a security threat. Throughout the 1990s, increased cooperation between border control and law enforcement agencies at the EU border has created a functional continuum between border control, terrorism, international crime and migration (Bigo 1994; Huysmans 2000). Decision-making on asylum and migration gradually moved away from the human rights and humanitarian fields of policy making to enter the security and policing domains (Rudge 1989). The war of terrorism in the twenty-first century has accelerated the conflation of migration with EU's homeland security concerns. This institutional outlook has also permeated the public and media narrative. As the policy response to human migration became more militarised, the need to 'strengthen cooperation' and 'increase resilience' to effectively resist and recover from the negative effects of 'uncontrolled movements of people' became common parlance in NATO and EU strategic documents (NATO 2012, 2018; European Commission 2017; and chapter by Anholt and Wagner in this volume).

The securitisation of migration has led to a neglect of humanitarian considerations when dealing with human beings fleeing their countries and trying to reach Europe. Human rights commitments have been increasingly subordinated to the political imperative of preventing the arrival of asylum seekers and migrants from the Middle East and North Africa. The priority is not to protect people on the move, but to protect the border from the desperate people trying to cross it.

A 'Comprehensive Approach' in the Region and Across Public and Private Sectors

In the twenty-first century, Europe has taken 'unprecedented levels of peacetime defensive action' to contain human migration (Landau 2018). The European Border and Coast Guard Agency (Frontex) has enjoyed a massive expansion of its budget, mandate, and capabilities since its creation in 2005. Military assets are regularly deployed to patrol and protect borders. But the EU's objective of stemming arrivals requires measures that exceed those that can be taken by EU border control agencies and military organisations.

It is for that reason that EU governments have actively sought concerted action across the region. The animating idea behind NATO and EU engagement with countries in the Mediterranean basin is the stabilisation of the neighbourhood to enhance European security, combat terrorism and effectively manage population movements at the main geographic gateways used by African migrants to reach Europe such as the Spain–Morocco and Italy–Libya sea crossings. These agreements have provided the necessary resources and infrastructure to patrol borders, prevent departures, detain migrants, and ensure re-admission back into North Africa.

The set of carrots and sticks put in place over time to ensure active compliance has not been limited to Europe's southern neighbours. It has also extended to the private sector, civil society organisations, and even individual citizens. The threat of being prosecuted for abetting illegal immigration was consistently used in the early 2000s, when Italian courts prosecuted fishermen and captains of commercial vessels for rescuing undocumented migrants encountered at sea and bringing them to safety in Italian ports. The captain and crew of the German NGO ship, Cap Anamur, were also prosecuted for aiding illegal immigration after rescuing 37 migrants at sea close to Lampedusa and bringing them to safety in Italy. Even if the rescue of people at risk of drowning at sea remained a paramount obligation under international maritime law, Italy's use of domestic prosecution as deterrence made SAR a risky activity for ship captains and crews (del Valle 2016).

The gradual enactment of carrier sanctions legislation went a step further by extending the responsibility of migration control from the government to the private sector (Menz 2011; Rodenhäuser 2014; Scholten 2015). Carrier personnel are required to control migrants' documentation at the point of embarkation and deny boarding to undocumented migrants. Under this legislation, personnel working for air, land, and sea transportation companies have become a first-instance immigration control, having to deal not only with economic migrants, but also with asylum seekers who may need international protection. Penalties are imposed by EU countries on transport operators who fail to exercise this control. This pressure has co-opted transport companies into actively contributing to the efforts of EU states to prevent arrivals. The limited availability of data on carrier sanction implementation across Europe (Baird 2017) raises serious questions about the transparency and accountability of privatised border management functions, and obscures any understanding of the impact that these practices have on the right to seek asylum.

The Rise and Fall of Civilian-Led Migrant Rescue in the Mediterranean

A Window of Opportunity for NGOs to Save Lives at Sea (2014–2015)

The human cost of migration deterrence policies has been high: figures from the International Organization of Migration (IOM) show that, since the year 2000, at least 35,000 people have died trying to cross the Mediterranean Sea (IOM 2018).

Drownings at the southern European border had been a regular occurrence for years, but the end of Qaddafi's rule in Libya in 2011 unleashed the perfect storm. Even if regime change was supported by several European leaders, and the NATO-led military intervention proved critical to tip the balance of power, the fall of Qaddafi also had the unintended effect of creating the ideal conditions for an upsurge of departures of asylum seekers from the Libyan coast towards Europe. The smuggling and trafficking industry thrived amidst Libya's chaos. The EU's policy focus on reinforcing border restrictions and the lack of any viable safe and legal alternatives for people trying to flee Libya exacerbated the incentives for a very lucrative illegal 'mobility market' to flourish (Crepeau 2015).

As the number of attempted crossings in fragile wooden and rubber boats grew, death numbers increased. In late 2011 the Dutch operational section of MSF conceived and discussed the first proposal for the deployment of a ship to rescue migrants at sea in an attempt to reduce mortality in the central Mediterranean. After a difficult internal debate, the proposal was finally shelved by MSF's management team. I have described MSF's internal deliberations around the possibility of launching SAR operations elsewhere (del Valle 2016). Central to the decision to reject the proposal was the uncertainty about the role the organisation could play. Italian courts had set a precedent by prosecuting civilians who had rescued migrants in the early 2000s, which raised serious doubts about the organisation's chances of cooperating productively with Italian authorities on the disembarkation of migrants. In addition, the divisive nature of the migration debate in Europe raised questions about the potential reaction from the public and donors to a potential intervention.

The public outcry around more than 360 deaths resulting from the Lampedusa shipwrecks in 2013 led to calls for political action. Operation Mare Nostrum, led by the Italian Navy, was launched in late 2013 to rescue migrants at sea. Despite it having rescued over 150,000 people, Mare Nostrum was maligned as a 'pull factor', further incentivizing migrants to cross the Mediterranean. Under political pressure from the EU, and lack of financial support, Mare Nostrum was terminated in late 2014. The Frontex-led Operation Triton was deployed as a defensive mission to patrol borders within 30 nautical miles of European shores to deter further attempts of reaching Europe.

The withdrawal of SAR capacities in the Mediterranean region, where most drownings were historically registered, created a vacuum that NGOs quickly moved into fill. A small NGO called Migrant Offshore Aid Station (MOAS) was created in 2014 with the vision of saving lives at sea. Médecins Sans Frontières (MSF) joined forces with MOAS in 2015. The joint rescue operation was launched in April 2015. The objective to save lives was coupled with a call on European governments to increase SAR capacity at sea and open safe and legal alternatives for asylum seekers and migrants to enter Europe in order to prevent further loss of life (del Valle 2016). Given the complexity of the operation, MSF adopted a consistent policy to distance itself from both EU border control and law enforcement agencies, and from smuggling or trafficking networks operating in North Africa (del Valle 2016). This choice was based on the logic under which humanitarian organisations work. For operations to be viable they need to take distance from the interests and conflicting agendas of different players. Humanitarian agencies seek to remain neutral in conflict and impartial in polarized political settings, focusing on assisting those who need it most, regardless of other considerations.

In late April, 1200 people drowned in a single week. Media reported widely, and the EU response was to launch the EU Common Security and Defense Policy (CSDP) military operation EUNAVFOR Med Sophia. While EU public rhetoric emphasised the humanitarian objective of 'saving lives', the core purpose of Sophia remained law enforcement and border protection. Operation Sophia's mandate to neutralise and disrupt smugglers' networks and infrastructure, capturing and destroying boats used to transport refugees across the Mediterranean, confirmed the military rationale shaping the EU response to irregular migration.

As EU states poured funding into deploying military assets to fight human smuggling, civil society in Europe mobilised to increase SAR capabilities. MSF added two more boats to rescue efforts. In the months that followed, other established NGOs such as Save the Children followed suit, and groups of European citizens mobilised in Germany, France, and Spain to create small NGOs with the single objective of rescuing migrants at sea. Organisations such as Sea Watch, Sea Eye, Proactiva Open Arms, Jugend Rettet, and SoS Méditerranée were created between 2015 and 2016. In less than one year, there were 13 active NGO boats patrolling the international waters north of Libya, all working in coordination with the MRCC in Rome. This unprecedented mobilisation of European civil society, supported by public donations, allowed NGOs to carry out lifesaving rescue operations on a daily basis. NGOs offered journalists access to their ships and the media was able to cover the 'migration crisis' live, as events occurred. The 'crisis' made top headlines across European news outlets in 2015. The images of human beings risking their lives on flimsy overcrowded boats became ubiquitous a central political and moral dilemma for Europe.

A sense of urgency spread across parliaments and government offices in European capitals and in Brussels. The European Council convened several meetings, but the inability to reach a consensus on the way forward became evident. The main stumbling block was the lack of a wider EU agreement on how to share the responsibility of assisting refugees and migrants who arrived in EU territory. Few countries wanted to offer asylum or even temporary shelter to those who arrived in Italy.

Amidst this political deadlock and bitter divisions, the rapid deployment of NGOs prevented loss of life on a massive scale. Between 2014 and 2017, NGOs alone rescued and brought to safety 110,000 men, women, and children (Cusumano and Pattison 2018). Research has shown that the deployment of NGOs significantly improved maritime safety (Heller and Pezzani 2016; Steinhilper and Gruijters 2018). By 2016, NGOs were a critically important rescue actor in the Mediterranean, responsible for around 26% of rescues (Arsenijevic et al. 2017). Given the situation in Libya and beyond, tens of thousands of people continued to attempt the crossing and deaths were still inevitable, but the proportion of those dying at sea was significantly reduced.

The Backlash Against Migration: Return to Deterrence and Externalisation in Turkey (2015–2016)

It was clear from the outset that the operational space for civilian SAR was a delicate balance which could not be taken for granted for various reasons. First, the presence of NGOs facilitated and massively increased media coverage. The visibility of the crisis at sea mounted pressure on EU governments to act and made divisions inside Europe painfully evident. Finger pointing abounded and collective action seemed impossible.

Second, MSF and other NGOs offered a narrative of the crisis which was openly critical of European migration policy. The position upheld by MSF was that, for as long as EU governments remained unwilling to offer safe and legal alternatives to asylum seekers and migrants, people would continue to risk their lives at sea in the hands of human smugglers and traffickers. On a practical level, MSF criticised the attempt to stem migration as ineffective because a poor understanding of the economy of smuggling had helped the business boom. The EU's deliberate withdrawal of SAR capabilities as a deterrence tactic was both morally reprehensible and misguided. Both the need for SAR and the smuggling business could be eliminated by offering mobility options in line with

Europe's legal and moral commitments. However, these were extremely thorny propositions for EU politicians, who were also under pressure from right-wing ethno-nationalist groups using the crisis to call for further restrictions on immigration.

The arrival of refugees fleeing war in Syria, Afghanistan, and Iraq in Greece and Eastern Europe increased the pressure in late 2015. Leaders in different EU states reacted with an eye on the unstable mood of their domestic constituencies. This resulted in contradictory measures being enacted by different actors, which exacerbated tensions internally within many countries, and between EU member states. Border fences were quickly erected, and several EU member states unilaterally re-established border controls at strategic routes within the Schengen area to prevent the entry of asylum seekers and migrants into their territory. The lack of solidarity between southern and northern European countries left Italy and Greece feeling abandoned by their EU partners, who sheltered behind the provisions of the Dublin Regulation and boycotted every attempt by the EU Commission to negotiate quotas to share the responsibility for asylum seekers amongst member states.

The coordinated terrorist attacks killing 130 people and injuring 400 in several venues in Paris in November 2015 were a turning point for the EU response to refugees. The Islamic State of Iraq and the Levant (ISIL) claimed responsibility, saying the attacks were retaliation for the French airstrikes in Syria and Iraq. The French Prime Minister, Manuel Valls, contended that some of the killers had taken advantage of Europe's migrant crisis to 'slip in' across the border unnoticed (*France24* 2015). Even if subsequent police investigations would prove this assertion misleading, terrorism was unambiguously attributed to migration in the public record. This narrative neglected facts and bypassed important questions about the radicalisation of European youths, but fitted perfectly under the EU and NATO paradigm that had for years identified movements of people across EU borders as a security risk. EU ministers gathered immediately after the Paris Attacks for emergency talks to tighten immigration controls. To be safe again, Europe needed to 'regain control' of its borders.

Stoking fear proved to be an profitable tactic for many politicians who, on the back of an openly xenophobic, anti-immigration discourse, made significant electoral gains in France, Britain, Hungary, and Italy itself. In other EU countries, anti-immigration rhetoric was progressively adopted by otherwise more moderate voices. The leaders of the few countries that initially stepped up to offer asylum—most notably, Germany and Sweden, quickly felt the political pressure to limit their hospitality. EU leaders in power, even those with more progressive ideologies, effectively found themselves performing a treacherous balancing act: they could either enact visible border controls that were strict enough to appease electorates' anxieties linked to migration and undercut public support of far-right parties, or risk allowing those parties to gain more power, which would ultimately challenge fundamental democratic values across the continent.

Returning asylum seekers and migrants who had arrived in Europe back to their countries of origin and preventing further arrivals, became attractive propositions for EU leaders in power across the entire political spectrum. Regardless of ideological considerations, a pragmatic alliance of European leaders which could ensure a level of cooperation of countries neighbouring Europe would serve two immediate political objectives. First, it would curb fears in the electorate and show EU leaders were taking concerted action to 'regain control' of their borders. Second, it would help circumvent the political deadlock which had hitherto divided European leaders. If people could be returned and prevented from getting to Europe in the first place, then the politically sensitive issue of distributing the responsibility to host them amongst EU member states could be avoided.

The EU–Turkey refugee agreement was signed in March 2016 and enjoyed support from all EU member states and the EU Commission. The EU would provide EUR six billion funding over three years to the Erdogan regime on the condition that asylum seekers and migrants who had arrived in Greece would be returned to Turkey. Turkey also committed to preventing the further departure of boats from its shores. In return, Turkish nationals would be granted visa-free travel to Europe and, once the number of irregular arrivals in the EU dropped, a voluntary humanitarian scheme to transfer Syrians from Turkey to other European countries would be implemented. In an unprecedented move, the European Commission's launched its largest ever humanitarian aid programme through its Directorate-General for European Civil Protection and Humanitarian Aid Operations (DG ECHO), in order to ensure financial incentives for aid agencies to set up operations in Turkey to assist refugees outside of Europe's borders (EU Commission 2015, 2016).

MSF and other aid agencies strongly objected to the EU's abdication of responsibility and publicly criticised the agreement with Turkey to keep refugees away from European shores. MSF also decried the use of humanitarian aid in Turkey as part of the refugee containment strategy. The EU–Turkey deal marked a historic turning point in the relationship between MSF and the EU. After a difficult internal debate, in June 2016, MSF made the controversial decision to no longer accept funding from any EU member state, Norway, or EU institutions in protest of European policy towards asylum seekers and migrants (MSF 2016; *Reuters* 2016). It was the first time in its history that MSF distanced itself from European institutional funding across the board and for all its projects around the world. The cancelling of grants represented a reduction of EUR 60 million in MSF's operational income.

From 'Search and Rescue' to 'Interception and Return': Externalisation in Libya (2016–2017)

MSF teams conducted exploratory missions into migrant detention centres in Libya in early 2016. The assessments confirmed what MSF staff aboard rescue ships in the Mediterranean had been hearing from the people they rescued for over a year. Sub-Saharan African migrants transiting through Libya were arbitrarily detained in overcrowded spaces and subjected to routine beatings, extortion for money, and deprivation of food, water, and basic sanitation. MSF negotiated access with Libyan authorities, and expanded its operations into several detention centres around Tripoli in July 2016. By extending services to Libya, MSF was aware of the extremely difficult challenge ahead: maintaining its access to improve health services, nutrition and sanitation conditions in these centres, whilst at the same time bearing witness to the situation, and challenging the inhumane treatment inflicted on asylum seekers and migrants arbitrarily detained.

In April 2016 France, Britain and Spain had re-deployed ambassadors in Tripoli to reinforce the legitimacy of the embattled Government of National Accord (GNA) brokered by the UN (see chapter by Varvelli and Villa in this volume). Italy quickly announced plans to reopen its embassy as well. Libya remained fragmented and conflict-ridden. The EU's agenda to stabilise Libya had two primary objectives: combatting terrorism and the local affiliate of the ISIL, and stemming migration across the Mediterranean. The EU Border Assistance Mission in Libya

(EUBAM), established in 2013 under the EU's Common Security and Defence Policy (CSDP), was extended in 2015 to support the Libyan authorities in 'improving and developing the security of the country's borders' (EUBAM mandate 2013 and 2015). After the EU–Turkey deal, it was a matter of time before the EU would seek a similar agreement with Libya to prevent asylum seekers and migrants from reaching Europe.

On 20 June 2016, the Council of the European Union expanded Operation Sophia's mandate to provide 'capacity building' to the Libyan Coast Guard (LCG) with the stated purpose of contributing to 'save lives at sea' (EU Council 2016). By providing assets and training to the LCG, the MRCC would hand over SAR coordination to Tripoli, ensuring that migrants who departed from Libyan shores could be intercepted, 'rescued', and returned to Libya. The humanitarian discourse of 'saving lives' became once again a useful rhetorical device to justify an operation, but this time it would ultimately fulfill the objective of preventing arrivals in Europe.

Within MSF's leadership there was an acute awareness of the increasingly delicate political balance in which the SAR operation was unfolding. The organisation continued to advocate privately and publicly for the opening of safe and legal routes for asylum seekers and migrants, and publicly denounced EU cooperation with Libya as condoning and validating arbitrary detention and human rights violations. But few within MSF had any illusions about the possibility of influencing European leaders. The choice to facilitate the externalisation of EU borders, and the containment of migrants in Libya was made by EU leaders in spite of the human cost it would have on the people intercepted and returned to detention. In the months that followed, LCG speedboats were involved in intimidating and attacking NGO rescue ships. In August 2016, MSF's boat Bourbon Argos was boarded and fired upon by the LCG. Sea Watch, Mission Lifeline, and Jugend Rettet all denounced the LCG for the use of violence against NGOs and migrants, and the failure to conduct effective SAR, but European cooperation and funding to the LCG continued nevertheless.

The space for NGO-led SAR was shrinking fast. MSF had been extremely flexible in cooperating and following the lead of the MRCC throughout the SAR operation. But there were certainly limits on how far MSF would go to accommodate the shifting function of SAR. What would MSF do if the MRCC instructed MSF boats to turn around and disembark migrants in Libya? Would MSF transfer migrants to LCG boats knowing they would be taken back to Libya? MSF's first-hand experience of detention conditions and human rights abuses in Libya made it ethically impossible for the organisation to comply with such instructions. The possibility of MSF SAR operations becoming co-opted into an 'interception and return' effort had been discussed internally since 2015, and remained a red line. If that moment were to come, MSF would have no choice but to refuse to follow instructions from the rescue coordination authorities, and face the consequences.

Crimes of Solidarity: The Crackdown on SAR NGOs (2017–2018)

Hostility directed at migrants quickly extended to the NGOs who were rescuing them at sea. Throughout 2016, MSF experienced a sharp increase in resentment voiced through social media when reporting about their SAR missions at sea. Even if a level of opposition had been expected as part of the operation from the outset, the increased polarisation of the debate was palpable. Online expressions of support for MSF's rescue work continued side-by-side with increasingly vicious attacks for helping 'illegals' reach Europe.

Frontex's 'Risk Analysis Report' for 2017 became the first official EU document to blame the NGO rescuers for the crisis at sea. Mirroring the allegations used to discontinue the Mare Nostrum operation, Frontex's Director, Fabrice Leggeri, went on record in media interviews stating that NGOs constituted a pull-factor for people in Libya and that they were not cooperating sufficiently with law enforcement agencies in combatting smuggling and trafficking (*Guardian* 2017). In Italy, this narrative was weaponised by anti-immigration parties who peddled the notion of NGOs acting as 'taxis of the sea' to aid human trafficking. Europe was being 'invaded' by 'illegal immigrants', and action had to be taken to neutralise the NGOs who were aiding these invaders. The attorney general of the Italian city of Catania then announced that he would start an investigation on allegations of collusion between NGOs and human smugglers (*Reuters* 2017).

Even if the allegations of collusion were refuted by NGOs and discredited by independent reports and analysts (Crawley et al. 2016; Heller and Pezzani 2017), the Italian Senate Defense Committee set up a Commission of Enquiry. The Commission found no evidence of collusion, but asked for rescue NGOs' to be better regulated (Cusumano

2017). The Italian Interior Ministry followed up on the Italian Parliament's request in July by drafting a Code of Conduct and demanding that it be signed by NGOs operating SAR ships without delay. The draft text of the Code of Conduct was leaked to the media (*Euronews* 2017) and presented to NGOs along with a threat: those who did not sign would no longer be granted access to Italian ports. With general elections approaching the pressure of anti-immigration parties was acute, and the sense of urgency to be seen as bringing NGOs 'under control' was evident.

The Italian move to draft and implement a Code of Conduct took NGOs by surprise. NGOs operating offshore Libya had always operated transparently, under the direction of the MRCC, and in accordance with the international legal provisions regulating maritime rescue. NGOs were divided in their response. Some, such as MOAS, Save the Children, Sea-Eye and Proactiva Open Arms decided to sign the Code of Conduct. Others, including MSF, saw the Code as both redundant and counterproductive. The limitation of operational transfers between NGO boats risked reducing the overall effectiveness of the SAR effort. Furthermore, the imposition of the presence of the armed judiciary police aboard NGO boats to participate in the fight against smuggling was seen as an attempt to co-opt the work of NGOs for border policing activities. This would compromise the independence of NGOs and the impartiality of the rescue effort (Cusumano 2017). When the amendments proposed by NGOs were not accepted, several NGOs, including MSF, refused to subscribe. However, SoS Méditerranée, MSF's partner on board of the Aquarius, decided to sign. Time would show that accepting the Code would make no difference: the campaign against NGOs recuing migrants had been unleashed, and made no distinction between signatories and non-signatories. All NGOs would eventually be driven out of the sea.

The judicial offensive against NGOs started before the ink on the signatures of the Code of Conduct had dried. Only one day after the German NGO, Jugend Rettet, announced it would not sign the Code of Conduct, Italian police impounded its ship, the Iuventa, in the port of Lampedusa as part of an investigation led by a prosecutor in the Sicilian city of Trapani. In the months that followed, an unprecedented deployment of resources using infiltrated agents, satellite eavesdropping, radar tracings, and information provided by secret services was led to prosecutions against NGOs for alleged collusion with human traffickers and aiding illegal immigration. Predictably, none of the investigations initiated against NGOs by Italian prosecutors in Trapani, Catania, Ragusa or Palermo have found any evidence of wrongdoing, and all cases so far have been closed or archived without any convictions. But the impounding of boats belonging to Proactiva Open Arms, SeaWatch and Jugend Rettet had the desired immediate effect of thwarting NGO SAR operations in the Mediterranean. In the medium term, the negative media coverage would also reduce public donations, seriously limiting the ability of many NGOs to operate.

In late 2017, the MRCC started referring the few NGOs left at sea to the LCG as the new rescue coordinating authority, regardless of its track record of threats against NGOs, its poor SAR capacity, and its known use of violence against migrants intercepted at sea. When boats in distress were located, the MRCC instructed NGO boats to stand by and delay assistance waiting for the LCG to take over the rescue and return migrants back to Libya. In early August, Proactiva Open Arms publicly released video footage of the LCG approaching their boat and opening fire. A few days later, the Italian MRCC sent a letter to all NGOs warning that the security of rescue teams at sea could no longer be guaranteed. MSF decided to reduce its operations to a single boat, the Aquarius, operated jointly with SoS Méditerranée. Other NGOs followed suit by suspending their operations.

In March 2018 Italian authorities impounded Proactiva Open Arms's ship, and detained crew members after they had refused to hand over rescued migrants to the Libyan Coast Guard at sea. Even if charges had to be dropped and the ship released thereafter, Proactiva decided to stop its rescue operations a few weeks later. By the summer of 2018 the Aquarius, operated jointly by SoS Med and MSF, was the only boat still in operation. The final blow was the closure of Italian ports. The Aquarius was denied docking rights on June 10th and was left adrift for a week with 629 migrant passengers who, were finally disembarked in Spain. Gibraltar stripped Aquarius of its flag the same month, forcing it to cease its operations. The Aquarius was not the only ship forbidden to disembark the people it had rescued at sea. Even the Diciotti, an Italian Coast Guard vessel, was not allowed to disembark 177 migrants it had rescued for almost two weeks. The situation was resolved after the migrants on board started a hunger strike and a prosecutor in Catania opened an investigation on Salvini for the illegal confinement of the migrants on board.

It took Aquarius three weeks to secure a new registration from Panama. It went back to sea, but on August 10th, it was again denied the authorisation to disembark, and caught in a standoff between European governments to decide the fate of 141 migrants on board. The last trip of the Aquarius was in late September. After rescuing 58 migrants in international waters, the instruction to transfer people to a Libyan patrol boat finally came. Knowing that people would be returned to Libya, SoS Med and MSF refused to obey. Citing political pressure from Europe, Panama revoked Aquarius' registration and withdrew its flag. The 58 migrants on board were eventually disembarked in Malta after a week at sea. The Aquarius then became stateless, docked in the port of Marseille. As MSF and SoS campaigned to obtain a new flag to resume operations, the Public Prosecutor's office in Catania issued an order to impound the Aquarius and placed its operating personnel under investigation. The Aquarius had been forcibly immobilised.

Analysis and Conclusions

The collective action of a handful of European-based NGOs improved maritime safety and prevented deaths in the Mediterranean on a massive scale between 2014 and 2018 (Steinhilper and Gruijters 2018; Cusumano and Pattison 2018). The rapid expansion of NGO-led SAR, which saved tens of thousands of lives at sea, was made possible by two factors.

First, the active collaboration between NGOs, the MRCC, and the Italian Coast Guard to locate and rescue migrants from boats in distress. The MRCC played a central role in actively assigning rescue and transfer duties to NGO boats. NGO boats operated strictly under its command: no boat was rescued, no transfer or medical evacuation was made, and no migrants were disembarked without directions from or coordination with the MRCC.

The second crucial factor enabling SAR operations was the cooperation of the Italian Government to allow disembarkation of rescued people in Italian ports. NGOs were directed towards the Sicilian ports of Pozzallo, Siracusa, Augusta and Catania, where most disembarkations took place. MSF and other agencies were at times critical of the shortcomings in the reception system in Italy, calling on authorities to live up to their responsibilities to offer adequate protection and assistance to asylum seekers and migrants. Despite the shortcomings, the authorities' willingness to facilitate disembarkations and allow the work of NGOs, United Nations agencies, and the Red Cross in Italian reception centres enabled their lifesaving operations.

The alignment between the NGO's objective to save lives and the operational purpose of the Italian MRCC and Coast Guard temporarily suited the political needs of EU leaders between 2015 and 2016. After the tragic loss of life in Lampedusa in 2013 and the discontinuation of the Mare Nostrum operations at the end of 2014, large segments of European public opinion and civil society supported NGOs deployed at sea to save lives. Public donations in Germany, France, Spain, and other countries enabled the creation of small, single-purpose NGOs dedicated to maritime rescue. Cooperation with these NGOs became essential for the MRCC to fulfill its mission, as commercial vessels crossing the Mediterranean were neither interested nor technically equipped to carry out rescues.

The lack of solidarity between European countries to host asylum seekers turned what could have been a manageable issue into a political crisis favouring the growth of anti-immigration parties. The rhetoric of these parties was anchored in a narrative of alienation of migrants and securitization of borders which had developed in Europe for decades. This toxic combination would ultimately bring maritime rescue and disembarkation of asylum seekers and migrants in Italy under attack, eliminating the space for the MRCC to cooperate with NGOs to save lives.

The Problem of 'Unity of Purpose':
Lessons not Learnt on Civil-Military Cooperation

The notion of civil-military cooperation (CIMIC) as an integral part of modern warfare operations rests on the premise that civilian and military capabilities need to be coordinated to ensure mutual support towards a shared outcome. Since the legitimacy and effectiveness of humanitarian agencies operating in war zones relies on their independence, neutrality and impartiality to carve a safe space to operate, an association of these agencies with belligerents in conflict, which is implied by the notion of CIMIC, has been controversial from the outset. Within the polarisation of the so-called 'war on terror' in the twenty-first century, US Secretary of State Colin Powell's notorious portrayal of NGOs as 'force multipliers' and an important part of the US 'combat team' in Afghanistan (Powell 2001) encapsulated the problem posed by the attempts to co-opt NGOs into supporting military objectives of parties to conflict. For years, MSF and the International Committee of the Red Cross (ICRC) have had frank exchanges with NATO commanders on the CIMIC doctrine to explain the negative implications of this alleged 'unity of purpose' (MSF 2009).

Even if the Mediterranean was not a conflict zone, it presented similar challenges. MSF rejected from the outset the notion of having a 'unity of purpose' with law enforcement or border control agencies. MSF did not reject the work of these agencies, but was clear on the limits of its own role: rescue and medical assistance of migrants at sea, and disembarkation in a place of safety. Inquiring into the legal status of people rescued, or cooperation in a 'war on smugglers' were beyond its mandate. What operations required was the recognition of practical reality: Civilian law enforcement agencies, military assets and humanitarian NGOs operated along the European maritime border, but with different mandates and roles.

Consistent with this logic, MSF's operational practice was to enhance the mutual understanding of the respective mandates of actors operating at sea, taking every opportunity to emphasise the differences in function and purpose between law enforcement agencies and humanitarian NGOs. For MSF, 'unity of purpose' was neither conceivable nor necessary beyond the practical need to operate in a coordinated fashion to prevent loss of life. Most NGOs followed a similar logic, and neither the MRCC nor the Italian Coast Guard exerted pressure on NGOs to act beyond their humanitarian mandate. Search and Rescue NGOs were invited to participate in the Shared Awareness and De-confliction in the Mediterranean (Shade Med) forum alongside representatives of nations and organisations operating in the Mediterranean. The presence of NGOs is such forum illustrates both their willingness to cooperate to increase the operational effectiveness of the rescue effort, and the Italian Coast Guard and Navy's acknowledgement of the importance of NGOs' work.

In contrast to the Italian armed forces, Frontex officials showed very little awareness of humanitarian principles. The predominance of a 'police' mindset rendered the agency unable to appreciate the limited role of NGOs and their objections to subordinating their rescue efforts to immigration control.

The criminalisation of the work of NGOs by Italian judiciary and police forces reveals a similarly poor understanding of the rationale and limitations of the work of humanitarian NGOs. When NGOs objected to the presence of police personnel on board, as the Code of Conduct drafted by the Interior Ministry prescribed, the 'law enforcement' mindset prevailed once again. These institutions seemed conditioned to react by spying on NGOs, issuing arrest warrants, and impounding boats on the assumption that humanitarian workers had something to hide.

These institutional shortcomings in reacting effectively to the complexity of humanitarian operations at the European border, coupled with deliberate scapegoating campaigns conducted by increasingly influential anti-immigration parties vying for political power in the Italian elections, ultimately condemned the valuable work of NGOs on the basis of the unfounded allegation that rescue efforts somehow promoted and facilitated illegal immigration.

The decision to close Italian ports to asylum seekers and migrants, and the political pressure to strip the Aquarius of its flag were the last blows to NGO-led search and rescue in the Mediterranean. The closure of ports will not only affect NGOs, but is bound to limit the efforts of the Italian Coast Guard, and is likely to discourage commercial vessels from fulfilling their legal duty to assist boats in distress at sea.

The Human Cost of Deterrence and the Hard Choices for Civil Society

The political imperative to stem migration will continue to result in loss of human lives at sea. Italy's shifting policy towards SAR in the Mediterranean shows that while criminalisation does have a deterrence effect on potential rescuers, it is unlikely to deter migrants from attempting the crossing. The morally questionable tactic of withdrawing SAR capabilities as a deterrence measure has been tried before. When Mare Nostrum was ended, people continued to attempt the crossing and deaths increased (Steinhilper and Gruijters 2018). Preliminary figures from 2018 seem to suggest that the crackdown on NGO-led SAR could have similarly negative consequences for maritime safety. According to the United Nations High Commissioner for Refugees (UNHCR), the number of migrants crossing from Libya to Italy has gone down when compared to 2017, but the proportion of those who die on the way has risen (UNHCR 2018).

The human cost of European deterrence efforts is not limited to deaths at sea. European support for the arbitrary detention of asylum seekers and migrants in countries at the southern border of Europe, where human rights abuses have been well documented, raises fundamental questions about the legality and moral legitimacy of European migration management strategies.

Within Europe itself, the marginalisation and social exclusion of asylum seekers and migrants will confront the EU with the need to consider measures to ensure member states comply with legal standards and live up their commitment to fundamental democratic values. Not doing so will certainly contribute to a further undermining the credibility and viability of the European project as a whole.

Individuals and organisations assisting asylum seekers and migrants in contemporary Europe will continue to face a hostile political environment for the foreseeable future. The humanitarian ethos that considers all lives as equally valuable has become a subversive idea in a context of rising xenophobia. European ports are closed and solidarity towards asylum seekers is being criminalised. Political considerations have eliminated the space for cooperation between humanitarian NGOs and state actors, civil or military, in the Mediterranean basin. As state policy deprives groups of people from basic rights, humanitarian organizations will be confronted with regulations that condemn human beings to suffering or neglect. Operating in this environment will force NGOs to grapple with fundamental legal and moral questions around the limits of compliance, principled abstention, and the choice for civil disobedience.

References

Acosta, A., & Wiesbrock, A. (Eds.). (2015). *Global Migration: Old Assumptions, New Dynamics*. Denver: Praeger.

Arsenijevic, J., Manzi, M., & Zachariah, R. (2017). Defending Humanity at Sea. *Médecins Sans Frontières (MSF) Operational Research Unit (LuxOr)*. http://searchandrescue.msf.org/assets/uploads/files/170831-%20Report_Analysis_SAR_Final.pdf.

Baird, T. (2017). Carrier Sanctions in Europe: A Comparison of Trends in 10 Countries. *European Journal of Migration and Law, 19*(3), 307–334.

Bigo, D. (1994). The European Internal Security Field: Stakes and Rivalries in a Newly Developing Area of Police Intervention. In M. Anderson & M. den Boer (Eds.), *Policing Across National Boundaries* (pp. 161–173). London: Pinter.

Bourbeau, P. (2015). Migration, Resilience and Security: Responses to New Inflows of Asylum Seekers and Migrants. *Journal of Ethnic and Migration Studies, 41*(12), 1958–1977.

Crawley, H., Duvell, F., Jones, K., McMahon, S., & Sigona, N. (2016). *Destination Europe? Understanding the Dynamics and Drivers of Mediterranean Migration* (MEDMIG Project Final Report). http://www.medmig.info/wp-content/uploads/2016/12/research-brief-destination-europe.pdf. Accessed 21 March 2019.

Crepeau, F. (2015). *From Enforced Closure to Regulated Mobility* (RCIS Working Paper No. 2015/4).

Cusumano, E. (2017). Straightjacketing Migrant Rescuers? The Code of Conduct on Maritime NGOs. *Mediterranean Politics, 24*(1), 106–114.

Cusumano, E. (2019). Migrant Rescue as Organized Hypocrisy: EU Maritime Missions Offshore Libya Between Humanitarianism and Border Control. *Cooperation and Conflict, 54*(1), 3–24.

Cusumano, E., & Pattison, J. (2018). The Non-governmental Provision of Search and Rescue in the Mediterranean and the Abdication of State Responsibility. *Cambridge Review of International Affairs, 31*(1), 53–75.

del Valle, H. (2016). Search and Rescue in the Mediterranean Sea: Negotiating Political Differences. *Humanitarianism and the Migration Crisis, Refugee Survey Quarterly, 35*(2), 22–40.

EU Commission. (2015, November 24). *EU-Turkey Cooperation: A €3 Billion Refugee Facility for Turkey*. Brussels: Press Release.

EU Commission. (2016, September 8). *EU Announces More Projects Under the Facility for Refugees in Turkey: €348 Million in Humanitarian Aid to Refugees in Turkey*, Brussels.

EU Council. (2016, June 20). Extension and Expansion of EUNAVFOR MED Operation Sophia Mandate.

EUBAM Mandate (2013 and 2015). Council Decision 2013/233/CFSP of 22 May 2013 on the European Union Integrated Border Management Assistance Mission in Libya (EUBAM Libya) (OJ L 138, 24.5.2013, p. 15) and Council Decision (CFSP) 2015/2276 of 7 December 2015 amending and extending Decision 2013/233/CFSP on the European Union Integrated Border Management Assistance Mission in Libya (EUBAM Libya) (OJ L 322, 8.12.2015, p. 51).

Euronews. (2017). *Italy's Code of Conduct for NGOs Involved in Migrant Rescue: Text.* https://www.euronews.com/2017/08/03/text-of-italys-code-of-conduct-for-ngos-involved-in-migrant-rescue. Accessed 21 March 2019.

European Commission. (2017, July 6). *A Strategic Approach to Resilience in the EU's External Action.* Joint Communication to the European Parliament and the Council, Brussels.

Faist, T. (1995). Boundaries of Welfare States: Immigrants and Social Rights in the National and Supranational Level. In R. Miles & D. Thranhardt (Eds.), *Migration and European Integration: The Dynamics of Inclusion and Exclusion* (pp. 177–195). London: Pinter.

France24. (2015, November 19). *Paris Attack Terrorists Used Refugee Chaos to Enter France, Says PM Valls.* https://www.france24.com/en/20151119-paris-attackers-slip-refugee-migrant-crisis-terrorism. Accessed 21 March 2019.

Frontex—European Border and Coast Guard Agency. *Risk Analysis F.*

Guardian. (2017, February 27). *NGO Rescues off Libya Encourage Traffickers, Says EU Border Chief.*

Heller, C., & Pezzani, L. (2016). *Death by Rescue.* Forensic Architecture Agency.

Heller, C., & Pezzani, L. (2017). *Blaming the Rescuers.* Forensic Architecture Agency.

Huysmans, J. (2000). The European Union and the Securitization of Migration. *JCMS: Journal of Common Market Studies, 38*(5), 751–777.

International Organization for Migration (IOM). (undated). *Missing Migrants Project Data.* https://missingmigrants.iom.int/region/mediterranean. Accessed 21 March 2019.

Landau, L. (2018). A Chronotope of Containment Development: Europe's Migrant Crisis and Africa's Reterritorialisation. *Antipode, 51*(1), 169–186.

Lentin, A. (2008). Europe and the Silence About Race. *European Journal of Social Theory, 11*(4), 487–503.

Menz, G. (2011). Neo-Liberalism, Privatization and the Outsourcing of Migration Management: A Five-Country Comparison. *Competition & Change, 15*(2), 116–135.

Matthijs, K., Neels, K., Timmermann, C., Haers, J., & Mels, S. (Eds.). (2015). *Population Change in Europe, the Middle-East and North Africa: Beyond the Demographic Divide.* Farnham: Ashgate.

Médecins Sans Frontières (MSF). (2009). *Speech by MSF President Christophe Fournier at NATO's Allied Rapid Reaction Corps Conference*, Rheindahlen, Germany. https://www.msf.org/nato-speech-christophe-fournier. Accessed 21 March 2019.

Médecins Sans Frontières (MSF). (2016). *MSF to No Longer Take Funds from EU Member States and Institutions.*

Médecins Sans Frontières (MSF). (2018a, September 23). *Italian Government Pressures Panama to Stop Aquarius' Rescues on World's Deadliest Maritime Route.* MSF Press Release.

Médecins Sans Frontières (MSF). (2018b). *Sinister Attacks by Italian Authorities on Life Saving Search and Rescue in the Mediterranean.*

NATO. (2012). CIMIC Field Handbook (4th Edition, 2016), Civil Military Cooperation Centre of Excellence (CCOE). Available at: https://www.cimic-coe.org/wpcontent/uploads/2014/06/CFHB-4-0-CONTENT-1-5-E-Book-2.pdf (last accessed, June 2019).

NATO—North Atlantic Treaty Organization. (2018). *Resilience and Article 3*.
Papademetriou, D. (Ed.). (2006). *Europe and Its Immigrants in the 21st Century: A New Deal or a Continuing Dialogue of the Deaf?* Washington, DC and Lisbon: Migration Policy Institute and Luso-American Foundation.
Powell, C. (2001, October 26). *Remarks to the National Foreign Policy Conference for Leaders of Nongovernmental Organizations*. National Foreign Policy Conference for Leaders of Nongovernmental Organizations, Washington, DC.
Reuters. (2016, June 17). *MSF Spurns EU Funding Over 'Shameful' Turkey Migrant Deal*.
Reuters. (2017, February). *Italian Court Investigates Whether Smugglers Finance Rescue Boats*.
Rodenhäuser, T. (2014). Another Brick in the Wall: Carrier Sanctions and the Privatization of Immigration Control. *International Journal of Refugee Law, 26*(2), 223–247.
RT France. (2018). *Les jeunes du Rassemblement National (ex-FN) et de la Ligue italienne unis contre la «submersion migratoire»*.
Rudge, P. (1989). European Initiatives on Asylum. In D. Joly & R. Cohen (Eds.), *Reluctant Hosts—Europe and Its Refugees*. Avebury: Aldershot.
Scholten, S. (2015). *The Privatisation of Immigration Control Through Carrier Sanctions: The Role of Private Transport Companies in Dutch and British Immigration Control*. Leiden: Brill.
Steinhilper, E., & Gruijters, R. (2018). A Contested Crisis: Policy Narratives and Empirical Evidence on Border Deaths in the Mediterranean. *Sociology, 52*(3), 515–533.
United Nations High Commissioner for Refugees (UNHCR). (2018). *Desperate Journeys: Refugees and Migrants Arriving in Europe and at Europe's Borders*.

CHAPTER 15

Conclusions

Eugenio Cusumano and Nathan Cooper

Despite the frequent critiques received from academics, the concept of resilience did not lose traction among policy-makers. On the contrary, as shown in the introduction, references to resilience have become pervasive in key strategic documents such as the EU Global Strategy (EUGS) and the Wales and Warsaw NATO summits conclusions. In fact, one could say that the very notion of resilience has itself proven remarkably resilient to criticism.

This concluding chapter draws on the insights gathered throughout this volume to reappraise resilience, its merits, and its limitations as an analytical compass guiding the formulation of foreign and security policies towards the Middle East, Maghreb, and Sahel regions. To this end, we will reassess both the heuristic utility of resilience as a theoretical concept and the advantages and drawbacks of resilience-based policy-making in light of the evidence provided by the case studies.

The chapter will be divided as follows. The first section focuses on the merits of resilience, arguing that the term can serve as four-pronged conceptual bridge. By acknowledging that crises may be inevitable and Western initiatives have often proved unable to rebuild and transform

E. Cusumano (✉) · N. Cooper
University of Leiden, Leiden, The Netherlands
e-mail: e.cusumano@hum.leidenuniv.nl

© The Author(s) 2020
E. Cusumano and S. Hofmaier (eds.),
Projecting Resilience Across the Mediterranean,
https://doi.org/10.1007/978-3-030-23641-0_15

target countries, resilience-based thinking helps bridge the gap between expectations and reality. Moreover, resilience provides a bridge between foreign providers of aid and capacity-building and the institutions and societies of recipient states by stressing the need for locally owned, tailored solutions to fragility. Furthermore, resilience connects policy and academic communities, offering a platform for dialogue between scholars and practitioners and enabling civil-military interaction. Last, resilience bridges the diverging interests of EU and NATO member states, acting as a catalyst of consensus-building between and within each organisation thanks to its constructive ambiguity.

The second section formulates some critiques to the usage of resilience as a foreign policy concept, reappraising the fuzziness and empirical indeterminacy of the term acknowledged by previous scholarship against the backdrop of countries at the Southern end of the Mediterranean basin. Most notably, we stress that both the properties and the empirical referents of resilience are often unspecified. Existing strategic documents rarely clarify the nature of external shocks and who the exact beneficiaries of resilience-building strategies are. While most initiatives purportedly apply to state institutions, societies, and individuals alike, these goals may not necessarily go hand in hand. Prioritising the short-term resilience of authoritarian state institutions may yield short-term stability but also hinder long-term efforts towards democratisation and socioeconomic inclusion, thus weakening societal resilience. Without a more open appraisal of the potential trade-offs between long and short-term approaches and between state and societal resilience-building strategies, there is a risk that resilience and its implementation will become too ambiguous to be constructive. In order to overcome these limitations, the third section tackles the key questions raised by the concept of resilience, such as resilience *for whom* and resilience *to what*, but also *why, how*, and *who* should pursue resilience. These questions should not only lie at the heart of academic research, but also need to be addressed by policy-makers when formulating and evaluating foreign policy initiatives vis-à-vis countries at the Southern side of the Mediterranean basin.

The last section provides some directions on the way ahead by taking stock of the empirical evidence collected by the contributors to this volume in order to draw some lessons and develop policy recommendations. Specifically, we stress the importance of EU-NATO synergy and civil-military cooperation as an integral part of a comprehensive and inclusive approach to resilience-building in the Middle East, Maghreb, and Sahel regions. By including and reaching out to practitioners from military, international, and non-governmental organisations as well as academics, it is our hope that this volume can both serve as an example of civil-military cooperation and provide a modest contribution towards bringing the key questions elaborated below into the policy debate.

Reappraising Resilience: A Conceptual Bridge

Although there is some validity in the academic critique that resilience may be a stretched concept, the success of catchwords in Euro-Atlantic policy circles lies more on the frequency and pervasiveness of their use rather than in their analytical rigour (Cusumano and Corbe 2018). We believe that the key reason resilience has been used so widely in the policy debate is its ability to bridge the gap between different epistemic and policy communities and across seemingly irreconcilable priorities and expectations within the EU and NATO. As a result, resilience has proved capable of serving as a bridging concept, namely a term facilitating interdisciplinary research agendas and knowledge production, connecting academia with policy realms, and stimulating dialogue between previously separate groups (Baggio et al. 2015). Drawing on the chapters of this volume as well as previous scholarship, we identify four main areas in which resilience offers the greatest potential as a bridging concept.

Bridging Expectations and Reality

The aftermath of the Arab uprisings prompted scholars and practitioners alike to call for a reality check in EU and US foreign policy-making. Following this line of argument, the concept of resilience can serve as a timely bridge between expectations and reality, reconciling transformative ideals focusing on promoting democracy, human rights, and sustainable development with the chronic fragility and entrenched authoritarianism of most countries at the Southern end of the Mediterranean basin. Such a process of expectation management may provide the groundwork for more realistic foreign policies grounded in 'principled pragmatism' (European Union 2016; Biscop 2016).

Like the concept of hybrid threats, resilience reflects the awareness that crises can be neither anticipated nor resolved in full. As such, the pervasiveness of resilience in policy debate does not only betray Western societies' growing awareness of their own fragility, exemplified by the financial crisis, the fears raised by large-scale human mobility, and the rise of populism and extremism in the European and US political arenas. Resilience-based thinking is also informed by the understanding that Western actors' ability to project their influence over third countries and (re)shape their political trajectory is severely limited. This sobering awareness is not just an acknowledgment that NATO and EU member states' capabilities and political rarely suffice in pursuing ambitious transformative goals, but also an admission of scholars and practitioners' epistemological limits. For Chandler, resilience presupposes ontological complexity in that crises are essentially beyond the limit of government reason (2014a: 55, 2014b). International actors must therefore be prepared for 'unknown risks, adaption, learning by doing, and flexibility as a way to embrace… rather than completely eliminate uncertainty' (Juncos 2018: 561; Evans and Reid 2014). If pre-defined solutions to crises do not exist and uncertainty severely constrains rational decision-making, resilience projection efforts must inevitably consist of tentative solutions based on trial and error rather than overly ambitious normative agendas. Protracted conflict and instability have been increasingly accepted as the new normal in EU and NATO policy discourse, and are therefore seen as something to be mitigated and managed rather than solved in full.

This shift is evident in the EUGS's emphasis on principled pragmatism, which resonates more closely with today's pessimistic *zeitgeist* and a sobering reappraisal of EU and Western democracies' ability to act as normative powers promoting human rights, liberal democracy, and economic prosperity beyond their borders. The aftermath of the Arab uprisings, seen as having caused massive instability while achieving very limited democratisation, played a significant role in reshaping rhetoric and policy priorities alike. By occupying a middle ground between democracy promotion and stabilisation agendas, resilience has not only been elected as the new *leitmotiv* of EU external action at large, but also become especially pervasive in the European Neighbourhood Policy (ENP) and the Euro-Mediterranean partnership in particular.

The concept of resilience may therefore help bridge the capabilities-expectations gap long lamented in EU external relations scholarship (Hill 1993; Toje 2008). As noted by Snyder and Vinjamuri (2012) in their case for pragmatism in foreign policy, when resources are scarce and consensus is hard to achieve 'actors who strongly emphasise principles and normative consistency inevitably set themselves up for charges of bad faith' (443). Recent scholarship has noted that the mismatch between ambitious goals and the difficulty for the EU to reach consensus and deploy sufficient resources in the pursuit of such objectives has caused a systematic gap between talk and action (Cusumano 2019a). As the cornerstone of more realistic and pragmatic foreign policy, resilience offers an antidote to overly ambitious commitments that may too easily be criticised as naïve, hypocritical, or patronising. As explained below, resilience may therefore be especially useful in order to avoid the accusation that NATO and EU countries impose neo-colonial agendas on developing countries by serving as a bridge between the beneficiaries of capacity-building and development aid and their foreign sponsors.

Bridging Providers of Reform and Local Societies

Acknowledging that the EU, NATO, and their members can only manage and contain crises rather than solve them on their own highlights the importance of local actors in development and capacity-building projects.

As noted by Juncos (2016, 2018) and Anholt and Wagner in this volume, resilience can therefore narrow the divide separating providers of capacity-building from local societies by stressing the importance of tailored solutions and local ownership of foreign-sponsored reform projects. Several contributors to this volume have noted that local ownership is increasingly understood by NATO, the EU, and their member states as a precondition for success in institution-building, military training and development projects alike. Accordingly, cultural awareness of the local context, the involvement of local institutions and civil society in the planning and implementation of reform projects, and the participation of regional security forces in the conduct of crisis management operations are crucial ingredients for projecting resilience. Resilience can therefore serve as a forceful reminder that in order to avoid being criticised as the imposition of patronising, one-size-fits all templates on recipient countries, Euro-Atlantic foreign policy initiatives in the Middle East, Maghreb and Sahel should be constantly adapted to the specificities of each local context.

Scholars in this volume have identified a variety of strategies aimed at developing local ownership. For instance, Giumelli explains that Tunisian and Egyptian institutions were involved in the drafting of EU restrictive measures targeting perpetrators of human rights abuses. As noted by Ruffa, Rietjens and Nygren, the extensive deployment of African peacekeepers equipped United Nations (UN) operation MINUSMA in Mali with extensive cultural and situational awareness. As further explained in the next section, however, the quest for local ownership is often stymied by organisational constraints as well as policy and ethical dilemmas. For instance, Raineri and Baldaro as well as Pounds, El Alam and Keijzer acknowledge that NATO and EU military forces have prioritised a narrow understanding of resilience as preparedness against external shocks. To some extent, this is a matter of diplomatic and political opportunity. Turning a blind eye to recipients' sociopolitical dysfunctions by focusing on external threats may help overcome local institutions' resistance against capacity-building initiatives. Building resilience in the Middle East, Maghreb and Sahel regions, however, often requires first and foremost addressing endogenous political and socioeconomic fragilities.

Bridging Divides Within and Between Academic and Policy Communities

Several scholars have noted that resilience facilitates interdisciplinary dialogue and holistic research agendas cross-cutting the divide between academic disciplines. Bourbeau, for instance, describes this potential as an 'intra-social sciences bridging concept' (2018: 119). Indeed, most of the obstacles to resilience identified in the current volume require insights from different subfields in international relations, ranging from security to development studies, and different disciplines, including anthropology, demography, economics, agricultural studies, and health sciences. Resilience has also helped bring together different practitioners' communities. As noted by Anholt and Wagner, sharing the resilience jargon has enabled and facilitated dialogue between security experts, humanitarians, development, and environmental specialists from governments, international organisations, NGOs, and the private sector alike. Moreover, as this volume testifies, resilience is a conceptual tool bringing together academics and practitioners. The recent emphasis on resilience has magnified the possibility for dialogue between scholars and policy-makers, thus helping to bridge the oft-lamented gap between academia and policy.

Last, the concept of resilience can forge novel synergies between civilian and military actors, serving as an enabler of civil-military interaction. Preparedness against hybrid threats that are primarily non-military in nature presupposes civil-military cooperation by requiring the involvement of a large range of civilian actors in national security policy-making and implementation (Corbe and Cusumano 2018). Tight interactions between civilian government agencies, non-governmental organisations, firms, and military organisations are all the more crucial in order to project resilience abroad. As noted by Ruzza in this volume, dialogue and coordination between shipping companies, international institutions, international organisations, and their member states helped develop an effective response against piracy off the Horn of Africa.

Bridging Divides Between and Within NATO and the EU

The effectiveness of counter-piracy initiatives also derives from the combined efforts of the EU and NATO, which both deployed maritime missions in the Indian Ocean. NATO and the EU's common embrace of resilience can facilitate EU–NATO cooperation, providing a common lexicon for the two organisations to work together. As highlighted in this volume's introduction, NATO and the EU's usage of the concept varies. Nevertheless, both organisations share a genuine commitment to enhancing the preparedness of state institutions and societies at Europe's Eastern and Southern borders alike. The convenient conceptual looseness of resilience allows for a degree of constructive ambiguity, acting as a catalyst for consensus-building between and within increasingly divided alliances and organisations. This constructive ambiguity may be especially useful at a time when the election of Donald Trump as US president raised concerns about the future of NATO and transatlantic relations at large. Indeed, resilience may help narrow the widening transatlantic rift by leveraging on the US and the EU's common interest in stability at NATO's Southern borders while simultaneously resonating with Washington's increasing reluctance to get directly involved in crisis management abroad and European capitals' unwillingness to completely relinquish their human rights and democratisation agenda.

Furthermore, resilience allows for bridging consensus gaps within both NATO and EU by narrowing the increasing divergence between member states' threat perceptions and strategic priorities. This divide is both sectorial and geographic. Eastern European states as well as the US and the UK have consistently prioritised NATO's traditional mission of ensuring Europe's territorial defence. This inevitably entails that NATO and EU efforts should remain geared towards the East, and focus mainly if not exclusively on deterring Russia and preventing the destabilisation of vulnerable countries in Northern and Eastern Europe. Southern European member states, however, increasingly regard

NATO's traditional mission as overly restrictive and peripheral to their own security interests, demanding that NATO put greater emphasis on projecting stability across its southern borders. As explained by Varvelli and Villa, the latest NATO power projection initiative—operation Unified Protector—effectively turned the tide of the Libyan civil war, but was not followed by any meaningful post-conflict stabilisation initiatives. The ensuing chaos and large increase in irregular migration caused significant frustration in Italy, where populist forces fiercely criticised NATO as inconsequential or even detrimental to Rome's national interests. Fellow EU member states' failure to redistribute the asylum seekers rescued in the Mediterranean sea further fuelled the grievances of Southern European NATO and EU member states like Italy, Greece, and Spain, causing a rise in Euroscepticism (Cusumano 2019b).

Van der Linde, Franza, and Stapesma note that Europe's energy security concerns too have primarily focused on gas disruptions from Russia. Countries at Europe's southern borders, by contrast, have received much less attention even if energy supply disruptions in the Southern Mediterranean have been more frequent than along the Russian–Ukrainian transit corridor. As illustrated by Larsen and Koehler, however, NATO attention towards countries in the Middle East and Maghreb has recently increased. The recent creation of a Southern Hub in Naples is a case in point. As activities that can be directed towards the East and the South alike, projecting stability and resilience are tasks that all NATO member states should see as resonating with their own security interests. As a loose, overarching concept all member states can tentatively agree on, resilience can thus help narrow the growing divergences and ease the tension within NATO and the EU alike, acting as an important catalyst of consensus-building.

Critiques to Resilience

Although the concept of resilience has several merits, contributors to this volume have also acknowledged a number of drawbacks, adding to the criticism already formulated by the existing literature.

First, states and international organisations alike have long sought to assist countries beyond their borders in strengthening their local institutions and civil society. As such, the latest emphasis on resilience may be nothing but a rediscovery of the wheel. As noted by Larsen and Koehler in Chapter 3, NATO has projected stability outside its borders at least since the end of the Cold War. Anholt and Wagner too stress significant continuities between the EU's resilience-based Global Strategy and Neighbourhood Policy and the EU's previous policies towards countries at the Southern end of the Mediterranean basin. Kaunert, Léonard, and Wertman also observe that the latest emphasis on resilience has left EU counterterrorism cooperation with countries in the Middle East and North Africa substantially unchanged. Likewise, Giumelli shows that the usage of sanctions and restrictive measures have also been largely unaffected by the turn to resilience. Hence, the critique that resilience may be nothing but old wine in new bottles is not entirely off the mark. As warned by Badarin and Schumacher, the unwarranted use of a novel concept is not merely redundant: rebranding as new policies that are in fact characterised by continuity rather than change has policy and normative implications alike. Pitching resilience as an innovation without actually revising the goals and means of existing foreign policies may only create an artificial watershed that deludes advocates of new approaches, confounds recipients of reform, and disrupts the institutional memory of the organisations providing capacity-building and development assistance by discarding as inapplicable the lessons and best practices obtained from relevant past initiatives.

Moreover, as noted above, resilience is a fuzzy concept. As concluded by Joseph in his recent analysis, resilience ultimately means different things to different actors (2018: 18). Although the malleability of a concept may be convenient as a tool of consensus-building, vague concepts also entail challenges for researchers and policy-makers alike. This is especially true for non-directly observable phenomena like resilience. Since resilience cannot be observed without being tested, whether or not a state or community is resilient only becomes visible in hindsight, once it has (or has not) proven able to resist shocks. Such an ex post reasoning, however, would condemn policy action to chasing rather than anticipating crises by seeking to mitigate shocks and disturbances that have already occurred. Turning resilience into an objectively operationalisable goal that allows for early warning mechanisms, timely crisis prevention initiatives, swift action, and objective policy evaluation requires a clear identification of the properties of the concept. These properties could then serve as indicators to measure existing fragilities before the resilience of a specific country or community is tested by a shock. In the effort to turn the concept into a concrete guidance on how to enhance military preparedness, NATO has identified seven baseline requirements for national resilience (*NATO Review* 2016; Cusumano and Corbe 2018). As noted by Pounds, El Alam, and Keijzer, however, these requirements are useful for NATO members, but ill-suited for Middle Eastern countries like Lebanon, whose vulnerabilities primarily derive from Beirut's consociational and fragmented power structure, exposure to regional powers' interference, and poverty among the native and large refugee population. Since resilience is often conceptualised as the opposite of fragility, one could identify resilience-building with all the measures taken to address states' institutional and socioeconomic fragility, using the extensive literature on the subject as a source of policy directions. However, fragility too is an elusive concept that often betrays a Western-centric, Westphalian understanding of the state (Pospisil and Kühn 2016; Nay 2013).

Existing definitions identify resilience with the ability to withstand and recover from shocks. As noted by Bourbeau (2018), what amounts to a shock is often contentious: shocks, like threats, are at least to some extent socially constructed phenomena. As such, certain disturbances may be inflated or overlooked depending on actors' missions, organisational cultures, and parochial agendas. Disagreement exists not only on the nature, but also on the locus of these shocks. Owing to the EU and NATO's understanding of resilience as preparedness against the destabilisation triggered by hybrid threats posed by hostile foreign actors, current resilience-building initiatives have often been conceived of as the attempt to increase countries' ability to withstand external shocks. In Bourbeau's words, resilience-building initiatives at the Southern end of the Mediterranean basin have focused on the left pole of the 'exogenous/endogenous dichotomy', a simplistic divide which offers 'fragile foundations upon which to theorise our understanding of resilience in world politics' (2018: 12). As noted by several contributors, crisis management and capacity-building missions in the Middle East, Maghreb, and Sahel clearly display a bias towards prioritising exogenous shocks. For instance, Raineri and Baldaro show that EU capacity-building missions in the Sahel have focused on preparedness against foreign militants and terrorist networks, organised crime, and large-scale immigration. This has translated into a marginalisation of Sahelian countries' domestic fragilities arising from extreme poverty, patronage politics, and the abuses committed by local security forces.

In sum, the different properties of resilient entities and the definition and locus of shocks frequently remain ill-specified. Moreover, the empirical referents of resilience are often insufficiently clear as well. Consequently, there is considerable vagueness regarding who exactly resilience-building initiatives should apply to. Three different empirical referents have been identified: individuals, societies, and state institutions, or states at large. Existing resilience-building strategies often mention state, societal, and individual resilience together, presenting them as two sides of the same coin. According to the EUGS, for instance, resilience is not limited to government institutions' ability to reform, but 'encompasses all individuals and the whole of society' (24). States are resilient when 'societies … have a hope for the future' (26). This conveniently loose formulation obscures some thorny trade-offs between state and societal resilience. Far from always increasing societal resilience, strengthening authoritarian states' institutional effectiveness by means of capacity-building may have a negative impact on individuals' fundamental freedoms and societies' internal pluralism. The ambiguous relationship between state and societal resilience reflects a broader problem: whether we should prioritise short-term approaches to security challenges or work for long-term solutions. Although focusing on strengthening the security forces of states with shaky democratic credentials and a poor human rights record may yield quicker pay-offs, this is arguably detrimental to the long-term resilience of society, communities, and individuals. Ultimately, resilience-building can only disguise but not solve the most vexed dilemma of Western countries' foreign and security policies, namely whether to prioritise stability at the price of condoning authoritarian governments' repressive policies or to promote their long-term democratisation despite the risks of short-term instability. This stability-democratisation dilemma has forcefully manifested itself in several cases covered in the volume. As noted by Amadio Viceré and Frontini, for instance, both the EU and NATO have eventually converged towards giving an implicit blessing to Egypt's return to authoritarianism. Badarin and Schumacher concur with this finding, identifying the prioritisation of stabilisation over democratisation as an overarching feature of the revised European Neighourhood policy at large.

If this dilemma is not tackled explicitly, resilience may ultimately be too ambiguous to be truly constructive. Excessive ambiguity might only serve the purpose of preserving a flimsy façade of consensus while delaying any meaningful discussion on how to address strategic disagreement within NATO and the EU. Moreover, as stressed by Badarin and Schumacher, ambiguity over foreign policy priorities may be problematic for agenda-setting. An ill-specified commitment to simultaneously enhancing both state and societal resilience tells us little on whether priority should be given to ongoing unrest and conflicts such as Libya's, post-conflict reconstruction and national reconciliation in Syria, Egypt's re-authoritarisation, extreme poverty in the Sahel region or other severe forms of instability and human suffering. The absence of objective criteria to measure resilience and weigh the relative importance of its different components also hinders policy evaluation and blurs the transparency and accountability of capacity-building missions and development projects. Last, excessive ambiguity may increase the risk that foreign policy agendas will prove unable to manage stakeholders' expectations, fail to reconcile rhetoric and reality, and therefore be denounced as forms of organised hypocrisy camouflaging parochial security and economic interests. In order to ease the challenges arising from the ambiguity of resilience, academics and practitioners alike should not shy away from answering some key pressing questions, which we will elaborate in the section below.

Elucidating Resilience: Key Questions

Scholars and policy-makers alike are inevitably confronted with fleshing out the concept of resilience by asking themselves basic and yet crucial questions, the same that could be asked to the concept of security (Baldwin 1997).

First, resilience-building inevitably requires asking ourselves whose resilience we are to enhance, or *resilience for whom*. Resilience-building initiatives have often simultaneously targeted individuals, societies, and state institutions alike. As already stressed above, however, the possibility to enhance state and societal resilience at once cannot be taken for granted. State and societal resilience may not only be at cross-purposes with each other, but are also very broad notions even when taken in isolation. The pursuit of state resilience begs the question of which government institutions should be strengthened: while capacity-building may enhance the ability of military and law enforcement institutions to cope with external threats and internal unrest, enhancing states' ability to reform would also require broader institutional reforms embracing parliaments, the judiciary, and the government institutions providing basic public services. In ethnically fragmented communities, societal resilience may also be too broad of a concept to serve as a template for action. Knowing how to enhance societal resilience requires acknowledging socioeconomic, ethnic, and religious cleavages, identifying whether priority should be given to those suffering from extreme poverty, oppressed minorities, or refugees and internally displaced persons.

The question of *resilience for whom* is inextricably linked to the question of *resilience to what*. As noted above, shocks and disturbances can hardly be pinned down objectively. Consequently, someone's shock may ultimately be someone else's adaptation strategy. Migration is a case in point. Although European states and societies may see large-scale irregular migrations as a shock or even a threat, human mobility is often the only available coping strategy for communities struggling with conflict, oppression, and extreme deprivation (Bourbeau 2015). These seemingly abstract theoretical questions have a host of policy implications. Is resilience-building an activity to be explicitly directed at preparing against an identifiable national security threat, either conventional or hybrid? Or should projecting resilience be primarily meant to address domestic fragilities arising from extreme poverty, vulnerability to pandemic diseases, and environmental degradation? As shown by several contributors to this volume, this is a pressing question for EU and UN crisis management and capacity-building in the Sahel region. In the absence of clearer directions, military organisations, aid agencies, and NGOs alike may prioritise short-term, easily measurable objectives. Such objectives, in turn, may be too easily informed and sometimes distorted by the organisational cultures, standard operating procedures, and parochial priorities of each of these actors. Military organisations' tendency to see resilience as preparedness against external shocks is a case in point.

In some cases, identifying specific shocks with public opinion priorities may serve the strategic purpose of easing collective action and mobilising resources within international organisations, an increasingly difficult endeavour at the time of growing disagreement within the Euro-Atlantic community. Most notably, member states' eagerness to tackle irregular migrations has enabled EU institutions to mobilise military and law enforcement personnel for maritime border control missions that also rescued a large number of migrants in distress. As forcefully illustrated by Del Valle, however, restricting human mobility eventually became the primary focus of EU migration management. Consequently, short-term activities with thorny legal and ethical implications gained priority over both humanitarian tasks and more inclusive attempts to tackle the root causes of migrations. As noted by Ruzza, the convergence of strong international norms and economic interests can serve as an effective trigger for more effective and less contentious forms of collective action. The existence of anti-piracy norms enabled NATO and the EU to act swiftly and effectively in order to safeguard safety of navigation in the Western Indian Ocean.

Relatedly, there is a need to go over the question of what the ultimate goal of resilience-building is, or in other words *why resilience* should be projected abroad. How much is resilience-building dictated by a concern for the well-being of African and Middle Eastern communities relative to European states' interest in a stable neighbourhood? Although one can surely argue that investing long-term economic development and democracy promotion would be beneficial to both recipients of assistance and members of the Euro-Atlantic community, thereby amounting to a form of enlightened self-interest, this is not necessarily the case for more short-term approaches, which may prioritise authoritarian governments' ability to stifle social unrest, combat international terrorism, and support European migration management efforts. Presenting such policies as inspired by a normative commitment to the well-being of societies at the Southern end of the Mediterranean basin may only trigger accusations of hypocrisy and spur further resentment.

Fourth, *how* is resilience to be most effectively promoted? The answer to this policy dilemma is not only inextricably linked with previous questions such as resilience to what and for whom, but also evokes a fifth question, namely *who* is to promote resilience. Thanks to their resources and expeditionary capabilities, military organisations can offer an important contribution to different types of resilience-building initiatives, ranging from deterrence and crisis management to capacity-building and disaster relief. Enhancing societal resilience, however, requires resources and expertise that military organisations alone cannot provide. As further elaborated below, effective cooperation between militaries and public and private civilian organisations is therefore warranted.

Although the complexity of resilience-building belies overarching, one-size-fits-all solutions, the extensive empirical evidence provided by the case studies examined in this volume allows for identifying some lessons learnt and best practices. It is to these that we now turn.

Projecting Resilience: The Way Ahead

Existing literature has already identified a number of policy directions for effective resilience-building. For instance, Juncos (2018: 9–10) stresses the importance of local ownership through bottom-up reforms, institutional flexibility cross-cutting traditional policy silos and artificial divides between internal and external security, and a joined-up approach between different international organisations and between public, commercial, and non-governmental actors. The evidence collected from the cases examined in this volume confirms and further elucidates these recommendations.

To begin with, several contributors concur in noting that projecting resilience across the Mediterranean requires EU-NATO cooperation. Thanks to its bases in the Mediterranean and its deterrence and force projection capabilities, NATO can play a crucial role at the hard end of the crisis spectrum, as epitomised by operation Unified Protector in Libya. Moreover, NATO's prestige among armed forces worldwide makes initiatives like the NATO Mediterranean Dialogue effective platforms for military diplomacy and norm diffusion. As noted by Larsen and Koehler, making membership to the NATO Mediterranean dialogue and the provision of NATO military assistance explicitly conditional upon the fulfilment of certain democratic and human rights criteria may enable NATO with the possibility to socialise foreign military organisations into international humanitarian law, civilian control of the military, and other key norms.

As stressed by several contributors, however, projecting resilience is much more than force projection and foreign military training: it also requires fully fledged institutional and economic reforms as well as effective development cooperation. NATO's narrow mandate as a security organisation and its perceived alignment with US security interests, often seen with suspicion by countries in the broader Middle East, severely limits the scope of NATO's resilience-building efforts. By contrast, the EU can contribute to a larger array of initiatives thanks to its much wider policy portfolio and extensive economic clout. Most notably, the EU is the largest provider of international development worldwide, and has dedicated significant financial resources to countries at its South through frameworks such as the ENP European Neighbourhood Instrument (ENI) (Schumacher et al. 2017). The EU's ability to contribute to the stabilisation of countries at the Southern end of the Mediterranean does not solely relate to the direct provision of aid. Granting access to the EU common market also provides vital economic opportunities for neighbouring countries. As noted by Franza, Van der Linde, and Stapersma, European countries' demand for fossil fuels is a key source of revenues for countries like Algeria and Libya. The consequences of EU energy diversification and decarbonisation agendas on countries in the Southern Neighbourhood should therefore be carefully assessed.

Geographic proximity and economic wherewithal maximise the effectiveness of EU 'governance by conditionality' (Lavenex and Schimmelfennig 2009), allowing the EU to leverage on 'money, markets, and mobility' by making development aid, access to the common market, and visa liberalisation contingent upon democracy and human rights criteria. As illustrated by the case of Ukraine and the broader Eastern Neighbourhood, however, EU economic and soft power instruments lack the military deterrence capabilities required to prevent revisionist powers to act as spoilers (Gehring et al. 2017; Rogers 2017). Other regional powers' interference is a formidable obstacle to conflict resolution and stabilisation in several countries in the Southern Neighbourhood too, such as Syria, Lebanon, and Libya. An effective division of labour between NATO and the EU would not only reduce the risk of inconsistencies, overlap, and duplications in the activities of the two organisations, but also enable fruitful synergies. Indeed, joint EU–NATO efforts are crucial for effective resilience-building. As noted by Varvelli and Villa, without the post-conflict stabilisation and reconstruction capabilities that only the EU can provide, NATO military interventions like operation Unified Protector in Libya are unlikely to translate into long-term stabilisation. As such, EU–NATO cooperation from the earliest stages of crisis management is warranted. The July 2018 Joint Declaration on EU–NATO Cooperation, where the presidents of the EU Council and Commission and NATO Secretary General have stressed that their efforts are 'mutually reinforcing', is therefore a valuable step forward (NATO 2018). To date, however, EU–NATO joint efforts have primarily focused on protecting European member states from hybrid threats rather than enhancing the resilience of states at Europe's Southern borders.

Cooperation between international organisations should not be limited to the EU and NATO. The UN and the African Union (AU) alike are heavily involved in the Sahel region, as shown by UN operation MINUSMA and the hybrid UN–AU mission UNAMID in Darfur.

The simultaneous deployment of European and African peacekeepers can combine European armed forces' military effectiveness with African soldiers' cultural awareness, thereby offering an important contribution to crisis management and resilience-building in Mali and beyond. Such forms of cooperation, however, are not without externalities and challenges. The involvement of peacekeepers from neighbouring authoritarian states, for instance, may tarnish the impartiality and legitimacy of UN operations (Karlsrud 2019). Moreover, as noted by Ruffa, Rietjens, and Nygren, lack of interoperability and mistrust between European and African forces has weakened the effectiveness of UN operations.

Cooperation in resilience-building should not be limited to crisis management and capacity-building operations, nor should it solely involve international organisations and their member states' military forces, foreign ministries, and development agencies. As shown by the Regional Refugee and Resilience Plan (3RP) in Syria—a network involving 270 partners, including UN agencies and international and local NGOs—societal resilience-building has the potential to mobilise a wide range of actors from both governments and civil society (UNHCR 2018). Civil society also plays a key role in migration management thanks to NGOs' support for development projects, management of refugee camps, and involvement in maritime rescue operations. As argued by Del Valle, however, European border agencies' unfamiliarity with humanitarian principles and their prioritisation of border control over human security eventually compromised an otherwise successful novel form of cooperation between humanitarian NGOs and European navies and coast guards. Mutual interest in political stability, freedom of navigation and economic development may provide a more solid platform for dialogue between state actors and the commercial sector both at sea and land. The chapters by Franza, Van Der Linde, and Stapersma as well as Ruzza highlight the importance of for-profit organisations like the extractive and shipping industries and the need to involve them in resilience-building initiatives across the Mediterranean.

As epitomised by the examples above, projecting resilience requires a comprehensive approach ensuring deconfliction, coordination, and cooperation between military organisations, governments, international organisations' agencies, NGOs, and commercial actors. In brief, projecting resilience requires civil-military cooperation. As a provider of training and the custodian of NATO-CIMIC doctrine, organisations like the NATO Centre of Excellence on Civil-Military Cooperation (CCOE), which generously sponsored this research project, can therefore play a meaningful role in enabling this dialogue. Even at a time when strains in Transatlantic relations, growing disagreement among European countries, and societal divides over contentious, heavily politicised issues like irregular migration hinder cooperation at the strategic level, a modicum of coordination can still be fostered by means of bottom-up initiatives. The Contact Group on Piracy off the Coast of Somalia and the shared awareness and deconfliction (SHADE) conferences, organised in response to both piracy in the Western Indian Ocean and migration across the Mediterranean, are a case in point.

We hope that our volume too can provide a modest contribution to strengthening this dialogue. By bringing together academics, military officers, government and international organisations officials, think tank analysts, and humanitarian workers, the book we had the privilege of editing has not only attempted to advance the scholarship on resilience and crisis management in the Middle East, Maghreb and Sahel regions, but has also sought to provide a small stepping stone in bridging the gap between civilian and military actors and between academic and policy communities.

REFERENCES

Baggio, J. A., Brown, K., & Hellebrandt, D. (2015). Boundary Object or Bridging Concept? A Citation Network Analysis of Resilience. *Ecology and Society, 20*(2), 2–12.

Baldwin, D. (1997). The Concept of Security. *Review of International Studies, 23*, 5–27.

Biscop, S. (2016). *The EU Global Strategy: Realpolitik with European Characteristics* (Egmont Institute Policy Brief, 75).

Bourbeau, P. (2015). Migration, Resilience, and Security: Responses to New Inflows of Asylum Seekers and Migrants. *Journal of Ethnic and Migration Studies, 41*(12), 1958–1977.

Bourbeau, P. (2018). *On Resilience: Genealogy, Logics, and World Politics*. Cambridge: Cambridge University Press.

Chandler, D. (2014a). Beyond Neoliberalism: Resilience, the New Art of Governing Complexity. *Resilience, 2*(1), 47–63.

Chandler, D. (2014b). *Resilience: The Governance of Complexity*. Abingdon: Routledge.

Corbe, M., & Cusumano, E. (2018). Conclusions. In E. Cusumano & M. Corbe (Eds.), *A Civil-Military Response to Hybrid Threats* (pp. 303–312). Basingstoke: Palgrave.

Cusumano, E. (2019a). Migrant Rescue as Organized Hypocrisy: EU Maritime Missions Offshore Libya Between Humanitarianism and Border Control. *Cooperation and Conflict, 54*(1), 3–24.

Cusumano, E. (2019b). Straightjacketing Migrant Rescuers? The Code of Conduct on Maritime NGOs. *Mediterranean Politics, 24*(1), 106–114.

Cusumano, E., & Corbe, M. (2018). Introduction. In E. Cusumano & M. Corbe (Eds.), *A Civil-Military Response to Hybrid Threats* (pp. 1–14). Basingstoke: Palgrave.

European Union. (2016, June). *Shared Vision, Common Action: A Stronger Europe: A Global Strategy for the European Union's Foreign and Security Policy*. Brussels.

Evans, B., & Reid, J. (2014). *Resilient Life: The Art of Living Dangerously*. Cambridge: Polity Press.

Gehring, T., Urbanski, K., & Oberthür, S. (2017). The European Union as an Inadvertent Great Power: EU Actorness and the Ukraine Crisis. *JCMS: Journal of Common Market Studies, 55*(4), 727–743.

Hill, C. (1993). The Capability-Expectations Gap, or Conceptualizing Europe's International Role. *Journal of Common Market Studies, 31*(3), 305–328.

Joseph, J. (2018). *Varieties of Resilience*. Cambridge: Cambridge University Press.

Juncos, A. (2016). Resilience as the New EU Foreign Policy Paradigm: A Pragmatist Turn? *European Security, 26*(1), 1–18.

Juncos, A. (2018). Resilience in Peacebuilding: Contesting Uncertainty, Ambiguity, and Complexity. *Contemporary Security Policy, 39*(4), 559–574.

Karlsrud, J. (2019). From Liberal Peacebuilding to Stabilization and Counterterrorism. *International Peacekeeping, 26*(1), 1–21.

Lavenex, S., & Schimmelfennig, F. (2009). EU Rules Beyond EU Borders: Theorizing External Governance in European Politics. *Journal of European Public Policy, 16*(6), 791–812.

NATO. (2018, July 10). *Joint Declaration on EU-NATO Cooperation*. https://www.nato.int/cps/en/natohq/official_texts_156626.htm. Accessed 26 April 2019.

NATO Review. (2016). Resilience: A Core Element of Collective Defence. https://www.nato.int/docu/review/2016/Also-in-2016/nato-defence-cyber-resilience/EN/index.htm. Accessed 26 April 2019.

Nay, O. (2013). Fragile and Failed States: Critical Perspectives on Conceptual Hybrids. *International Political Science Review, 34*(3), 326–341.

Pospisil, J., & Kühn, F. (2016). The Resilient State: New Regulatory Modes in International Approaches to State Building? *Third World Quarterly, 37*, 1–16.

Rogers, J. (2017). Reinforcing Deterrence Through Societal Resilience: Countering Hybrid Threats in the Baltic Region. In E. Cusumano & M. Corbe (Eds.), *A Civil-Military Response to Hybrid Threats* (pp. 259–281). Basingstoke: Palgrave.

Schumacher, T., Andreas, M., & Thomas, D. (Eds.). (2017). *The Routledge Handbook on the European Neighbourhood Policy*. London: Routledge.

Snyder, J., & Vinjamuri, L. (2012). Principled Pragmatism and the Logic of Consequences. *International Theory*, 4(3), 434–448.

Toje, A. (2008). The Consensus-Expectations Gap: Explaining Europe's Ineffective Foreign Policy. *Security Dialogue*, 39(1), 121–141.

United Nations Refugee Agency (UNHCR). (2018). *Regional Refugee and Resilience Plan 2018–19: Regional Strategic Overview*.

Index

A
Action Plan on Combating Terrorism, 91
Active Learning Network for Accountability and Performance in Humanitarian Action (ALNAP), 23
Afghanistan, 3, 49, 51–53, 55, 56, 109, 154, 156, 279, 287
African-led International Support Mission in Mali (AFISMA), 193, 194
African Union (AU), 49, 50, 56, 149, 175, 194, 232, 235, 310
Airborne Warning & Control System (AWACS), 56
Algeria, 2, 11, 49, 52, 75, 93–95, 97, 126–128, 130–134, 140, 142, 254, 310
Alliance's Partnership Action Plan on Defence Institution Building (PAP-DIB), 53
Allied Command Transformation (ACT), 41
Allied Maritime Command, 165, 235
All Sources Information Fusion Unit (ASIFU), 195–197, 199
Al-Qaeda in the Islamic Maghreb (AQIM), 96, 175, 193
Ansar Dine, 193
Anti-Money Laundering and Countering Financing of Terrorism (AML/CFT), 97
Anti-Money Laundering and Countering Financing of Terrorism Global Initiative, 97
Armed groups, 23, 158, 164, 176, 177, 180, 182, 193, 194
Article 4, North Atlantic Treaty (Washington Treaty), 50
Article 5, North Atlantic Treaty (Washington Treaty), 156
Article 8, Lisbon Treaty, 69
Article 8, Treaty on the European Union, 69
Article 21, Treaty on the European Union, 81
Article 29, Treaty on the European Union, 105

Association Agreement, 65, 216, 219, 250
Asylum seekers, 13, 269, 272–275, 277–282, 286, 287, 289, 290, 302
Azawad, 192, 193

B
Benghazi, 114–116, 154, 157, 159, 162, 256
Best Management Practices (BMPs), 13, 236
Brussels Summit, NATO, 53, 254

C
Cairo Declaration on Counterterrorism and the Rule of Law 2011, 98
Capacity-building, 11, 171, 172, 175, 182, 190, 221, 296, 299, 300, 303–308, 311
Carrier sanctions, 275
Centre of Excellence (COE), 219, 221, 222
Chicago Summit, NATO, 259
Civil-military cooperation (CIMIC), 4, 13, 218, 241, 287, 296, 297, 300, 311
Civil-Military Cooperation Centre of Excellence (CCOE), 1, 219, 311
Civil-military relations, 53
Civil society actor (CSO), 210
Civil Society Facility Humanitarian assistance, 256
Climate change, 22, 75, 80, 138, 192
Clingendael International Energy Programme (CIEP), viii, xi
Code of Conduct for NGOs, 284, 289
Combined Maritime Forces (CMF), 231, 233, 234, 236, 240

Combined Task Force 151 (CTF-151), 232–236, 238, 240–242
Common Foreign and Security Policy (CFSP), 105–107
Common Security and Defence Policy (CSDP), 11, 92, 171, 172, 175, 181, 183, 184, 232, 237, 277, 282
Comprehensive approach (CA), 14, 21, 183, 184, 311
Comprehensive sanctions, 104
Concentrated Solar Power (CSP), 139–141
Conflict Armament Research (CAR), 109, 182
Contact Group on Piracy off the Coast of Somalia (CGPCS), 235, 237, 240, 312
Counter piracy operations, 240
Counter-terrorism, 10, 49, 88–95, 97–99, 194, 254, 255, 260
Counter-Terrorism in the Middle East and North Africa Region (CT MENA), 98
Crisis governance, 23, 24

D
Daesh/Islamic State/Islamic State of Iraq and the Levant/Islamic State of Iraq and al-Sham (IS/ISIL/ISIS), 90, 92, 93, 96, 134, 160, 162, 279, 281
Deep and Comprehensive Free Trade Agreement (DCFTA), 251, 252, 256
Defence and Related Security Capacity Building (DCB), 51, 254
Defence capacity building, 259
de Hoop Scheffer, J., 39
Democracy promotion, 65, 80, 109, 248, 250, 256, 298, 308

Democratic People's Republic of North Korea (DPRK), 103, 109
Deterrence, 2, 3, 37, 38, 46, 55, 57, 98, 165, 252, 275, 278, 289, 290, 308–310
Development assistance, 14, 23, 27, 28, 71, 303
Diplomacy, 2, 165, 171, 253, 309
Directorate-General for European Civil Protection and Humanitarian Aid Operations (DG ECHO), 280
Disarmament, demobilisation and reintegration programme (DDR), 164
Disaster risk reduction (DRR), 70

E
Early warning capacity, 252
Eastern neighbourhood, 43, 138, 143, 310
Economic growth, 69, 129, 257
Economic shocks, 192
Effective governance, 220
Egypt, 10, 12, 29, 42, 47, 49, 50, 52, 73, 76, 77, 79, 93–95, 98, 99, 104, 109–112, 117–120, 126–130, 135, 137, 149, 156, 162, 163, 247, 248, 254–261, 305, 306
Energy resources, 138, 142
Energy security, 10, 125–127, 129, 130, 133, 138, 142, 143, 257, 302
Enhanced Forward Presence (EFP), 55
Enhanced Oil Recovery (EOR), 131
Enhanced Partnership Interoperability Programs, 51
Environmental degradation, 192, 307
EU 4th Anti-Money Laundering Directive, 96

EU Border Assistance Mission (EUBAM) in Libya, 96, 160, 281
EU Capacity Building Mission in Niger (EUCAP Sahel Niger), 11, 92, 171–175, 181
EU Counter-Terrorism Coordinator, 89, 91
EU Global Strategy for Foreign and Security Policy (EUGS), 66
EU internal security cooperation, 88, 99
Euro-Arab Dialogue, 64, 94
Euro-Atlantic diplomacy, 12, 248, 260
Euro-Atlantic region, 2, 8
Eurojust, 97
Euro-Mediterranean Partnership/Barcelona Process (EMP), 64, 250
Euromed Justice, 97
Euromed Police, 97
European Bank for Reconstruction and Development (EBRD), 126
European Border and Coast Guard Agency (Frontex), 274
European Commission (EC), 19, 64–78, 80, 91, 93, 95, 97, 108, 126, 256
European Council (EC), 17, 22, 76–78, 91, 114, 116, 278
European Court of Justice (ECJ), 107
European Economic Community (EEC), 64, 104, 105
European Endowment for Democracy, 256
European External Action Service (EEAS), 70, 78, 174, 176, 248, 250, 252, 258
European Neighbourhood Policy (ENP), 3, 9, 64–70, 72, 73, 75, 76, 79, 89, 90, 94, 120, 138, 216, 217, 250, 251, 256, 257, 298, 309

European Parliament (EP), 87, 90–93, 257
European Security Strategy (ESS), 17–22, 64, 67, 69, 91, 250
European Union Capacity-Building Mission in Somalia (EUCAP Somalia or EUCAP Nestor), 13, 232, 233, 236, 240
European Union (EU), 2–4, 6–14, 17, 18, 20–22, 25, 29, 31, 40, 45, 47, 48, 51, 53, 56, 64–68, 70–72, 74, 75, 77–81, 87–99, 103–108, 110–120, 125, 126, 130–132, 136, 138, 139, 141, 143, 147, 149, 150, 159–161, 163, 165, 171, 172, 175, 178, 179, 182–184, 199, 206, 212, 215–222, 232–236, 239–241, 247, 248, 250–252, 255–261, 272–283, 290, 297–305, 307–310
European Union Military Staff (EUMS), 232
European Union Naval Force (EUNAVFOR) Atalanta, 13, 232, 234, 236
European Union Naval Force in the Mediterranean (EUNAVFOR Med or EUNAVFOR Sophia), 53, 116, 165, 277
European Union Training Mission Mali (EUTM Mali), 175, 181
EU sanctions, 103–105, 108, 117
EU Special Envoy to Libya, 159
External shocks, 7, 8, 11, 71, 104, 117, 169, 171, 172, 296, 300, 304, 307

F
Fleet Exercise Web (FEXWEB), 234
Floating Storage Regasification Unit (FSRU), 135

Foreign Affairs Council (FAC), 251, 257
Former Yugoslav Republic of Macedonia (FYROM), 44, 109
Fragile states, 28, 71, 169, 200
Freedom and Justice Party (FJP), 254, 256, 259

G
Gasdotto Algeria Sardegna Italia (GALSI), 132
Gas resources, 132, 137
General National Accord (GNA), 161
General National Congress (GNC), 115, 116, 158, 159, 161, 162
General System of Preference (GSP), 105
Global Counterterrorism Forum (GCTF), 98
Good governance, 53, 91, 217
Government of National Accord (GNA), 2, 115, 116, 157, 161–163, 281
Groupe d'Action Rapide - Surveillance et Intervention au Sahel (GAR-SI SAHEL), 179
Group of Five for the Sahel/*Force conjointe du G5 Sahel* (G5 Sahel/G5S or FC-G5S), 48, 50, 176, 178, 181, 191, 192
Gulf Cooperation Council (GCC), 48–50, 95, 156
Gulf countries, 49, 50, 127

H
Hezbollah, 96, 164, 207, 208, 210, 216–218, 220, 222
High Representative of the European Union for Foreign Affairs and Security Policy (HP), 18

High risk area (HRA), 232, 235–237, 239, 240, 242
Home-grown terrorists, 88
Host societies, 23, 29
House of Representatives (HoR), 115, 116, 158, 159, 161, 162
Humanitarian agencies, 287
Humanitarian assistance/aid, 2, 20, 28, 44, 194, 199, 217, 218, 230, 280, 281
Humanitarian crises, 71
Humanitarian principles, 13, 30, 288, 311
Human rights, 9, 10, 18–20, 68, 69, 77, 80, 81, 90, 93, 95, 98, 99, 105, 108, 109, 111, 112, 114, 118, 170, 172, 176, 179, 192, 193, 250, 251, 254, 257, 259, 273, 274, 282, 283, 290, 297–299, 301, 305, 309, 310
Human security, 12, 18, 261, 311
Human smuggling and trafficking, 96

I
Immigration, 67, 160, 271, 274, 279, 284, 288, 289
Implementation Force in the Former Yugoslavia (IFOR), 44
Improvised explosive device (IED), 195
Individual Cooperation Programme (ICP), 258
Individual Partnership and Cooperation Programme (IPCP), 52, 54, 254
Inequality, 207, 214, 219, 220, 222
Integrated Border Management (IBM), 96, 218
International Chamber of Commerce (ICC), 236
International Committee of the Red Cross (ICRC), 288
International Criminal Court (ICC), 114
International Criminal Tribunal for the former Yugoslavia (ICTY), 109
International humanitarian law (IHL), 309
Internationally Recommended Transit Corridor (IRTC), 233, 234, 237
International Maritime Bureau (IMB), 13, 229, 236, 239
International Maritime Organization (IMO), 228, 235, 236
Interoperability, 30, 174, 242, 311
Iran, 48–50, 103, 105, 109, 136, 205, 207, 208, 221, 222, 232
Iraq, 29, 49, 52, 53, 89, 94, 95, 97, 98, 154, 156, 250, 279
Irregular migration, 11, 20, 171, 173, 174, 176, 183, 252, 258, 277, 302, 307, 312
Istanbul Cooperation Initiative (ICI), 45, 48–51
Italian-Libyan Treaty on Friendship, Partnership and Cooperation, 150
Italy, 53, 131–134, 138, 143, 150, 151, 157, 159–161, 165, 166, 231, 253, 254, 256, 269, 271, 275, 278, 279, 281, 283, 286, 287, 289, 302

J
Joint Mission Analysis Centre (JMAC), 197
Joint Operational Command (JOC), 197
Jordan, 10, 29, 31, 49–51, 77–79, 93–95, 97, 99, 135, 156, 217

K
Kosovo Force (KFOR), 44

L

League of Arab States (LAS), 48, 50
Lebanon, 3, 10, 12, 23, 29, 77–79, 93, 95–97, 126, 128, 129, 135, 137, 151, 205–219, 221–223, 304, 310
Libya, 2, 3, 10, 11, 13, 46, 47, 49, 53, 67, 73, 96, 104, 109, 110, 114, 116–120, 126–130, 133, 134, 137, 140, 142, 147–155, 157–166, 170, 172, 173, 182, 183, 192, 253, 254, 256, 269, 275–278, 281–286, 289, 306, 309, 310
Libyan Coast Guard (LCG), 53, 282, 283, 285
Libyan National Army (LNA), 2, 162
Libyan Political Agreement (LPA), 115
Liquefied natural gas (LNG), 132–137
Lisbon Treaty (LT), 65, 248
Lone wolf terrorists, 87

M

Mali, 3, 11, 12, 48, 169–171, 173, 175–178, 181–184, 190–200, 299, 311
Malian Defence and Security Forces (MDSF), 192, 193
Maritime Rescue and Coordination Center (MRCC), 270, 271, 277, 282, 284–288
Maritime Security Centre—Horn of Africa (MSCHOA), 232, 235–237, 240
Maritime Security Patrol Area (MSPA), 231, 233, 234, 236, 237
Measures of the Euro-Mediterranean Partnership (MEDA), 65
Médecins Sans Frontières (MSF), 13, 30, 269–271, 276–278, 281–286, 288

Mediterranean Dialogue (MD), 45, 47–51, 215, 253, 258–260, 309
Mediterranean region, 96, 126, 276
Mediterranean Sea, 134, 152, 156, 275, 302
Member State (MS), 19, 39, 269
Middle East and North Africa (MENA) region, 10, 12, 18, 45, 47–49, 55, 57, 88–90, 92–95, 97, 99, 103, 104, 110, 117, 120, 126, 127, 129, 138, 141, 143, 149, 151, 155, 248, 250, 252, 258, 259, 261
Middle East Eye (MEE), 111
Migrant Offshore Aid Station (MOAS), 276, 284
Migration, 2, 20, 56, 68, 75, 80, 96, 116, 143, 160, 173, 174, 178, 180, 181, 216, 241, 251, 254, 255, 258, 261, 272–276, 278–281, 289, 307, 308, 311, 312
Migration crisis, 116, 277
Military Orientation and Programming Law (LOPM), 177, 180
Modernisation of the Administration of Justice programme, 99
Mogherini, Federica, 18, 73, 216, 248
Moldova, 51, 64
Movement for Unity and Jihad in West Africa, 193
Muslim Brotherhood, 254–256, 259

N

National Committee for the Rehabilitation of Democracy and the Restoration of the State in Mali, 193
National Determined Contributions (NDCs), 139
National institutions, 119, 212
National Movement for the Liberation of Azawad (MNLA), 192–194

National Transitional Council (NTC) of Libya, 115, 162
NATO-Russia Founding Act, 43
NATO Secretary General, 39, 153, 310
Natural Gas Liquids (NGL), 131
Naval Coordination Cell (NAVCO), 232
Naval operations, 234
Neighbourhood Investment Facility, 256
Neoliberalism, 25
Niger, 11, 48, 149, 169, 172–176, 182–184, 191
No-fly zone (NFZ), 114, 150, 152, 154, 156, 162
Non-governmental organisation (NGOs), 3, 4, 13, 18, 19, 29, 269–271, 276–278, 282–289, 297, 300, 301, 307, 311
North Atlantic Council (NAC), 40, 153
North Atlantic Treaty Organisation (NATO), 1–4, 6–14, 37–58, 73, 115, 125, 126, 138, 143, 147, 149–153, 155–157, 162, 165, 166, 205, 206, 211, 215, 216, 218–222, 230, 231, 233–236, 240, 241, 247, 248, 252–254, 258–262, 273, 274, 279, 288, 295–305, 308–310
Nuclear (non-) proliferation, 109

O
Offshore resources, 137, 138
Oil, 3, 11, 113, 114, 116, 127, 129–131, 133, 134, 137, 139, 142, 143, 148, 149, 158, 160, 162, 165, 166, 239
Organization for Security and Co-operation in Europe (OSCE), 40, 45, 51, 56, 73

Orientation and Programming of Internal Security Law (LOPSI), 179

P
Panama Maritime Authority (PMA), 270
Partnership Cooperation Menu (PCM), 54
Partnership for Peace (PfP), 43, 50, 51
Partnership Priorities (PP), 76–79, 216, 258
Peacekeeping missions, 12, 155, 198, 200
Petroleum Facility Guard (PFG), 134
Piracy, 13, 227–242, 301, 312
Political and Security Committee (PSC), 105
Preventing/countering violent extremism (P/CVE), 95
Projecting stability, 8, 9, 13, 38–42, 44–47, 54–57, 215, 260, 302

Q
Qaddafi/Gaddafi, 11, 110, 114, 115, 118, 147–155, 157, 158, 162, 172, 182, 192, 275
Qatar, 48–50, 156

R
Radicalisation, 11, 63, 75, 77, 87, 90, 92–94, 171, 174, 182, 252, 279
Rasmussen, Anders Fogh, 259
Regional Refugee and Resilience Plan (3RP), 28, 29, 218, 311
Reserve-to-Production Ratio (R/P), 131
Resilience, 1–14, 18–31, 63, 66, 67, 70–81, 88, 99, 103, 104, 117, 119, 120, 125, 134, 144,

169–173, 175, 177, 181–184, 189–192, 194–196, 198–200, 205, 206, 210, 211, 215, 216, 219, 222, 227, 228, 237, 238, 240, 247, 248, 250–252, 258, 260, 261, 295–312
Resilience-based governance, 18, 24
Resilience building, 258, 308
Restrictive measures, 10, 103–110, 112–115, 117–120, 299, 303
Rule of law, 10, 20, 42, 68, 77, 81, 93, 95, 98, 99, 111, 153, 173, 216, 249, 251, 254
Russian Federation, 64, 109
Russian–Ukrainian transit corridor, 10, 143, 302

S
Sahel region, 4, 182, 189, 190, 192, 295, 296, 300, 306, 307, 310, 312
Sahel states, 169, 171, 182, 183
Sanctions, 10, 103–110, 112–121, 134, 149, 193, 270, 303
Saudi Arabia, 48, 49, 95, 141, 156, 163, 205, 208, 221, 232, 249
Search and rescue (SAR), 13, 270, 271, 275–278, 282–286, 288, 289
Security-development nexus, 2, 72
Security sector governance, 47, 52, 53
Security sector reform (SSR), 54, 98, 175–177
Serval French Military Operation, 194
Shared awareness and deconfliction (SHADE), 234–238, 240–242, 312
Single Support Frameworks (SSF), 76, 79
Social cohesion, 111, 192
Solar Photovoltaics (Solar PV), 140
Somalia, 230–233, 237, 240
Somali National Armed Forces (SNAF), 232

Sophia, EU CSDP operation. *See* European Union Naval Force in the Mediterranean (EUNAVFOR Med or EUNAVFOR Sophia)
SoS Méditerranée (SoS Med), 269–271, 277, 285, 286
Southern and Eastern Mediterranean (SEMED), 2, 10, 126, 127, 129, 130, 134, 136–144, 205
Southern Gas Corridor (SGC), 136
Southern neighbourhood, 3, 9, 10, 18, 31, 32, 38, 46, 63, 65–76, 79–81, 88, 93, 95, 96, 119, 144, 250, 251, 260, 310
Special Representative for the Southern Mediterranean Region to the UN, 159
Special Representatives of the Secretary General (SRSGs), 197
Stabilisation *Force* in Bosnia and Herzegovina (SFOR), 44
Stability, 2, 8, 9, 13, 22, 39–44, 53, 54, 56, 57, 76, 78, 79, 94, 99, 116, 137, 147, 163–165, 169–171, 183, 191, 205, 210, 211, 213–215, 219, 222, 247, 248, 250, 251, 253, 258, 259, 301, 302, 305, 311
Stoltenberg, Jens, 39, 56, 57
Strategy for Combatting Radicalization and Recruitment to Terrorism, 91
Support for Partnership, Reform and Inclusive Growth Programme (SPRING Programme), 251, 256
Supreme Headquarters Allied Powers Europe (SHAPE), 53
Syria, 2, 10, 23, 47, 49, 65, 67, 73, 89, 90, 92, 95, 96, 104, 109, 110, 112–114, 117–120, 126–130, 137, 205–208, 213, 214, 217, 219, 221, 222, 250, 279, 306, 310, 311

T

Targeted sanctions, 10, 104
Technical Assistance to the Commonwealth of Independent States (TACIS), 65
Terrorism, 10, 11, 22, 56, 67, 68, 77, 87–99, 105, 108, 109, 116, 149, 150, 170, 172–174, 176, 180–182, 216, 234, 252–254, 258, 261, 273, 274, 279, 281, 308
Total Primary Energy Supply per Capita (TPES/Pop), 127, 128
Training Mission in Afghanistan (NTM-A NATO), 53
Training Mission in Iraq (NTM-I NATO), 53
Transnational organised crime, 96
Treaty of Maastricht, 104
Treaty of Rome, 104, 108
Treaty of the European Union (TEU), 105
Treaty on the Functioning of the European Union (TFEU), 106
Tripoli, 2, 115, 116, 150, 151, 153, 154, 159–163, 281, 282
Troop-/police-contributing countries (T/PCCs), 195
Tunisia, 10, 12, 42, 93, 95–98, 104, 109–112, 114, 117–120, 126, 128, 132, 137, 144, 160, 162, 247–254, 260, 261
Turkey, 28, 29, 93, 95, 98, 126, 128–130, 135–137, 143, 151, 157, 160, 217, 260, 280, 281

U

Ukraine, 7, 64, 67, 90, 136, 254, 310
UN Development Programme (UNDP), 6, 28, 29, 169, 174, 182, 214, 218
Unified Protector NATO operation, 11, 152, 153, 156, 253, 302, 309, 310
Union for the Mediterranean (UfM), 64, 150, 250
Union of Soviet Socialist Republics (USSR), 43
United Arab Emirates (UAE), 48, 49, 163
United Kingdom (UK), 5, 64, 113, 114, 131, 148–152, 155, 156, 160, 161, 219, 231, 256, 301
United Kingdom Marine Trade Operations (UKMTO), 231, 234
United Nations (UN), 3, 12, 18, 40, 51, 56, 79, 105, 108, 110, 114–117, 149, 150, 152, 153, 155, 160, 161, 163, 164, 189–192, 194–200, 206, 215, 217–220, 231, 235, 281, 287, 299, 307, 310, 311
United Nations Conference on Trade and Development (UNCTAD), 79, 239
United Nations Convention of the Law of the Sea (UNCLOS), 228
United Nations Department for Safety and Security (UNDSS), 197
United Nations Development Group (UNDG), 30
United Nations Framework Convention on Climate Change (UNFCCC), 139, 142
United Nations General Assembly (UNGA), 29, 30
United Nations High Commissioner for Refugees (UNHCR), 23, 29, 31, 77, 218, 289, 311

United Nations Mission in Kosovo (UNMIK), 155
United Nations Multidimensional Integrated Stabilization Mission in Mali (MINUSMA), 12, 176, 179, 190, 191, 194–199, 299, 310
United Nations Office for West Africa and the Sahel, 190
United Nations Office on Drugs and Crime (UNODC), 166
United Nations Policy (UNPOL), 197
United Nations Secretary General, 29, 191
United Nations Security Council (UNSC), 105, 108, 114, 115, 149, 151–153, 155, 161, 162, 175, 190, 193, 207, 208, 233, 235
United States Central Command (CENTCOM), 50
United States Maritime Liaison Office (MARLO), 231

Unmanned aerial vehicles (UAVs), 195
UN Office for the Coordination of Humanitarian Affairs (UNOCHA), 28, 192, 198
UN peacekeeping operations, 12, 190, 194, 195
UN Support Mission in Libya (UNSMIL), 153, 160

W
Wales Summit, NATO, 6, 51
Warsaw Summit, NATO, 6, 9, 38, 39, 45, 57, 215
Weapons of mass destruction (WMD), 67, 108, 150
Working Party of Foreign Relations Counsellors (RELEX), 106
World Food Programme (WFP), 230, 232
World Humanitarian Summit (WHS), 23, 25, 28–30